Understanding Neighbourhood Dynamics

Maarten van Ham • David Manley • Nick Bailey
Ludi Simpson • Duncan Maclennan
Editors

Understanding Neighbourhood Dynamics

New Insights for Neighbourhood Effects Research

Springer

Editors
Maarten van Ham
OTB Research Institute for the Built
Environment
Delft University of Technology
Delft, The Netherlands

Nick Bailey
School of Social and Political Sciences
Urban Studies
University of Glasgow
Glasgow, UK

Duncan Maclennan
Centre for Housing Research
School of Geography and Geosciences
University of St. Andrews
Fife, UK

David Manley
School of Geographical Sciences
University of Bristol
Bristol, UK

Ludi Simpson
The Cathie Marsh Centre for Census
and Survey Research (CCSR)
School of Social Sciences
University of Manchester
Manchester, UK

ISBN 978-94-007-4853-8 ISBN 978-94-007-4854-5 (eBook)
DOI 10.1007/978-94-007-4854-5
Springer Dordrecht Heidelberg New York London

Library of Congress Control Number: 2012949186

Printed on acid-free paper

Springer is part of Springer Science+Business Media (www.springer.com)

Preface

There is a wide belief in neighbourhood effects: the idea that living in disadvantaged neighbourhoods can have a negative effect on residents' life chances over and above the effect of their individual characteristics. A central question in the neighbourhood effects literature is whether living in a disadvantaged neighbourhood causes people to be poor, to suffer poor health and to have lower general wellbeing, or whether people at greater risk of poverty, who tend to have worse health and lower wellbeing, simply live in these neighbourhoods because living in more affluent ones costs too much. The answer to this question has major consequences for policy responses to deprived neighbourhoods.

This book brings together a collection of chapters which argue that neighbourhood effects cannot be fully understood without also understanding neighbourhoods more generally, but particularly the processes behind neighbourhood change. Surprisingly, given the awareness of (self) selection processes, the neighbourhood effects literature pays scant attention to the literature on selective residential mobility into and out of neighbourhoods. To further our understanding of neighbourhood effects, it is necessary to take a dynamic view of neighbourhoods, focussing on the neighbourhood as a transitory area in constant flux rather than viewing the neighbourhood as a static object. At present there is insufficient understanding either of the processes which create population turnover or change within individual neighbourhoods or of those which lead to or maintain neighbourhood segregation more generally. Both sets of processes need to be understood to further our knowledge of neighbourhood dynamics and hence neighbourhood effects.

The book has been designed to enrich neighbourhood effects research with insights from the closely related, but currently largely separate, literatures on neighbourhood dynamics. The book will be of interest to those who want to know more about what causes neighbourhoods to change, and what makes households choose to live in certain neighbourhoods. These insights are important for our understanding of cities and for the formulation of urban, housing and social policy. Collectively, the chapters in this book offer a state-of-the-art overview of literature on neighbourhood dynamics, including empirical contributions from the UK, Australia, Sweden, The Netherlands and the USA.

Many of the contributions in this book were presented at the seminar Understanding Dynamic Neighbourhoods on 8 and 9 September 2010 at the University of Manchester. The seminar was part of a wider ESRC Seminar Series, Challenges in neighbourhood effects research: does it really matter where you live and what are the implications for policy (RES-451-26-0704). The first book based on this seminar series, *Neighbourhood Effects Research: New Perspectives*, appeared in 2012 with Springer. The seminar series, and the associated book series with Springer, is the result of a collaboration between researchers from OTB Research Institute for the Built Environment at Delft University of Technology, the School of Geographical Sciences at the University of Bristol, the Centre for Housing Research at the University of St. Andrews, Urban Studies at the University of Glasgow and the Cathie Marsh Centre for Census and Survey Research at the University of Manchester.

Delft, NL — Maarten van Ham
Bristol, UK — David Manley
Glasgow, UK — Nick Bailey
Manchester, UK — Ludi Simpson
St. Andrews, UK — Duncan Maclennan

Acknowledgements

The editors would like to acknowledge the financial support from the Economic and Social Research Council in the form of an ESRC Seminar Series grant (RES-451-26-0704). The editors also wish to acknowledge the generous financial and staff time support of OTB Research Institute for the Built Environment at Delft University of Technology and the Centre for Housing Research (CHR) at the University of St. Andrews. The editors would like to express their thanks to all the authors for submitting their initial manuscripts on schedule, responding positively to comments and suggestions from the editors and delivering final versions of chapters with minimum delay. We are also grateful to Graeme Sandeman, the cartographer of the School of Geography and Geosciences at the University of St. Andrews, who has redrawn the graphs and maps, and to Martine de Jong-Lansbergen from OTB Research Institute for the Built Environment at Delft University of Technology for all her work on the layout of the book.

Contents

Contributors

Manuel B. Aalbers Department of Geography, Planning and International Development Studies, University of Amsterdam, Amsterdam, The Netherlands

Nick Bailey Urban Studies, School of Social and Political Sciences, University of Glasgow, Glasgow, Scotland, UK

Helen Barnes Social Disadvantage Research Centre, Oxford Institute of Social Policy, University of Oxford, Oxford, UK

Gideon Bolt Faculty of Geosciences, Utrecht University, Utrecht, The Netherlands

Åsa Bråmå Centrum för kommunstrategiska studier, Linköpings universitet, Norrköping, Sweden

William A.V. Clark Department of Geography, University of California, Los Angeles, CA, USA

Karien Dekker Faculty of Social Sciences, Sociology, Utrecht University, Utrecht, The Netherlands

Nissa Finney Cathie Marsh Centre for Census and Survey Research (CCSR), School of Social Sciences, University of Manchester, Manchester, UK

Stephen Jivraj Cathie Marsh Centre for Census and Survey Research (CCSR), School of Social Sciences, University of Manchester, Manchester, UK

Mark Livingston Urban Studies, School of Social and Political Sciences, University of Glasgow, Glasgow, Scotland, UK

Duncan Maclennan Centre for Housing Research, School of Geography and Geosciences, University of St. Andrews, Fife, UK

David Manley School of Geographical Sciences, University of Bristol, Clifton, Bristol, UK

David Mclennan Social Disadvantage Research Centre, Oxford Institute of Social Policy, University of Oxford, Oxford, UK

Geoffrey Meen Department of Economics, School of Politics, Economics and International Relations, The University of Reading, Reading, UK

Julia Meen Oxford Archaeology, Janus House, Osney Mead, Oxford, UK

Gerald Mollenhorst Faculty of Social and Behavioural Sciences, Sociology, Utrecht University, Utrecht, The Netherlands

Christian Nygaard Department of Economics, School of Politics, Economics and International Relations, The University of Reading, Reading, UK

Matthieu Permentier The Netherlands Institute of Social Research/SCP, The Hague, The Netherlands

Hanneke Posthumus Faculty of Geosciences, Utrecht University, Utrecht, The Netherlands

Natasha Rivers Centre for Studies in Demography and Ecology, University of Washington, Seattle, WA, USA

Veronique Schutjens Faculty of Geosciences, Utrecht University, Utrecht, The Netherlands

Ludi Simpson The Cathie Marsh Centre for Census and Survey Research (CCSR), School of Social Sciences, University of Manchester, Manchester, UK

Maarten van Ham OTB Research Institute for the Built Environment, Delft University of Technology, Delft, The Netherlands

Ronald van Kempen Faculty of Geosciences, Utrecht University, Utrecht, The Netherlands

Beate Völker Faculty of Social and Behavioural Sciences, Sociology, Utrecht University, Utrecht, The Netherlands

Chapter 1
Understanding Neighbourhood Dynamics: New Insights for Neighbourhood Effects Research

Maarten van Ham, David Manley, Nick Bailey, Ludi Simpson, and Duncan Maclennan

Introduction

To date, one of the main challenges in the neighbourhood effects literature has been to identify causality – that is, a causal effect of living in a poverty concentration neighbourhood on an individual over and beyond their own characteristics. A previous volume with Springer (Neighbourhood Effect Research: New perspectives; van Ham et al. 2012b) offered new perspectives on neighbourhood effects through state of the art research, and refocused the debate on neighbourhood effects. The research presented

M. van Ham (✉)
OTB Research Institute for the Built Environment, Delft University of Technology, P.O. Box 5030, 2600 GA Delft, The Netherlands
e-mail: m.vanham@tudelft.nl

D. Manley
School of Geographical Sciences, University of Bristol, University Road, Clifton, Bristol BS8 1SS, UK
e-mail: d.manley@bristol.ac.uk

N. Bailey
Urban Studies, School of Social and Political Sciences, University of Glasgow, Glasgow G12 8RS, Scotland, UK
e-mail: nick.bailey@glasgow.ac.uk

L. Simpson
The Cathie Marsh Centre for Census and Survey Research (CCSR), School of Social Sciences, University of Manchester, Humanities Bridgeford Street, Manchester M13 9PL, UK
e-mail: Ludi.Simpson@manchester.ac.uk

D. Maclennan
Centre for Housing Research, School of Geography and Geosciences, University of St. Andrews, Fife KY16 9AL, UK
e-mail: dm103@st-andrews.ac.uk

M. van Ham et al. (eds.), *Understanding Neighbourhood Dynamics: New Insights for Neighbourhood Effects Research*, DOI 10.1007/978-94-007-4854-5_1,

in this volume is a direct response to one of the major findings of the previous book: the challenge presented by the highly structured and non-random distribution of individuals over space and time into specific neighbourhoods. A substantial problem for researchers attempting to establish whether neighbourhood effects are present is that selective inflows of households into neighbourhoods can significantly bias the outcome of studies trying to measure these effects (see Duncan et al. 1997; Hedman 2011; Hedman and van Ham 2011; Galster 2008; van Ham and Manley 2010).

This book places neighbourhood selection at the centre of the neighbourhood effects literature and argues that neighbourhood effects cannot be fully understood without understanding neighbourhoods more generally, and in particular the drivers and processes behind neighbourhood population change, such as selective mobility into and out of neighbourhoods. Surprisingly, given the latent awareness of both (self) selection processes and discrimination by institutions, the neighbourhood effects literature pays scant attention to the literature on selective residential mobility or neighbourhood dynamics in general. Looking further into the future there is a clear agenda for neighbourhood effects researchers as a group: to move forward, we must understand better the processes of neighbourhood selection, and we must incorporate this understanding in our studies of neighbourhood effects.

Developing a better understanding of the mechanisms behind neighbourhood dynamics is also beneficial for a number of cognate literatures. The housing choice literature focuses mainly on characteristics of dwellings. These dwelling characteristics are not independent from neighbourhood choice as different neighbourhoods offer different types of dwellings. An improved understanding of neighbourhood choice is also crucial for our understanding of neighbourhood change. Changes in the demographic or socioeconomic structure of neighbourhood populations can in part be explained through selective inflow (and outflow) of households. As a result of the issues discussed in this volume, we will also be able to reach a better understanding of (the causes of) residential segregation. Whilst segregation is frequently conceptualised as a static state, making linkages with neighbourhood sorting enables segregation to be better understood as a process. Determining how households end up in certain neighbourhoods will enrich the segregation debate.

This volume is not, however, merely concerned with connecting disparate sets of academic literature. Within a wider context, developing a better understanding of neighbourhoods is also important for policy. Belief in the presence of neighbourhood effects is often one of the major justifications for the use of area based initiatives (ABIs) as a means to break the cycle of disadvantage and negative individual outcomes (see for instance Tunstall 2011). The central question in the neighbourhood effects literature is whether living in a disadvantaged neighbourhood causes people to be poorer, to suffer worse health and to have lower general wellbeing, or whether these people with greater risks of poverty simply live in these neighbourhoods because living in more affluent ones costs too much (see Cheshire 2012). The answer to this deceptively simple question has major consequences for policy responses to deprived neighbourhoods.

In addition, selective mobility into and out of target areas is often seen as a weakness of ABIs, diluting the impact on the target areas. Those able to take the most advantage of the ABI outcomes are also the most likely to move out of the neighbourhood after the ABI. The process of (self) selection by households out of neighbourhoods serves to frustrate attempts to engineer more mixed population compositions. Post-ABI, the process of selective mobility can re-sort the population so that the neighbourhood level gains are lost. There is also the issue that residents who are displaced by the ABI might end up in other disadvantaged neighbourhoods, where they might be exposed again to negative neighbourhood effects. A broader understanding of what motivates individuals and households to move into and out of neighbourhoods and what characteristics are most likely to lead to moves will aid the formulation of ABIs that can better target intended populations.

Definition of Neighbourhood

An issue that must be dealt with before we go any further concerns the notion of neighbourhood itself. The definition of neighbourhood can vary from person to person, even between individuals living relatively close to each other. There is a long line of literature that has attempted to define neighbourhoods, including the multi-scalar approach of Suttles (1972) or the exploration of the spatial extent of communities in Chicago by Hunter (1982). More recently, Galster (2001, p. 2111) noted that 'neighbourhood' is a "term that is hard to define precisely, but everyone knows it when they see it [...] Yet, even a cursory survey of definitions in the literature reveals some crucial differences in what the implicit 'it' is". The diversity of definitions can become even more problematic when neighbourhoods need to be made operational for research. Frequently, the approach taken to defining neighbourhoods is borne out of pragmatism: the definition matches the economic and administrative units that are employed by governments and other agencies for collecting statistics and organising civic functions. Some authors have suggested that it is better to create bespoke neighbourhoods depending on the object under study. A bespoke neighbourhood can, for example, be defined as consisting of the nearest 500 individuals (see for example Östh et al. in press) or as an area in which there is a relatively high level of homogeneity (see for example Manley et al. 2006). Galster (2001) presents one of the few comprehensive studies of "what" a neighbourhood could be, and demonstrates the wide variety of definitions in existence. He starts by highlighting that neighbourhood can be thought of in an ecological sense and emphasises the importance of social organisation, geographical connectedness, and shared identities with a common boundary (p. 2111). Within this discussion, Galster presents ten dimensions along which neighbourhood definitions can be judged, including aspects such as the type of buildings, infrastructure, demographic characteristics, class and status of residents, tax and public service groupings, environmental characteristics, spatial proximity, political, social interactive and sentimental characteristics. These multiple dimensions of neighbourhood classification further demonstrate the potential idiosyncrasies that can exist in attempting to define concepts that are highly variable. Nevertheless, there is "no doubt ... about the importance of neighbourhoods" (Hulchanski 2007, p. 3). In the chapters that follow in this book, the authors have all used their own definitions of neighbourhood driven by the unique perspective (and the data utilised) that their research requires.

Neighbourhoods as Dynamic Places

Neighbourhoods are not static entities: they are dynamic places that constantly change in terms of their composition, definition and relationships with the surrounding environment. They are places that are in continual flux as households and individuals move in and out, but they also change as the population in-situ changes – grows or shrinks through births and deaths, matures through ageing. As Hulchanski (2007, p. 1) notes, "[a]lthough some neighbourhoods change very little in their physical, social, and demographic composition over time, others may change significantly in the course of a few years". Some neighbourhoods change very quickly as the result of single or multiple external shocks, such as large scale neighbourhood demolition and (re)generation, or more slowly as the patterns of residential mobility change. Understanding neighbourhoods and their role in the wider urban context is crucial in developing a better understanding of how the neighbourhoods that we study develop, replicate and change over time.

A prime example of a study of neighbourhood change is by Hulchanski (2007), using Canadian Census data for the city of Toronto from 1970 through to 2005. Hulchanski took a long term perspective on neighbourhood development and change. His work demonstrates how, over time, the city of Toronto has diverged from a place of relative neighbourhood homogeneity, with many neighbourhoods in which the residents earned 'middle incomes' to one of marked social and economic divisions. Hulchanski describes this as changing from a city of neighbourhoods to a "city of disparities" (p. 10). Within this process, some neighbourhoods have experienced gentrification, others have experienced downgrading in terms of their position in the urban neighbourhood hierarchy. The analysis is very powerful and provides a rich account of a wide set of processes. However, like many neighbourhood studies, the data used are (repeated) cross sectional, and as such can only be used to describe patterns and not to investigate causes or processes. As a consequence, these studies cannot show *how* the change comes about. In order to do this, and to make connections with the residential mobility literature, it is necessary to use longitudinal data of neighbourhoods and individual residential histories.

Theories of Change

There are numerous theoretical frameworks that can be used to understand the dynamics of neighbourhoods (see for instance Grigsby et al. 1987). The sheer breadth of theories demonstrates the complexity of the subject and highlights that there are many competing arguments that set out to detail the processes that lead to the residential patterns observed in neighbourhoods. This introductory chapter only gives a brief overview of causes of neighbourhood change as each chapter in this book already expands on the theories and frameworks that they adopt. In broad terms, we can group the causes into three categories. The first set of causes places household behaviour as central. Households "choose"[1] to live in (or leave) certain neighbourhoods and by their decisions they can alter the population composition of neighbourhoods. A second set deals with demographic and socio-economic change of neighbourhood residents (the non-movers) while the third relates to external shocks to the neighbourhood, including structural changes to the labour market and large scale (re)generations and gentrification. Within this third set are theories about the role of institutions such as banks, lending agencies and local and national governments which influence the composition of neighbourhoods, intentionally or otherwise.

There is a lively debate on the causes of household behaviour leading to neighbourhood change. Much of the literature focuses on the importance of (self) selection (or sorting) into neighbourhoods based on preferences. This can be contrasted with the literature on the role of discrimination by housing 'gatekeepers' such as financial institutions and social housing providers. The current debate on neighbourhood sorting is frequently seen as originating from the work of Schelling (1969, 1971). Schelling theorised that small differences in preferences with regard to (for example the ethnicity of) neighbours, can lead to a system with highly segregated neighbourhoods. Clark (1991) investigated Schelling's hypothesis empirically using US data from telephone surveys conducted in Omaha, Kansas City, Milwaukee, Cincinnati, and Los Angeles as part of a litigation related to desegregated cities (Clark 1991, p. 9). Analysis based on the responses of the interviewees appears to confirm that Schelling's hypothesis was broadly correct, and that even very small preferences to live with own-group ethnic members could lead to highly segregated communities. If we assume that preferences are a substantial and important driver of neighbourhood sorting and residential choice, then the processes that form such preferences are also important. There is a wide literature that suggests that many individuals wish to live in neighbourhoods that are very similar to the neighbourhoods in which they grew up (Feijten et al. 2008). Moreover, the experience of individuals in terms of the places in which they grew up has been demonstrated to be important when seeking to understand the subsequent residential career of individuals (see van Ham et al. 2012).

It is important to ensure that the role of preferences is not overstated. Schelling's work depends on group preferences as a means to drive neighbourhood residential sorting and relies on households being able to express and act on their preferences and desires. It is clear that having the luxury to act out such idealised choice sets is not always going to be possible or realistic for all sections of the population. In contrast to Schelling's preference models, some authors have demonstrated that discrimination is a key driver behind segregation and residential sorting. For instance, authors have highlighted the importance of discrimination within housing markets, either through realtors 'steering' potential buyers (e.g. on the basis of ethnicity)

[1] Not all households are free to choose where they live, with choice being mediated by tenures and financial means. For many tenants in the social sector there is very limited freedom of choice (see for example Manley and van Ham 2011; van Ham 2012).

or finance companies making credit harder to obtain for some groups (see for instance Galster 1976). Using mortgage data from the United States of America, Immergluck (2009) has investigated the geography of foreclosures and has concluded that not only is the spatial patterning of foreclosures distinct but there is also a clear racial (ethnic) dimension. In the European context Aalbers (2011, 2012, this volume) has investigated the process of redlining and the restrictions of credit by neighbourhood and ethnicity, showing that ethnic financial discrimination is present in many forms. Ethnic discrimination is not restricted to the owner occupied market. Henderson and Karn (1984, 1987) investigated the allocations of social housing across the city of Birmingham (United Kingdom) and demonstrated that ethnic minority households were excluded from some neighbourhoods when housing officers thought that the neighbourhood already contained a 'sufficient' share of ethnic minority households, or if the (ethnic minority) household was not considered 'deserving' of the dwelling or neighbourhood in question. A decade later evidence of similar practices was uncovered in the British city of Oldham where households identified as belonging to Asian ethnic minority groups were actively segregated through the process of social housing allocations (CRE 1993). What these literatures demonstrate that there are important drivers behind residential sorting that move far beyond the concept of preferences and self-sorting mechanisms.

While there are many drivers of change which revolve around households changing their residential location, neighbourhoods also alter their population composition through residential immobility. Demographic change can be a very important driver of neighbourhood change. For instance, the apparent segregation of ethnic minority groups in the north of England during the early 2000s was initially presumed to be the result of Schelling-style 'self-selection'. In fact, research showed it was a consequence of differing demographic traits between the minority and majority ethnic populations which saw ethnic minority families increasing in size while the majority White households tended to reduce in relative terms. Selective mobility was not found to be a large contributor to changes in segregation (Simpson 2004; Finney and Simpson 2009). In-situ change of households may result in large changes of neighbourhood populations over time. Populations age, young people leave the parental home, new households form, children are born, people get and lose jobs, and health situations change. These socio-economic and demographic dynamics of households will influence the composition of neighbourhood populations. Such changes can lead to changes in the services and facilities available in neighbourhoods, which in turn might alter the types of households that will look to move to these neighbourhoods, which will reinforce the altered profile or through replacement populations result in static neighbourhood characteristics.

The final set of causes of neighbourhood change can loosely be grouped around the idea of external 'shocks'. These are distinct from the mechanisms discussed above which relate to changes based on the behaviour of households. One of the most obvious shocks comes when neighbourhoods are (re)generated.[2] In the most

[2] This is written as (re)generation to signify that on many occasions the process of regeneration requires to wholesale removal of both the social and physical neighbourhood before rebuilding takes place and it is, therefore, more akin to the 'generation' of a new neighbourhood.

extreme cases, this leads to the removal and dispersal of the neighbourhood population and the destruction of the physical infrastructure. The new neighbourhoods that are built in place are frequently comprised of completely different types of housing, and therefore households, and so the population of the neighbourhood can completely change in a relatively short amount of time. Other external shocks include gentrification. Some scholars, notably Slater (2006), have been highlighting the importance of gentrification as a driver of neighbourhood change for some time, and after a relative hiatus in the academic discourse, attention appears to be being paid to the process once again. The last of the external shock mechanisms we highlight refers to how neighbourhoods relate to the wider economic setting in which they are located. These changes have been particularly prevalent in the older industrial towns and cities of Western countries. Extreme examples can be identified in places such as Detroit (USA), but a large number of cities in the US and Europe have undergone seismic changes in their labour markets since the 1960s and 1970s, with profound impacts on the neighbourhoods within them. As manufacturing industry and therefore manual jobs have relocated elsewhere, previously vibrant neighbourhoods have declined to places where there are roads of empty houses, where apparently few people want to live. These are neighbourhoods that, as a result of the external economy have become undesirable. While national welfare systems have cushioned these shocks to a greater or lesser extent, changes in welfare systems have tended to reinforce decline in these places (Wacquant 2008).

Challenges

There is now a vast neighbourhood effects literature (some 18,000 papers, book chapters and reports, van Ham et al. 2012a) but relatively little of the research covered in that body of work genuinely links theory to empirics and demonstrates the existence of causal neighbourhood effects by empirical investigation. One recent example that shows what can be achieved when these connections are made is the research completed by Beatriz Caicedo Valasquez at the University of Bristol in a Ph.D. investigation into the impact of the neighbourhood environment on adolescent behaviour in Colombia (Valasquez 2012). The careful formulation of a theoretical framework of potential causal transmission pathways lead to clear hypotheses of causal mechanisms which were subsequently tested by empirical analysis. Thus, a major challenge for researchers investigating neighbourhood effects is to make a more explicit connection between theory and empirical investigation.

A second challenge is to pay much more attention to the definition and spatial scale of neighbourhoods. This is connected to the previous challenge as the spatial scale of the investigation cannot be seen separate from the hypotheses which are tested. The challenge, therefore, is to make the question of spatial scale explicit and to operationalize neighbourhoods in ways which make sense with respect to the causal mechanism(s) being investigated. There is little point in investigating large scale neighbourhoods if the causal mechanisms hypothesised are thought to work at a very local scale and vice versa. Finally, the third challenge for neighbourhood effects research is the collection and use of detailed longitudinal data enabling research over a long time scale. It is unlikely that exposure to a negative set of circumstances for a short period of time will have the same impact on the individual as a long term or repeated exposure (see Galster 2012). Thus, studies must seek not to investigate yearly or even five yearly outcomes. Rather studies should seek to examine as much of the life course as is possible adopting a 20 or even 30 year horizon of study and incorporating exposure time as well (see van Ham et al. 2012, for recent advances along these lines using Swedish data).

Book Structure and Contents

The remainder of this book is organised around 11 chapters by researchers from Australia, The Netherlands, Sweden, the United Kingdom and the United States of America. The first chapter by Bailey, Barnes, Livingston and Mclennan provides an explicit link between the neighbourhood population dynamics literature and the neighbourhood effects literature. Next, Meen, Nygaard and Meen offer a long-term perspective to neighbourhood change and the (im)possibilities of policy changing the history of a neighbourhood. Aalbers highlights the influence of financial institutions on neighbourhood dynamics and change. Then there are two chapters, one by Posthumus, Bolt and van Kempen and one by Bråmå which investigate the effects of urban renewal on neighbourhoods and the rest of the city. The next two chapters – by Völker, Mollenhorst and Schutjens, and by Permentier – investigate the link between neighbourhood characteristics and residential mobility decisions of residents. Jivraj and Finney offer a holistic and integrative view of neighbourhood dynamics by investigating both the effects of mobility into and out of neighbourhoods and in-situ change of neighbourhood residents. The chapter by Dekker investigates the relationship between neighbourhood ethnic and socio-economic composition and satisfaction with the neighbourhood. The final chapter by Clark and Rivers focusses on ethnic sorting across neighbourhoods. There are several important links between chapters in the book. For example, several chapters focus on the ethnic dimensions of neighbourhood dynamics. Much of the literature on neighbourhood population change is concerned with changing ethnic compositions of neighbourhoods. The causes of these changes are debated and chapters discuss, and test, various theories of change. The remainder of this introductory chapter provides a detailed overview and summary of all the book chapters.

Chapter 2 by Nick Bailey, Helen Barnes, Mark Livingston and David Mclennan starts with the observation that non-random sorting of residents into neighbourhoods provides neighbourhood effects researchers with a major challenge. The neighbourhoods which people choose reflect their incomes and other factors and, as a result, neighbourhood characteristics are endogenous, causing bias in models of neighbourhood effects. So understanding neighbourhood choice is at the heart of a better understanding of neighbourhood effects. This chapter reviews what is known about patterns of wresidential mobility and selective migration, in order to provide a clearer understanding of these dynamics on which to build research on neighbourhood effects.

The literature review discusses three findings of research on residential mobility and population turnover which receive broad support. The first is that neighbourhood characteristics have a relatively weak influence on the desire to move, on moving intentions and on actual mobility. The second is that general indicators of satisfaction with the neighbourhood appear to be more closely related to the desire to move and to moving intentions than indicators measuring specific aspects of the neighbourhood. And the third is that neighbourhood change may be a stronger driver for moving intentions than current neighbourhood characteristics.

The literature review continues to discuss how differences in residential mobility rates between social groups (selective migration) can lead to changes in the social composition of a neighbourhood. It is argued that this area of research is less well developed than the residential mobility literature. This section of the chapter presents five initial conclusions or hypotheses. First, selective migration processes are difficult to study, being sensitive to measurement error, and we should be particularly cautious of results as a consequence. Second, while there is general support for the view that selective migration can lead to spatial segregation, the influence it has on this process is relatively weak, and studies are far from consistent in their findings. Third, mobility associated with ageing and the life-course plays a fundamental role in selective migration flows, frequently cutting across other factors. Fourth, selective migration is not the only process at work in driving neighbourhood change, nor is it necessarily the most important. Fifth, the relative importance of selective migration and other processes may vary between different kinds of place.

The literature review concludes that residential mobility and selective migration are both heavily influenced by ageing and life-course events, where a "demographic conveyor" brings younger adults to lower income areas, most of whom will soon move on to better places. It also concludes that neighbourhood context may be defined as much by flows as by static or cross-sectional characteristics (see also the chapter by Nissa Finney). As a consequence, complex neighbourhood typologies can be constructed. Finally, the chapter concludes that responses to a given neighbourhood context may be more varied and subjective than previously assumed. It is suggested that objective neighbourhood characteristics themselves may matter less than how individuals respond to them, and these responses are generally not very well understood using quantitative modelling.

The chapter ends with a discussion of the relative strengths of some recently-developed data sources in the UK, and their potential to shed new light on residential mobility and selective migration. An overview is given of longitudinal survey data, census-based longitudinal data, and administrative sources. No one kind of data source is likely to provide researchers of neighbourhood dynamics with everything they need but combinations of different kinds of data have great potential.

Chapter 3 by Geoff Meen, Christian Nygaard and Julia Meen is concerned with understanding why urban structures arise, persist and change, with a specific focus on long term neighbourhood change. They argue that, typically, neighbourhoods exhibit persistence in social structures over very long periods of time. Relative spatial patterns of wealth and poverty within cities can remain broadly unchanged for decades if not centuries. Analysing long term neighbourhood change is challenging as long-term time series data are not readily available. The chapter starts with a discussion of initial urban population distributions and argues that geography and geology are crucial in understanding these early distributions, using Melbourne, Australia as a case study. Meen, Nygaard and Meen argue that once initial social patterns become established, they become locked in by the history of development. Path dependence in the development of neighbourhoods may arise not only from geology, but also because of the longevity of the housing stock, which creates spatial lock-in. Next, the chapter considers whether spatial structures persist over time and the extent to which structures change in response to large external shocks. Neighbourhood change may occur both gradually or in discrete jumps and it is suggested that neighbourhood change takes place in response to four types of shocks: exogenous innovations, such as wars; policy innovations, such as slum clearance and major regeneration schemes; technological innovations; and endogenous change, such as migration. The authors conclude that these shocks occur irregularly and have to be very large to have any impact.

In the remainder of this chapter, the authors review three strands of research: approaches based on social interactions; tests of non-linear thresholds and spatial variations in local housing supply elasticities from cross-sectional data; and evidence based on very long-run data sets. Out of these three strands, social interaction models are highlighted as the most elegant approach for explaining the dynamics of change, but these models are also the most difficult to test empirically. The chapter therefore presents evidence from related approaches, mainly based on the work of Schelling (1971), which illustrate how interactions can lead to segregation as a stable state, but also how structural change in neighbourhoods can result from purely random shocks which take neighbourhoods to a threshold or topping point. The second strand of research examines the empirical evidence for thresholds, using a cross-section model of local house prices. These models show some support for the idea that some of the most deprived neighbourhoods become stuck in poverty traps and that only very large sums of money can reduce deprivation and to promote such areas to a take-off point where they become self-sustaining. More modest policy changes may be insufficient and therefore stable patterns emerge. Finally, the third strand of research discussed provides evidence of long-run change since the nineteenth century. Such a long term approach is needed because there is limited evidence of change over shorter periods. In a case study for London, this approach suggests that post-war slum clearance programmes have locked-in or even increased social stratification.

Chapter 4 by Manuel Aalbers argues that the actions of mortgage lenders can play an important role in understanding the trajectories of some of the most deprived neighbourhoods in Western cities. In his chapter he makes a distinction between social and abstract space, where social space refers to how people think about the places where they live, and where abstract space refers to how institutions think about spaces for political or economic gain. It is argued that mortgage lenders conceptualise neighbourhoods in abstract space and use the notion of the neighbourhood as a means to reduce their risk or to extract profit, and as such can exercise destructive powers over the neighbourhood.

Through the practice of redlining, mortgage lenders may write of whole neighbourhoods as being too risky for investment. This is an example of place-based discrimination or social exclusion where mortgage lenders reduce risk not by excluding specific individuals, but by excluding whole areas. As a result, homeowners in such neighbourhoods might be unable to sell their dwelling, becoming trapped in their neighbourhoods. Others are unable to buy in these areas because lenders deny them access. In some cases, mortgage lenders require higher interest rates or down-payments to lend in particular areas. Aalbers calls this practice 'yellowlining' and sees it as an example of sub-prime predatory lending where mortage lenders target the most vulnerable in society to extract maximum profit.

Aalbers argues that redlining and place-based predatory sub-prime lending are not opposites as is sometimes argued, but are two adjacent positions on a continuum of exclusionary lending practices. The practices of redlining and predatory lending are in many ways very similar and can have similar effects on neighbourhoods. Both can be categorised as a neighbourhood effect, where the neighbourhood you live in not only has a direct causal effect on your ability to obtain a loan, but also on the conditions of that loan. Redlining and predatory lending disproportionally hit the same socio-economic groups: low-income groups and ethnic minorities. The discussion on redlining in the US has been connected to debates on the causes of ethnic segregation. Redlining is named explicitly as a form of an institutionalised discriminatory practice leading to segregation in both the US and the Netherlands. Although the key factor in red-lining is place-based, it is suggested that the underlying cause, in some cases, may be race-based.

To illustrate how redlining and predatory lending affect neighbourhoods, two case studies are discussed: a neighbourhood in Rotterdam, the Netherlands and one in Cleveland, Ohio, USA. Research in Rotterdam showed that neighbourhood decline was one of the reasons for lenders to redline the area, but also that redlining was a major cause of the further decline of the area. Aalbers demonstrates that a limited number of neighbourhood characteristics (high shares of low-income households, unemployed, and ethnic-minorities) are able to accurately predict 80% of the redlined cases. The case of the neighbourhood in Cleveland shows that mortgage lender practices not only hit individual borrowers, but also resulted in housing abandonment at the neighbourhood level. As such, these practices have severe spill-over effects on house prices, crime and neighbourhood decline. Aalbers clearly illustrates that the neighbourhood in which you live can enable or constrain you in obtaining a mortgage, and as such can also influence the trajectory of a neighbourhood as a whole.

Chapter 5 by Hanneke Posthumus, Gideon Bolt and Ronald van Kempen presents a study investigating forced moves as a result of neighbourhood renewal programmes in three cities in the Netherlands. It is argued that an underlying motivation for many urban renewal programmes is to create social mix in areas which are characterized by concentrations of low incomes. Such a mix is thought to be beneficial to mitigate assumed neighbourhood effects, although this is highly debated. The main instrument for social mix policies is the mixing of housing types and tenures and, through this, the mixing of socio-economic groups. Creating a mix of housing tenures and reducing the density in neighbourhoods implies that part of the population has to move elsewhere. Little is known about the neighbourhood careers of these displaced households. It is argued that, if such forced movers move to other deprived neighbourhoods, then the policies have not reduced the assumed negative effects of living in a deprived neighbourhood for them. This chapter asks two questions. First, how can neighbourhoods to which displaced households move be characterized? Second, how do the neighbourhoods to which many displaced households move, differ from their previous neighbourhoods?

To answer these questions, data is used from three Netherlands cities: Breda, Ede, and Rotterdam. Previous regeneration schemes during the 1970s and 1980s focused on the pre-WWII neighbourhoods in Rotterdam. During this period of neighbourhood renewal, residents were rehoused in renovated properties mainly in the same neighbourhood and as a result most of these neighbourhoods remained amongst the poorest in the city after the urban renewal process. Nowadays, the urban restructuring process is more focused on post-WWII neighbourhoods with a large proportion of social rented dwellings. In medium sized cities like Breda and Ede, these post-WWII neighbourhoods are amongst the worst in terms of income and unemployment. In Rotterdam, however, the post-WWII neighbourhoods currently targeted for restructuring are not always the worst. For all three cities, data was available on those who were forced to relocate due to urban renewal. Although the allocation systems varied between the three cities, all those forced to move received some form of assistance or a priority status in finding a new dwelling.

The results show that despite the wide variety of neighbourhoods to which displaced households move, there is a tendency for households to concentrate in neighbourhoods with certain characteristics. These neighbourhoods are in general near their old neighbourhood, have inexpensive housing stock, a low average socio-economic status, and a large share of ethnic minorities. In all three cities it was observed that restructured and receiving neighbourhoods are relatively similar in characteristics. However, forced movers in Breda and Ede are slightly more likely to move to a better neighbourhood than their neighbourhood of origin, while in Rotterdam they tend to move down the neighbourhood hierarchy. This is most likely a result of the structure of the local housing market opportunities.

The re-concentration of displaced households in rather similar neighbourhoods can have negative effects for these receiving neighbourhoods, although relative numbers of displaced residents are small in comparison with the total population of the receiving neighbourhoods. In any case, the re-concentration of displaced households implies that mixing – and the assumed positive effects – does not take place at a city-wide scale. Ultimately, this means that urban restructuring does not automatically result in more mixed neighbourhoods as some neighbourhoods might become more and not less segregated as a result.

Chapter 6 by Åsa Bråmå also investigates the relocation of residents who were forced to leave a renewal area but takes an alternative perspective. The focus of the chapter is on the effects of neighbourhood regeneration on the population composition of the regenerated neighbourhood, as well as on the changing position of the neighbourhood in the overall hierarchy of neighbourhoods within the city. The impact of neighbourhood regeneration on the wider city environment has received little attention in the literature, and has broad implications for our understanding of processes of neighbourhood change. In the literature review Bråmå focuses on the side effects of neighbourhood regeneration for other parts of the city. In particular spill over (or replacement) effects and displacement effects are discussed, two processes which are strongly related. There is some evidence in the literature that, through displacement, social upgrading of a neighbourhood is a 'zero sum game' when considered across the city as a whole. Various types of displacement – derived from the gentrification literature – are discussed: direct last-resident displacement; direct chain displacement; exclusionary displacement; and displacement pressure.

The case study area in this chapter is a large housing estate (Ringdansen) situated in Norrköping, Sweden. Before regeneration, the neighbourhood had a very bad reputation, and was one of the poorest neighbourhoods in the city, and avoided by more affluent city residents. It was generally seen as a place of last resort in the local housing market. From 1996 the neighbourhood underwent a major regeneration programme, consisting of both physical changes to the housing stock and social projects. Also the name of the neighbourhood was changed to avoid associations with the pre-regeneration period. To investigate the effects of regeneration on the neighbourhood population of Ringdansen and other neighbourhoods in the city, longitudinal, geo-coded data from the GeoSweden database was used. This dataset includes annual demographic, socioeconomic and geographic information on all individuals who have resided in Sweden between 1990 and 2008.

The analyses showed that the regeneration programme had raised the neighbourhood's position in the overall hierarchy of neighbourhoods in the city of Norrköping's. However, the chapter discusses how this relative change has occurred not only as a result of the regeneration of Ringshansen, but also as a consequence of other neighbourhoods in the city gaining worse reputations. The increasing number of neighbourhoods at the bottom of the hierarchy in Norrköping comprise mainly of the rental neighbourhoods in the neighbouring district of Hageby. The deteriorating situation in Hageby seems to be the result not of direct displacement of the socioeconomically weak residents from Ringdansen, but of exclusionary displacement of vulnerable households from Ringdansen. The rent increases following the regeneration of Ringdansen has resulted in a redirection of migration flows consisting of the most vulnerable groups away from Ringdansen towards other more affordable destinations, mainly Hageby.

The results of this study have wider implications for our understanding of neighbourhood change. The study shows very clearly how change in a particular neighbourhood in a city cannot be seen separately from developments in other parts of the same city. Neighbourhood regeneration is likely to affect the surrounding neighbourhoods as well as more distant parts of the city, and this should be taken into account in regeneration policy. There is a real risk that regenerating one neighbourhood will cause problems in other parts of the city, thereby reducing the overall effects of investment in neighbourhood regeneration.

Chapter 7 by Beate Völker, Gerald Mollenhorst and Veronique Schutjens reports findings from research in the Netherlands that links the level of neighbourhood social capital and the change in neighbourhood social capital between 2002 and

2006 with moving intentions and actual moves. The chapter starts with the observation that increasing attention is being paid to the role of the neighbourhood in the literature. It is also noted that the literature on social capital has grown enormously over the last few decades, and that although there are some important links to be made between the two literatures, these are often explicit. The main underlying hypothesis is that those who live in a neighbourhood with high levels of macro level social capital are better off than others, even when they themselves do not have many actual social ties themselves. If neighbourhoods with high levels of macro social capital are good for you, than it can be hypothesised that those living in neighbourhoods that lack of macro level social capital are more likely to develop an intention to leave their neighbourhood and act on this desire. The research question addressed in this chapter is: Does the amount of neighbourhood social capital and its change between 2002 and 2006 affect an individual's intention to leave the neighbourhood and an individual's moving behaviour?

The chapter briefly reviews the literature on moving intentions and actual moving behaviour and links this literature to the social capital literature. Social capital at the macro level is defined as the degree to which residents have friendly relationships with each other and assume that they can ask each other for help. As such, macro level social capital will enhance the feelings of belonging and community and can be expected to discourage residents from expressing an intention to move, or from actually moving. It was hypothesised that the more neighbourhood social capital available, the less likely people are to state that they want to leave the neighbourhood. Those on low incomes are thought to be most dependent on neighbourhood social capital, and are therefore thought to be the least likely to express an intention to move in neighbourhoods with high levels of social capital. A drop in neighbourhood social capital is expected to have a positive effect on pre-move thoughts and actual moving behaviour, especially for the better off.

The study uses 2002 and 2006 data from the Netherlands Housing Demand Survey (Woon), which is a national representative sample of citizens of the Netherlands. Neighbourhood social capital is estimated using an ecometric procedure, which accounts for systematic respondent biases in the perception of social capital. The analyses indeed confirm that low and decreasing neighbourhood social capital stimulates moving intentions and actual moving behaviour. It is suggested that to get a better understanding of the interactions between moving intentions, moving behaviour and social capital, future work should inquire more deeply into the conditions which cause social capital in neighbourhoods to change.

Chapter 8 by Matthieu Permentier focuses on neighbourhood reputations as a factor in understanding neighbourhood dynamics. The reputation of a neighbourhood is thought to affect selective inflow-and out-flow of residents, which might result in stable neighbourhood characteristics, or in gradual or rapid neighbourhood change. The neighbourhood effects literature places great importance on neighbourhood reputations as it is hypothesized that living in a neighbourhood with a poor reputation reflects on the individuals living there, and can reduce their ability to, for example, get a job, or might have a negative effect on their self-esteem. Poor neighbourhood reputations might also be a problem in neighbourhood renewal, where although a neighbourhood has received major investments and major changes in the social and physical structures have been made, the neighbourhood might still suffer from a poor reputation for historical reasons, reducing the effect of urban renewal because more affluent city residents do not consider living in these places.

The chapter discusses in detail the literature on neighbourhood reputations. It is argued that neighbourhood reputations are based on a collective shared view of neighbourhoods, and that reputations are thought to differ between residents and non-residents. Therefore a distinction is made between internal and external reputations. The notion of neighbourhood reputations also contains a stratification element: the reputation reflects the individual status of the residents. As a result, the neighbourhood can be used as a symbol of residents' socio-cultural and/or socio-economic position in society and their preferences. This leads to a hierarchy of neighbourhoods based on their reputation.

In this chapter, Permentier focuses on one aspect of selective outflow of neighbourhood residents: their intentions to leave their neighbourhood, and how these intentions are influenced by neighbourhood characteristics such as (perceived) neighbourhood reputations. A clear distinction is made between neighbourhood (dis)satisfaction and neighbourhood reputations. For instance, people might be satisfied with their neighbourhood, but might still want to leave because they believe that others have a negative view on their neighbourhood. Although neighbourhood reputations are likely to have a substantial impact on residential mobility, and on the dynamics of neighbourhoods, the literature on residential mobility seldom includes the neighbourhood's reputation as an explanatory variable. The empirical analyses in this chapter are based on a survey from 2006 in the Netherlands city of Utrecht. More than 1,300 respondents in 24 different neighbourhoods were asked about the reputation of their neighbourhood, and how they think others perceive this reputation.

The results show that a negative perception of neighbourhood reputation increases the probability that residents will express an intention to leave the neighbourhood. This result holds even when people are satisfied with their current neighbourhood. This is important as it is suggested that neigbourhood satisfaction and neighbourhood reputation are two partly separate factors. This result will contribute to our understanding of individual residential mobility behaviour, neighbourhood dynamics and understanding the success of neighbourhood renewal. The results suggest that for neighbourhood regeneration to be successful, it is important to change the image of the neighbourhood, to make it more attractive for other city residents.

Chapter 9 by Stephen Jivraj investigates socioeconomic neighbourhood change. Most studies investigating neighbourhood change use repeated cross-sectional data to document how neighbourhood characteristics change over time. Although such analysis can be useful, it cannot give insight into the causes of change. The population composition of a neighbourhood can change because of compositional differences in the in-flow and out-flow of residents. Neighbourhood population characteristics can also change because the characteristics of sitting residents change (for example their employment status). In this study Jivraj explores the causes of neighbourhood change by investigating how the effect of residential mobility of low income primary school-aged pupils in England compares with other components of change in the concentration of low income pupils in an area. Because the effect of residential mobility on the change in the concentration of low income pupils in an area is likely to vary between different spatial scales, the analyses are carried out for four different geographical units. The components analysed are the net effect of internal migration (residential mobility), entry and exit to and from the primary school system (school turnover), late entry and early exit to and from the primary school system (a proxy for international migration), and improved and declined socioeconomic status without moving (in-situ change).

Pupils who claim Free School Meals (FSM) are used as a proxy for low income households, a method which is used widely in educational research. To be eligible for FSM, a child must be living in a household claiming a means-tested income benefit. The analysis is conducted at different spatial scales using the FSM indicator recorded in the English School Census and the Townsend deprivation index. The School Census records details of all state school pupils in England and is derived from an electronic administrative form completed by each school. The inclusion of a unique pupil number allows pupils to be followed over time. Data derived from the School Census is averaged for each isolated component over consecutive 1 year periods between 2002–03 and 2006–07. Change in the concentration of FSM pupils for each component is measured at Local Authority District, Statistical Ward, Lower Level Super Output Area and Output Area levels.

The results show that the two dominant components of neighbourhood change are in-situ change and residential mobility. In-situ change, which refers to households changing their income status, either by improving or declining their income while staying in the same neighbourhood, decreased the concentration of FSM pupils at every spatial scale. The effect of residential mobility was not as strong as that of in-situ change, and it increased the concentration of FSM pupils in the most deprived areas. The effect of both of these components is greatest in deprived areas where in-situ change marginally decreases the concentration of FSM pupils whereas residential mobility marginally increases the concentration of FSM pupils. These results are consistent across spatial scales, however, the effects are accentuated the finer the spatial granularity.

The results of this study have significance for our understanding of neighbourhood change especially in deprived neighbourhoods. It is often assumed that selective mobility is the greatest driver of neighbourhood change, but this study seems to indicate that in-situ change is more important. It must be said however, that the data used was from 2002 to 2007, a period in which the use of FSM dropped in the whole of England. Repeating the analysis using more recent data from the economic crisis might reveal different patterns. In-situ change can be expected to be even more important than selective migration during the economic crisis and can be expected to increase the concentration of poverty. The effects of migration are hard to predict as the crisis might prevent people from moving at all. However, if only certain people are moving (those forced to) the effect of selective migration might be quite large.

Chapter 10 by Nissa Finney argues that there is a return to concerns about ethnic difference, ethnic conflict and ethnic residential segregation in cities. In the context of changing residential ethnic mix, static conceptualisations of neighbourhoods do not help to understand the social meaning of neighbourhoods. She argues that neighbourhoods are dynamic and in constant flux, and that categorisations of neighbourhoods should be based on dynamic factors. The ethnic make-up of a neighbourhood is determined by constant demographic processes of births, deaths, in-migration and out-migration. This chapter contributes to the literatures about ethnic neighbourhoods by examining neighbourhoods in terms of their demographic functions. It suggests that neighbourhoods can be thought about in terms of their population change, and the mechanisms of that change. The chapter contributes to debates about the demographic function of neighbourhoods by examining how population dynamics of ethnic groups vary within and between areas, and whether areas play the same demographic role for all ethnic groups. The chapter has three specific aims: first, to describe the geography of population dynamics of ethnic groups in neighbourhoods; second, to provide a conceptualisation and operationalization of ethnic group population dynamics of neighbourhoods; and third, to present an indication of how population dynamics relate to social cohesion.

The chapter uses a typology of population dynamics which characterises the relationship between natural change and migration for each ethnic group across neighbourhoods. The typology has a number of categories based on population growth and decline. The chapter uses estimates of components of population change for wards of Britain for the decade 1991–2001 and results from the 2005 Citizenship Survey. Finney finds considerable variation in ethnic group population dynamics (in terms of the relative importance of natural change and migration) and their geographies which are not accounted for in existing models of demographic and mobility transitions. To an extent ethnic differences can be interpreted in terms of group age structures and immigration histories. These differences might disappear when minority populations mature, but this is not necessarily the case. Finney found clear ethnic differences in geographic patterns of population dynamics, with urban-rural differences in migration behaviour for the white population, but not so much for minority groups.

The chapter proposes a four category typology of ethnic group population dynamics which accounts for dynamics in population change in 70% of Britain's wards. The categories of ethnic group population dynamics are Family Growth/White migration loss, Attractor, Replacement and Multi-ethnic Growth, for each of which there are clear geographies. The categorisation demonstrates that neighbourhoods can have different demographic functions for different ethnic groups. A neighbourhood can operate a single demographic function for one ethnic group, or multiple demographic functions for a set of ethnic sub-populations.

It was hypothesised that dynamic neighbourhoods would have low levels of community cohesion due to increases in diversity. However, descriptive results from the 2005 Citizenship Survey do not indicate this to be the case. Lowest levels of neighbourhood belonging and cohesion were found to be associated with Family Growth/White Migration Loss areas. The chapter does not show why this is the case, but suggests that future research should focus on a combination of diversity and population instability. The chapter finally suggests that using a categorisation of neighbourhood ethnic group population dynamics as an alternative to static measures of ethnic composition may provide alternative and more nuanced understandings of the effects of diverse neighbourhoods.

Starting with the observation that there is an increasing interest in neighbourhood effects, both from academics and policy makers Chap. 11 by Karien Dekker argues that an often neglected subject is neighbourhood satisfaction. Many policies designed to reduce the assumed negative effects of living in deprived neighbourhoods aim to create neighbourhoods of opportunity, places where people choose to live, and where people are satisfied with their residential environment (both physical and social). However neighbourhood satisfaction may be important in understanding why certain groups are more likely to leave deprived neighbourhoods than others. Of specific interest in this chapter is the relationship between neighbourhood deprivation and the share of ethnic minorities in the neighbourhood.

It is clear from the literature that white populations avoid neighbourhoods with a high proportion of ethnic minorities. It is not very clear however, whether this is because white people explicitly seek to avoid ethnic minorities, or because they avoid the neighbourhoods where ethnic minorities are concentrated: often neighbourhoods with low average incomes, high levels of crime, and poor services. This is known as the racial proxy hypothesis, which states that race (or ethnicity in the non-American context) is a proxy for other neighbourhood characteristics. In other words, if a regression model controls for socio-economic characteristics of the neighbourhoods (income), the ethnic composition of the neighbourhood should not have an effect on people's mobility behaviour.

The aim of this chapter is to increase our understanding of neighbourhood satisfaction, with a specific focus on testing the racial proxy hypothesis. The study uses a combination of survey data and Netherlands neighbourhood statistics. Dekker found some mixed evidence to support the racial proxy hypothesis, but the evidence against the hypothesis was overwhelming. Respondents were found to have negative attitudes with regard to living in neighbourhoods with high shares of low income residents and ethnic minorities. The negative effects on satisfaction with the neighbourhood of living in an ethnic minority concentration neighbourhood seem to be increasing over time. It is carefully concluded that in today's society in the Netherlands, the racial proxy hypothesis is not valid anymore, partly because of rising ethnic and religious tensions. The chapter concludes that neighbourhood regeneration policies should focus more on social problems in neighbourhoods and less on physical problems.

Chapter 12 by Clark and Rivers starts with a discussion of the literature on the causes of ethnic and racial segregation. They highlight three different perspectives on why segregation in neighbourhoods occurs. The first perspective focuses on differences in budget constraints between ethnic groups. The second perspective focuses on preferences with regard to the ethnicity of neighbours and social networks of whites and ethnic minorities. The third perspective emphasizes housing market discrimination and the role of real estate agents and lending institutions as gatekeepers in the residential mobility process. Clark and Rivers observe that the literatures on these three perspectives are currently largely separate, and that the role of income is underplayed in the literature on differences in neighbourhood choice between ethnic and racial groups. They also note that the literature shows clear indications that income, household situation (dual earners), employment status, and homeownership all work together in neighbourhood sorting. On the other hand there is clear evidence that the differential willingness to live with combinations of other races and ethnicities is an important factor in creating separation across neighbourhoods and communities. Whether whites are avoiding non-white neighbourhoods because they do not want to live with non-whites, or whether they avoid other characteristics of these neighbourhoods which are associated with race is still debated.

The main body of the chapter is concerned with selection: who chooses what kind of neighbourhood and the relationship of that choice to household characteristics. The research uses data from the panel study of income dynamics (PSID) for the years 1999–2005 and data from the decennial census of population and housing. They first examine the patterns of selectivity in neighbourhood choices by neighbourhood racial and ethnic composition and then socio economic status. Second, they pose the question to what extent moves reinforce current ethnic and socio-economic distributions. Third, they ask the question whether the selection for majority-own race and majority white areas, and the selection across the socio-economic status scale differ by income, education, age, and by ethnicity.

The study clearly shows that choice and sorting outcomes reinforce existing patterns of ethnic and racial segregation in neighbourhoods, that strong ethno centric preferences by race and ethnicity means that racial separation is likely to remain important in cities, and that socio-economic status combined with racial preferences increase the levels of segregation in the urban fabric. The study shows that many people choose neighbourhoods which are similar in race and ethnic composition than their neighbourhood of origin. Blacks have the highest probability of remaining in minority concentration areas. Hispanics show the greatest range in neighbourhood outcomes. Neighbourhood outcomes by socio-economic status are more diverse than those by race and ethnicity, although most people choose a neighbourhood similar to their previous one.

This chapter re-emphasises that sorting within the existing urban fabric is a powerful factor in understanding processes of neighbourhood formation and neighbourhood change. When moving, not all households end up in a neighbourhood with the same characteristics as their neighbourhood of origin and it is this change which changes the urban fabric. There is clear evidence that ethnic and racial groups are advantaged when they have greater resources. Money matters in the choices of ethnic combinations and in moving up the status scale. According to Clark and Rivers this would not be remarkable except that there is substantial US literature which continues to downplay income and wealth as critical variables in neighbourhood selection.

References

Aalbers, M. (2011). *Place, exclusion and mortgage markets*. Oxford: Wiley.

Aalbers, M. (2012). How do mortgage lenders influence neighbourhood dynamics? Redlining and predatory lending. In M. van Ham, D. Manley, N. Bailey, L. Simpson, & D. Maclennan (Eds.), *Understanding neighbourhood dynamics: New insights for neighbourhood effects research*. Dordrecht: Springer.

Cheshire, P. (2012). Policies for mixed communities: Still looking for evidence? In M. van Ham, D. Manley, N. Bailey, L. Simpson, & D. Maclennan (Eds.), *Neighbourhood effects research: New perspectives* (pp. 267–294). Dordrecht: Springer.

Clark, W. (1991). Residential preferences and neighbourhood racial segregation: A test of the Schelling segregation model. *Demography, 28*(1), 1–19.

Commission for Racial Equality (CRE). (1993). *Housing allocations in Oldham: Report of a formal investigation*. London: CRE.

Duncan, G. J., Connell, J. P., & Klebanov, P. K. (1997). Conceptual and methodological issues in estimating causal effects of neighborhoods and family conditions on individual development. In J. Brooks-Gunn, G. J. Duncan, & J. Lawrence (Eds.), *Neighborhood poverty* (Context and consequences for children, Vol. 1, pp. 219–250). New York: Russell Sage.

Feijten, P., Hooimeijer, P., & Mulder, C. H. (2008). Residential experience and residential environment choice over the life-course. *Urban Studies, 45*(1), 141–162.

Finney, N., & Simpson, L. (2009). *Sleepwalking to segregation: Challenging myths about race and migration?* Bristol: Policy Press.

Galster, G. (1976). Prejudice versus preference: What do we really know about housing market discrimination? *Journal of Regional Analysis and Policy, 6*(1), 17–27.

Galster, G. (2001). On the nature of neighbourhood. *Urban Studies, 38*(12), 2111–2124.

Galster, G. (2008). Quantifying the effect of neighbourhood on individuals: Challenges, alternatives approaches, and promising directions. *Schmollers Jahrbuch, 128*(1), 1–42.

Galster, G. (2012). The mechanism(s) of neighbourhood effects: Theory, evidence, and policy implications. In M. van Ham, D. Manley, N. Bailey, L. Simpson, & D. Maclennan (Eds.), *Neighbourhood effects research: New perspectives* (pp. 23–56). Dordrecht: Springer.

Grigsby, W., Baratz, M., Galster, G., & Maclennan, D. (1987). The dynamic of neighborhood change and decline. *Progress in Planning, 28*(1), 1–76.

Hedman, L. (2011). *Residential mobility and neighbourhood effects: A holistic approach* (Geografiska Regionstudier, Nr 88). Uppsala: Uppsala Universitet.

Hedman, L., & van Ham, M. (2011). Understanding neighbourhood effects: Selection bias and residential mobility. In M. van Ham, D. Manley, N. Bailey, L. Simpson, & D. Maclennan (Eds.), *Neighbourhood effects research: New perspectives* (pp. 79–100). Dordrecht: Springer.

Henderson, J., & Karn, V. (1984). Race, class and the allocation of public housing in Britain. *Urban Studies, 21*(1), 115–128.

Henderson, J., & Karn, V. (1987). *Race, class and state housing, inequality and the allocation of council housing in Britain*. Aldershot: Gower.

Hulchanski, D. (2007). *The three cities within Toronto. Centre for urban and community studies* (Research Bulletin 41). Toronto: University of Toronto.

Hunter, A. (1982). *Symbolic communities: The persistence and change of Chicago's local communities* (Studies of urban society series). Chicago: University of Chicago Press.

Immergluck, D. (2009). *Foreclosed: High risk lending, deregulation and the undermining of America's mortgage market*. Ithaca: Cornell University Press.

Manley, D., & van Ham, M. (2011). Choice-based letting, ethnicity and segregation in England. *Urban Studies, 48*(14), 3125–3143.

Manley, D., Flowerdew, R., & Steel, D. (2006). Scales, levels and processes: Studying spatial patterns of British census variables. *Computers, Environment and Urban Systems, 30*(2), 143–160.

Östh, J., Malmberg, B., & Andersson, E. (in press). Analysing segregation using individual neighbourhoods. In C. Lloyd, I. Shuttleworth, & D. Wong. (Eds.), *Segregation*. Bristol: Policy Press.

Schelling, T. C. (1969). Models of segregation. *The American Economic Review, 59*(2), 488–493.

Schelling, T. C. (1971). Dynamic models of segregation. *Journal of Mathematical Sociology, 1*(1), 143–186.

Simpson, L. (2004). Statistics of racial segregation: Measures, evidence and policy. *Urban Studies, 41*(3), 661–681.

Slater, T. (2006). The eviction of critical perspectives from gentrification research. *International Journal of Urban and Regional Research, 30*(4), 737–757.
Suttles, G. D. (1972). *The social construction of communities*. Chicago: University of Chicago Press.
Tunstall, R. (2011). *How much tenure mix is there in England, how has this changed 1981–2001 and what are the policy implications*? Paper presented at European Network of Housing Research, Toulouse, France.
Valasquez, B. C. (2012). *Individual and neighbourhood determinants of adolescent aggressive behaviour: A multilevel analysis*. Unpublished Ph.D. thesis, University of Bristol, UK.
van Ham, M. (2012). Economics of housing choice. In S. J. Smith, M. Elsinga, L. Fox-O'Mahony, S. E. Ong, & S. Wachter (Eds.), *The international encyclopaedia of housing and home* (Entry 94). Oxford: Elsevier.
van Ham, M., & Manley, D. (2010). The effect of neighbourhood housing tenure mix on labour market outcomes: A longitudinal investigation of neighbourhood effects. *Journal of Economic Geography, 10*(2), 257–282.
van Ham, M., Hedman, L., Manley, D., Coulter, R., & Östh, J. (2012) *Intergenerational transmission of neighbourhood poverty in Sweden. An innovative analysis of individual neighbourhood histories*. IZA Discussion Paper No. 6572 (www.iza.org).
van Ham, M., Manley, D., Bailey, N., Simpson, L., & Maclennan, D. (2012a). Introduction. In M. van Ham, D. Manley, N. Bailey, L. Simpson, & D. Maclennan (Eds.), *Neighbourhood effects research: New perspectives* (pp. 1–22). Dordrecht: Springer.
van Ham, M., Manley, D., Bailey, N., Simpson, L., & Maclennan, D. (Eds.). (2012b). *Neighbourhood effects research: New perspectives*. Dordrecht: Springer.
Wacquant, L. (2008). *Urban outcasts: A comparative sociology of advanced marginality*. Cambridge: Polity Press.

Chapter 2
Understanding Neighbourhood Population Dynamics for Neighbourhood Effects Research: A Review of Recent Evidence and Data Source Developments

Nick Bailey, Helen Barnes, Mark Livingston, and David Mclennan

Introduction

The area effects literature is concerned with the impacts of neighbourhood context on individual opportunities or outcomes. Studying such effects would be much simpler if individuals were randomly allocated to neighbourhoods and were not permitted to move between them. Unfortunately for social researchers (but fortunately for almost everyone else), most people have a large amount of choice over their neighbourhood location, collecting a diverse set of experiences and exposures over their life-course. As a result, places experience a through-flow of residents and the potential for a change in their composition.

These processes of neighbourhood selection by households provide neighbourhood effects researchers with a number of methodological challenges (Ginther et al. 2000; Dietz 2002; Galster et al. 2008). First, the neighbourhoods in which people live reflect individual characteristics, not least household incomes but also tastes and preferences, which shape or constrain neighbourhood choice. As a result, neighbourhood characteristics cannot be considered as exogenous (or fixed), rather they are endogenous. If this endogeneity is ignored when modelling, estimates of neighbourhood effects will tend to be biased. Second, if we do not fully control for the effects of parental or family background, this may also lead to biased estimates of neighbourhood effects as a result of the hidden selection of particular groups into

N. Bailey (✉) • M. Livingston
Urban Studies, School of Social and Political Sciences, University of Glasgow,
25 Bute Gardens, Glasgow G12 8RS, Scotland, UK
e-mail: nick.bailey@glasgow.ac.uk; mark.livingston@glasgow.ac.uk

H. Barnes • D. Mclennan
Social Disadvantage Research Centre, Oxford Institute of Social Policy,
University of Oxford, Barnett House, 32 Wellington Square, Oxford OX1 2ER, UK
e-mail: helen.barnes@spi.ox.ac.uk; david.mclennan@spi.ox.ac.uk

M. van Ham et al. (eds.), *Understanding Neighbourhood Dynamics: New Insights for Neighbourhood Effects Research*, DOI 10.1007/978-94-007-4854-5_2,

particular places. The direction of these biases may be upward or downward, leading to over- or under-estimation of the true scale of neighbourhood effects (Galster 2008).

Various responses to these problems have been identified (Dietz 2002; Galster 2008; Galster et al. 2008) although all too often the problems have simply been ignored (van Ham and Feijten 2008; Hedman and van Ham 2011). Several statistical techniques have been suggested and implemented with varying degrees of success. Alternative responses have included imposing a measure of control on the situation by assigning residents more or less at random to new neighbourhoods (as with the Moving to Opportunity program in the US, for example) or taking advantage of 'natural' quasi-experiments (Oreopoulos 2003; Briggs et al. 2010). Researchers have also tried to focus retrospectively on non-movers and explore the impacts of neighbourhood change on that group (Boyle et al. 2004). A common issue with these approaches is whether it is safe to generalise from such atypical groups or experiences.

This chapter does not seek to add to the extensive literature on these methodological issues directly. Rather, its aim is to review what is known about patterns of residential mobility and selective migration, in order to provide a clearer understanding of these dynamics on which to build research on neighbourhood effects. As well as reviewing existing research, the chapter discusses the relative strengths of some recently-developed data sources in the UK, and their potential to shed new light on residential mobility and selective migration.

Why Understanding Population Dynamics Aids Neighbourhood Effects Research

A better understanding of neighbourhood dynamics would be valuable for neighbourhood effects researchers for two main reasons. First, research focussed on individual residential mobility aids our understanding of the interaction between people and their neighbourhood contexts. Research into the factors which shape people's desire to remain or leave, and their actual mobility, provides important insights into the aspects of neighbourhood context which are perceived as important by them. This in turn may help our understanding of the characteristics which we need to measure in neighbourhood effects studies. It is well-recognised in principle that individuals have different definitions of the boundaries of their 'neighbourhood' as well as different experiences or exposures in the same place (Suttles 1972; Galster 2001). Exploring how people's mobility intentions and practices vary in response to the same context may also deepen our understanding of these variations. Most directly, actual mobility affects individual exposures to a neighbourhood and, hence, the 'dosage' of that neighbourhood that they receive (Ellen and Turner 1997; Galster 2012). Broadly, we expect dosage to rise with time so understanding who spends longer in which kinds of place may be valuable when trying to identify the groups most exposed to different contexts.

Second, research focussed on neighbourhood mobility patterns aids our understanding of how those contexts vary and, in particular, how they change. The sum of individual mobility decisions – the turnover rate for a neighbourhood – is part of the context within which individuals live. The impacts or meaning of turnover rates are still debated: low turnover may be portrayed as stability or as isolation, high turnover as instability or as openness or connection (Bailey and Livingston 2007). Nevertheless, it is a contextual variable that has appeared in many studies (Shaw and McKay 1942; Kasarda and Janowitz 1974; Sampson et al. 1997). The selective migration flows which result from individual decisions are fundamental processes reproducing the system of neighbourhoods but also driving change within it. The sorting and re-sorting of people across space gives rise to segregation and, in turn, to the possibility of neighbourhood effects. Many studies portray selective migration as the only factor giving rise to segregation but there is growing recognition of a wider range of processes at work (Finney and Simpson 2009; Bailey 2012). Understanding the relative contribution of selective migration *and other processes* to changes in segregation may aid our understanding of how neighbourhood effects operate.

Insights from Recent Research

In this section, we summarise some insights from recent research on residential mobility and selective migration. We have not conducted a full systematic review, so the conclusions are presented as hypotheses which require further testing.

Residential Mobility and Population Turnover

We begin by examining research which looks at frequencies or rates of moving. Here, there are two related issues: what makes people wish to leave (or remain in) particular kinds of place; and which places have high (or low) levels of turnover and why. The basic theoretical model for residential mobility sees 'residential stress' arising from a mismatch between *desired* housing and neighbourhood characteristics, and *current* ones, with stress leading to a desire to move. Such desires may or may not turn into more concrete intentions to move, and these may or may not lead to actual mobility. A failure to achieve a move in the face of residential stress may be the source of a range of negative impacts on individual well-being, including worse health (Kearns and Parkes 2003). Alternatively, stress may be released through adaptation – the adjustment of individual aspirations to circumstances (Andersen 2008). Understanding what produces residential stress or what prevents it from being released through mobility or adaptation may therefore be of value for wider studies of neighbourhood effects. More generally, the research on neighbourhood satisfaction, desire to move and actual mobility help us understand how people respond to different kinds of place.

As well as factors 'pushing' people to (want to) move, some factors 'pull' them towards other locations (family or employment connections, for example) while others restrain them from moving or 'pull' them back to their current neighbourhood (Confusingly, the term 'pull factor' is used in the literature to describe both). The latter may include emotional or functional attachments which build up over a period of time (Kasarda and Janowitz 1974). The development of these attachments may also be shaped by neighbourhood characteristics including levels of turnover (Bailey et al. 2012). Other important barriers to mobility include financial costs, particularly for those on low incomes. The drivers of a desire to move may therefore differ from those for expecting to move or actually moving (Coulter et al. 2010; Lu 1999).

Another kind of analysis looks at neighbourhoods rather than individuals, and seeks to understand the factors which drive aggregate levels of population turnover. The key question is the extent to which turnover is wholly explained by compositional factors or, conversely, whether neighbourhood context also plays a role. To put this another way, does a given neighbourhood have high turnover because it is home to the kinds of people who tend to move often (young, single renters, for example) or is turnover high because there is something about the neighbourhood as a place to live which causes people to move on sooner than they would otherwise have done? In relation to deprived neighbourhoods, there are some interesting differences in national preconceptions about turnover. In the UK, the policy discourse has portrayed many deprived neighbourhoods as 'unstable' or suffering from an excess of mobility although there is little evidence to support this (Bailey and Livingston 2007; Beatty et al. 2009). Policy efforts have focused on improving the neighbourhood environment, and on promoting social mix and stability. In France, by comparison, the policy discourse is based on the belief that deprived places are marked by problems of stasis or a lack of turnover, leading to isolation (Pan Ké Shon 2010).

In recent studies, three findings appear to receive broad support. First, *neighbourhood characteristics have a relatively weak influence on the desire to move, on moving intentions and on actual mobility.* This was the main finding from Rossi's (1980) study which began as an attempt to understand which aspects of the neighbourhood influenced mobility but which concluded by arguing that it is individual housing requirements and hence life-stage transitions that are key. This has been reinforced by recent work (Kearns and Parkes 2003; Parkes and Kearns 2003; van Ham and Feijten 2008; Beatty et al. 2009; Rabe and Taylor 2010). Although a very wide range of neighbourhood factors have been examined, individual socio-demographic characteristics and housing satisfaction are consistently shown to be more important.

Studies of neighbourhood turnover reinforce these findings. At the aggregate level, turnover is driven by composition rather than context (Bailey and Livingston 2007; van Ham and Clark 2009; Beatty et al. 2009). Some neighbourhood characteristics do have modest associations with higher turnover. Bailey and Livingston (2007) show that neighbourhood deprivation is associated with marginally higher turnover, even once demographics have been taken into account. On the other hand,

Beatty et al.'s (2009) study showed that neither factors relating to general satisfaction with accommodation nor those relating to satisfaction with the area were significant, nor were more specific indices of crime and lawlessness, or environmental problems.

Neighbourhood context has stronger impacts on the desire to move or moving intentions than on actual mobility (Kearns and Parkes 2003; Beatty et al. 2009). For example, Kearns and Parkes (2003) directly compare the impact of neighbourhood perceptions on moving intentions at one time with actual moves 4 years later. The contribution of home and neighbourhood perceptions to the goodness-of-fit of the model is much less in the case of actual moves than moving intentions (measured by the reduction in deviance scores). Overall dissatisfaction with immediate surroundings is a significant influence on moving intentions but not on actual mobility. Parkes and Kearns (2003) show very similar results for moving intentions. The gap between the desire to move and actually moving is greater for those on low incomes.

Second, *general indicators of satisfaction with the neighbourhood appear to be more closely related to the desire to move and to moving intentions than indicators measuring specific aspects of the neighbourhood.* Kearns and Parkes (2003) look at both moving intentions and actual mobility, and compare the impacts on these of overall neighbourhood satisfaction and of indices measuring nine specific aspects of the home and neighbourhood. Overall dissatisfaction measures have the stronger impact; see also Parkes and Kearns (2003). Similarly, Beatty et al. (2009) show that indices measuring specific problems with crime and lawlessness, and with environmental problems were not significant, although three measures of social capital or attachment were weakly significant; the latter may indicate the restraining influence of personal ties. A related finding is that subjective perceptions of neighbourhood characteristics appear to play a more important role in explaining mobility than objective neighbourhood characteristics (Lee et al. 1994; Rabe and Taylor 2010).

In addition, there is some evidence that different groups of people are sensitive to different aspects of the neighbourhood context. Van Ham and Feijten (2008) show that objective neighbourhood characteristics are only weak influences on individual desires to move. However, they also find that higher status groups (those on higher incomes, owners or Whites) appear more sensitive to the presence of lower status groups in their neighbourhood and therefore are more likely to wish to leave as the proportion of people in such groups rises. This finding closely parallels work on place attachment which shows similar interactions, both in relation to ethnicity and in relation to socio-economic characteristics (Charles 2003; Dekker and Bolt 2005; Bailey et al. 2012).

Third, *neighbourhood change may be a stronger driver for moving intentions than current neighbourhood characteristics.* As several studies have recognised, resident surveys may be limited in what they can tell us about people's views about different kinds of place because they capture most people in places where they have chosen to live – albeit that some people have fewer (if any) choices (van Ham and Clark 2009). The finding that people are generally happy to remain is not surprising. Some studies have therefore looked at how people react when neighbourhoods change around them. Feijten and van Ham (2009) find no impact from changes in neighbourhood socio-economic status on desire to move but they do show that a high level of turnover and an increase in the (non-Western) minority ethnic population increases the desire to leave to a modest extent (although this disappears when residents' subjective opinions about neighbourhood change are controlled for). Parkes and Kearns (2003) show perceptions of rising neighbourhood disorder are associated with declining neighbourhood satisfaction and with an increased desire to leave. Kearns and Parkes (2003) showed that the perception of neighbourhood decline was associated with an increased desire to leave but with reduced ability to do so. Van Ham and Clark (2009) show that a rise in the proportion of the population from minority ethnic groups is associated with an increased turnover rate.

Qualitative research on place attachment reinforces this, showing that, although people in general tend to express an indifference to the level of ethnic mix in their neighbourhood, a rapid rise in ethnic mix may trigger strong reactions from some amongst the White majority group (Livingston et al. 2010). This may be an expression of racism, at least in part, but others have argued that Whites (and non-Whites) may express lower satisfaction with neighbourhoods with high concentrations of minority ethnic groups partly because those neighbourhoods tend to be poorer; race or ethnicity is a 'proxy' for income and other neighbourhood quality attributes (Harris 1999, 2001).

Selective Migration, Neighbourhood Change and Migration Typologies

In this section, we are concerned with evidence on how differences in residential mobility rates between social groups (selective migration) can lead to changes in the social composition of a neighbourhood or even overall levels of spatial segregation. We are concerned here with the characteristics of migrants, not just numbers, and with the relative contribution of selective migration to neighbourhood change in comparison with other processes. In general, it is worth noting that this is an area where the evidence base is a lot less well-developed than for residential mobility.

We would make five initial conclusions or hypotheses. First, *selective migration processes are difficult to study, being sensitive to measurement error, and we should be particularly cautious of the results of these studies as a consequence*. Gross turnover is measured by the addition of two flows (in- and out-migrants), but net flows are measured by the difference. Measurement errors are the same for gross and net flows but are proportionately much larger in the latter. With selective migration, the situation is even worse as we are interested in the difference in net flows between two groups. This tends to be an even smaller number with even larger errors proportionately. The potential for 'noise' to swamp any 'signal' is very great and there is a corresponding danger that any biases in measurement may have a substantial influence on results.

Bailey and Livingston (2007, 2008) review the different methods that have been used to study selective migration. They stress the inherent weakness of estimates derived from 'mover surveys' in particular. First, the number of cases in survey-based studies tends to be small because of the high costs of tracing out-movers. Second, where studies report response rates, these tend to be lower for out-migrants compared with in-migrants. The concern must be that more deprived out-migrants are more likely to be missed, leading to biased estimates of net flows (out-migrants appear less deprived than they actually are) and hence biased estimates of selective migration. Third, studies that look at only one neighbourhood or small group of neighbourhoods cannot tell us where out-migrants go to or where in-migrants come from. The aggregate effect on all deprived neighbourhoods, or the wider neighbourhood system, is not clear. Around half the migrants into and out of deprived neighbourhoods in England and Scotland come from or go to other deprived neighbourhoods (Bailey and Livingston 2007). We should be very cautious therefore in generalising from such evidence.

Census-based studies offer both much greater scale and full geographic coverage but they suffer from the 'thinness' of data collected. In the UK, in particular, the absence of an income question in the Census limits the scope for analysis. Elsewhere, there has been growing use of longitudinal sample surveys and data from population registers. In the US, for example, Gramlich et al. (1992), Massey et al. (1994) and Quillian (1999) all use data from the Population Study of Income Dynamics, linked to Census tract data. There has been relatively little work on longitudinal data in the UK context, although there is growing scope to undertake such work through the linkage of neighbourhood variables to data from large-scale surveys such as the British Household Panel Study and its replacement, Understanding Society.

Second, *while there is general support for the view that selective migration works to increase spatial segregation, the effect appears relatively weak, and studies are not consistent in their findings.* One widely cited study is that by Cheshire et al. (1998). This uses a mover survey to examine selectivity in relation to employment status for a single neighbourhood in London. They argue that selective migration is significant, undermining efforts to change the composition of the neighbourhood. Larger studies based on mover surveys have found less clear evidence. In the United States, Coulton et al. (2009) found that selective migration appeared to *reduce* concentrations of poverty in their set of nine deprived neighbourhoods. The latter work is limited by the fact that status is measured only before the moves take place; if the out-movers were people who had seen an improvement in their situation, the impact of migration would look rather different. In the UK, Cole et al. (2007) draw on the results of their evaluation of a major neighbourhood regeneration programme, which included a mover survey across 39 deprived neighbourhoods. Like Cheshire et al., they conclude that selective migration tended to increased concentrations of unemployment in deprived areas but they also found that it reduced concentrations of poor health and raised average educational attainment.

Other studies have used a range of Census data sources with much wider geographic coverage. In relation to educational attainment, Bailey and Livingston (2008) conclude that selective migration exists but is very weak overall. Shuttleworth and colleagues (Shuttleworth and Barr 2009; Shuttleworth et al. 2010) provide a similar analysis for Northern Ireland. They identify some selective migration processes: people with higher educational qualifications are less likely to move to a more deprived neighbourhood and more likely to move to a non-deprived neighbourhood. For people moving to more deprived neighbourhoods, however, the rates for those with and without qualifications are actually strikingly similar. Like Bailey and Livingston (2008), their conclusion is that these processes have had "relatively small impacts on population patterns because people move short distances to areas similar to those they left" (Shuttleworth et al. 2010: p. 18). Jivraj (2012, this volume) reaches broadly similar conclusions.

Health researchers have made quite an intensive study of the selectivity of migration with respect to health. Their interest has been in trying to remove or control for the effects of selective migration in order to use inequalities in health between areas to assess changes in health inequalities more generally. Norman and colleagues (2005) show that morbidity and mortality rates rise in the most deprived areas as a result of selective migration, and that the out-migration of relatively healthy adults is a key factor here. Others, such as Connolly and O'Reilly (2007), find the opposite result: "overall migration … did not substantially alter the distribution of health through time, partly because the migrants out of the deprived and affluent areas were replaced by in-migrants with similar levels of health" (p. 1004). They cite a number of other studies, some that supported this view but others equally that contradict it.

Third, *mobility associated with ageing and the life-course plays a fundamental role in selective migration flows, frequently cutting across other factors*. This finding is the logical complement to the evidence discussed above about the importance of the life course for neighbourhood turnover but is not so widely acknowledged. Bailey and Livingston (2007) showed how there is a tendency for young adults in their 20s to move down the neighbourhood hierarchy, associated with the low resources they have at the start of their housing and neighbourhood careers. Older adults (particularly those in their 30s and 40s) tend to move up the hierarchy, reflecting their improving labour market and financial position. This age-related churning of the population through the neighbourhood system is illustrated in Fig. 2.1 below.

We might term this churning the "demographic conveyor". The analogy here is with a term used in climate science where slow-moving but massive ocean currents – such as the "North Atlantic conveyor" – have recently been understood to have quite fundamental impacts on the redistribution of energy around the Earth and hence on variations in climatic conditions (Houghton 2009). The "demographic conveyor" term is designed to convey the same impression. It provides a slow but steady overturning of population across the system, not redistributing 'energy' but bringing relatively young, healthy and well-educated adults into more deprived neighbourhoods. Further work is needed to unpack these flows, to explore their composition and impacts in more detail.

Fourth, *selective migration is not the only process at work in driving neighbourhood change, nor is it necessarily the most important*. Other processes may reinforce or reduce the impacts of selective migration. A small but growing number of studies have attempted to measure the relative contribution to neighbourhood change of these processes.

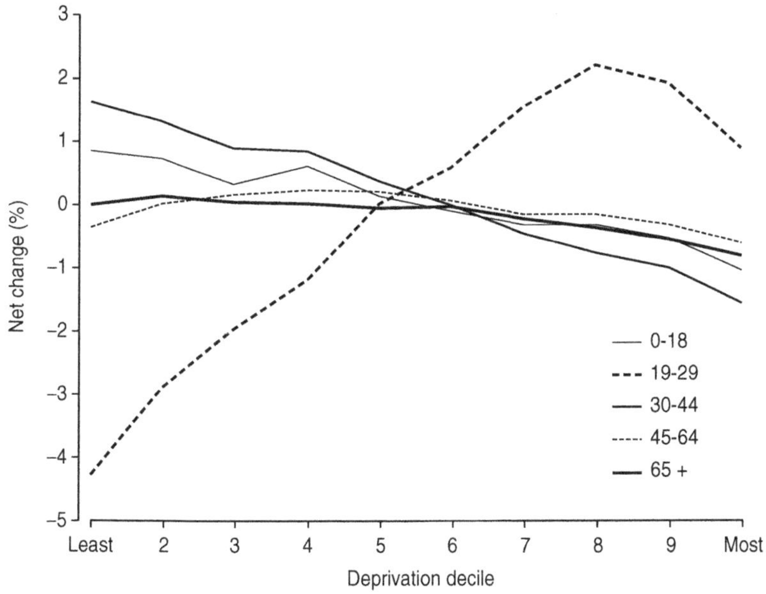

Fig. 2.1 Selective migration by age – England and Scotland, 2000–1 (Source: 2001 Census, Commissioned Tables C0572 © Crown copyright; Notes: This figure is a population-weighted average of results for England and Scotland; see Bailey and Livingston (2007: p. 49) for figures for individual countries)

One stream of work has examined the processes which alter the spatial concentration of ethnic groups over time. This has placed particular emphasis on the role played by natural change. Simpson (2004) for the UK and Musterd and De Vos (2007) for the Netherlands both show that changes in the concentrations of particular minority ethnic groups result from two opposing processes – net out- migration of the minority ethnic populations from areas of existing concentration, offset by higher levels of natural growth which tend to maintain those concentrations. These results directly challenge notions of active 'self-segregation' by minority ethnic groups which have been prevalent in policy discourses (Simpson et al. 2008).

In terms of socio-economic status, it is more common to contrast the effects of selective migration with those of social mobility or status change for non-movers. In the US, for example, Coulton et al. (2009) disaggregate changes in neighbourhood poverty rates into two main components: stayer change (improvement or worsening in poverty rates for non-movers); and mover change (differences in poverty rates for in- and out-movers i.e. selective migration). Their evidence shows that selective migration produced a small *reduction* in the poverty rates for their set of nine neighbourhoods (around 0.3% over a 3 year period) which was more than offset by a *rise* in poverty rates for non-movers (around 0.5%).

These different approaches have been combined and extended in a more comprehensive framework by Bailey (2012). That paper identifies a total of nine different processes which account for changes in neighbourhood composition over time, and hence changes in spatial segregation. These include selective migration, status change and natural change but also the impacts of other kinds of 'entry' to or 'exit' from the population: ageing into or out of the target range (in the case of the working age population, for example); moves to or from the communal establishment population; and migration into or out of the country. With longitudinal studies, sample attrition and sample accretion may also play a role. Using data from the Scottish Longitudinal Study, Bailey provides an initial study of the scale and nature of these flows in practice. The results support the view that selective migration flows have relatively modest impacts overall. Status changes for individuals were much more important in explaining changes in neighbourhood level spatial segregation.

Fifth, *the relative importance of selective migration and other processes may vary between different kinds of place*. Significant variations are apparent at the neighbourhood level. Some of these variations reflect broader regional factors at work. For example, opportunities for residential mobility are shaped by the state of the labour market and the housing system (see for example Bailey and Livingston 2008, in relation to variations in selective migration). Other variations are more localised.

This diversity of flows can be used to build new typologies of places and to explore whether these differences in context affect neighbourhood processes or relationships. Robson et al. (2008) construct a typology of deprived neighbourhood by looking at the origins and destinations of migrants. Their ideal-types are: transit, escalator, isolate and improver. 'Transit' neighbourhoods are characterised by flows from and to less deprived neighbourhoods, so there is a continually changing group of less deprived residents within the area. By contrast, 'isolate' neighbourhoods see migration exchanges through horizontal moves to or from other deprived locations. In the United States, Coulton et al. (2009) take a similar approach.

In her work on ethnicity, Finney (2012) takes this approach further in two senses. First she constructs her typology by examining the relative contribution of migration flows and natural change to changes in the size of each ethnic group in the neighbourhood. Second, she combines measures for the majority (White) population with those for minority ethnic groups so that her typology reflects both how the balance between ethnic groups is changing, the processes driving this change and whether this change occurs in the context of population growth or decline. She then illustrates how this might be used to understand residents' perceptions of community cohesion.

Summary

Three general points emerge from this short review. First, residential mobility and selective migration are both very heavily influenced by ageing and life-course events. Mobility and turnover remain driven fundamentally by demographics. Less widely appreciated, perhaps, is the impact on selective migration flows. There is a "demographic conveyor" bringing younger adults to start their neighbourhood careers in lower income areas, from which many will move on after relatively short periods of time. The effect is not equally strong in all deprived areas, nor is it necessarily the dominant flow in any particular area, but it is a process that underlies much else that is going on in the neighbourhood system. Lack of income (or low resources more generally) among young adults is what underpins this movement since it is what constrains their choices within the housing system, but they tend to be younger, healthier and better educated than the average for the neighbourhoods they enter.

Second, neighbourhood context may be defined as much by flows as by static or cross-sectional characteristics, and these flows are not limited to population turnover. While turnover has long been seen as a potential influence on a range of neighbourhood attributes, the studies discussed above highlight a much wider range of dynamics. Complex typologies can be constructed, the effects of which we have only just begun to explore. It should be stressed however that measuring a range of flows for small areas is likely to be difficult due to the problems of small numbers and the resulting 'noise'.

Third, there is the suggestion from research on residential mobility that responses to a given neighbourhood context may be more varied and subjective than previously assumed. There appears to be significant diversity in the ways in which people react to the same neighbourhood context. Neighbourhoods are multidimensional and what people value or what concerns them may be quite varied as a result. Objective neighbourhood characteristics may matter less than how individuals perceive or respond to their neighbourhood, and these responses may be shaped by factors that have not previously been included within quantitative modelling. Examining how different personality traits shape responses might be one way forward. Another would be to take more account of individuals' routes into particular places, or their histories or ties to other places.

Data Source Developments

As with work on neighbourhood effects, research into population dynamics is very demanding in data terms. If we wish to understand how places shape mobility intentions, we need data on both people and the places in which they live. For individuals, we want obvious socio-demographic characteristics for them, but we also want to know about their perceptions of their neighbourhood, and their relationships to it through social networks or affective attachments. We also want to be able to locate them within their households. For their neighbourhood, we want to understand not only the current composition but also the direction of change or trajectory. If we wish to study mobility outcomes, we need data that links people to the places they lived some time earlier. And if we wish to study how places change over time, we need to understand all the various flows that can impact on this, not just selective migration.

Until recently, research efforts have been hampered by the lack of longitudinal data for individuals linked to appropriate geographic units. However, there have been important developments in the UK in recent years. These include developments in longitudinal survey data, Census-based longitudinal data, and administrative data. These developments increase the potential value of these datasets for studying residential mobility and neighbourhood dynamics. We review these changes for each kind of data in turn.

Longitudinal Survey Data

The major UK longitudinal survey is the British Household Panel Study (BHPS) which has been running since 1991. Until recently, the opportunity to study neighbourhood change was limited by the fact that geographical identifiers were not provided below the level of Local Authority; in the UK, these are far too large to stand as proxies for neighbourhoods, having a median population around 110,000. More recently, a version of the BHPS has been made available with small area identifiers attached; these are for units with populations of around 1–2,000. This is potentially a major resource which has yet to be fully exploited. It offers scope to attach a wide variety of neighbourhood context measures, including those on trajectories and on flows. In 2009 the BHPS was replaced by the larger Understanding Society longitudinal study, which will improve matters further as the sample size rises to 40,000 households or 100,000 individuals.

The major advantage of this kind of data compared with Census or administrative sources is the ability to capture information on a wide range of individual perceptions of place. Barrages of questions on neighbourhood perceptions could be included for some or all respondents and repeated at varying intervals. Even with this size of sample, however, it is obviously not possible to provide data for individual neighbourhoods based on aggregate responses. The clustering within the sample is also relatively weak. The sample is clustered with an average of 18 households in each sampled postcode sector, which is likely to yield an average of 10 or 11 households interviewed. Postcode sectors are relatively large units for neighbourhood research, and uneven in size.

Census-Based Longitudinal Data

The UK Census provides some longitudinal data in the form of the question about place of residence one year previously. This can be used to measure the scale of net migration flows and estimate their impacts on neighbourhood composition (Bailey and Livingston 2008). It has the advantage of full population coverage and hence detail for small areas but it has the major limitation that data on personal characteristics are quite limited and measured only at the time of the Census (i.e. after any moves have taken place).

There are now three longitudinal datasets which combine data for a sample of individuals from successive Censuses. The Office for National Statistics (ONS) Longitudinal Study for England and Wales (ONS-LS) has been linking data for 1% of the population since 1971. The Scottish Longitudinal Study (SLS) has data from 1991 and 2001, and covers 5% of the population. There is also the Northern Ireland Longitudinal Study (NILS) which covers 28% of the population but started only in 2001. All three sources have linked this Census data to a range of health data, and to population registers that capture births and deaths. To use this data to assess the impacts of flows on neighbourhoods requires a set of stable neighbourhood boundaries over time, such as those developed in Scotland.

Data on neighbourhood context can be obtained by aggregating from individual data where there are sufficient cases or by attaching data from other Census or administrative sources. This can cover trajectories and flows potentially. Data on individuals is limited, however, with no data on subjective perceptions and not even a question on incomes. The impacts of selective migration can only be assessed through indicators such as social class, employment status or educational attainment. There is the danger that these may mask income or wealth differences, as discussed above. Finding ways to link the Longitudinal Study data to sources other than health service data or vital registrations would be a huge potential benefit. Links to administrative data on benefits or taxes would be particularly valuable since they would add most value in terms of measures of income.

Administrative Sources

Administrative data is information collected by organisations primarily for their own operational purposes. Large datasets are held by a range of public sector organisations. Administrative data sources can provide rich information on the trajectories of individuals and how these impact on neighbourhood change. In combination with other data, such information can contribute significantly to research into selective migration and neighbourhood change. We look briefly at three possibilities.

First, patient register data provides a good means of measuring migration flows. Data on individuals is captured when they register with a new doctor. Although registrations are known to vary by sex and age, it is considered the best source of data for tracking the movement of individuals at lower geographical levels (ONS 2010). On the other hand, it has relatively limited information on individual characteristics: only gender, age and address. The Office for National Statistics (ONS) uses this data, in combination with other sources, to produce estimates of internal migration within the UK and this is available at small area level (Lower Super Output Areas).

Second, the Work and Pensions Longitudinal Study (WPLS) is a dataset constructed by the Department for Work and Pensions (DWP). It links together benefit data held by DWP with data on employment, earnings, savings, tax credits and pensions from Her Majesty's Revenue and Customs (HMRC). The WPLS was introduced in 2004 but contains data back to 1999 and already contains hundreds of millions of records. There are several separate datasets linked by various individual identifiers (some based on fuzzy matching procedures). The sensitive nature of the data means that access is highly restricted.

Individual data is limited but the scale of the datasets gives the potential to aggregate to neighbourhood level to produce measures of context. In theory, these could provide measures of neighbourhood trajectories and even of flows. In practice, the quality of the address information is rather variable which may limit the value of this data. Where people are on benefits, and particularly on benefits that require frequent attendance at administrative offices, changes of address tends to be captured well. For those in employment, particularly higher paid jobs, address information is much less complete. Researchers at the Social Disadvantage Research Centre (SDRC) at the University of Oxford have used this data source to explore the individual-level employment transitions and geographical movements occurring in deprived neighbourhoods (Barnes et al. 2011). Better address data on individuals in work could be obtained by combining data from the WPLS with the patient register data discussed above. This is currently being considered by SDRC as part of research for the ESRC-funded Administrative Data Liaison Service (ADLS).[1]

Third, there is data on children available from the National Pupil Database (NPD). This was introduced in 2002 and is managed by the Department for Education (DfE). For each academic year the NPD contains information on pupil and school characteristics (e.g. age, gender, ethnicity, postcode, free school meal status, special educational needs, and attendance) from the Schools Census[2] and National Curriculum key stage attainment data. Data collection is a statutory requirement in England and Wales for all maintained schools. In a typical year information on approximately eight million pupils is included in the NPD. The NPD is one of the most accessible administrative datasets, and has been widely used for research purposes; see Jivraj (2012, this volume) for example.

Using information on home postcode, it is possible to track the geographical movement of pupils between time-points. Pupil characteristics such as ethnicity or FSM status (a proxy for income poverty) can be examined to see which pupils move and how this may contribute to neighbourhood change. Such analysis was undertaken as part of the national evaluation of the NDC programme in a study on the challenges to raising the educational attainment of children living in NDC areas which explored pupil mobility, including a comparison of the characteristics of 'inmovers' and 'outmovers' (Whitworth et al. 2009; Jivraj 2012).

[1] The ADLS act as an intermediary between academic researchers and data holding organisations to provide information, aid with communication and promote the use of administrative data. For more information see http://www.adls.ac.uk/

[2] Prior to 2007 this was known as the Pupil Level Annual School Census (PLASC).

Table 2.1 Comparing data sources for research on neighbourhood dynamics

	Longitudinal survey data	Census longitudinal data	Administrative sources
Individual data			
Socio-demographic characteristics over time	Yes	Limited	Limited
Individuals and households	Yes	Yes	Limited
Perceptions of neighbourhoods, networks, attachments	Possible	No	No
Neighbourhood data			
Socio-demographic composition	Possible to attach	Yes/possible to attach	Yes/possible to attach
Aggregate perceptions, networks, attachments	Limited	No	No
Trajectories and flows	Possible to attach	Yes/possible to attach	Yes/possible to attach

Summary

Table 2.1 provides a summary of the relative strengths and weaknesses of the three different types of data. Though some of these reflect peculiarities of the UK situation, many are likely to reflect similar issues in other countries. No one kind of data source is likely to provide researchers of neighbourhood dynamics with everything they need but combinations of different kinds of data have greater potential. One approach would involve the merger of longitudinal survey data which provides rich details on individuals and households with data on neighbourhoods characteristics and dynamics from Census or administrative sources. Some work has been done in this way but much more could be developed. A second approach would involve the merger of different kinds of administrative dataset to provide more complete coverage of status changes and residential mobility, as noted in relation to the patient register and the WPLS datasets above. A third approach would be based around adding to the data on individuals in the Census longitudinal datasets by matching it to greater range of administrative data, not just health records. In particular, the scope to derive information on incomes and benefits from the WPLS has great potential. Each of these approaches would present significant practical challenges, not least negotiating permissions, but they have great potential to add enormous value.

Conclusions

This chapter provides a review of recent studies on residential mobility and selective migration, and of the current state of datasets available to researchers of neighbourhood dynamics in the UK. The review was driven by the concern to provide some useful insights for neighbourhood effects researchers so it is to this issue that we return now.

Overall, the review makes it difficult to retain a conception of neighbourhoods as rigid containers for a more-or-less fixed group of people subject to the same set of experiences or reacting to these experiences in the same kinds of way. In general terms, neighbourhood effects research needs to get to grips with this complexity far more than it has managed previously. In this sense, the chapter reinforces many of the points made by Galster (2012) in the previous volume. He advocated using a 'pharmacological metaphor' of 'dosage-response relationships' to draw attention to a variety of dimensions in the possible relationship between neighbourhood context and individual response. On the 'dosage' side, these included a recognition of the importance of individual and neighbourhood dynamics: 'duration' of exposure (a function of individual mobility); 'consistency' (a function of the stability of neighbourhood characteristics over time); and trajectory (the direction of change for individuals or areas). On the 'response' side, these included questions about the 'universality' or variability of responses and the role of complex mediating factors including individual agency ('antidotes' or 'buffers'). The research on neighbourhood dynamics reinforces the need to take account of each of these dimensions.

More specifically, we might make three particular suggestions for future research. The first of these is about recognising the *subjectivity* of the neighbourhood experience. Individuals not only have different perceptions of their neighbourhood's boundaries and characteristics, they also experience places differently and respond to those experiences differently. The effect of a given neighbourhood context is therefore likely to vary between individuals. Recognising this contingency may help to bring neighbourhood effects into clearer focus. Variations may run along the lines of groups or characteristics which social researchers are used to measuring; the meaning of ethnic mix depends on an individual's ethnicity, for example. Other variations may depend on characteristics which quantitative researchers have rarely tried to capture. These might reflect personal histories or prior experiences; the kinds of place you grew up in or came from may shape your experiences of your current area. They might be influenced by trajectories and expectations of future moves – whether you see yourself living somewhere else in a few years time. They may be shaped by psychological attributes such as confidence, extroversion and so on.

Related to this first point, the second suggestion would be to focus on people experiencing *residential stress* as a result of the area in which they live. These are people expressing a desire to move because of neighbourhood characteristics. People do not have to be perceive a harm in order for it to be damaging but, if people are expressing such negative judgements on their area, they might provide particularly useful insights into causal mechanisms. Focussing on the 'frustrated movers' might be particularly helpful.

The third suggestion is to pay greater attention to *neighbourhood dynamics and flows*. Not only do people flow through places receiving varying durations of 'dose', places change too and change through different processes or flows. Neighbourhood trajectories may be as important as neighbourhood characteristics. A declining area may have lower satisfaction than one of similar status which is stable or on the rise, as existing research has shown. This may also lead to different patterns of socialising or of attachment, or produce different levels of stress for residents. Going further, research could focus on the different combinations of flow which underpin trajectories. An 'upward' trajectory produced by selective migration (e.g. through gentrification and displacement) is likely to be experienced quite differently to the same trajectory produced through upward mobility for existing residents. New typologies of dynamics and flows are needed to try to capture these variations.

The challenges of responding to neighbourhood population dynamics appear quite substantial, even daunting. The good news is that data sources have continued to develop, at least in the UK, as discussed in the second section of the paper. These developments have not been driven by a neighbourhoods agenda in most cases but they can meet at least some of the increasing demands of neighbourhoods researchers. Individual sources each contain limitations but, if we can solve the practical challenges and legal barriers, there is great scope for novel combinations of sources to provide fresh insights. Defending and extending these developments is therefore a critical task in the current fiscal climate.

Acknowledgements We are grateful to the participants at the seminar in Manchester, and to the editors and referees for helpful feedback on the earlier drafts of this chapter. Census output is Crown copyright and is reproduced with the permission of the Controller of HMSO and the Queen's Printer for Scotland.

References

Andersen, H. S. (2008). Why do residents want to leave deprived neighbourhoods? The importance of residents' subjective evaluations of their neighbourhood and its reputation. *Journal of Housing and the Built Environment, 23*(2), 79–101.

Bailey, N. (2012). How spatial segregation changes over time: Sorting out the sorting processes. *Environment and Planning A, 44*(3), 705–722.

Bailey, N., & Livingston, M. (2007). *Population turnover and area deprivation*. Bristol: Policy Press.

Bailey, N., & Livingston, M. (2008). Selective migration and area deprivation: Evidence from 2001 census migration data for England and Scotland. *Urban Studies, 45*(4), 943–961.

Bailey, N., Kearns, A., & Livingston, M. (2012). Place attachment in deprived neighbourhoods: The impacts of population turnover and social mix. *Housing Studies, 27*(4), 1–24.

Barnes, H., Garratt, E., McLennan, D., & Noble, M. (2011). *Understanding the worklessness dynamics of deprived areas*, DWP Research Report 779, London: Department for Work and Pensions.

Beatty, T., Lawless, P., Pearson, S., & Wilson, I. (2009). *Residential mobility and outcome change in deprived areas: Evidence from the new deal for communities programme*. London: CLG.

Boyle, P., Norman, P., & Rees, P. (2004). Changing places. Do changes in the relative deprivation of areas influence limiting long-term illness and mortality among non-migrant people living in non-deprived households? *Social Science & Medicine, 58*(12), 2459–2471.

Charles, C. Z. (2003). The dynamics of racial residential segregation. *Annual Review of Sociology, 29*(1), 167–207.

Cheshire, P., Flynn, N., & Jones, D. A. (1998). *Harlesden city challenge: Final evaluation*. London: LSE.

Cole, I., Lawless, P., Manning, J., & Wilson, I. (2007). *The moving escalator? Patterns of residential mobility in new deal for communities areas. Research report 32*. London: DCLG.

Connolly, S., & O'Reilly, D. (2007). The contribution of migration to changes in the distribution of health over time: Five-year follow-up study in northern Ireland. *Social Science & Medicine, 65*(5), 1004–1011.

Coulter, R., van Ham, M., & Feijten, P. (2010). *A longitudinal analysis of moving desires, expectations and actual moving behaviours* (Discussion Paper 5277). Bonn: IZA. http://ftp.iza.org/dp5277.pdf

Coulton, C., Teodos, B., & Turner, M. A. (2009). *Family mobility and neighbourhood change: New evidence and implications for community initiatives*. Washington, DC: Urban Institute.

de Souza Briggs, X., Popkin, S. J., & Goering, J. M. (2010). *Moving to opportunity: The story of an American experiment to fight ghetto poverty*. Oxford: Oxford University Press.

Dekker, K., & Bolt, G. (2005). Social cohesion in post-war estates in the Netherlands: Differences between socioeconomic and ethnic groups. *Urban Studies, 42*(13), 2447–2470.

Dietz, R. D. (2002). The estimation of neighborhood effects in the social sciences: An interdisciplinary approach. *Social Science Research, 31*(4), 539–575.

Ellen, I. G., & Turner, M. A. (1997). Does neighbourhood matter? Assessing recent evidence. *Housing Policy Debate, 8*(4), 833–866.

Feijten, P., & van Ham, M. (2009). Neighbourhood change… reason to leave? *Urban Studies, 46*(10), 2103–2122.

Finney, N. (2012). How ethnic mix changes and what this means for integration: Understanding neighbourhood population dynamics of ethnic groups. In M. van Ham et al. (Eds.), *Understanding neighbourhood dynamics: New insights for neighbourhood effects research*. Dordrecht: Springer.

Finney, N., & Simpson, L. (2009). Population dynamics: The roles of natural change and migration in producing the ethnic mosaic. *Journal of Ethnic and Migration Studies, 35*(9), 1479–1496.

Galster, G. (2001). On the nature of neighbourhood. *Urban Studies, 38*(12), 2111–2124.

Galster, G. (2008). Quantifying the effect of neighbourhood on individuals: Challenges, alternative approaches, and promising directions. *Schmollers Jahrbuch, 128*(1), 7–48.

Galster, G. (2012). The mechanism(s) of neighbourhood effects: Theory, evidence and policy implications. In M. van Ham, D. Manley, N. Bailey, L. Simpson, & D. Maclennan (Eds.), *Neighbourhood effects research: New perspectives* (pp. 23–56). Dordrecht: Springer.

Galster, G., Andersson, R., Musterd, S., & Kauppinen, T. M. (2008). Does neighbourhood income mix affect earnings of adults? New evidence from Sweden. *Journal of Urban Economics, 63*(3), 858–870.

Ginther, D., Haveman, R., & Wolfe, B. (2000). Neighborhood attributes as determinants of children's outcomes: How robust are the relationships? *Journal of Human Resources, 35*(4), 603–642.

Gramlich, E., Laren, D., & Sealand, N. (1992). Moving into and out of poor urban areas. *Journal of Policy Analysis and Management, 11*(2), 273–287.

Harris, D. R. (1999). "Property values drop when blacks move in, because…": Racial and socioeconomic determinants of neighborhood desirability. *American Sociological Review, 64*(3), 461–479.

Harris, D. R. (2001). Why are Whites and Blacks averse to Black neighbors? *Social Science Research, 30*(1), 100–116.

Hedman, L., & van Ham, M. (2011). Understanding neighbourhood effects: Selection bias and residential mobility. In M. van Ham et al. (Eds.), *Neighbourhood effects research: New perspectives*. Dordrecht: Springer.

Houghton, J. (2009). *Global warming: The complete briefing* (4th ed.). Cambridge: Cambridge University Press.

Jivraj, S. (2012). The components of socioeconomic neighbourhood change: An analysis of school census data at varying spatial scales in England. In M. van Ham et al. (Eds.), *Understanding neighbourhood dynamics: New insights for neighbourhood effects research*. Dordrecht: Springer.

Kasarda, J. D., & Janowitz, M. (1974). Community attachment in mass society. *American Sociological Review, 39*, 328–339.

Kearns, A., & Parkes, A. (2003). Living in and leaving poor neighbourhood conditions in England. *Housing Studies, 18*(6), 827–851.

Lee, B. A., Oropesa, R. S., & Kanan, J. W. (1994). Neighborhood context and residential mobility. *Demography, 31*(2), 249–270.

Livingston, M., Bailey, N., & Kearns, A. (2010). Neighbourhood attachment in deprived areas: Evidence from the north of England. *Journal of Housing and the Built Environment, 25*(4), 409–427.

Lu, M. (1999). Determinants of residential satisfaction: Ordered logit vs. regression models. *Growth and Change, 30*(2), 264–287.

Massey, D. S., Gross, A. B., & Shibuya, K. (1994). Migration, segregation and the geographic concentration of poverty. *American Sociological Review, 59*(3), 425–445.

Musterd, S., & De Vos, S. (2007). Residential dynamics in ethnic concentrations. *Housing Studies, 22*(3), 333–353.

Norman, P., Boyle, P., & Rees, P. (2005). Selective migration, health and deprivation: A longitudinal analysis. *Social Science & Medicine, 60*(12), 2755–2771.

Office for National Statistics (ONS) (2010). *Estimating internal migration: customer guidance notes*. London: ONS.

Oreopoulos, P. (2003). The long-run consequences of living in a poor neighbourhood. *Quarterly Journal of Economics, 118*(4), 1533–1575.

Pan Ké Shon, J.-L. (2010). The ambivalent nature of ethnic segregation in France's disadvantaged neighbourhoods. *Urban Studies, 47*(8), 1603–1623.

Parkes, A., & Kearns, A. (2003). Residential perceptions and housing mobility in Scotland: An analysis of the longitudinal Scottish house condition survey 1991–96. *Housing Studies, 18*(5), 673–701.

Quillian, L. (1999). Migration patterns and the growth of high-poverty neighborhoods, 1970–1990. *The American Journal of Sociology, 105*(1), 1.

Rabe, B., & Taylor, M. (2010). Residential mobility, quality of neighbourhood and life course events. *Journal of the Royal Statistical Society: Series A (Statistics in Society), 173*(3), 531–555.

Robson, B., Lymperopoulou, K., & Rae, A. (2008). People on the move: Exploring the functional roles of deprived neighbourhoods. *Environment and Planning A, 40*(11), 2693–2714.

Rossi, P. H. (1980). *Why families move* (2nd ed.). London: Sage.

Sampson, R., Raudenbush, S. W., & Earls, F. (1997). Neighborhoods and violent crime: A multi-level study of collective efficacy. *Science, 277*(5328), 918–924.

Shaw, C. R., & McKay, H. D. (1942). *Juvenile delinquency and urban areas*. Chicago: University of Chicago Press.

Shuttleworth, I., & Barr, P. (2009). *Tilting the balance? Population redistribution through internal migration in Northern Ireland, 2001–7*. Paper presented at the Fifth International Conference on Population Geographies, Dartmouth College, New Hampshire.

Shuttleworth, I., Gould, M., & Barr, P. (2010, April 14–18). *Short-distance migration, residential segregation and spatial scale: Perspectives from the Northern Ireland longitudinal study*. Paper presented at the AAG, Washington, DC.

Simpson, L. (2004). Statistics of racial segregation: Measures, evidence and policy. *Urban Studies, 41*(3), 661–681.

Simpson, L., Gavalas, V., & Finney, N. (2008). Population dynamics in ethnically diverse towns: The long-term implications of immigration. *Urban Studies, 45*(1), 163–183.

Suttles, G. (1972). *The social construction of communities*. Chicago: University of Chicago Press.

van Ham, M., & Clark, W. A. V. (2009). Neighbourhood mobility in context: Household moves and changing neighbourhoods in the Netherland. *Environment and Planning A, 41*(6), 1442–1459.

van Ham, M., & Feijten, P. (2008). Who wants to leave the neighbourhood? The effect of being different from the neighbourhood population on wishes to move. *Environment and Planning A, 40*(5), 1151–1170.

Whitworth, A., Wilkinson, K., McLennan, D., Noble, M., & Anttila, C. (2009). *Raising educational attainment in deprived areas: The challenges of geography and residential mobility for area-based initiatives*. London: CLG.

Chapter 3
The Causes of Long-Term Neighbourhood Change

Geoffrey Meen, Christian Nygaard, and Julia Meen

Introduction

In recent years, a considerable amount of research has been conducted into the impact of neighbourhood structures on economic performance. This is a technically difficult area, where the key issue is whether location has an effect on outcomes independently of the socio-economic characteristics of an individual and his/her family. However, the question is, perhaps, less pressing if neighbourhoods are constantly evolving, so that, for example, no neighbourhood remains permanently impoverished. The processes by which local areas change, or remain impervious to change, provide the focus of this chapter. Amongst the key issues in dynamic neighbourhood economics are: (i) the factors that determine the initial distribution of populations and development patterns, (ii) the reasons why some neighbourhoods maintain their primacy, even when any initial advantages disappear, (iii) the factors that influence patterns of segregation or mixing, (iv) the determinants of neighbourhood change. These are the questions which this chapter begins to address. As discussed below, a feature of most urban structures is that relative spatial patterns of wealth and poverty can remain broadly unchanged or persist for decades if not centuries. Many factors contribute to this, including the geography/geology and the history of physical development. Once an area becomes developed, property rights and other interests generate lock-in to existing spatial structures. This causes problems for conventional empirical analysis. First, time-series data sets are rarely

G. Meen (✉) • C. Nygaard
Department of Economics, School of Politics, Economics and International Relations, The University of Reading, Whiteknights, Reading RG6 6AA, UK
e-mail: g.p.meen@reading.ac.uk; c.a.b.nygaard@reading.ac.uk

J. Meen
Oxford Archaeology, Janus House, Osney Mead, Oxford OX2 0ES, UK
e-mail: Julia.meen@oxfordarch.co.uk

M. van Ham et al. (eds.), *Understanding Neighbourhood Dynamics: New Insights for Neighbourhood Effects Research*, DOI 10.1007/978-94-007-4854-5_3,

sufficiently long to discover major evidence of any change. Second, if change does eventually occur, it may be sudden and exhibit a highly non-linear process. Third, in practice, the most appropriate localised data sets are often unavailable.

These problems imply that one approach alone is unlikely to unravel the complexities of neighbourhood change. Therefore, this chapter brings together the results of a number of different strands of research from recent years undertaken by the authors. This includes work on spatial poverty traps and spatial lock-in, local variations in housing supply elasticities, self-organisation, and work on long-run data sets, notably for London from the mid nineteenth century, designed to deal with the issue of persistence, which cannot be taken into account on more conventional, shorter data sets. All the strands have shortcomings, but contribute to the overall evidence base.

The remainder of this chapter is organised as follows. The next section considers original neighbourhood population distributions. One school of thought suggests that initial natural advantages give rise to patterns of population and industry that are reinforced over time, because of increasing returns. There are a number of primarily US studies in the literature (e.g. for New York and Boston), of why cities developed, but the main case study in this chapter is Melbourne in Australia. Melbourne has the advantage that its history can be traced very closely from its initial European settlement in the 1830s. The impact of geology on the location of wealthy neighbourhoods stands out very clearly and this still influences the distribution today. The next section provides a further case study, in this instance for London, to demonstrate issues that relate to very long-run urban change – the persistence of residential patterns, the non-linearity of change and the importance of slum clearance programmes. The next three sections consider three different strands of research. The work on spatial poverty traps and supply elasticities uses cross-section data and searches for evidence of non-linearity and local supply variations. The work on self-organisation uses cellular automata, whereas the work on long-run data sets uses convergence tests for London between 1881 and 2001, paying particular attention to the impact of slum clearance programmes.

Initial Population Distributions

The natural advantages of any area, e.g. closeness to natural resources, ports, transport hubs, or soil fertility, ensure that such locations are able to establish an advantage which, through increasing returns, may be sustained over long periods of time, because of the externalities associated with agglomeration. In this case, history and path dependence (the way in which institutions and structures from the past influence current choices, see North 2005) are crucial to explaining spatial structure. Glaeser (2005a, b) considers the historical development of New York and Boston respectively. He suggests that, despite the current strength of both cities, over the long term, the two have experienced different trajectories. Apart from short periods, New York has experienced almost continuous growth, whereas Boston had to re-invent itself in order to counteract declining fortunes. Initially, both cities had natural advantages, for example, the superiority of New York's deep water port and its connection to the Great Lakes, or Boston's religious foundations, which promoted social cohesion and put an emphasis on education. But their subsequent status is strongly related to their ability to attract high-skilled workers and to act as an information hub.

However, these studies do not consider distributions within cities and Melbourne provides a useful case study. For those outside Australia, Melbourne may seem a surprising choice, but, as mentioned above, its history is well-defined from the period of European settlement. Melbourne experienced major shocks, notably in the 1850s and 1880s (a gold rush in the former and a speculative boom in the latter – the period known as "Marvellous Melbourne", Davison 2005), which led, in 1891, to Melbourne having the second highest rateable value (after London) of any city in the British Empire (Briggs 1963, p. 278).

Figure 3.1 sets out some of the features of Melbourne, which played a major part in an explanation of the original development patterns. European settlement from the 1830s took place primarily on the relatively fertile alluvial flats and mudstones/sandstones, which now form the CBD and parts of the eastern suburbs. The western districts beyond the Maribyrnong River are dominated by basalt rock and were quickly established as the industrial areas of the city, aided by the proximity to the bay. Similarly, to the East of the CBD, along the western bank of the Yarra River (Melbourne's main river), the working class districts of Fitzroy, Collingwood and Richmond are all based on basalt rock. In fact the western bank at this point provides a further social divide and the wealthy districts of Hawthorn and Kew on the eastern bank lie on mudstone/sandstone and also have a higher elevation, looking across the city. More generally, higher elevations attracted the wealthy. For example, within working-class North Melbourne, the Hotham Hill area attracted wealthy residents. Many of their residences are still there today, whereas the slums in the valley have been swept away.[1]

A simple regression of the average house price in 2004 in each Melbourne postcode on the different rock formations in each area (distinguishing between sedimentary, metamorphic and igneous) reveals significant differences in price patterns. Dwellings built on sedimentary rocks have prices approximately one third higher than those built on igneous rocks (such as in the western districts). Geological structure clearly is an exogenous variable to modern house prices. As noted above, elevation is one factor still likely to have an influence – Kew and Hawthorn, for example, in the eastern suburbs lie on sedimentary rocks. But this is not the whole story. The alluvial flats are typically still high priced, despite the fact that the original advantages in terms of soil fertility are, arguably, now less of an issue. Even without allowing for any more modern innovations to city structure the R^2 is 0.12 and 0.20 if location co-ordinates are added. Persistence, built on geology, still seems to be important in Melbourne.

[1] The valley was still experiencing heavy flooding in 2010.

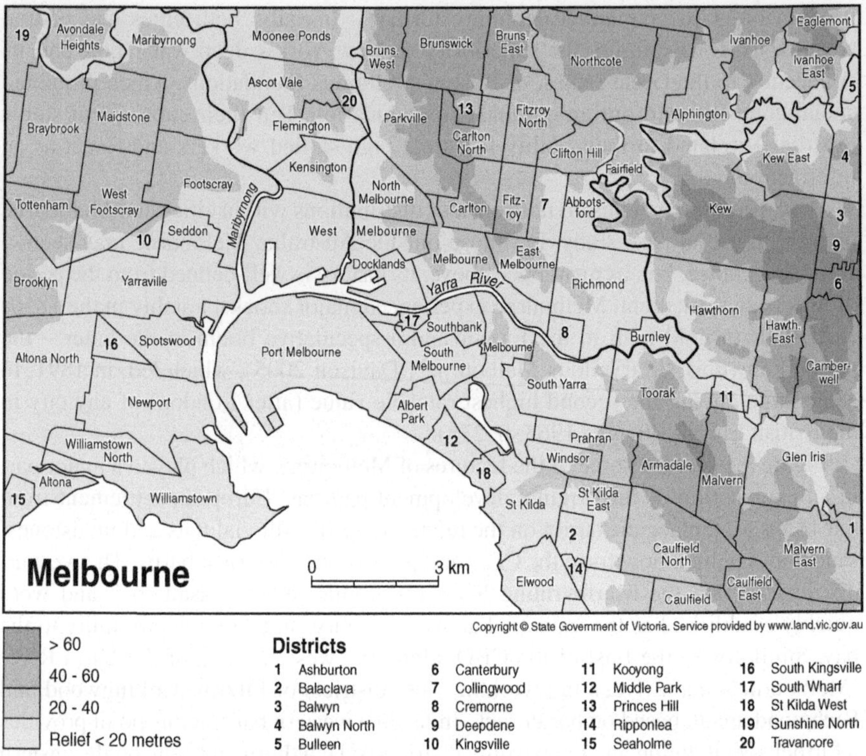

Fig. 3.1 Melbourne and its suburbs

Melbourne's rivers were equally as important for the location of the wealthier areas as geology. Original development took place just upstream from the Yarra Falls, which provided a natural divide between the tidal brackish water downstream and the upstream freshwater. Until the destruction of the falls in the 1880s, the lower level provided a basin for shipping; trade expanded rapidly particularly after the discovery of the Victorian goldfields in the 1850s. Excise duties provided the most important revenue source for the colony and the (third) Customs House on the banks of the pool, which still stands as a museum, was completed in 1876 and remains one of Melbourne's most elegant buildings, reflecting its importance. By contrast, the original development around the Maribyrnong River (the second largest river) was primarily working class and industrial since it consisted of salt water and early graziers favoured the upper reaches with freshwater tributaries. A further set of issues arises from planning. The grid pattern of Melbourne's CBD was set out by surveyor Robert Hoddle in 1837, mainly determined by geography, and extended versions, to allow for urban sprawl, remain in place today.

Nevertheless, despite the argument that historical patterns are crucial to understanding today's distributions, they are certainly not identical. The idea of geological determinism, irrespective of subsequent human geography and economic processes, is unappealing (as evidence from the R^2 above indicates). Originally working class neighbourhoods such as Richmond, Fitzroy and Collingwood have all been gentrified to some extent, because of their inner city locations. Furthermore, the river quality of the Maribyrnong has improved, industrial development in some parts has been replaced by high quality housing, and the western basalt districts are being developed for housing as part of the Melbourne growth areas, as the Eastern suburbs become increasingly congested. Therefore, economic processes operate in addition to historical constraints. Nevertheless if path dependence exists, empirical analysis should reveal some relationship between current patterns of segregation and the patterns in the first half of the nineteenth century.

Path dependence may arise not only from geology, but also because of the longevity of the housing stock. Glaeser and Gyourko (2005) suggest that modern work on urban dynamics ignores the link with housing and the physical structure of cities. In their model, cities exhibit asymmetric responses to periods of growth and decline; because of the durability of the housing stock, cities grow faster than they decline. Typically, demolition rates of older properties in declining areas are low, rather than being replaced as they become economically obsolete. Consequently, the spatial structures of these areas of a city change only slowly, with the poorest elements of the population trapped there. This is a further example of spatial lock-in; once areas have been developed, it becomes difficult to change the basic characteristics of an area.

Issues in Long-Run Change

A further question is the extent to which areas, initially established because of their natural advantages, have managed to preserve their position over time, even if the initial advantages have become irrelevant for subsequent development. Empirical studies of this form have used much longer data sets than typically appear in time-series econometrics. Studies consider two key questions: (i) whether spatial structures persist; (ii) the extent to which structures change in response to large external shocks or whether they eventually return to their initial positions. Research by Davis and Weinstein (2002, 2008) and Bosker et al. (2007) concentrate on the effects of World War II bombings – the former in the case of Japan and the latter for Germany. Davis and Weinstein conclude that the growth rates of bombed Japanese cities recovered in the post-war period, despite the widespread destruction and find that, by 1960, US bombing had little effect on relative city sizes. By contrast, Bosker et al. (2007) find evidence that large shocks may be sufficient to shift city population distributions permanently. Looking at the Vietnam war, Miguel and Roland (2011) suggest that US bombings had little permanent effect on local poverty rates.

A more descriptive approach considers summary measures of the spatial distribution of disadvantaged households and how these measures change over time. For example, have the populations of cities or other spatial entities become more polarised in terms of wealth or have they converged? The spatial scale of analysis depends on data availability, which is usually determined by administrative boundaries. In the case of the UK, studies are often based on sub-divisions of local authorities, such as wards.

Meen et al. (2005) constructed Indices of Dissimilarity for unemployment rates in the wards of all the English local authorities in 2001. He found that, not only do the older, northern authorities have higher unemployment rates, but they also exhibit a higher degree of segregation within the authorities. Furthermore, the most segregated authorities have generally remained in this position for the previous 30 years, despite the stance of government policy to improve social mixing. Indeed, Dorling et al. (2007) find that spatial poverty patterns have widened. Consequently, UK data suggest that there is a high degree of stability in the relative positions of local areas.

At one level, the persistence of segregation within cities should cause little surprise – conventional location theory suggests that segregated communities are likely to be the norm and reflects the income elasticity of housing demand; therefore policy is fighting against deeply-rooted market processes. However, the predicted position becomes slightly more complex once some of the assumptions of the standard monocentric model are relaxed, particularly if neighbourhood externalities such as pollution, environmental quality and crime rates are taken into account. Whereas the standard model predicts that wealthier households are likely to be concentrated in the city suburbs, this is not necessarily the case if inner cities have their own attractions, raising the quality of life (Brueckner et al. 1999). But, even in this extended model, segregation between wealthy and poor households remains the likely outcome.

But, as comparative static models, standard location theory contributes little to explaining the dynamics of change and alternative approaches are required. As noted above, dissimilarity indices suggest little change in spatial structure over the last 30 years in the UK, but change clearly does take place, if sufficiently long time periods are considered, for example through urban sprawl.

In principle, change may occur both gradually or in discrete jumps and Meen (2009) suggests that neighbourhood change takes place in response to four types of shocks:

(i) Exogenous innovations: examples are wars, acts of terrorism, acts of God.
(ii) Policy innovations: these include major infrastructure changes, e.g. new road networks, new social housing estates, slum clearance and major regeneration schemes.
(iii) Technology innovations: for example, the Industrial Revolution, powered flight, motorised transport.
(iv) Endogenous change: migration is the most notable, both in to and out of an area, where the flows have different compositions in terms of economic status.

Discrete jumps occur, with the exception of (iv), irregularly. Furthermore, shocks may have to be very large to have any discernible impact (and, as in the case of Davis and Weinstein above, areas can still return to their original positions). A lock-in of spatial structures may occur because major area redevelopment only takes place occasionally. Meen and Nygaard (2011) show that, in parts of the East End of London, local areas changed little between the mid to late nineteenth century and World War II – the area was dominated by poor quality terraced housing. But, subsequently, the area changed because of the destruction of properties arising from the heavy bombing of the docks in the war (London Topographical Society 2005, Map 65), although the street layouts remained broadly the same until the early 1990s. It was not until the major redevelopments associated with the Docklands – driven by the London Docklands Development Corporation between 1981 and 1998 – that the structure fundamentally altered. Therefore, large shocks – war and policy in this instance – were necessary for change to happen.

Figure 3.2 shows the importance of the different slum clearance programmes that were in operation in London from 1860 until the mid 1970s. The cleared areas are calculated by plotting changes at individual property levels onto historical GIS maps and shows that a high proportion of East, North East and South London were redeveloped over the hundred years. But development was piecemeal rather than to a general plan. As Thurley (2010) argues, the failure to implement grand plans for London, particularly in the nineteenth century, compared with other European capitals, such as Paris and Vienna, reflect the triumph of commercial and individual interests over the wider public good, the lack of a strong city-wide government until the formation of the London County Council, the under-representation of London MPs in Parliament and the unwillingness of Parliament to spend on London infrastructure projects. More generally, the diversity of property rights makes wholesale development difficult. Since the density of housing is high, obtaining agreement for rebuilding over a large number of individual owners contributes to the lock-in of existing structures. However, the effect of slum clearance programmes on urban change is not clear a priori. On the one hand, the improved environment and better quality housing may attract wealthier households. But on the other hand, if the older properties are replaced with newer social sector housing estates, the clearances could lock in the segregation of poorer households.

Self-Organisation and Social Interactions

Persistence in segregated, spatial patterns, coupled with periods of infrequent but major structural shifts are consistent with self-organisation arising from the properties of complex systems. However, segregation arising from self-organisation has different policy implications from the case in which segregation arises from the standard location model, discussed above. In the latter, segregation is the outcome of the optimal decisions by individual households. In the absence of externalities, it is an efficient outcome and does not necessarily merit government intervention. By contrast, patterns of segregation under self-organisation arise from the interdependencies between the decisions of households, leading to a form of externality and possible market failure. This can be demonstrated from the classic Schelling

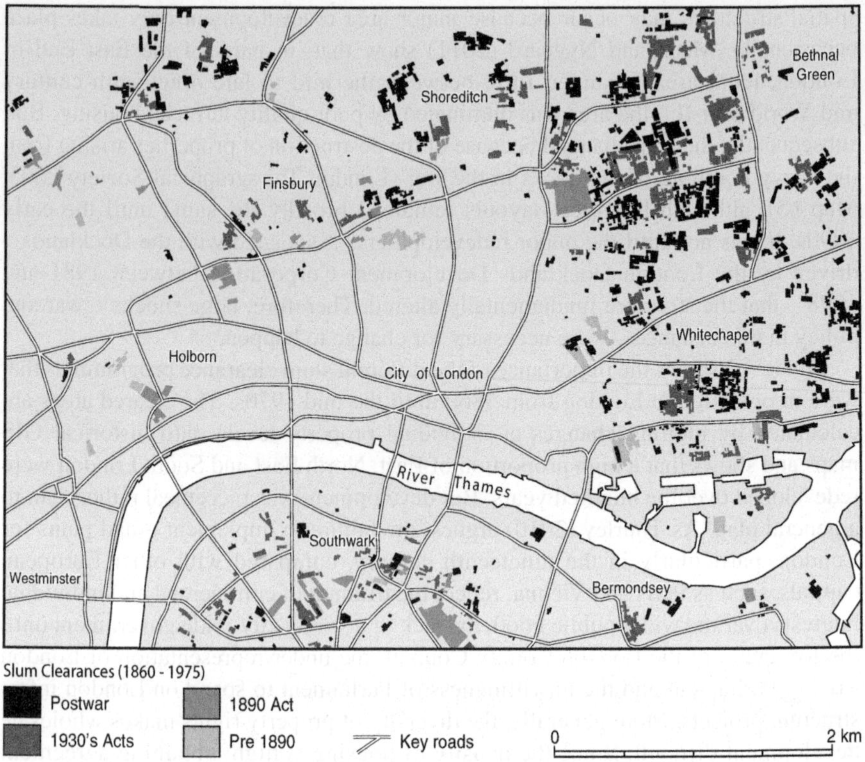

Fig. 3.2 Slum clearance programmes in London 1860–1975 (Source: Slum clearance representation maps (authors' calculation) are based on copies of LCC representation maps stored at the London Metropolitan Archives and are derived from Historic Ordinance Survey County Series 1:2500 1st revision (1893–1915) and 2nd revision (1906–1939) from EDINA Digimap and Landmark information Group. The nineteenth century Thames and docks is from Gregory et al. (2009) and nineteenth century main roads are from Mooney et al. (2009))

(1971) model, which shows that mild preferences about the characteristics of your neighbours (these may be ethnic or social status for example) lead to more highly segregated communities than would be expected. Furthermore, more recent developments of the basic Schelling approach, (See for instance Young 1998, 2001; Krugman 1996) show that segregation is a stochastically-stable state. Even if complete integration were to occur, then small random shocks are likely to lead to a complete breakdown of the structure, eventually leading to segregated communities.

The principles of self-organisation within neighbourhoods can be demonstrated using agent-based cellular automata models (CA). Furthermore, they show how structural change can occur in response to a series of purely random shocks, which take areas to a threshold or tipping point. As a demonstration, taken from Meen and Meen (2003), consider two groups of agents equal in number – rich (light) and poor (dark). These are initially randomly distributed in locations on a flat plain lattice,

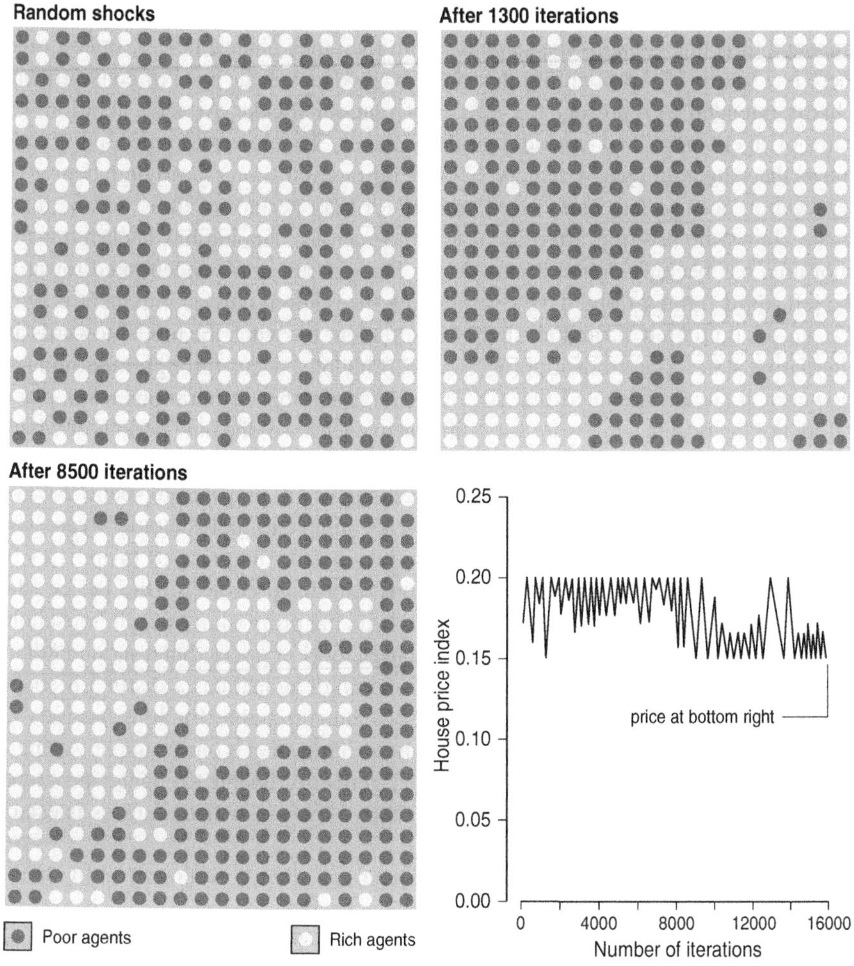

Fig. 3.3 Tipping in a random matching model (Source: Based on Meen and Meen (2003))

representing a city (first frame of Fig. 3.3). The rich are assumed to have an income of 1 and poor have 0.75. Each agent is defined as content if she lives in a neighbourhood where a minimum of 35%[2] of agents are of the same type. The neighbourhood is taken as the eight squares surrounding the agent. Under the rules of the game, two agents are chosen at random and may change places. If the contentment of one

[2] The precise percentage is unimportant. Fully integrated communities might imply 50%.

increases, but the other falls, no move takes place. But if the contentment of one rises and the other remains the same (or both rise) they change places. In addition, there is a small (2%) probability that they swap whatever the level of contentment. This is intended to represent the effects of random shocks. At each iteration, all pairs of agent meet and consider trading places. The second frame of Fig. 3.3 shows the state after approximately 1,300 iterations and shows that a high degree of segregation occurs. This state may continue for long periods of time, but the third frame shows the position after about 8,500 iterations. Tipping has occurred – the poor area has become rich and vice versa. The rich are now concentrated towards the left (third frame of Fig. 3.3). Even though the random move component is only 2%, an accumulation of random shocks is sufficient to switch the model towards an alternative state. Therefore, tipping can, in principle, occur through randomness. However, it should be noted that (i) a very large number of iterations takes place before tipping occurs – these are very infrequent events; (ii) the time periods at which tipping occurs is unpredictable.

To show this in different form, suppose all agents are prepared to spend 20% of their income on housing. Therefore, prices are higher in high income areas. The final frame plots a time series over the iterations for the price of properties in a neighbourhood located towards the bottom right-hand corner of the lattice (the average over nine squares). The price depends on the proportion of each household type in the neighbourhood and shows initial high level of prices, but a sudden fall as neighbourhood tipping occurs. The price function demonstrates a distinct S-shape and illustrates the point that neighbourhoods remain stable for long periods of time, but when they switch, they switch quickly. Gentrification is one example. A single (rich) household moving to a declining area is, generally, unable to change its nature, but once a group of households of similar status moves in, a critical mass is established, sufficient to generate area take off.

This is an example of more general peer group effects, where an individual's behaviour depends not only on his or her own characteristics, but also on the behaviour of peers, including their location choices. The role of peer group effects has been discussed in quantitative models of criminal behaviour and schooling, for example (Glaeser et al. 1996). In such models, an individual's educational performance depends not only on likely future returns to education, but also on the attitude towards education of the peer group. Poor performance by adolescent males is sometimes attributed to this source. The interactions between peers can lead to social multipliers, cumulative causation, increasing returns and poverty traps, since initial small shocks are reinforced through peer group interactions.

Non-linear Change, Implications for Neighbourhoods and the Local Price Elasticity of Supply

Models of complex systems using social interactions and peer groups imply non-linear threshold outcomes of which local poverty traps can be one manifestation. Durlauf (2006, p. 143) suggests that, formally, poverty traps are limiting cases of economic immobility or are states in which the persistence of economic conditions is arbitrarily long. However, in the current state of development, it remains the case that spatial models in the CA tradition are based on simple rules of behaviour, rather than on fully estimated models (see, for example, Bossomaier et al. 2007; Gilbert et al. 2009). Although Blume and Durlauf (2001) and Durlauf (1997) show how social interaction models can be related to conventional discrete choice models, in practice, there are few micro data sets that are available at neighbourhood level, that allow the models to be adequately estimated. Consequently, tests of non-linearity have taken rather different routes. A series of papers Quercia and Galster (1997), Galster and Zobel (1998), Galster et al. (2000), Galster (2002) investigates the evidence for non-linear thresholds in the US.

As a second-best alternative to estimating the neighbourhood social interactions model directly, one approach is to test whether there is any evidence of poverty traps in local areas on more aggregated data. Meen (2009) investigated the evidence for non-linearity in cross-section house price data for English local authority districts, using a logistic function, (3.1), where prices are related to a set of indicators – deprivation, incomes, the number of households and the dwelling stock. Using a variety of tests for non-linearity, some support for a threshold was found. The relationships between house prices and deprivation for 2001 and 2004 are shown in Fig. 3.4.

$$y_i = 1 - \frac{b_1}{1 + e^{(c_2 + c_3 \mathrm{IMD}_i + c_4 (H/HH)_i + c_5 (\mathrm{INC})_i + \varepsilon_{1i})}} \tag{3.1}$$

y_i = local authority house prices relative to the maximum regional price in which the local authority exists
IMD = Index of Multiple Deprivation (relative to regional average)
H = number of owner-occupied dwellings (relative to regional average)
HH = number of households (relative to regional average)
INC = household income (relative to regional average)
ε = error term
i denotes a spatial subscript (i.e. the local authority)

In Fig. 3.4 thresholds lie at approximate values of ±30 (expressed as deviations from the mean level of deprivation) and the curves become almost completely flat at values of approximately ±70. The main implication is that policy would have to reduce deprivation in any area to a value of approximately 30, before it will "take off" of its own accord. If regeneration expenditures only reduce deprivation from, say, 70–60, the impact is very modest. Escape for any area as a whole (as opposed to individuals in the area) from poverty traps requires the most deprived local areas to reach the take-off points. As above, periodically, areas may experience large shocks that bring them to those points through wars, natural disasters or technological change. But more modest policy changes may be insufficient. The required government expenditures for the most deprived areas to reach the take-off point may be prohibitive. Consequently, stable patterns emerge.

In Fig. 3.4, the values are an index, but to give a feel for the magnitudes involved, in the North West the maximum value of the index for a local authority district is 28

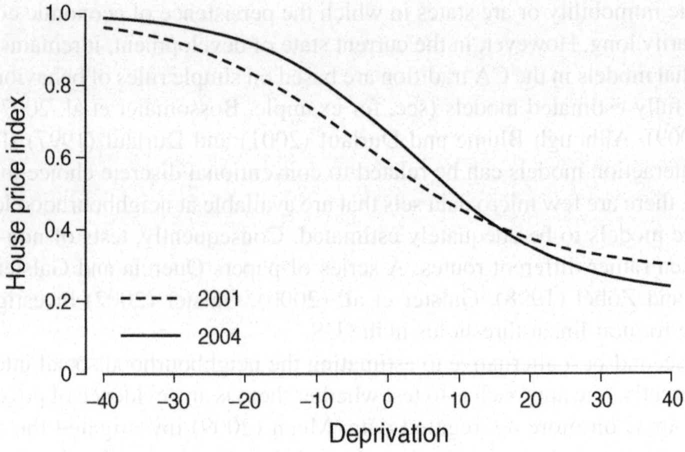

Fig. 3.4 Relationship between English local authority house prices and deprivation (Source: Based on Meen (2009))

in Knowsley, (after subtracting the regional average value). Therefore, even the most deprived local authorities are only just around the threshold. In fact, most districts lie in the steepest part of the curve. The implication is that no local authority can be "written off" as a whole – even the most deprived local authorities have their wealthy parts. This is hardly surprising since most local authorities have a mixture of "good" and "bad" areas and suggests the need to look at deprivation at a finer spatial level. In terms of Census Output Areas (OAs) for the Northern regions of England, Meen (2009) calculates that approximately 1 % of OAs have deprivation scores above 70, but the percentage is much lower in the South East. Nevertheless, in terms of regeneration expenditures, this is a significant number of areas that are potentially stuck in poverty traps. Furthermore, since, by implication, the expected capital gain in the most deprived areas is lower than in areas that lie on the steepest part of the curve, private investors or owner-occupiers are less likely to be attracted to the former.

A second strand of research using local cross-section data examines the extent to which historical land-use patterns affect the price elasticity of new housing supply (Meen and Nygaard 2011). In the absence of land-use policy restrictions, it might be expected that the price elasticity of housing supply would be higher on green field sites, since redevelopment of existing sites is more expensive (see Fig. 3.2 above). In fact, using a sample of Medium Level Super Output Areas (MSOAs) along the Thames Valley to the East and West of London, the price elasticity is noticeably higher on brownfield sites, reflecting the strength of policy aimed at encouraging development on the latter. However, even taking policy into account, historical land-use patterns and geography still have a major impact on the supply of new homes.

Evidence of Change from Long-Run Data Sets

If spatial patterns are highly persistent, rather than using cross-section data, a preferable approach is to employ very long-run information. But the typical data sets employed by time-series econometricians, say 40 or 50 years, are unlikely to reveal full evidence of change, because the shocks identified in the section on long-run change take place rarely. Although appealing, the disadvantage of using long-run data is that they are generally unavailable off-the-shelf and have to be painstakingly compiled from original sources. In this section, the evidence is considered whether the distribution of the most disadvantaged areas has changed over time, in particular, whether the areas of lowest social status in 1881 have caught up with the better areas by 2001. Although the section on long-run change identified a range of shocks that could change spatial structures, slum clearance programmes are, arguably, amongst the most important and receive particular attention. Results are taken from Meen and Nygaard (2010) and refer to Central London.

But, first, it was argued above that the required data at fine spatial scales, necessary to estimate social interaction models, are not generally available in the UK. An exception arises from nineteenth century data, where, from digitised census records, names, addresses and occupations are available for all census years between 1851 and 1901. Individual records after that date are not yet available under the 100 year rule. However, the nineteenth century data imply that panels of individual movements can be constructed over 50 years and, furthermore, based on the occupations of residents in the areas, measures of area social status can be constructed at very fine spatial scales. For the tests described below, the nineteenth century London parishes are divided into five groups – North, South, Central, East and West. In each of the groups, 100 male household heads are sampled, based on the 1881 census, and are tracked backwards and forwards between 1851 and 1901, along with their eldest male child and father. In addition, information is collected for 1881 on the occupational status of the immediate neighbours of the household heads, which are used to construct neighbourhood status indicators.

Therefore, it is possible to construct panel data sets throughout the second half of the nineteenth century, although even small samples are highly labour-intensive. These can be used to trace the development of local areas and also to follow the migration patterns of individuals (Meen et al. 2007). As an example of the information available, one head of household, George Sewell, who lived at 33 Great Saffron Hill (Central London) at the time of the 1881 census can be tracked. George was aged 34, but had not moved far from his birth location of Clerkenwell. He was a brass finisher by trade. Although he was widowed, he lived with his one son Joseph, aged 11, who was still at school. Overall ten people lived at Number 33, which was below the average density for the street of 14 persons per dwelling. By 1891, George (45) had remarried to Louisa (37) and they lived with five children, George (16), Ada (15), Henry (6), William (4), and Stephen (2). They lived in two rooms at 22 St

Helena Place and George was employed as a Dipper and Burnisher.[3] In 1901, they still lived in the same two rooms, although George junior and Ada had moved on by this time. George was now recorded as aged 53 and was still married to Louisa (47). The sons Henry (16), William (14) and Steven (12) were still there and Henry is noted as being "feeble minded from childhood" and had no employment. William was a hawker and Steven a paper distributor. George, himself, was still a Dipper and Burnisher.

Returning to George's eldest son Joseph (by previous marriage), in 1891 he was now aged 21 and was living in two rooms at 5 Smithfield with his uncle William Whales, William's wife and three children. Joseph was still single and was employed as a glass beveller. By 1901, Joseph had moved to occupy 2 rooms at 20 Malta Street in Clerkenwell. Now aged 30 at the time of the census, he was a sheet glass worker and was married to Rosaline (29) – a french polisher. She was also born in Clerkenwell. They had a daughter called Rosaline (7). Nine people in total lived at number 20.

It is also possible to work backwards from the 1881 census to 1851. For example, in 1871, George was 25 and married to his 25 year-old first wife, living with their 1-year old son. They lived at the same address as in 1881 and George was still a Brass Finisher. In 1861, 17 year-old George lived with his parents in Hatton Wall (around the corner from Saffron Hill) along with his brother Henry (22) and sister Ellen (14). George is recorded as a labourer. In 1851, George (7) lived with his parents and brother and sister at 12, Gunpowder Alley in the parish of St Brides. His father's name is difficult to decipher, but he was a labourer, born in Gloucestershire; his mother, Henrietta, was born in St Pancras. This one example, traces the history of three generations of the Sewell family in the nineteenth century. Therefore, it is feasible to conduct empirical studies of intergenerational persistence. Furthermore, micro migration studies can be conducted. This one example suggests that intergenerational persistence in occupation and location is strong and, since George never moved more than a short distance from his place of birth, moves were very short distance, consistent with one of Ravenstein's (1885) laws of migration.

Moreover, since the same information on neighbours can also be compiled, it is possible to build up neighbourhood profiles. Meen et al. (2007) discuss the historical development of Saffron Hill (the street in which George Sewell lived in 1881) to the current day. In the eighteenth century, the Saffron Hill area was notorious as an overcrowded slum, frequented by criminals, despite lying only a kilometre from the British Museum. In 1831 Saffron Hill was described as a steep, narrow, undrained way, comprising rotting Jacobean, Stuart and early Georgian tenements. But over the following two centuries, Saffron Hill was transformed by each of the four changes highlighted in the section on long-run change. First, much of the area was torn down as part of two major improvement schemes between 1841 and 1878, which included the construction of the Metropolitan Line – London's first underground railway. These improvement schemes were, however, limited in their effect

[3] A dipper was responsible for glazing in the pottery trade.

in alleviating poverty. Writing in the 1850s and 1860s, Henry Mayhew (Neuburg 1985), highlights Greater Saffron Hill as an area of low-grade lodging houses. In the absence of cheap public transport, most unskilled workers had to travel to work on foot and, therefore, had to live close to their places of employment. Improvement schemes, therefore, added to the over-crowding in the surrounding areas in the short run (Yelling 1986, p. 15). Second, the parish of Saffron Hill as a whole experienced a sharp rise in population in the first half of the century, reaching its peak around 1830, but by the end of the century, migration to Outer London and transport improvements meant that population was under half of that a 100 years earlier. Third, the detailed maps of the London Topological Society (2005) show that large parts of Saffron Hill were almost completely destroyed or damaged beyond repair in the Blitz and, although the street remains narrow, few of the original buildings now exist. Indeed the bottom end of the road, near Holborn, consists of prime office space.

A number of issues arise from this selective illustration of one small area of London's history. First, in the nineteenth Century, areas of high wealth were located close to areas of high poverty. Since walking was the main means of transport, extremes could easily be found within a kilometre of each other. Although advances in transport took place rapidly through the second half of the nineteenth century, cheap fares did not allow suburbanisation of the poor until early in the twentieth century. Second, over long periods of time, the statuses and uses of locations, which are now classified as central London, appear to have changed considerably. Areas that were once deprived do not necessarily remain deprived.[4] Third, although the buildings have changed considerably, the street lay out has changed less. Saffron Hill is still narrow and it is fairly easy to track many of the earlier thoroughfares and most of the smaller streets that appear on nineteenth Century maps are still there today. London did not experience the same transformation seen in Paris and other major European capitals in the nineteenth century. Similarly, proposed slum demolition schemes in London, following the 1875 Artisans' and Labourers' Dwellings Improvement Act, were focussed on discrete sites rather than a general plan (Yelling 1986, p. 17). Sites were not necessarily physically adjacent nor involved a re-shaping of the city. Indeed, there appears to have been a deliberate attempt to avoid Haussman's grand designs for Paris as an unacceptable concentration of power and an assault on private property. Finally, households in the nineteenth century typically moved only short distances, contributing to a preservation of patterns of poverty.

Even in the absence of full estimation of the micro location model, it is still possible to test some of the underlying ideas and to examine the extent to which the poorer London areas have caught up with the richer neighbourhoods between 1881 and 2001. This question is considered in Meen and Nygaard (2010), where policy induced changes, notably slum clearance programmes are the main focus of

---

[4] However, Orford et al. (2002), comparing data on social status from the 1991 Census and from the Booth maps highlight the stability of spatial poverty patterns over the last 100 years, although they find a degree of convergence over that period.

attention. The empirical work is based on the conventional convergence tests, more commonly employed in the regional growth convergence literature (Barro 1991; Barro and Sala-i-Martin 1991, 1992). Tests of whether poor regions or countries catch up with richer entities in the long run are based on Eq. (3.2).

$$\ln(y_{i,t+T} / y_{i,t}) = \alpha + \beta \ln(y_{i,t}) + \gamma X_{i,t} + \varepsilon_{i,t} \quad (3.2)$$

where i represents the spatial entity; $y_{i,t}$ is usually per capita GDP; $\varepsilon_{i,t}$ is an error term; $X_{i,t}$ is a set of variables that control for differing steady-state growth rates across the areas. The dependent variable is measured over a time interval of T years. Therefore, according to (3.2), growth rates can vary because of differences in the factors that determine the steady-state or because of differences in the initial positions. β-convergence implies that the poorest countries/regions grow faster than the richest. Empirically, β-convergence indicates that there is a negative relationship between the initial level of per capita income and its rate of growth over time.

Absolute convergence takes place when poorer areas grow faster than the richer whatever their characteristics, whereas conditional convergence implies that an area grows faster the further it is from its own steady state. This gives rise to the possibility that, under conditional convergence, richer areas could still grow faster than poorer regions according to differences in structural and policy variables that affect each area's steady state. There is no necessary tendency to convergence if areas have different steady states.

However, measures of per capita GDP are not available for local neighbourhoods throughout history. Therefore, in line with the sample described above, Meen and Nygaard (2010) use the standardised share of household heads in social classes (iv) and (v) in 1881 and 2001 as the dependent variable in each neighbourhood. These classes broadly correspond to the unskilled occupations. Since the exact addresses of all sample members in 1881 are known, it is possible to match the sample to modern Medium Level Super Output Areas (MSOAs), which are used as the basic spatial unit of analysis. This generates a sample of 3,124 household heads for 101 MSOAs shown in Fig. 3.5 in Inner London. In this case, β_I becomes a measure of the extent to which social class structure persists across the 120 years. Significant positive values denote persistence, whereas negative values indicate a reduction in segregation over time.

As noted above, there is no necessary tendency to convergence if areas have different steady states, determined by the variables in X_i. In Meen and Nygaard (2010), the main variable affecting the steady state is the proportion of each MSOA's land area that has undergone slum clearance since 1881, distinguishing between the different clearance acts. The hypothesis is that slum clearance changes the steady state percentage of heads in the lower classes in each MSOA. But the effects of the programmes could be either negative or positive.

Two key results emerge. First, across the Inner London MSOAs, there is evidence of slow conditional convergence at a rate of approximately 0.6% per annum. Second, four measures are tested – land cleared prior to 1890 (the London County Council was established in 1889, see Yelling (1982) for a description of the LCC's programmes up to 1907), clearances under the 1891 Act, programmes under the

Fig. 3.5 The sample of medium level super output areas (Source: The 2001 MSOA and 1961 Local Government District boundaries are based on data provided through EDINA UKBORDERS with the support of the ESRC and JISC and uses boundary material which is copyright of the Great Britain Historic GIS Project, Portsmouth University)

Acts of the 1930s and post-war clearances between 1950 and 1975. Of these variables, only the last has any significant effect on the percentage change in the proportion of heads in classes (iv) and (v). Furthermore, the coefficient is positive. This implies that post-war schemes locked-in or even increased the social stratification established amongst the earlier generations. The construction of large social housing estates on cleared land is an obvious factor. There are a number of possible interpretations of the insignificant effects from the earlier schemes. First, many of these schemes were small and piecemeal and may simply have been too small to have had an effect across the MSOA as a whole. Furthermore, although many of the earlier developments reduced densities, they were replaced with properties with rents too high for the poorest households. But the displaced households only moved short distances in order to remain close to work. Therefore, there may have been only a limited effect within the wider MSOAs. Third, although untestable on this data set, the clearance programmes may have temporarily improved the relative positions of the most deprived areas, but, in the long term, they returned to their previous states.

Conclusions

This chapter is concerned with the long-term processes that lead to neighbourhood formation and persistence. In terms of the initial establishment of social hierarchies, the role of geography and geology are investigated. The chapter suggests that, once these initial social patterns become established, they become locked in by the history of development – buildings and infrastructure are long lasting, demolitions are infrequent and the diverse nature of property rights (and the necessity of compensation) makes large-scale redevelopment difficult. In principle, social interactions models provide the most elegant approach to explaining the dynamics of change. But, given data deficiencies, these models are the most difficult to test directly. Therefore, this chapter presents evidence from a number of different, but related approaches, including theoretical models using cellular automata, arising from the Schelling (1971) tradition. These demonstrate how interactions lead to segregation as a stochastically stable state, but it is possible that an accumulation of random shocks can, on occasions, tip an area to a different state. Gentrification is a possible example. Models of this form suggest non-linear thresholds. A second class of model examines the empirical evidence for thresholds, using a cross-section model of local house prices. Although caution is necessary, some support exists, which suggests that the most deprived areas become stuck in poverty traps and large sums are required to promote such areas to a take-off point where they become self-sustaining. The analysis suggests that approximately 1 % of census output areas in the North of England are in this position, but smaller percentages in the South. Furthermore, the chapter finds that new housing supply is also strongly affected by historical development patterns and geography. The third strand of the chapter provides evidence of long-run change since the nineteenth century (necessary because there is limited evidence of change over shorter time periods). This requires the construction of novel data sets, derived partly from census records and partly from detailed planning drawings for slum clearance programmes. This is a painstaking process. However, results suggest that, although there is evidence of conditional convergence between the poorest and richest MSOAs, post-war slum clearance programmes have locked-in or even increased social stratification.

Perhaps the key message that arises from this chapter is that any changes in neighbourhood residential patterns are slow. They do not respond quickly to variations in market prices and spatial patterns are persistent. Therefore, the question of whether neighbourhood has an independent effect on economic outcomes, raised in the neighbourhood effects literature, is real.

There are a number of possible extensions to the research. First, although fully estimated social interactions models cannot be constructed on modern data, the nineteenth century panel can be used. However, there are doubts whether nineteenth century conclusions can be extrapolated to the twenty-first century. Second, the set of conditioning variables used in the convergence tests can be extended. The emphasis in this chapter is on slum clearance, but further work could consider the development of railway networks and roads for example. This is feasible through the use of historical GIS techniques. In addition, the work of Davis and Weinstein considers the effects of World War II bombings on Japanese cities. Using the detailed maps of the London Topological Society (2005), it is feasible to add bomb damage during the Blitz as an additional conditioning variable. However, the construction of the required data sets is time consuming.

References

Barro, R. (1991). Economic growth in a cross-section of countries. *Quarterly Journal of Economics, 106*(2), 407–443.

Barro, R., & Sala-i-Martin, X. (1991). Convergence Across States and Regions. *Brookings Papers on Economic Activity, 22*(1), 107–182.

Barro, R., & Sala-i-Martin, X. (1992). Convergence. *Journal of Political Economy, 100*(2), 223–251.

Blume, L. E., & Durlauf, S. N. (2001). The interactions-based approach to socioeconomic behaviour. In S. Durlauf & H. P. Young (Eds.), *Social dynamics* (pp. 15–44). Cambridge: The MIT Press.

Bosker, M., Brakman, S., Garretsen, H., & Schramm, M. (2007). Looking for multiple equilibria when geography matters: German city growth and the WWII shock. *Journal of Urban Economics, 61*, 152–169.

Bossomaier, T., Amri, S., & Thompson, J. (2007). Agent-based modelling of house price evolution. *Proceedings of the 2007 IEEE Symposium on Artificial Life,* http://researchoutput.csu.edu.au/R/?func=dbin-jump-full&object_id=3301&local_base=GEN01-CSU01

Briggs, A. (1963). *Victorian cities*. London: Penguin Books.

Brueckner, J., Thisse, J.-F., & Zenou, Y. (1999). Why is Central Paris rich and Downtown Detroit poor? An amenity-based theory. *European Economic Review, 43*(1), 91–107.

Davis, D. R., & Weinstein, D. E. (2002). Bones, bombs, and break points: The geography of economic activity. *American Economic Review, 92*(5), 1269–1289.

Davis, D. R., & Weinstein, D. E. (2008). In search for multiple equilibria in urban industrial structure. *Journal of Regional Science, 48*(1), 29–65.

Davison, G. (2005). *The rise and fall of marvellous Melbourne*. Melbourne: Melbourne University Publishing.

Dorling, D., Rigby, J., Wheeler, B., Ballas, D., Thomas, B., Fahmy, E., Gordon, D., & Lupton, R. (2007). *Poverty, wealth and place in Britain, 1968 to 2005*. Bristol: Policy Press.

Durlauf, S. N. (1997). Statistical mechanics approaches to socioeconomic behavior. In W. B. Arthur, S. N. Durlauf, & D. Lane (Eds.), *The economy as an evolving complex system II* (pp. 81–104). Reading: Addison-Wesley.

Durlauf, S. N. (2006). Groups, social influences, and inequality. In S. Bowles, S. N. Durlauf, & K. Hoff (Eds.), *Poverty traps* (pp. 141–175). Princeton: Princeton University Press.

Galster, G. C. (2002). An economic efficiency analysis of deconcentrating poverty populations. *Journal of Housing Economics, 11*(4), 303–329.

Galster, G. C., & Zobel, A. (1998). Will dispersed housing programmes reduce social problems in the US? *Housing Studies, 13*(5), 605–622.

Galster, G. C., Quercia, R. G., & Cortes, A. (2000). Identifying neighbourhood thresholds: An empirical investigation. *Housing Policy Debate, 11*(3), 701–732.

Gilbert, N., Hawksworth, J. C., & Swinney, P. A. (2009). *An agent-based model of the English housing market*. Association for the Advancement of Artificial Intelligence, http://www.aaai.org/Papers/Symposia/Spring/2009/SS-09-09/SS09-09-007.pdf

Glaeser, E. L. (2005a). Urban colossus: Why is New York America's largest city? *FRBNY Economic Policy Review, 12*, 7–24.

Glaeser, E. L. (2005b). Reinventing Boston 1630–2003. *Journal of Economic Geography, 5*(2), 119–153.

Glaeser, E. L., & Gyourko, J. (2005). Urban decline and durable housing. *Journal of Political Economy, 113*(2), 345–375.

Glaeser, E. L., Sacredote, B., & Scheinkman, J. A. (1996). Crime and social interactions. *Quarterly Journal of Economics, 111*(2), 507–548.

Gregory, I., Southall, H., & Mooney, G. (2009). *London's rivers in the late 19th century*. ESRI Shapefile, Edina ShareGeo Open.

Krugman, P. (1996). *The self-organizing economy*. Oxford: Blackwell.

London Topological Society. (2005). *The London County Council bomb damage maps 1939–1945* (LTS Publication No. 164). London Topological Society and London Metropolitan Archives.

Meen, G. P. (2009). Modelling local spatial poverty traps in England. *Housing Studies, 24*(1), 127–147.

Meen, D., & Meen, G. (2003). Social behaviour as a basis for modelling the urban housing market: A review. *Urban Studies, 40*(5–6), 917–935.

Meen, G., & Nygaard, C. (2010). *Slum clearances and long-run urban change: The case of London 1881–2001*. University of Reading, Department of Economics, Working Paper.

Meen, G., & Nygaard, C. (2011). Local housing supply and the impact of history and geography. *Urban Studies, 48*(14), 3107–3124.

Meen, G., Gibb, K., Goody, J., & McGrath, T. (2005). *Economic segregation in England*. York: The Policy Press.

Meen, G., Meen, J., & Nygaard, C. (2007). *A tale of two Victorian cities in the 21st century*. PRRES Conference Paper, Perth.

Miguel, E., & Roland, G. (2011). The long-run impact of bombing Vietnam. *Journal of Development Economics, 96*(1), 1–15.

Mooney, G., Southall, H., & Gregory, I. (2009). *London's roads in the late 19th century*. ESRI Shapefile, Edina ShareGeo Open.

Neuburg, V. (1985). *London labour and London poor, selections from the writings of Henry Mayhew*. London: Penguin.

North, D. C. (2005). *Understanding the process of economic change*. Princeton: Princeton University Press.

Orford, S., Dorling, D., Mitchell, R., Shaw, M., & Davey-Smith, G. (2002). Life and death of the people of London: A historical GIS of Charles Booth's inquiry. *Health & Place, 8*(1), 25–35.

Quercia, R. G., & Galster, G. C. (1997). Threshold effects and the expected benefits of attracting middle-income households to the central city. *Housing Policy Debate, 8*(2), 409–435.

Ravenstein, E. G. (1885). The laws of migration. *Journal of the Royal Statistical Society of London, 48*(2), 167–235.

Schelling, T. (1971). Dynamic models of segregation. *Journal of Mathematical Sociology, 1*(1), 143–186.

Thurley, S. (2010). *Town and Crown: Why London never became an imperial capital*. http://www.gresham.ac.uk/event.asp?PageId=4&EventId=990. Accessed 11 June 2011.

Yelling, J. A. (1982). L.C.C. Slum Clearance policies, 1889–1907. *Transactions of the Institute of British Geographers, New Series, 7*(3), 292–303.

Yelling, J. A. (1986). *Slums and slum clearance in Victorian London* (London series in economic geography, Vol. 10). London: Allen and Unwin.

Young, H. P. (1998). *Individual strategy and social structure. An evolutionary theory of institutions*. Princeton: Princeton University Press.

Young, H. P. (2001). The dynamics of conformity. In S. N. Durlauf & H. P. Young (Eds.), *Social dynamics* (pp. 133–154). Cambridge: The MIT Press.

Chapter 4
How Do Mortgage Lenders Influence Neighbourhood Dynamics? Redlining and Predatory Lending

Manuel B. Aalbers

Introduction

Many studies see neighbourhood change as the result of a "natural" process (e.g. Downs 1973; Grigsby et al. 1987); put simply, the idea is that when neighbourhoods get older the population inevitably changes and the housing stock ages. Alternatively, scholars have made links between social-economic developments on an (inter-) national level and neighbourhood change at the local level (e.g. Walker 1981; Wilson 1996), for instance unfavourable economic conditions or suburbanization are seen as causes of neighbourhood decline. This chapter users a so-called socio-spatial approach that argues that neighbourhood change is not only the result of demographic change and changing housing preferences or of structural changes in the economy, but also of the actions of abstract space makers such as mortgage lenders landlords, real estate brokers and developers (Feagin and Parker 1990; Gottdiener 1994; Gotham 2002a; Aalbers 2011). This approach, building on seminal contributions by Lefebvre (1991), Harvey (1985), Smith (1979) and Soja (1980) was developed as a response to natural models of neighbourhood change and to the invasion-succession model in particular.[1]

A core assumption of the socio-spatial approach is that urban development does 'not develop out of an inevitable and unalterable structural necessity, but rather in a contingent manner; [it] result[s] from the conscious actions taken by individual decision makers in various class, race, gender, and community-based groups, acting under particular historical circumstances' (Feagin and Parker 1990, p. 12). This emphasis on agency brings people back into the analysis and emphasizes the centrality

[1] This chapter builds on Aalbers (2006, 2009, 2011).

M.B. Aalbers (✉)
Department of Geography, Planning and International Development Studies, University of Amsterdam, Plantage Muidergracht 14, 1018 TZ Amsterdam, The Netherlands
e-mail: m.b.aalbers@uva.nl

M. van Ham et al. (eds.), *Understanding Neighbourhood Dynamics: New Insights for Neighbourhood Effects Research*, DOI 10.1007/978-94-007-4854-5_4,

of action and conflict in determining the shape of the built environment. It also suggests that researchers should look beyond the usual indicators of change such as income levels and residential mobility by digging deeper to uncover the actions of the "abstracts space makers".

Without neglecting the primordial characteristic of space, the socio-spatial approach sees space as a social product in which all aspects of life, whether economic, political or cultural, are negotiated through the operation of power relations (Soja 1980). The French sociologist and philosopher Henri Lefebvre (1991) makes an important distinction between social space and abstract space: social space refers to the how people think about the place where they live whereas abstract space refers to how government and real estate actors think about space for political or economic gain. Abstract space is a tool of power that produces a homogenizing, hierarchical representation of space. Neither abstract nor social space, however, are homogeneous but, rather, as sets of relations. In social space, heterogeneity is characterized by coexistence and simultaneity (although this does not necessarily mean in peaceful coexistence), in abstract space by hierarchies and fragmentation.

In Downs' life-cycle theory of neighbourhood change (Downs 1973) not only succession but all neighbourhood decline is considered a natural consequence of an aging building stock. He ignores locally contingent conditions as well as the actions of abstract space makers. According to the socio-spatial approach, abstract space makers are not merely automata of the price mechanism, who steer the *natural* operation of the market, but can actively structure the process of neighbourhood change, through actions such as speculation, blockbusting, milking, redlining and pushing predatory loans – the latter two actions are the focus of this chapter. Moreover, there is no such thing as the *natural* operation of the real estate market, just as there is no such thing as a *natural* market since 'the market itself is a *social* product' (Smith 1996, p. 62, emphasis added). Market actors such as landlords, real estate brokers and lenders should be seen as intentionally and unintentionally restructuring the local real estate market and thus possibly producing or contributing to process of neighbourhood change.

The notion of abstract space helps us to understand how places, such as neighbourhoods, are not only shaped and moulded by those who live there but also by outside actors that make decisions that directly and indirectly affect the lives of the people in that neighbourhood. In this chapter I apply this notion to the question how mortgage lenders influence neighbourhood dynamics. Neighbourhoods may be "written off" by lenders (abstract space), but can be considered desirable living environments by others (social space). Neighbourhoods may also be considered good spaces to extract money from in a way that does not benefit the residents of these neighbourhoods. Lenders and other financial institutions can provide the essential underpinning for positive social development, but they also have destructive power (Jacobs 1961): the power to deny credit loans, known as redlining (see below), or to push unsuitable loans, known as predatory lending (see below). Both these processes affect neighbourhoods and local communities, as we will see in the following sections.

Mortgage redlining is the identification of an area, usually a neighbourhood or zip code area, where no mortgage loans are issued, which is a form of place-based financial and social exclusion. Mortgage applicants are excluded *from* obtaining housing by denying them mortgages in redlined neighbourhoods. Current homeowners are excluded *through* housing because they are unable to sell their house, becoming trapped in their neighbourhood. Redlining can also be defined as the identification in abstract space of a specific area where mortgage loans to buy a house are not granted and is also known as "credit blacklisting". The concept is based on a hierarchical representation of space. The usual justification for redlining is that the lender wants to limit the risks in an area that is deteriorating (abstract space). The lender discriminates against a whole class of risks rather than distinguishing among individual risks.

Sub-prime lending is often defined as lending to a low-income borrower with poor credit, but this would be a misrepresentation of the essence of sub-prime lending, which is lending at higher fees and interest rates whether or not the borrower actually has bad credit or a low income. Sub-prime loans are pushed on borrowers – low and moderate-income as well as middle and high-income – because they bring in more money, not just because lenders are pushed to sell them. Commenting on the sub-prime mortgage crisis, neither the media nor economists ever pass an opportunity to point out that many borrowers took out loans they could not afford. This is correct, but in most cases this was not because borrowers were eager to take on large loans even though they had bad credit. A majority of the sub-prime loans went to borrowers with prime credit (Brooks and Simon 2007). This implies that lenders systematically overcharged borrowers.

A subset of sub-prime lending is known as predatory lending. Predatory lenders charge excessive fees and interest rates and originated loans that were not beneficial for borrowers. Originally predatory lending was seen as a small part of the sub-prime mortgage market, but predatory lending is not an exception but rather something very common in sub-prime lending. Often homeowners do not have a full understanding of the mortgage lending process and fail to hire experts, not only at the time of mortgage origination, but also when the first payment problems arise (Engel and McCoy 2002). Predatory lending, then, is another way in which abstract space makers, exploit vulnerable neighbourhoods and its residents.

Redlining and predatory lending are generally considered opposite movements in mortgage lending because redlining excludes people from loans while predatory lending includes and then exploits people through loans. In the next section, I will argue that despite this important contradiction, redlining and predatory lending are in many ways very similar and have similar effects on neighbourhoods. I will continue to argue that both these processes in mortgage lending constitute neighbourhood effects. To illustrate my argument, I will briefly discuss cases of redlining and predatory lending and how they impact on the neighbourhoods in which they are played out. The redlining case study comes is the Tarwewijk in the Dutch city of Rotterdam, the predatory lending case study the Slavic Village in the American city of Cleveland, Ohio, a formerly redlined area. In the Rotterdam case I do this based on an empirical study (Aalbers 2006) that included neighbourhood observations and interviews with 22 abstract space makers (lenders, real estate and mortgage brokers, landlords and government officials) and 40 social space makers (citizens, undocumented migrants and shopkeepers). The Cleveland case is based on a literature review. Both redlining and predatory lending are widely researched in the United States although there is also historical or recent evidence of redlining from Canada, South Africa, Australia, Italy, the Netherlands and the United Kingdom (for an overview see Aalbers 2011). Predatory lending in an exclusively American concept, but loan sharks are active around the globe; and, as Ferguson (2009) shows, usury is of all times.

Similarities Between Redlining and Predatory Lending

The two extremes of geographical disparities are, on the one hand, areas where full mortgages (100% loan-to-value) or low down-payment mortgages are granted on advantageous conditions (greenlining), and on the other hand areas where no mortgages are granted whatsoever (redlining). Greenlining can be defined as the provision of mortgage loans under normal, advantageous conditions; it constitutes the provision of loans to areas of which mortgage lenders are eager to provide mortgage loans because the area is considered low-risk (of course loan applications can still be rejected because the lender considers either the collateral or the applicant high-risk). We can only speak of redlining when mortgage loan applications are rejected solely based on place-based factors, implying that even low-risk applicants would be rejected. Some authors have included disadvantageous loan conditions based on place-based factors in their definition of redlining, but I prefer to use the term yellowlining for such conditions. Yellowlining includes higher down-payment requirements and higher interest rates, if these are based on place-based factors; for example, if lenders normally charge a 5% interest rate, but raise it to 8% only in certain neighbourhoods, these neighbourhoods can be considered yellowlined – or, in other words: if sub-prime lending is performed on place-based factors it can be defined as yellowlining. Furthermore, redlining and place-based sub-prime lending, i.e. yellowlining, are not opposites, but two adjacent positions on a continuum that ranges from redlining on the most exclusionary side to greenlining on the most inclusionary side.

Predatory lending and redlining share at least six properties. First, they both describe lending patterns in financial markets and are mostly discussed in the context of mortgage markets. Second, both processes played a major role in the two biggest crises of the last 100 years: predatory lending in the financial crisis that started in 2007 and redlining in the Great Depression that started in 1929. The U.S. economic boom of the 1920s also led to a housing boom. Likewise, the Wall Street Crash of 1929 and the economic crisis of the 1930s was also a housing crisis. Widespread unemployment made it impossible for many homeowners to pay off their mortgage loans, resulting in foreclosures and tax sales. In addition, people who retained their job were often unable to refinance their loan after it expired after the usual 5 year maturity because of the withdrawal of financial institutions from the mortgage market, and therefore also lost their homes. In the early 1930s the average number of foreclosed mortgage loans was 250,000 per year and at some point exceeding more than 1,000 per day; half of all residential mortgages in the U.S. were in default (Dennis and Pinkowish 2004; Immergluck 2004).

One response to the crisis was the creation of the Home Owners Loan Corporation (HOLC) under the Roosevelt Administration. The HOLC was designed 'to provide emergency relief to homeowners by refinancing or purchasing defaulted mortgages' (Dennis and Pinkowish 2004, p. 7), in other words to forestall foreclosures. Thanks to the HOLC tens of thousands of borrowers were kept from losing their homes in the mid and late 1930s and, in addition, it refinanced more than one million mortgages, all on relatively low-interest rates (Gotham 2002b, p. 53). But by developing a neighbourhood rating system, the HOLC was also instrumental in implementing and institutionalizing redlining practices. The HOLC developed a neighborhood rating and mapping system comprising four colors corresponding to four different numbers and four different letter codes: green, First-grade or A referring to 'homogeneous neighborhoods ... hot spots ... in demand as residential locations in good times and bad ... American business and professional men'; blue, Second-grade or B referring to 'stable ... still good ... still desirable' areas that had 'reached their peak'; yellow, Third-grade or C referring to 'definitely declining ... heterogeneous' neighborhoods that attract 'undesirable element[s]' and are 'infiltrated by a lower grade population'; and lastly, red, Fourth-grade or D referring to neighborhoods 'in which the things taking place in C areas have already happened' as a result of 'detrimental influences in a pronounced degree' and where houses have 'little or no value today, having suffered a tremendous decline in values due to the colored element now controlling the district' (Jackson 1985, pp. 197–200). According to Jackson, Jewish neighborhoods, even the stable and affluent ones, would never be considered First-grade, while Black neighborhoods were by nature considered unstable and declining or depressed and habitually colored red. Crossney and Bartelt (2005), however, claim that the connection between ethnicity and lending is less strong, even though they admit it is clear that Black and mixed areas were more often redlined than homogenous White areas.

Although the HOLC is often blamed for *introducing* redlining policies and practices, it is important to note that the HOLC was simply following dominant ideas in real estate and mortgage markets, already practiced at the local level. However, the HOLC did *implement* and *institutionalize* redlining policies. As a government institution it did institutionalize already existing policies of redlining into government policies by designing redlining maps for more than 200 American cities. Fourth-grade, red-colored neighborhoods were no exception, but rarer on some city maps than on others. While the map of St. Louis County, for example, only shows a small number of neighborhoods colored red, the map of the city of Newark, NJ is full of redlined neighborhoods and no single neighborhood in Newark is colored green. Figure 4.1, the map for the city of Baltimore, shows a classic pattern: inner-city neighborhoods surrounding the central business district are colored red, the next

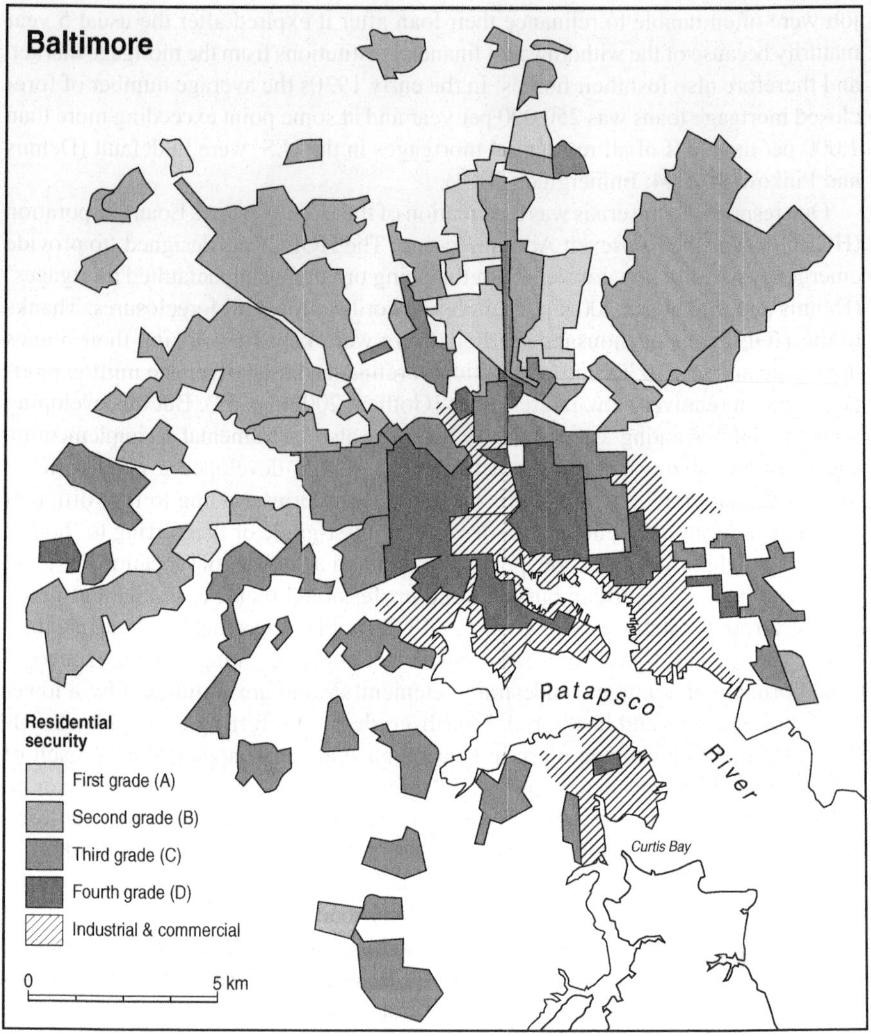

Fig. 4.1 Redlining map of Baltimore, 1930s (Source: National Archives, Washington, DC)

ring of neighborhoods and the older suburbs are largely colored yellow, while newer suburbs – albeit with a few exceptions – are colored blue or, less common, green. In addition, in a few years time, the number and size of redlined areas could dramatically increase as Hillier's analysis of the HOLC Residential Security Maps for Philadelphia clearly shows: in 2 years time the share of city-land redlined almost doubled to 34% (Hillier 2003).

Things were different in 2007 and 2008 when the default and foreclosure crisis was, to a great extent, a result of sub-prime and predatory lending. In the U.S. sub-prime mortgage lending had been growing rapidly, from about \$35 billion (5% of total mortgage originations) in 1994 to \$600 billion (20%) in 2006 (Avery et al. 2006).

In states such as Nevada, sub-prime loans accounted for more than 30% of the loans originated in 2006 (Nassar 2007). Many homeowners were unable to keep up with their loans, in particular since many of these loans were characterized by "interest rate reset" moments at which interest rates could easily double or triple. Many loans were designed in such a way that they looked cheap, but would, in fact, turn out more expensive. Borrowers were shown the initial, low interest rate while the higher interest rate is hidden in the small print of the mortgage contract, which is typically unreadable. Rising unemployment also resulted in an increase in the number of homeowners who were unable to keep up with their mortgage loan payments.

Third, both redlining and predatory lending disadvantage homeowners and borrowers: redlining by directly excluding borrowers who live in certain areas, predatory lending by charging higher rates for certain borrowers. As mentioned above, redlining does not only exclude potential homeowners from buying a house, it also excludes current homeowners because they cannot sell their houses and are therefore unable to move. Redlining simultaneously disables home ownership for one group and traps people in home ownership for another group.

It is often argued that sub-prime lending enabled home ownership for people that were formerly excluded from home ownership. In reality, most sub-prime loans were not enabling home ownership as more than half of them were refinance loans and second mortgages – in other words, loans for people who already owned a mortgaged property. In addition, sub-prime loans were sold to prime borrowers. Lenders could charge higher interest rates on sub-prime loans and thus make more money. For this reason lenders gave brokers bigger sales fees for selling sub-prime loans.

Fourth, redlining and predatory lending disproportionally hit the same social groups: low-income groups and racial minorities. Discussions on redlining have taken place primarily in the U.S. and have been connected to debates on the causes of segregation and to debates on forms of racial discrimination. Massey and Denton (1993) distinguish between three factors that cause segregation: prejudice, discrimination, and discriminatory institutionalized government policies including "public" redlining. Galster (1992) explicitly names redlining as a form of discriminatory practice leading to segregation. Not only American, but also Dutch research shows a very strong correlation between redlined neighbourhoods and neighbourhoods predominantly accommodating ethnic minority groups (Aalbers 2007). In the case of redlining, place-based exclusion often implies indirect race-based exclusion as ethnic minority groups are hit disproportionably hard by redlining practices. Even though the key factor in exclusion is clearly place-based, the underlying cause may be race-based as mortgage lenders may use zip code as a proxy for race. Since racial exclusion would amount to discrimination, lenders may resort to other methods to exclude certain racial or ethnic groups. Segregation, in a way, facilitates the indirect racial exclusion when direct racial exclusion is legally difficult. Yet, many countries have also outlawed either place-based discrimination or disparate impact on minorities. In the U.S. both the "disparate treatment" of minorities and the "disparate impact" on minorities are prohibited (for a discussion see Immergluck 2004; Ross and Yinger 2002). Furthermore, the U.S. has several housing- and finance-specific laws on discrimination, including the Fair Housing Act (1968), the Home Mortgage

Disclosure Act (1975) and the Community Reinvestment Act (1977). In the Netherlands, to give another example, the *Algemene Wet Gelijke Behandeling* (General Equal Treatment Act) not only prohibits direct but also indirect discrimination, and as a report by the *Commissie Gelijke Behandeling* (Equal Treatment Committee) shows several form of yellowlining and redlining in the Netherlands should be considered indirect racial discrimination (CGB 2006).

There is mounting evidence that sub-prime and predatory lenders use sophisticated marketing techniques to reach people with little education or prior lending experience (Carr and Schuetz 2001; Quercia et al. 2004; Newman 2009). Predatory loans were sold mostly in neighbourhoods with high shares of ethnic minority populations. Almost half of the loans in minority areas were predatory compared to 22% in white areas (Avery et al. 2007). African-Americans receive more than twice as many high-priced loans as Whites, even after controlling for the risk level of the borrower (Schloemer et al. 2006). It then comes as no surprise that foreclosures are concentrated in the neighbourhoods where the concentration of these groups is greater. These problems are not new: for at least 10 years researchers have pointed out how sub-prime and predatory lending target racial minority groups and result in rising default and foreclosure rates (e.g. Pennington-Cross 2002; Squires 2004; Wyly et al. 2006).

In the U.S., decades of financial deregulation have not resulted in wider access to mainstream financial services, but in a two-tier banking system with mainstream finance in most places next to a landscape of financial exclusion and predatory lending where banking services and the number of bank accounts have declined while fringe banking (pawn shops, payday lenders etc.) and predatory lending flourish (Caskey 1994; Dymski 1999; Immergluck 2009; Leyshon and Thrift 1997; Squires 2004). The heralded "end of redlining" may in fact just be "redlining by another name" – Squires (2004) speaks of "the new redlining" – in which the same social groups and places are no longer formally excluded but "overincluded" and thereby still exploited.

Fifth, both redlining and predatory lending have a clear geographical component. In the case of redlining, this is tautological as the idea of place-based exclusion is part of the definition of redlining. Redlining targets low-income neighbourhoods and ethnic neighbourhoods in particular. However, redlining not only affects low-income families and ethnic minorities but also everyone applying for a mortgage in a redlined neighbourhood. Because potential incoming homeowners either have their mortgage application declined, or if accepted experience a very difficult process in redlined neighbourhoods, current homeowners in these neighbourhoods cannot sell their houses for a decent price. Consequently, they are unable to move out and a minimum-choice neighbourhood is born.

In the case of predatory lending we see a clear concentration in certain neighbourhoods: predatory lending is either concentrated in areas that were redlined, or areas that would be redlined if such practices occurred currently (see also Hernandez 2009). Both quantitative and qualitative research show that 'subprime loans are making credit available in communities where credit likely historically has not been – and likely still is not – as readily available' (Goldstein 2004, p. 39). The old geography of place-based financial exclusion (redlining) has not disappeared, but has been replaced – and to a large extent *reproduced* – by a new geography of predatory lending and overinclusion. Moreover, sub-prime lenders exploit uneven development that resulted from these earlier rounds of urban exclusion. In other words, formerly redlined neighbourhoods do not enter the world of prime lending, but receive mortgage loans from the parallel lending world of sub-prime and predatory lenders and are therefore still financially excluded.

Sixth, the local impact of redlining and sub-prime lending are frighteningly similar, not just in who gets hit, but also what it does to neighbourhoods and communities that, in the end, get stripped of equity and opportunities. This is a point to which we will return below. Indeed, neighbourhoods become exploited not for the gain of its residents but rather for the gain of others, like speculators, mortgage brokers and financial institutions. In other words, and this leads us to the final shared characteristic, the type of agents involved in redlining and predatory lending – both the powerful ones and the exploited ones – are essentially the same. The main two differences seem to be exclusion versus overinclusion and the development of these processes. Overinclusion in many cases is a special case of exclusion.

With the foreclosure crisis that started in 2007, sub-prime and predatory lending have been decreasing fast and lenders have been going out of business in large numbers. And not only sub-prime lending has decreased; it has generally become more difficult that get a mortgage loan. Both *The Washington Independent* (Kane 2008) and *City Limits* (Markey 2010) are citing evidence that the same lenders have started charging higher fees for borrowers in certain zip codes, i.e. lenders have implemented another set of yellowlining policies. Likewise, in the Netherlands, newspaper *De Volkskrant* investigated the consequences of the financial crisis on bank lending and demonstrates that it is becoming much harder, if not close to impossible, to get hold of a mortgage in the ethnic minority neighbourhoods of Rotterdam and The Hague (Van den Eerenbeemt and Rengers 2009; see also Aalbers 2010).

Neighbourhood Effects

Discussions on redlining and predatory lending have taken place primarily in the U.S. and have been connected to debates on the causes of segregation and to debates on forms of racial discrimination. Race and place shape the opportunity structure of people, neighbourhoods and cities (Squires and Kubrin 2005); race and place are so intertwined that it is hard, and in some cases impossible, to disentangle them empirically. Analytically one has to see race and place in a dialectic relationship. Race-based and place-based exclusion intersect, as the places hit by exclusion are often inhabited predominately by ethnic minority groups. Holloway (1998) even argues that both race and place are insufficient in explaining lending discrimination; it is the interaction of race-based discrimination and the neighbourhood's racial composition that shapes lending discrimination.

By definition, social and financial exclusion are associated with and concentrated in certain places, and located at all scales (Gough et al. 2006), including that of the neighbourhood. Although its importance for social exclusion is sometimes overstated, we should also not make the mistake of suggesting that the neighbourhood is irrelevant for processes of exclusion. The neighbourhood plays a different part in different countries and cities, and is also contingent on the physical and social structure of the neighbourhood itself (Kesteloot et al. 2006). If one takes an individualized definition of exclusion location is insignificant as it is merely a place where poor people live. Then "excluded neighbourhoods" are simply seen as 'an aggregate of the conditions of the people who live in them' (Spicker 2001, p. 38). Neighbourhoods are then passive: they are places where poor people live, but they have no influence on poverty itself. Yet, there is another possibility, which is that neighbourhoods cause, affect, or intervene in exclusion processes in such a way that exclusion becomes exacerbated or limited, depending what happens on the neighbourhood level.

Before we continue it is useful to differentiate between exclusion *through* housing and exclusion *from* housing (e.g. Cameron and Field 2000). People are not only excluded *from* housing. *Through* their housing situation they can also be excluded from other things, like residential mortgage finance. Housing can act as a key element in social exclusion. In its most extreme form, one can think of homelessness and rough sleeping, but more widely we need to recognize that the housing system plays a role in shaping social exclusion (see Marsh and Mullins 1998, p. 750). Access to housing and the cost of housing, for example, make a big difference in what exclusion implies; while the condition of the housing stock and its environment directly influence the experience of exclusion. When speaking of the environment, we turn to exclusion *through* housing and to what the literature refers to as "neighbourhood effects".

Exclusion *through* housing does not focus on the lack of access to adequate housing, but rather on the role played by housing or by the neighbourhood as a causal factor generating other forms of social exclusion, especially from the labour market and civil society. The neighbourhood effects hypothesis is highly debated and there is not much clear evidence that neighbourhood effects exist (Van Ham and Manley 2010). Neighbourhood effect studies have often looked at the effects of the neighbourhood on social mobility and employment, but the effects of the neighbourhood may go much further, as suggested by many other studies (e.g. Briggs 1997; Ellen and Turner 1997; Musterd and Andersson 2005). The fear of crime, for example, is directly associated with perceptions of the physical deterioration of an area (Painter 1992, p. 182) and this fear may intensify already existing patterns of exclusion. In addition, neighbourhoods may be 'avoided or viewed with apprehension where a stereotype of a despised group combines with and reinforces a negative stereotype of place' (Sibley 1998, p. 120). In this way, 'the reputation of an area may also have an effect on its resources. People who live in "bad areas" may find it difficult to get credit; insurance premiums may be higher there; and residents may not be able to get commercial deliveries or taxi services' (Spicker 2001, p. 33).

While many neighbourhood effects studies focus primarily on employment and social mobility, it could be argued that redlining and yellowlining, i.e. place-based exclusion and overinclusion in the mortgage market, could be conceptualized as types of neighbourhood effects. Redlining serves as a prime example of exclusion from and through home ownership. For people who are denied a loan, redlining means exclusion *from* owner-occupation; for people who are unable to sell their house at a "decent" price and are forced to suffer a loss or are forced to give up their ambition to sell and relocate, redlining means exclusion *through* owner-occupation. In both cases the neighbourhood plays an important role; neighbourhood based factors may exclude anyone willing to buy in that neighbourhood, as well as those planning to sell.

Stuart (2003) shows very clearly how the way in which powerful actors such as lenders and brokers define a neighbourhood in abstract space has very clear consequences for what happens at the neighbourhood level. The dynamics of social space are such that they have to react to the dynamics of abstract space. This reaction can possibly counteract abstract space dynamics. In the Chicago neighbourhood Back of the Yards, for example, neighbourhood residents were able to successfully fight (in social space) the redlining of the neighbourhood (abstract space) by threatening to withdraw their savings from the banks if they continued their redlining practices (Jacobs 1961). But another reaction to abstract space dynamics in social space is the acceptance of the new situation, either passively by staying in the neighbourhood without resisting redlining policies or actively, for instance by "voting with your feet", and by moving out of the neighbourhood.

Likewise, place-based predatory lending presents a case of exclusion *through* housing. In many definitions of predatory lending, targeting low-income and ethnic minority areas is part of the definition (e.g. NCRC 2002; Squires 2004). As we have seen in the last section, predatory lending is heavily concentrated in these already disadvantaged neighbourhoods: living in a low-income or ethnic minority neighbourhood makes it more likely that predatory lenders will try to push their loans, even when controlling for income or credit score. Since predatory loans are the most unsuitable type of sub-prime loans, they cause more havoc in these areas, even to neighbourhood residents and institutions that are not locked into an abusive loan, as we will see below.

Predatory lenders make profit 'by stripping equity and wealth from home owners in underserved communities through highcost refinance loans' (Taylor et al. 2004, p. 27). Teaser rates and other tricks are used to sell these loans. Rapidly increasing interest rates and balloon payments (i.e. big sum not paid in regular intervals) are used to increase returns, and in some cases also to increase the likeliness of default. Repeated default then allows lenders to repossess homes and acquire equity. In this way lenders do not enable home ownership but effectively strip home equity from borrowers. In 2006, 13% of outstanding loans were sub-prime, but 60% of the loans in foreclosure were sub-prime, up from 30% in 2003 (Nassar 2007). Mortgage foreclosures not only hit individual borrowers and their families, but also result in housing abandonment at the neighbourhood level. It is not just defaulting borrowers who are hit; in addition, there are severe spill-over effects on housing prices, crime and neighbourhood decline (Immergluck 2009; Lardner 2008; Newman 2009).

To illustrate how both redlining and predatory lending affect neighbourhoods, the next two sections will briefly discuss two different cases: the impact of redlining on the Tarwewijk neighbourhood in Rotterdam and the impact of predatory lending and foreclosures on U.S. neighbourhoods, such as the Slavic Village in Cleveland, Ohio.

Redlining and Neighbourhood Decline: The Tarwewijk, Rotterdam

The Tarwewijk on the South bank of the Maas River is widely considered one of the most problematic neighbourhoods in the City of Rotterdam as well as in the Netherlands. The low level of maintenance of the private rented stock, and the high levels of drug use, dealing and related crime provided the neighbourhood with an infamous reputation. Residential mobility is extremely high, in particular in the Millinxbuurt, the eastern part of the neighbourhood where only 8% of the population had lived there longer than 5 years. Ethnically, the neighbourhood is highly mixed. At the time I started my research 37% were Dutch, 14% Surinamese, 10% Turkish, 9% (Netherlands') Antillean (i.e. from the Caribbean), and 30% belonged to other groups (COS 2001). For many ethnic groups this is an undercount as undocumented immigrants are not included in these data.

The formation of abstract space by mortgage banks defined the Tarwewijk as a loss-making neighbourhood. This resulted in the systematic exclusion and further disempowerment of socio-economically already weaker groups. Research on the Tarwewijk neighbourhood in Rotterdam shows that neighbourhood decline was one of the reasons for lenders to redline the area, but also that redlining fuelled neighbourhood decline (Aalbers 2006). As a result of redlining, residential turnover increased and housing maintenance was discouraged. Despite the actions of a local social housing association that was buying up deteriorated private rented housing units, dubious landlords acquired both former owner-occupied housing and private rented housing at prices far below the "normal" market value, often in cash.

In most of the 1990s the neighbourhood was heavily redlined by almost every lender and it continued to be redlined and yellowlined by some lenders in the early 2000s (see Fig. 4.2; more maps are included in Aalbers 2011). The high social mobility and the low popularity of the Tarwewijk resulted in it becoming a neighbourhood of last resort increasingly inhabited by those with the least options in the housing market. This includes not only the poor and the unemployed, but also drug users, marginal drug dealers and undocumented immigrants. The withholding of mortgage capital meant that current homeowners were unable to sell their house to people who needed a mortgage to pay for the house and were thus forced to stay in their house or sell the house at fire-sale prices to landlords. This resulted in what Harvey (1985) has called a "devalued place": a place in which capital becomes devalued as a result of its place-specific exclusion. The withdrawal of mortgage lenders, respected landlords and the better off from the Tarwewijk, which was inspired by the decline of the area, resulted in the further decline of the neighbourhood.

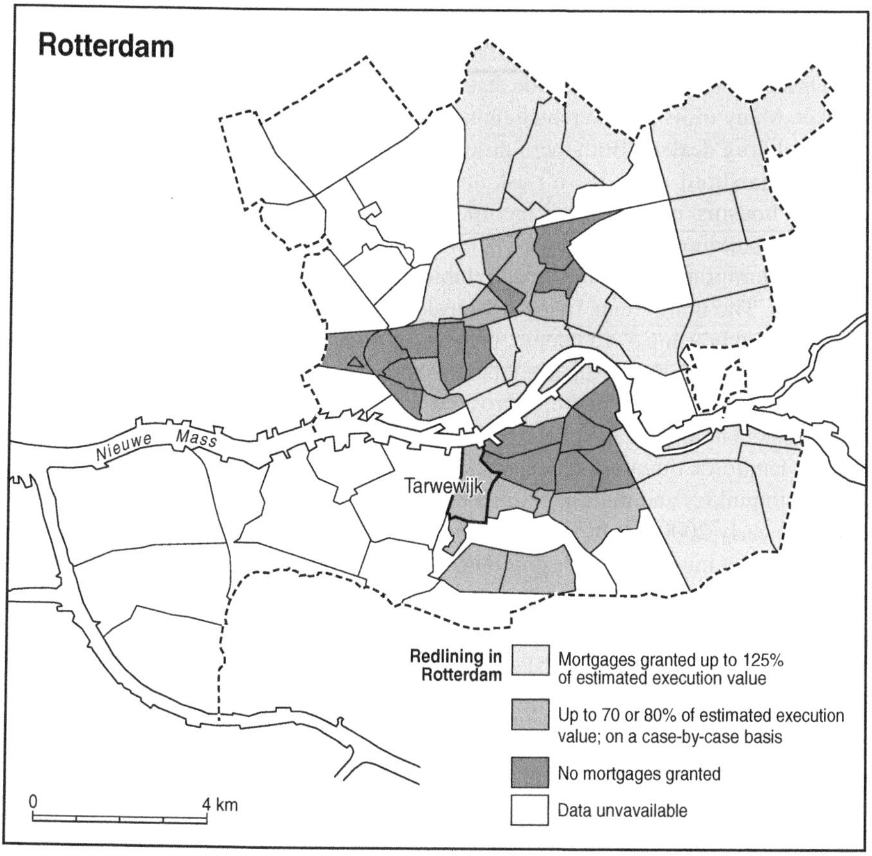

Fig. 4.2 Redrawn redlining map of Rotterdam showing the Tarwewijk neighbourhood, 1999 (Source: Aalbers 2011)

During the 1990s, larger, mostly reliable, landlords sold off their property to smaller, reliable landlords as well as to less reliable landlords. These larger landlords had seen their profits shrink while their maintenance expenses were rising. Facing neighbourhood decline, rising vacancy rates and the considerable investments needed, these landlords sold their property to landlords who have lower profit demands or who do not intend to invest a lot in the property. These landlords typically strive to maximize the value of their property by intensifying its use in order to increase cash flow. After some years, many of these landlords also sell their property, often to dubious landlords (in some cases criminals) who "milk" the property by letting it to those with very limited options (drug users, undocumented immigrants) or using it as a brothel or as a place in which to grow soft drugs. Milking is 'the deliberate undermaintenance of a rental property for the purpose of maximizing short-run monopoly profits' (Grigsby et al. 1987, p. 51). But milking the property is only one use; speculation and laundering black money are other uses. At that stage, property is no longer seen as a long term investment, but as a short term investment that is sometimes sold within a few weeks and where ownership becomes increasingly hard to trace.

It is not far-reaching to conclude that the Tarwewijk has a low status on the housing market. Many of its private rented units are let to undocumented immigrants and to marginal drug dealers. Both these groups not only have an interest in low rents, but also in a landlord that 'doesn't ask any questions'. The City District of Charlois (33,000 housing units), which incorporates the Tarwewijk, assumes there are at least 300 buildings (consisting of several units each) that accommodate undocumented immigrants. In some streets dubious landlords own at least a third of the buildings. The immigrants living here usually share a room with several people in an apartment housing 5–15 people. In these apartments every room is equipped with one or more bunk beds or with a number of mattresses. None of these "bed tenants" has a contract. Fifty to one hundred Euros a week is the common rent charged per bed. This means landlords can collect up to 6,000 Euros a month per apartment. On top of this, landlords often ask a deposit of anything up to 1,000 Euros. Some beds are also let to junkies and marginal drug dealers (who often use drug themselves).

In the early 2000s, redlining briefly became a hot issue in the City of Rotterdam and as a result most lenders discontinued, at least temporarily, their redlining activities. Around the same time a City agency started buying up properties in order to facilitate the renewal program of the area. As a result, housing prices are on the rise again. Furthermore, the City Department of Construction and Housing Supervision is addressing landlords whose housing maintenance is below the legal threshold. Landlords have three options: maintaining their housing stock, selling out to the City agency, or ignoring both the legal threats and the offer to buy. The first strategy is not very common, but both the second and the third are. One problem is that a number of landlords who sell out move on to buy up properties in the same or in other neighbourhoods. As Mr. Bergwerff, area manager for the City District, remarks: 'This landlord can buy new properties in adjacent streets with the money that he got. Out of the centre of attention, the slum landlords can continue their activities'. In other blocks and other neighbourhoods the process of housing degeneration, milking and speculation continues. This is indeed moving the problem, but since not all landlords follow this strategy, the overall problem becomes more manageable. Next to this, the City and the Court of Justice criminalize and prosecute any illegal activities these landlords may have undertaken. This is a process that requires patience, but is potentially more successful not only in combating the problems at stake but also in limiting the opportunities for landlords to take advantage of this situation.

Although the redlining practices cannot be held responsible for the milking and exploitation processes, the actions of these landlords were, of course, made easier by the redlining policies of mortgage lenders and the dispossession of properties by bona fide landlords. In the Tarwewijk, high residential mobility, drug use, drug dealing, crime, neighbourhood decline, redlining, and housing speculation feed upon one another. It is impossible to identify independent variables because every one of these processes is both cause and consequence of the other processes.

Elsewhere (Aalbers 2007) I have demonstrated that redlined areas of Rotterdam are neighbourhoods with high shares of low-income households, unemployed, ethnic-minorities and non-natives – all these variables individually accurately predict about 80% of the cases. Variables related to the share and value of owner-occupied dwellings also accurately predict a smaller percentage of the cases. With the use of discriminant analysis I was able to demonstrate that the interaction of group related variables involving ethnicity or income, on the one hand, with housing related variables, on the other hand, accurately predicts up to 95% of the cases. In other words, social-demographic characteristics together with housing market characteristics show what types of neighbourhoods are redlined: in Rotterdam these are low-income, high-immigrant neighbourhoods with a low share of owner-occupied units that also tend to be of low value. Safety levels, on average, are somewhat lower than elsewhere, but they are not necessarily the least safe areas. They are not necessarily neighbourhoods with a high population turnover, high vacancies or older dwellings.

Predatory Lending and Neighbourhood Decline: The Slavic Village, Cleveland

Although some cities in the Sunbelt are now hit harder than those in the Rustbelt, at the neighbourhood level the Rustbelt still tops the foreclosure lists. On the list of most foreclosed zip codes, four are now in Detroit; the Slavic Village in Cleveland, Ohio has the most foreclosure filings. Cleveland is one of the many U.S. Rustbelt cities that suffered from a loss of manufacturing jobs and a consequence population decline starting in the 1950s. In the beginning of that decade Cleveland had 914,000 residents; 60 years later it had only 397,000. A halving of the population is not uncommon for cities in America's Rustbelt, but what is striking about Cleveland is that it continued to lose population in all of these decades. Where the population of most other Rustbelt cities started to stabilize, Cleveland's merely slowed down in the 1990s when the city was known as 'The Comeback City', only to speed up again in the first decade of the twenty-first century, when the city lost 17% of its population, second only to Katrina-hit New Orleans.

In 2007, 7,000–8,000 foreclosures took place in Cleveland (Cohen 2008; Christie 2010). In Cuyahoga County, which includes Cleveland and surrounding suburbs and has an estimated population of 1.28 million, this number was around 15,000 in 2007 (Schiller and Hirsh 2008) and over 100,000, or about one in five properties, for the first 9 years of this century. In the County about 30% of subprime mortgage were either delinquent or in foreclosure by the summer of 2007 (Schwartz 2007), a share that has only increased since then. Predatory loans are responsible for 84% of all foreclosures in Cuyahoga County, African-Americans are disproportionally hit and so are minority and low-income neighbourhoods (Coulton et al. 2008). In all of Ohio, 45% of all mortgages are now underwater, meaning that the outstanding loan is larger than the estimated value; in Cleveland this is 55% (Christie 2010) and likely higher in the Slavic Village and other low income areas.

House prices in Cleveland have fallen dramatically. In 2005 the median sales price of a house was around $100,000, in early 2007 it was $62,000, a year later it was $15,500, a decrease of 75% in only 1 year (Mallach 2009)! The fall in prices is, at least in part, so dramatic because foreclosure sales now make up a large share of all sales and that brings down the median house prices considerably. Coulton et al. (2010) show how foreclosed properties used to sell for 60–80% of the previously estimated market value in 2004, but only for 10–40% of that value in 2009. Houses on Cleveland's East Side, that includes the Slavic Village, were selling for an average of 13% of their previously estimated market value in 2009 (Coulton et al. 2010). Median housing prices in the East Side declined from $25,000 to $4,575 from 2007 to 2008 (Mallach 2009). In this part of the city, almost 80% of the foreclosed properties sold for less than $10,000 in 2008 and 2009, up from only 4% in 2004. This was the case for 65% of the City of Cleveland and just over 40% of Cuyahoga County for foreclosure sales in 2008 and 2009 (Coulton et al. 2010). On eBay you can even buy houses starting at about $500.

The Slavic Village, also known as North and South Broadway, is often referred to as foreclosure's ground zero (Christie 2007). As its name suggests, the neighbourhood was once home to large groups of Slavic migrants: Poles, Czechs and Slovaks. From the 1950s onwards, the neighbourhood was hit hard by redlining, suburbanisation and the loss of manufacturing jobs (e.g. Krumholz et al. 2006). South Broadway's population declined from more than 60,000 in 1950 to less than 30,000 in 1990 and then down to about 21,500 in 2010 (Krumholz et al. 2006; City Data 2010). The decline in North Broadway was at least as dramatic; in 2010 it had just over 9,000 residents. The population has also changed colour. From an almost completely white neighbourhood, North Broadway has changed into an area that is 50% white, 40% black and 10% other (City Data 2010). South Broadway remains somewhat whiter. This makes the neighbourhood exceptionally mixed by Cleveland and national standards. The poverty rate in the Slavic Village increased from 13% in 1980, to 27% in 2000 and then to respectively 28 and 38% in South and North Broadway, higher than the city average but still behind neighbouring Kinsman where in 2010 56% of the residents lived below the poverty line (City Data 2010).

In the 1990s the Slavic Village, like the Comeback City at large, seemed to be a very resilient place, in part a result of the work of Slavic Village Development, a local non-profit community development corporation. But at the end of that decade predatory lenders became increasingly active in the neighbourhood and by 2005, 68% of the loan originations in the area where predatory (Cohen 2009). The result was a foreclosure epidemic. The Slavic Village was once a vivid neighbourhood but parts of it are now turning into a ghost town. Over the last few years, an average of two families per day were evicted, mostly as a result of foreclosures. About one in four houses has been in a foreclosure procedure over the last 5 years. In some streets a third of the houses are abandoned (Kotlowitz 2009).

The foreclosure crisis was exacerbated as a result of fraudulent flipping. This involves 'buyers, sellers, and appraisers, who obtain false documents in order to sell cheap, dilapidated properties in low income neighbourhoods for an inflated profit by taking advantage of relaxed mortgage lending restrictions' (Cohen 2009, p. 6).

Inaccurately high appraisals are key to these flipping schemes as higher appraisals allow for higher mortgages. Since Slavic Village Development had been renovating houses and subsequently selling them for higher prices, the artificially high appraisal values of the flippers' properties seemed credible. The inflated appraisals then also made new inflated appraisals possible, enabling the flippers to continue mortgage fraud, contributing to inflated housing prices. The lenders, in particular the predatory ones, were also complicit, albeit passively: they simply did not check the properties and were willing to provide loans with little documentation. Mortgage fraud was widespread within the Slavic Village. Cohen (2009) argues that mortgage fraud leads to the foreclosure of properties, devastates neighbourhoods by physical deterioration and a rise in crime, defrauds banking institutions and frustrates housing sales.

Foreclosing a house usually implies that it becomes vacant and vacant properties become vandalized as well as the victim of arson (Mallach 2009). In 2008 more than 60 fires were reported in vacant houses of Slavic Village (Kotlowitz 2009). Immergluck (2009) and Mallach (2009) explain how forecloses not only hit individuals borrowers, but also the neighbourhoods and cities in which they live. The spill-over effects for neighbourhoods are substantial and the costs for local governments vast and diverse. Besides borrowers and neighbourhoods, municipalities are also hit hard because tax income goes down due to foreclosed properties and lower real estate prices, while expenses are increasing as a result of foreclosures and property crime. Local governments around the country have cut expenses on education, infrastructure and social services. Of course the places that need the funding the most to counter the neighbourhood effects of predatory lending and foreclosures are often affected the most by budget cuts and can therefore do the least. It is estimated that one foreclosure lowers the price of a nearby house, on average, by 0.9% (Immergluck and Smith 2006). The cumulative effects can be devastating, as the case of the Slavic Village clearly demonstrates. Foreclosure costs for government are estimated to be around $30,000 (Moreno 1995; Apgar and Duda 2005) and for lenders around $50,000 (Kotlowitz 2009). Finally, there are psychological and emotional costs.

Due to foreclosures and owners losing their properties as a result of unpaid taxes the City owns thousands of parcels of tax-reverted land (Dewar 2006). The City of Cleveland and Cuyahoga County have to deal with an oversupply of housing and an undersupply of funds to demolish or renovate housing. $50–80 million may be needed to demolish the worst 10,000 houses. It has been argued that it is impossible to save all neighbourhoods that have been hit by the predatory and foreclosure crisis. As Weinstein (2008, p. 275) argues 'Limited resources should be deployed strategically, paying close attention to which neighborhoods have the existing housing stock and community amenities to compete for a pool of purchasers that had been shrinking even before credit standards tightened. Inevitably, this strategy will leave significant areas where parcels are abandoned or vacant.' Using indicators of housing market strength, the City developed a typology that classified the neighbourhoods within Cuyahoga County along a continuum of neighbourhood types, including "Regional Choice", "Stable", "Transitional", "Fragile", and "Distressed" (Reid 2011), thereby "imitating" a redlining map (Fig. 4.3), that like the HOLC maps of the

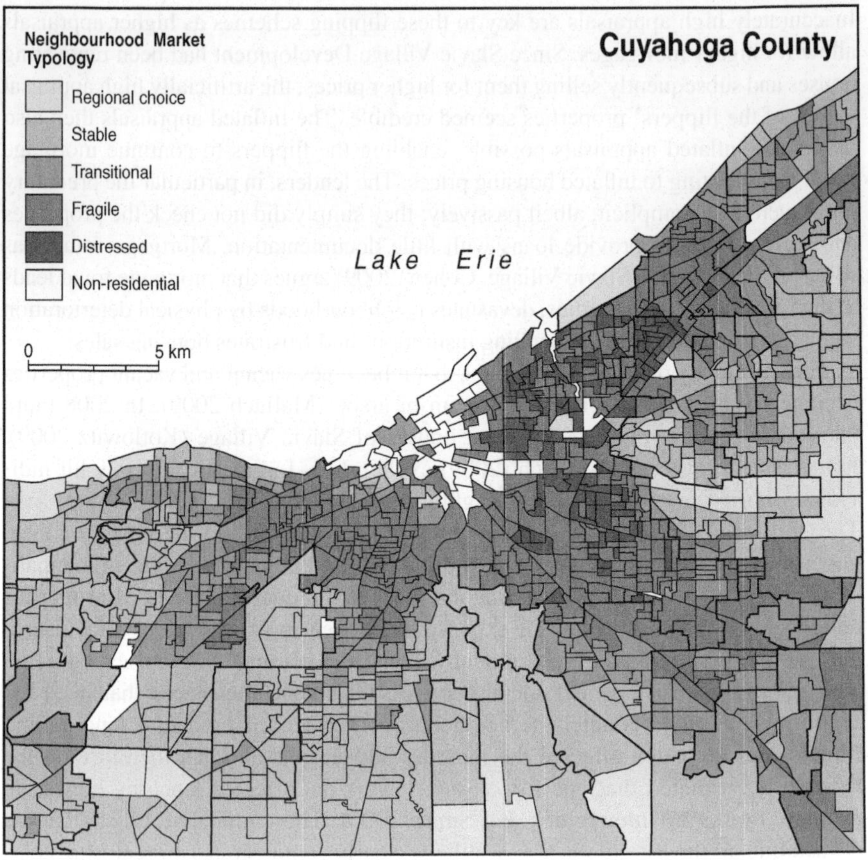

Fig. 4.3 Housing market typology map of Cuyahoga County, 2009 (Source: Adapted from City of Cleveland Department of Community Development)

1930s may both reflect and inspire lenders' redlining maps. The Slavic Village, like large parts of Cleveland's East Side, falls largely within the "fragile" and "distressed" categories. Some estimates say that 1,000 of the Slavic Village's 11,000 houses may need to be demolished. This comes to down about two-thirds of the estimated 2,200 vacant houses. Around 500 dwellings were already demolished by early 2011.

Next to the government, the courts and Slavic Village Development there is one important actor that could help stabilizing the Slavic Village: Third Federal Savings and Loan, an $11 billion thrift that was started in 1938 by the father of the current chief executive, supports the neighbourhood where it is headquartered. Since Third Federal continued to provide only "old-fashioned" prime loans, it lost a lot of market share to subprime and predatory lenders in the 1990s and early 2000s, but it is back in business in neighbourhoods like the Slavic Village. This lender's loans also have a foreclosure rate that is not only far below the Cleveland average, but even much lower than the national average (Schwartz 2007), demonstrating that foreclosures are not simply a result of a faltering economy, but mostly of bad overpriced loans.

Conclusions

Grigsby and colleagues (1987, p. 9) claim that 'succession must inevitably lead to decline if there exists within the community a poverty population of substantial size.' Downs' life-cycle theory goes a step further by arguing that not only succession itself is a natural process, but also that neighbourhood decline is inevitable for urban neighbourhoods (Downs 1973). In Downs' theory both local conditions and actions of real estate actors are ignored. In reality, real estate actors do not simply limit their risk in low-income neighbourhoods, but actively (through milking, or speculation) or passively (through redlining, or predatory lending) structure the process of neighbourhood decline. Concepts like "neighbourhood succession", "life-cycle" and "filtering" that are used to explain what is seen as the *natural* operation of the real estate market, distort the actual processes of neighbourhood decline by concealing agency as well as the social construction of place. The way these concepts are used also implies that "blaming the victim" and arguing that neighbourhood decline happens because landlords can no longer find tenants able to afford rents high enough to secure maintenance (e.g. Ahlbrandt and Brophy 1975), is not only untenable from a theoretical but also from an empirical point of view. A process like milking, for example, shows that it is possible to raise the rents while cutting back on expenses for maintenance. Explanations that equate the decline of a social group to the decline of a place are not only limited in their explanation, but also ultimately static, because they do not acknowledge the (often high) turnover in these kinds of neighbourhoods.

If the existence of any form of place-based exclusion can be demonstrated, it can be concluded that the neighbourhood matters. Then, the neighbourhood will make a difference for the individual mortgage loan applicant because it can either enable or constrain someone to reach a better position in life. Indeed, the concentration of excluded people in a neighbourhood may have an influence by itself on exclusion processes, and Spicker (2001, p. 34) therefore rightly claims that 'the problems of poor areas cannot be reduced to problems of poor people within those areas.'

These processes of place-based exclusion and overinclusion in the mortgage market constitute neighbourhood effects as location plays a role crucial in who can obtain a mortgage and under which conditions. This decision may very well be a result of a relatively large share of high-risk borrowers in a certain neighbourhood, but since exclusion is performed both on an individual basis *and* on a neighbourhood basis, the neighbourhood may be the decisive factor in the rejection of a mortgage loan application. It may come as no surprise that the type of neighbourhoods that were once faced with redlining are often the neighbourhoods that are also faced with high concentrations of sub-prime and predatory lending. These exclusionary processes are, at least in part, caused by other processes located at the level of the neighbourhood, but also give further shape to evolving patterns of neighbourhood change.

References

Aalbers, M. B. (2006). "When the banks withdraw, slum landlords take over": The structuration of neighbourhood decline through redlining, drug dealing, speculation and immigrant exploitation. *Urban Studies, 43*(7), 1061–1086.

Aalbers, M. B. (2007). What types of neighbourhoods are redlined? *Journal of Housing and the Built Environment, 22*(2), 177–198.

Aalbers, M. B. (2009). Geographies of the financial crisis. *Area, 41*(1), 34–42.

Aalbers, M. B. (2010). Redlining: Terug van weggeweest. *Rooilijn, 43*(1), 28–33.

Aalbers, M. B. (2011). *Place, exclusion, and mortgage markets*. Oxford: Wiley-Blackwell.

Ahlbrandt, R. S., & Brophy, P. (1975). *Neighborhood revitalization: Theory and practice*. Lexington: Lexington Books.

Apgar, W., & Duda, M. (2005). *Collateral damage: The municipal impact of today's mortgage foreclosure boom*. Washington, DC: Homeownership Preservation Foundation.

Avery, R. B., Brevoort, K. P., & Canner, G. B. (2006). Higher-priced home lending and the 2005 HMDA data. *Federal Reserve Bulletin, 92*, 123–166.

Avery, R. B., Brevoort, K. P., & Canner, G. B. (2007). The 2006 HMDA data. *Federal Reserve Bulletin, 93*, 73–109.

Briggs, X.d.S. (1997). Moving up versus moving out: Neighborhood effects in housing mobility programs. *Housing Policy Debate, 8*(1), 195–234.

Brooks, R., & Simon, R. (2007, December 3). As housing boomed, industry pushed loans to a broader market. *Wall Street Journal*, A1.

Cameron, S., & Field, A. (2000). Community, ethnicity and neighbourhood. *Housing Studies, 15*(6), 827–843.

Carr, J., & Schuetz, J. (2001). *Financial services in distressed communities: Framing the issue, finding solutions*. Washington, DC: Fannie Mae Foundation.

Caskey, J. (1994). *Fringe banking: Check-cashing outlets, pawnshops, and the poor*. New York: Russell Sage.

CGB. (2006). *Risicoselectie op grond van postcode en verblijfsstatus. Een onderzoek uit eigen beweging naar onderscheid door hypothecair financiers*. Utrecht: Commissie Gelijke Behandeling.

Christie, L. (2007, 19 November). Crime scene: Foreclosure. *CNN money*. http://money.cnn.com/2007/11/16/real_estate/suprime_and_crime/index.htm?cnn=yes

Christie, L. (2010, 14 January). Rescuing nation's foreclosure town. *CNN money.* http://money.cnn.com/video/news/2010/01/14/n_slavic_village_rescue.cnnmoney/

City Data. (2010). *Cleveland, Ohio*. Chicago: Advameg.

Cohen, J. R. (2008). *City of Cleveland v. Deutsche Bank National Trust, et al.*. Cleveland: Cohen Rosenthal & Kramer LLP.

Cohen, D. M. (2009). *Illegal flipping and neighborhood inequality: A Slavic village case study. A senior honors thesis*. Columbus: Ohio State University.

COS. (2001). *Several data sheets*. Rotterdam: Rotterdam Centrum voor Onderzoek en Sastistiek.

Coulton, C., Chan, T., Schramm, M., & Mikelbank, K. (2008). *Pathways to foreclosure: A longitudinal study of mortgage loans, Cleveland and Cuyahoga County, 2005–2008*. Cleveland: Center on Urban Poverty and Community Development.

Coulton, C., Schramm, M., & Hirsh, A. (2010). REO and beyond: The aftermath of the foreclosure crisis in Cuyahoga County, Ohio. In E. Rosengren & S. Pianalto (Eds.), *REO&vacant properties. Strategies for neighborhood stabilization* (pp. 47–54). Boston/Cleveland: Federal Reserve Banks of Boston and Cleveland.

Crossney, K. B., & Bartelt, D. W. (2005). The legacy of the home owners' loan corporation. *Housing Policy Debate, 16*(3/4), 547–574.

Dennis, M. W., & Pinkowish, T. J. (2004). *Residential mortgage lending: Principles and practices* (5th ed.). Mason: Thomson South-Western.

Dewar, M. (2006). Selling tax-reverted land: Lessons from Cleveland and Detroit. *Journal of the American Planning Association, 72*(2), 167–180.

Downs, A. (1973). *Opening up the suburbs: An urban strategy for America*. New Haven: Yale University Press.

Dymski, G. A. (1999). *The bank merger wave: The economic causes and social consequences of financial consolidation*. Armonk: Sharpe.

Ellen, I. G., & Turner, M. A. (1997). Does neighborhood matter? Assessing recent evidence. *Housing Policy Debate, 8*(4), 833–866.

Engel, K., & McCoy, P. (2002). A tale of three markets: The law and economics of predatory lending. *Texas Law Review, 80*(6), 1255–1381.

Feagin, J., & Parker, R. (1990). *Building American cities. The urban real estate game*. Englewood Cliffs: Prentice-Hall.

Ferguson, N. (2009). *The ascent of money. A financial history of the world*. New York: Penguin.

Galster, G. C. (1992). *Research on discrimination in housing and mortgage markets: Assessment and future directions*. Proceedings, Fannie Mae Annual Housing Conference. Washington, DC.

Goldstein, I. (2004). The economic consequences of predatory lending: A Philadelphia case study. In G. D. Squires (Ed.), *Why the poor pay more. How to stop predatory lending* (pp. 39–79). Westport: Praeger.

Gotham, K. F. (2002a). Beyond invasion and succession: School segregation, real estate blockbusting, and the political economy of neighborhood racial transition. *City and Community, 1*(1), 83–111.

Gotham, K. F. (2002b). *Race, real estate, and uneven development: The Kansas city experience, 1900–2000*. Albany: State University of New York Press.

Gottdiener, M. (1994). *The social production of urban space* (2nd ed.). Austin: University of Texas Press.

Gough, J., Eisenschitz, A., & McCulloch, A. (2006). *Spaces of social exclusion*. Abingdon: Routledge.

Grigsby, W., Baratz, M., Galster, G., & Maclennan, D. (1987). The dynamics of neighborhood change and decline. *Progress in Planning, 28*(1), 1–76.

Harvey, D. (1985). *The urbanization of capital: Studies in the history and theory of capitalist urbanization*. Oxford: Blackwell.

Hernandez, J. (2009). Redlining revisited: Mortgage lending patterns in Sacramento 1930-2004. *International Journal of Urban and Regional Research, 33*(2), 291–313.

Hillier, A. E. (2003). Redlining and the home owners' loan corporation. *Journal of Urban History, 29*(4), 394–420.

Holloway, S. R. (1998). Exploring the neighborhood contingency of race discrimination in mortgage lending in Columbus, Ohio. *Annals of the Association of American Geographers, 88*(2), 252–276.

Immergluck, D. (2004). *Credit to the community: Community reinvestment and fair lending policy in the United States*. Armonk: Sharpe.

Immergluck, D. (2009). *Foreclosed: High-risk lending, deregulation, and the undermining of America's mortgage market*. Ithaca: Cornell University Press.

Immergluck, D., & Smith, G. (2006). The external costs of foreclosure: The impact of single-family mortgage foreclosures on property values. *Housing Policy Debate, 17*(1), 57–79.

Jackson, K. T. (1985). *Crabgrass frontier: The suburbanization of the United States*. New York: Oxford University Press.

Jacobs, J. (1961). *The death and life of great American cities*. New York: Vintage.

Kane, M. (2008, May 15). Redlining redux: New mortgage industry policy could charge borrowers higher fees by zip code. *Washington Independent*. http://washingtonindependent.com/view/reconsidering

Kesteloot, C., Murie, A., & Musterd, S. (2006). European cities: Neighbourhood matters. In S. Musterd, A. Murie, & C. Kesteloot (Eds.), *Neighbourhoods of poverty: Urban social exclusion and integration in Europe* (pp. 219–238). Basingstoke: Palgrave Macmillan.

Kotlowitz, A. (2009, March 8). All boarded up. *New York Times*, 28. http://www.nytimes.com/2009/03/08/magazine/08Foreclosure-t.html.

Krumholz, N., Keating, W. D., Star, P. D., & Chupp, M. C. (2006). The long-term impact of CDCs on urban neighborhoods: Case studies of Cleveland's Broadway-Slavic village and Tremont neighborhoods. *Community Development: Journal of the Community Development Society, 37*(4), 33–52.

Lardner, J. (2008). *Beyond the mortgage meltdown: Addressing the current crisis, avoiding a future catastrophe*. Washington, DC: Demos.
Lefebvre, H. (1991). *The production of space*. Oxford: Blackwell.
Leyshon, A., & Thrift, N. (1997). *Money/space: Geographies of monetary transformation*. London: Routledge.
Mallach, A. (2009). *Addressing Ohio's foreclosure crisis: Taking the next steps*. Washington, DC: Brookings.
Markey, E. (2010, May 14). Banks redline minority communities again. *City Limits*. www.citylimits.org/news/articles/3996/banks-redline-minority-communities-again
Marsh, A., & Mullins, D. (1998). The social exclusion perspective and housing studies: Origins, applications and limitations. *Housing Studies, 13*(6), 749–759.
Massey, D. S., & Denton, N. A. (1993). *American apartheid: Segregation and the making of the underclass*. Cambridge, MA: Harvard University Press.
Moreno, A. (1995). *The cost-effectiveness of mortgage foreclosure prevention*. Minneapolis: Family Housing Fund.
Musterd, S., & Andersson, R. (2005). Housing mix, social mix and social opportunities. *Urban Affairs Review, 40*(6), 761–790.
Nassar, J. (2007). *Foreclosure, predatory mortgage and payday lending in America's cities*. Washington, DC: Testimony before the U.S. House Committee on Oversight and Government Reform.
NCRC. (2002). *Anti-predatory lending toolkit*. Washington, DC: National Community Reinvestment Coalition.
Newman, K. (2009). Post-industrial widgets: Capital flows and the production of the urban. *International Journal of Urban and Regional Research, 33*(2), 314–331.
Painter, K. (1992). Different worlds: The spatial, temporal and social dimensions of female victimization. In D. J. Evans, N. R. Fyfe, & D. T. Herbert (Eds.), *Crime, policing and place: Essays in environmental criminology* (pp. 164–195). London: Routledge.
Pennington-Cross, A. (2002). Subprime lending in the primary and secondary markets. *Journal of Housing Research, 13*(1), 31–50.
Quercia, R. G., Stegman, M., & Davis, W. R. (2004). Assessing the impact of North Carolina's anti-predatory lending law. *Housing Policy Debate, 15*(3), 573–602.
Reid, C. (2011). The neighborhood stabilization program: Strategically targeting public investments. *Community Investments, 23*(1), 23–33.
Ross, S. L., & Yinger, J. (2002). *The color of credit: Mortgage discrimination, research methodology, and fair-lending enforcement*. Cambridge, MA: MIT Press.
Schiller, Z., & Hirsh, A. (2008). *Foreclosure growth in Ohio 2008*. Cleveland: Policy Matters Ohio.
Schloemer, E., Li, W., Ernst, K., & Keest, K. (2006). *Losing ground: Foreclosures in the subprime market and their cost to homeowners*. Washington, DC: Center for Responsible Lending.
Schwartz, N. D. (2007, September 2). Can the mortgage crisis swallow a town? *New York Times*, 2. http://www.nytimes.com/2007/09/02/business/yourmoney/02village.html.
Sibley, D. (1998). The problematic nature of exclusion. *Geoforum, 29*(2), 119–121.
Smith, N. (1979). Toward a theory of gentrification: A back to the city movement by capital, not people. *Journal of the American Planning Association, 45*(4), 538–548.
Smith, N. (1996). *The new urban frontier. Gentrification and the revanchist city*. London: Routledge.
Soja, E. (1980). The socio-spatial dialectic. *Annals of the Association of American Geographers, 70*(2), 207–225.
Spicker, P. (2001). Poor areas and the "ecological fallacy." *Radical Statistics, 76*. www.radstats.org.uk/no076/index.htm
Squires, G. D. (Ed.). (2004). *Why the poor pay more: How to stop predatory lending*. Westport: Praeger.
Squires, G. D., & Kubrin, C. E. (2005). Privileged places: Race, uneven development and the geography of opportunity in urban America. *Urban Studies, 42*(1), 47–68.
Stuart, G. (2003). *Discriminating risk: The U.S. mortgage lending industry in the twentieth century*. Ithaca: Cornell University Press.
Taylor, J., Silver, J., & Berenbaum, D. (2004). The targets of predatory and discriminatory lending: Who are they and where do they live? In G. D. Squires (Ed.), *Why the poor pay more: How to stop predatory lending* (pp. 25–37). Westport: Praeger.

Van den Eerenbeemt, M., & Rengers, M. (2009, June 24). Geen hypotheken meer in Vogelaarwijk. *De Volkskrant*, 3.

Van Ham, M., & Manley, D. (2010). The effect of neighbourhood housing tenure mix on labour market outcomes: A longitudinal investigation of neighbourhood effects. *Journal of Economic Geography, 10*(2), 257–282.

Walker, R. (1981). A theory of suburbanization: Capitalism and the construction of urban space in the United States. In M. Dear & A. J. Scott (Eds.), *Urbanization and urban planning in capitalist society* (pp. 383–429). New York: Methuen.

Weinstein, A. C. (2008). The subprime mortgage crisis and local government: Immediate and future challenges. *Municipal Lawyer, 49*(3), 259–275.

Wilson, W. J. (1996). *When work disappears: The world of the new urban poor*. New York: Knopf.

Wyly, E. K., Atia, M., Foxcroft, H., Hammel, D., & Philips-Watts, K. (2006). American home: Predatory mortgage capital and neighbourhood spaces of race and class exploitation in the United States. *Geografiska Annaler B, 88*(1), 105–132.

Chapter 5
Urban Restructuring, Displaced Households and Neighbourhood Change: Results from Three Dutch Cities

Hanneke Posthumus, Gideon Bolt, and Ronald van Kempen

Introduction

In most European countries many neighbourhoods were explicitly planned and many dwellings were built in the first three decades after World War II. Housing production was considered necessary because of the postwar housing shortage and a growing number of households. Many of these dwellings were built in relatively large social housing estates, often in green and spacious environments. Although some mix of housing types did exist, large numbers of dwellings were built in rather monotonous apartment complexes and often they were affordable for households with low to medium incomes. Initially these areas were considered to be desirable by the new inhabitants: people moved there, because they liked it (Dekker and Van Kempen 2004).

Whereas the future for these neighbourhoods initially seemed promising, nowadays they are often perceived to be some of the most problematic areas of cities in Western European countries. Post-WWII neighbourhoods face a multitude of problems. First, the dwellings and public space have often been maintained poorly resulting in discomfort and physical deterioration. Second, the influx of households with low incomes and minority ethnic groups increased over time, which some, including the traditional inhabitants of these areas, have considered as a problematic issue (Slob et al. 2008). Many of the more prosperous families, who could afford more expensive dwellings, reacted to the neighbourhood changes by moving out of these neighbourhoods. This process created opportunities for new households – again often belonging to lower income and minority ethnic categories – to move to these neighbourhoods. The changing mix of households has negatively affected the social

H. Posthumus (✉) • G. Bolt • R. van Kempen
Faculty of Geosciences, Utrecht University,
P.O. Box 80.115, 3508 TC Utrecht, The Netherlands
e-mail: h.posthumus@uu.nl; g.s.bolt@uu.nl; r.vankempen@uu.nl

M. van Ham et al. (eds.), *Understanding Neighbourhood Dynamics: New Insights for Neighbourhood Effects Research*, DOI 10.1007/978-94-007-4854-5_5,

cohesion in post-WWII neighbourhoods because the traditional, more stable population (in terms of length of stay in the neighbourhood) was replaced by a more fluid population, who would typically move onwards within a few years.

A third problem that developed in many post-WWII neighbourhoods is a high unemployment level. Many newcomers in the post-WWII neighbourhoods did not have a job when moving there and a substantial number who did have one, lost their job as a consequence of economic restructuring in the last two decades and, more specifically, because of the economic and financial crisis during the last few years. The fourth and final problem of post-WWII neighbourhoods is a lack of safety. The physical environment of the neighbourhoods is such that it facilitates criminal activity especially when combined with a young population for whom there are few activities and who come from families with few financial resources. As a result criminality has increased in a number of post-WWII neighbourhoods in Western countries (Dekker and Van Kempen 2004; Andersen 2002; Wassenberg 2004; Swaroop and Morenoff 2006). As a consequence of all these developments, the liveability, popularity and reputation of post-WWII neighbourhoods have been increasingly under pressure (e.g., Dekker and Van Kempen 2004; Permentier et al. 2009).

Population mixing strategies have been implemented in post-WWII neighbourhoods both in the Netherlands as well as in many other European countries to reduce concentrations of residents with a weak socioeconomic position (Andersen and Van Kempen 2003; Ministry VROM 1997, 2000, 2007; Van Kempen and Bolt 2009). These strategies usually entail the demolition of parts of the original, inexpensive, social rented housing stock to be followed by the construction of more expensive rental and, especially, owner-occupied dwellings. Residents with a higher socioeconomic status than the average of the original residents would move to these dwellings, making the socioeconomic neighbourhood composition more mixed. The shifts in the physical structure and composition of the population resulting from this policy would reduce the problems many post-WWII neighbourhoods face (Ministry VROM 2008; Uitermark 2003).

The policy goal of a mixed neighbourhood population originates in the fear of the negative effects of spatial concentrations of the poor. There is a vast literature on the possible negative effects of these kinds of concentrations and much stems from the literature on American ghettos in general (Wilson 1987) and more specifically in the literature on neighbourhood effects (see for instance Leventhal and Brooks-Gunn 2000; Oberwittler 2007; Galster et al. 2008, 2010; Macintyre et al. 2008; Musterd et al. 2008). The main message in this literature is that spatial concentrations of the poor lead to negative effects: without the buffer of the middle class, the poor suffer a damaging social isolation (Wilson 1987, 1996; Atkinson and Kintrea 2000; Friedrichs 1998).

Ideas about the formation of ghettos and the negative ideas of living in ghettos are easily transported to Europe and adopted by politicians and policy makers as well as by some social scientists (for discussion see Van der Laan Bouma-Doff 2007; Van Kempen and Bolt 2012). European cities are definitely characterized by areas that can be called poor, distressed or disadvantaged and do contain concentrations of poor and minority ethnic groups. The reasoning is clear: if so many problems emerge from those concentration areas, as exemplified in the American literature, then something must be done to break these patterns of socio-economic and ethnic segregation and concentration. The logical alternative is to create a social and ethnic mix. Although mixing is a widespread policy goal, the effectiveness of such policies is much debated (Graham et al. 2009; Van Ham and Manley 2010; Joseph et al. 2007).

In the literature there has been much attention paid to the effects of mixed-housing policies on the targeted areas (e.g., Popkin et al. 2004; Kintrea 2007; Atkinson and Kintrea 2000; Van Beckhoven and Van Kempen 2003). The de-concentration of the (low-income) population, as well as a better mix between different income-groups are seen as positive effects of such a policy. Two of the major insights stemming from research into the effect of mixing strategies are that: (1) urban restructuring often improves the quality of dwellings and safety; but that (2) despite the increase in population mixing, the desired interaction between different population groups (such as more and less well-off residents, new and old inhabitants, natives and non-natives) in the neighbourhood rarely develops (e.g., Brooks et al. 2005; Kleinhans et al. 2007; Kleinhans and Van der Laan Bouma-Doff 2008; Van Beckhoven and Van Kempen 2003; Atkinson and Kintrea 2000).

The literature about the effects of restructuring policies on the neighbourhoods that have been restructured is extensive. Less attention, however, has been paid to the households that had to move to other neighbourhoods because of the restructuring process and on the effects of these moves on the receiving neighbourhoods. In this chapter our focus is specifically on the moves of these displaced households and on the type of neighbourhoods they move to. This is an important topic since the main aim of mixing policies both in the Netherlands as well as in other countries is to reduce problems in neighbourhoods by mixing their population. When the moves of displaced residents result in reconcentrations of the same people but in other neighbourhoods, problems are not be solved but simply moved. The policy logic of mixing policies implies that displaced residents need to move to a *different* type of neighbourhood than the one they leave in order to achieve an overall reduction in concentration related problems on a city-wide scale. Another important aim of mixing is to improve the situation of all residents, including those who are displaced, who are considered to be relatively deprived. Displaced residents would have limited chances for social mobility in their old neighbourhoods because of the presence of high concentrations of (other) deprived residents. These chances would, theoretically, increase by moving to neighbourhoods with better perspectives. Hence, it would be beneficial when displaced households move to a less deprived neighbourhood.

Because one of the goals of mixed communities policies is that displaced residents move to less deprived neighbourhoods than the neighbourhoods they left, it is important to answer the following question: *(a) How can neighbourhoods to which displaced households move be characterized?* To determine whether moves to neighbourhoods with certain characteristics also mean that displaced households move to "better" neighbourhoods we ask: *(b) How do the neighbourhoods to which many displaced households move, differ from their previous neighbourhoods?*

We acknowledge that the success of mixing policies does not solely depend on whether displaced residents do or do not move to neighbourhoods with certain characteristics. Only when the assumptions that a mixed population reduces neighbourhood problems and stimulates social mobility hold, could this be the case. Although this issue is pertinent, it is not within the scope of this paper.

In the next section we briefly analyse the insights from previous research and formulate several hypotheses about the type of neighbourhoods displaced households move to. These hypotheses are then tested using three different methods: (1) an analysis of the dispersal patterns; (2) an examination of the correlations between neighbourhood characteristics and the number of displaced households neighbourhoods receive; and (3) a comparison between neighbourhoods where restructuring takes place, neighbourhoods where many displaced residents settle, and other neighbourhoods. Based on these analyses the answers to the main questions will be formulated and reflected upon.

Previous Research

When neighbourhoods are restructured and change from areas with a large number of affordable rented dwellings into areas with a mix of housing types and tenures, a number of the original tenants will not be able to stay in the neighbourhood. They have to move elsewhere, because they cannot afford the rent or purchase of the new homes in that area. Obviously, this is often exactly the aim of a policy of restructuring: only by displacing a number of relatively poor households, a social mix can be achieved.

Characteristics of Neighbourhoods to Which the Displaced Move

The question is where do these displaced households move to? When the aim is to diminish spatial concentrations of low-income households, the idea is of course that the displaced households move to a large number of different areas, in order to avoid new concentrations of poverty elsewhere in the city or urban region. Some studies have shown that displaced households tend to move to a wide variety of neighbourhoods. However, the same studies have also shown that some neighbourhoods receive many more displaced households than others (Slob et al. 2008; Kingsley et al. 2003; Bolt and Van Kempen 2010). As such, re-concentration of low-income households does seem to take place, at least to a certain extent. The neighbourhoods to which many displaced residents move, have certain distinctive characteristics.

A first characteristic of neighbourhoods that receive many displaced residents is that they are often quite close to areas where the process of urban restructuring took place (Clampet-Lundquist 2004; Varady et al. 2001; Hartung and Henig 1997). This is to be expected because the lack of knowledge about more distant neighbourhoods stimulates residents to "choose" nearby neighbourhoods. Another possible reason for selecting an area close to the previous place is the possibility of maintaining one's local social networks.

Second, neighbourhoods to which many displaced residents move are characterized by a large inexpensive housing stock (Bolt and Van Kempen 2010; Pendall 2000; Varady and Walker 2000; Hartung and Henig 1997). The relatively unpopular dwellings that are listed for restructuring tend to be occupied by residents with a low income (Bolt et al. 2009). Their restricted budget forces them to choose another, inexpensive, dwelling when they have to move. As such, it can be expected that displaced households often move to neighbourhoods with a sizeable inexpensive housing stock.

Because of these housing characteristics, displaced residents are more likely to move to neighbourhoods where the populations means show a low average income, high rates of poverty, high levels of unemployment, high levels of welfare-dependency and low educational achievement (Oakley and Burchfield 2009; Hartung and Henig 1997; Pendall 2000; Kingsley et al. 2003). Similarly, other residents with a weak socioeconomic position are only able to access inexpensive dwellings which are overrepresented in certain neighbourhoods. Furthermore, it is possible that displaced residents prefer to live in neighbourhoods with many residents with a low socioeconomic status because it is easier to create a social safety net (Trudeau 2006). When many neighbours face similar difficulties they would be more willing to help another.

Finally, neighbourhoods that receive many displaced residents are characterized by a large share of ethnic minorities (Oakley and Burchfield 2009; Hartung and Henig 1997; Pendall 2000; Goetz 2002). One explanation for this finding is that minorities are overrepresented in neighbourhoods with an inexpensive housing stock because of their relatively weak socioeconomic position. Another explanation is that a large proportion of displaced residents also belong to an ethnic minority (Bolt et al. 2009) which results in their overrepresentation in neighbourhoods with a large share of minorities. This may be due to a preference to live among co-ethnics, but also to factors that restrict their choice on the housing market (Phillips 1998; Freeman 2000). As the immigrants among the ethnic minorities have on average less well-developed language skills than natives, and are less familiar with societal institutions and regulations, they tend to have more difficulties with the search process for a new dwelling (Bolt and Van Kempen 2010). Furthermore, discrimination (Galster 1999) and fear of racial harassment (Krysan and Farley 2002) may mean that ethnic minorities are less successful than non-minority households in obtaining a better place and thus "choose" from a limited number of neighbourhoods.

Neighbourhood Characteristics and Neighbourhood Problems

Displaced residents tend to move to nearby neighbourhoods with an inexpensive housing stock, low average income, and a large share of ethnic minorities. Apart from the proximity to their old neighbourhood, all other characteristics of neighbourhoods that receive many displaced residents have been related to the presence of neighbourhood problems (See for an intensive overview Sampson 2009; Sirgy and Cornwell 2002).

To start with, neighbourhoods with many (inexpensive) dwellings, specifically rented dwellings, experience more problems than neighbourhoods with a more expensive housing stock. It has been widely acknowledged that renters are less inclined than owners to invest in the maintenance of their dwelling and neighbourhood (Galster 1983; Dietz and Haurin 2003; Friedrichs and Blasius 2009). Furthermore, the owners of the rented stock (housing corporations, private owners, other institutions) are not always inclined to invest in all neighbourhoods and all dwellings equally. Investment in restructuring in one neighbourhood may result in little or no investment in other parts of the city. Consequently, physical deterioration can be relatively severe in neighbourhoods with many rented, inexpensive, dwellings in which no investment takes place.

According to the influential broken-windows thesis of Wilson and Kelling (1982), the physical deterioration of neighbourhoods may facilitate feelings of insecurity and illegal activities (see for instance Wyant 2008; Scarborough et al. 2010). However, Sampson et al. (1997) found that there is not a causal association between physical deterioration and crime (see also Sampson 2009). Instead, the level of social cohesion among residents is a crucial factor that affects both public disorder and crime (Sampson 2009). The rejection of the broken-windows hypothesis does not imply that the tenure distribution in the neighbourhood is irrelevant, as the level of social cohesion is found to be positively associated to homeownership (DiPasquale and Glaeser 1999; Dekker and Bolt 2005).

In addition, the level of social cohesion is strongly influenced by the socioeconomic status of neighbourhoods. In relatively poor neighbourhoods a lack of social organization and collective efficacy has been identified, resulting in higher levels of criminality (Sampson and Groves 1989; Sampson et al. 1997; Webster et al. 2006). Several studies have argued that poorer neighbourhoods hinder the social mobility of its residents because there are fewer opportunities to meet others with valuable resources (Galster et al. 2010; Musterd and Andersson 2006). Other studies have argued that mixing will not result in more social mobility because residents with different backgrounds are unlikely to interact with each other (Atkinson and Kintrea 2000; Kleinhans et al. 2007). The presence of a large share of minorities is also considered be problematic for neighbourhoods as it negatively affects the social cohesion in the neighbourhood (Laurence 2011; Putnam 2007) and restricts the socio-cultural integration of minorities (Gijsberts and Dagevos 2007; Vervoort et al. 2010). Furthermore, a number of authors have found that an influx of minorities has been found to increase the outflow of more prosperous residents increasing the problems associated with a population consisting of residents with a low socioeconomic status (Van Ham and Clark 2009).

Differences Between the Old and the New Neighbourhood

Even when displaced households move to relatively weak or problematic neighbourhoods, it is still possible that these new neighbourhoods are less deprived than the neighbourhoods that they exited. Therefore, our second main question is valid: How do the neighbourhoods to which many displaced households move, differ from their previous neighbourhoods? There is less literature on this topic: When the differences between the old and the new neighbourhood are examined, it is usually done on the basis of an analysis of questionnaires and interviews held with the displaced residents themselves (Kleinhans and Van der Laan Bouma-Doff 2008; Goetz 2002; Manzo et al. 2008; Varady and Walker 2000). Whilst there is, in principle, nothing wrong with this approach we should keep in mind that such subjective data may be biased. It is clear from the literature on residential mobility, for example, that people who recently moved usually evaluate their new situation positively. In some cases this positive view might be the result of a need to justify the move, or to adjust for the fact that they were forced to move. On the other hand, it might be expected that people are positive about their new situation, because in the case of urban restructuring people are often forced to move from the most deteriorated parts of the city and they do move to better places. A small change (a slightly safer neighbourhood, or some more facilities for children) can already be seen as a large improvement.

Other authors have taken an approach that used administrative data (see, e.g., Kingsley et al. 2003; Oakley and Burchfield 2009). The results from these kinds of studies are quite different. Although, some studies have shown that displaced residents move to better neighbourhoods, other studies have shown that this is generally not the case (Oakley and Burchfield 2009; Kingsley et al. 2003; Goetz 2002; Rubenstein 1988; Varady and Walker 2000). Compared to the international literature (mostly from the United States), the Dutch literature shows somewhat more positive outcomes: displaced residents have in general been able to improve their situation after moving. The progress they make is however often limited (Bolt and Van Kempen 2010; Slob et al. 2008; Kleinhans 2003; Kleinhans and Van der Laan Bouma-Doff 2008).

Hypotheses

Based on the literature outlined above, six hypotheses regarding the neighbourhoods displaced residents will move to can be formulated. Displaced residents tend to move to:

1. a limited number of neighbourhoods;
2. neighbourhoods near the restructuring projects from which they are displaced;
3. neighbourhoods with a large inexpensive housing stock;
4. neighbourhoods with a low average socioeconomic status;
5. neighbourhoods with a large proportion of ethnic minorities;
6. neighbourhoods that are rather similar but more popular than the neighbourhoods they leave.

Research Areas and Data

The data we use to test these hypotheses were collected from three Dutch cities: Rotterdam, Ede and Breda. We picked these cities in order to compare the dispersal patterns of displaced households in cities of different sizes. Until now, most research on the effects of urban restructuring has focused on large cities (Kleinhans 2003; Goetz 2002; Varady and Walker 2000). However, the effects of restructing in smaller cities may be different to those found in large cities for two reasons. First, medium sized cities have fewer neighbourhoods with a suitable housing stock for displaced households, which means that in theory these households have fewer choices between neighbourhoods. Second, in large cities, urban renewal policies have generally been carried out for a longer period of time compared to medium sized cities. In the 1970s and 1980s most of the urban renewal funds in the Netherlands were spent in the four largest cities (Amsterdam, Rotterdam, the Hague and Utrecht), as these cities had a large stock of old and deteriorated dwellings, especially in the pre-WWII part of the housing stock. In midsized cities the pre-WWII housing stock is relatively small. The present pre-WWII areas were considered to be less deteriorated. During this period a policy philosophy of "Building for the Neighbourhood", rather than promoting social mix was followed, which meant that new dwellings were built for the current inhabitants of the neighbourhood rather than for residents from outside. This resulted in a focus on renovating and rebuilding affordable rented dwellings. As a consequence, most of these neighbourhoods remained amongst the poorest of the city after the urban renewal process (Van Kempen and Bolt 2009). Nowadays, the urban restructuring process is much more focused on post-WWII neighbourhoods with a large proportion of social rented dwellings. In medium sized cities like Breda and Ede, these neighbourhoods are amongst the worst of the city. In Rotterdam, however, the neighbourhoods currently targeted for restructuring are not always the weakest. For displaced households there is more scope for improvement in Breda and Ede, as a household is less likely to move down the neighbourhood hierarchy because they are leaving neighbourhoods already at the bottom on the neighbourhood hierarchy. In Rotterdam, this is not the case as it is possible to move down as well as up the neighbourhood hierarchy.

Two types of data are used in the analysis. Firstly we use data from public databases that provide information about neighbourhood characteristics. The neighbourhood level is the lowest administrative level at which aggregated data are present. What constitutes a neighbourhood is defined by each municipality separately. They usually define neighbourhoods on the basis of natural borders, and architectural styles. Secondly we use data regarding the moving behaviour of displaced residents. We know the previous and present addresses, and by extension the neighbourhoods, of displaced households. Using these data we can depict dispersal patterns and by combining both dispersal and neighbourhood data we can gain greater insight into the relationships between the characteristics of neighbourhoods and the number of displaced households neighbourhoods receive.

Table 5.1 Core characteristics of Breda, Ede and Rotterdam

	Breda	Ede	Rotterdam
Total number of residents	172,085	107,588	587,130
% Ethnic minorities	11	7	34
Number of dwellings	75,886	41,408	289,337
% Owner-occupied dwellings	60	70	32
% Social rented dwellings	32	20	49
% Pre-WWII dwellings	16	12	32
Number of neighbourhoods	54	67	89
Average number of residents per neighbourhood	3,187	1,606	6,597
Average size of neighbourhoods (km^2)	2.39	4.76	3.02

Source: CBS Statline, Buurtmonitor Breda, Buurtmonitor Ede, Buurtmonitor Rotterdam

In Table 5.1 some of the main characteristics of the three selected cities are presented. Rotterdam is much larger than Breda and Ede. Ede is the smallest of the three areas in terms of the number of residents, but has more neighbourhoods than Breda. The proportion of ethnic minorities[1] is the highest in Rotterdam compared with Breda and Ede. In Breda and Ede the proportion of the population belonging to an ethnic minority is about the same. In comparison with Ede, the proportion of homeowners is somewhat smaller and the share of social rented dwellings somewhat larger in Breda. The housing market in Rotterdam consists of a considerably greater proportion of social rented dwellings than the housing market in the other two cities, and the housing stock in Rotterdam is on average much older, as almost a third of the dwellings has been built before WWII.

In *Breda* we followed households that were forced to leave their social rented dwelling because of urban restructuring between 2003 and 2009. In total 358 households moved in this period from restructuring projects in three neighbourhoods: Heuvel, De Geeren-Noord and Brabant Park. The displaced households moved to 34 different neighbourhoods. Information about the three restructured neighbourhoods in Breda is provided in Table 5.2a. This table shows that the restructured neighbourhoods are characterized by a very high proportion of social rented dwellings. Furthermore, there are few neighbourhoods with a lower average income than the restructured neighbourhoods in Breda.

In *Ede* we followed 507 households who were forced to relocate between 2003 and 2008. Restructuring projects took place in 20 neighbourhoods, but the largest projects took place in just three neighbourhoods: De Burgen, De Horsten and Uitvindersbuurt (434 displaced households in total). The displaced households moved to 30 different neighbourhoods. Table 5.2b shows that the proportion of social rented dwellings in restructured neighbourhoods in Ede is smaller than in the

[1] When we refer to ethnic minorities in The Netherlands, we use the following definition: a person belongs to an ethnic minority when at least one of his or her parents were born in a non-western country.

Table 5.2a Top three restructured neighbourhoods in Breda

	Heuvel	De Geeren-Noord	Brabantpark
Number of displaced households	85	147	126
% Total displaced households	24	41	35
Number of dwellings	3,125	1,410	4,210
% Social rented dwellings	66	72	44
% Neighbourhoods with a lower average income per income recipient	22	10	29
% Moves within the neighbourhood	49	9	33
% Moves to other neighbourhoods within the city	39	63	59
% Moves to other municipalities	12	28	8

Source: WonenBreburg, CBS Statline, Buurtmonitor Breda

Table 5.2b Top three restructured neighbourhoods in Ede

	De Burgen	De Horsten	Uitvindersbuurt
Number of displaced households	146	80	208
% Total displaced households	29	16	41
Number of dwellings	810	940	1,100
% Social rented dwellings	56	42	37
% Neighbourhoods with a lower average income per income recipient	12	16	23
% Moves within the neighbourhood	26	0	9
% Moves to other neighbourhoods within the city	61	78	80
% Moves to other municipalities	13	23	12

Source: Woonstede, CBS Statline, Buurtmonitor Ede

other two cities. The number of dwellings in the restructured neighbourhoods is also considerably smaller in Ede.

In *Rotterdam* we followed 2,818 residents who were forced to relocate in 2007, 2008 or 2009. Since the number of displaced residents is much larger in Rotterdam than in the other two cities, we only use three years of data. The three largest urban restructuring projects all took place in post-WWII neighbourhoods: Lombardijen, Zuidwijk and Hoogvliet-Zuid. The residents from the restructured neighbourhoods moved to 54 different neighbourhoods. Table 5.2c shows that the three largest restructuring projects in Rotterdam account for a considerably smaller proportion of displaced households than the three largest restructuring projects in Ede and Breda. Furthermore, a relatively large proportion of Rotterdam's neighbourhoods have a lower average income than the restructured neighbourhoods.

The rules and regulations surrounding the relocation process of those who were forced to move is one of the most important factors when investigating the outcomes of the relocation. There are some important differences in the rights people have in the three cities under investigation. The relocation process in Breda was organized according to a so-called 'option system'. This means that residents who have to move can indicate to what kind of dwelling (within the social housing sector) and

Table 5.2c Top three restructured neighbourhoods in Rotterdam

	Hoogvliet-Zuid	Lombardijen	Zuidwijk
Displaced households	261	290	251
% Total displaced households	9	10	9
Number of dwellings	10,105	6,895	6,720
% Social rented dwellings	58	56	75
% Neighbourhoods with a lower average income per income recipient	59	44	39
% Moves within the neighbourhood	58	33	16
% Moves to other neighbourhoods within the city	32	54	67
% Moves to other municipalities	10	13	18

Source: Maaskoepel, CBS Statline, Buurtmonitor Rotterdam

neighbourhood they want to move. Based on this information the housing corporation will offer a dwelling that matches the indicated options, as soon as such a dwelling becomes available. A suitable dwelling is always offered first to a household that has to move because of urban restructuring before it is offered to other social housing applicants. However, if three offers are turned down, the displaced resident loses their special status.

In *Ede* displaced residents have to search for a new dwelling themselves. Within the social renting sector this means that relocated residents have to access the weekly updated list of available dwellings. Residents who are forced to move because of restructuring receive a special priority status with which they will get certain types of dwellings before other prospective tenants. The type of priority status a displaced resident receives depends on the period they lived in the dwelling that will be demolished. When a resident has lived less than 7 years in the dwelling they receive a priority status for a similar type of dwelling. When a resident has lived between 7 and 12 years in the dwelling they receive a priority status for a single-family dwelling across a selected group of neighbourhoods, and when a resident has lived 12 years or more in the dwelling to be demolished they receive a priority status for all single-family dwellings in the local housing market area. As long as displaced residents apply for dwellings which match their priority status the dwelling will be offered to them before it is made available to other prospective tenants.

Like in Ede, displaced households in *Rotterdam* get a special status with which they get priority over other house seekers when they apply for social rented dwellings. In contrast to the situation in Ede, this priority status is similar for all displaced residents regardless of the length of time they have lived in the property. The priority status only holds for dwellings that are comparable to their previous dwelling in terms of type, size and price. It should be noted that comparability is a rather flexible concept. In practice it often turns out that only single-family dwellings in the social rented sector are not within reach for displaced residents. During the first 9 months residents have to try to find a new dwelling themselves, afterwards they receive help of the housing corporation for a period of 3 months. If they still do not have another dwelling after this period, a juridical procedure is started which can take about another 3 months.

Dispersal Patterns

An analysis of the dispersal patterns of displaced households is presented to examine our first two hypotheses: that displaced households move to a small number of neighbourhoods, which are frequently nearby their current location. Figure 5.1 shows the dispersal patterns of displaced households that moved out of their neighbourhood of origin but within the same municipality. For each city the moves from the three largest restructuring projects to other neighbourhoods within the city are depicted. The width of the lines indicates the size of the flows of displaced households between different neighbourhoods. These maps show first of all that displaced households moved to a large number of different neighbourhoods, but that moves to some neighbourhoods were much more common than moves to other neighbourhoods. Most neighbourhoods do not even receive a single displaced household. In each city the neighbourhood that received most displaced households accounts for around 10% of all displaced residents only.

The proportion of displaced residents who left their municipality differs between cities: the proportion is larger in Breda and Ede (17 and 14% respectively) than in Rotterdam (8%). Since Rotterdam is a larger city, it offers displaced residents more local choice, and less incentive to leave the municipality. The proportion of displaced households who moved within their neighbourhood is considerable in all cities. However, there are clear differences between cities. Whereas in Ede only 18% of the displaced households moved within their neighbourhood, in Breda this is 33%, and in Rotterdam even 43%. To some extent, this will be related to the size of the neighbourhood (Table 5.2a,b,c). As the neighbourhoods in Rotterdam are larger, there are more options for households who wish to stay within the neighbourhood. In Ede the neighbourhoods are relatively small, which gives on average fewer opportunities to move within a neighbourhood. Moving within the neighbourhood is further restricted here by the fact that a relatively large proportion of the social rented housing stock has been demolished.

Although displaced residents appear to re-concentrate in certain neighbourhoods, it is not the case that only a small number of neighbourhoods receive the large majority of displaced households. As such we can conclude that our first hypothesis that displaced households move to only a few neighbourhoods is only confirmed to a limited extent.

The maps in Fig. 5.1 also provide information regarding the distance between the old and new neighbourhood of displaced households from the largest restructuring projects in the selected cities. In Ede displaced residents were most likely to move to nearby neighbourhoods. Ede is a small city, so it is quite unlikely that people move over large distances. The more distant rural areas in the municipality did not attract many households. This largely has to do with the limited number of affordable dwellings in these areas. In Breda there is also a tendency to move to neighbourhoods near to their previous location, with the area of Heuvel as a clear exception. This pattern can be explained by the large proportion of displaced residents that moved *within* Heuvel (see Table 5.2a).

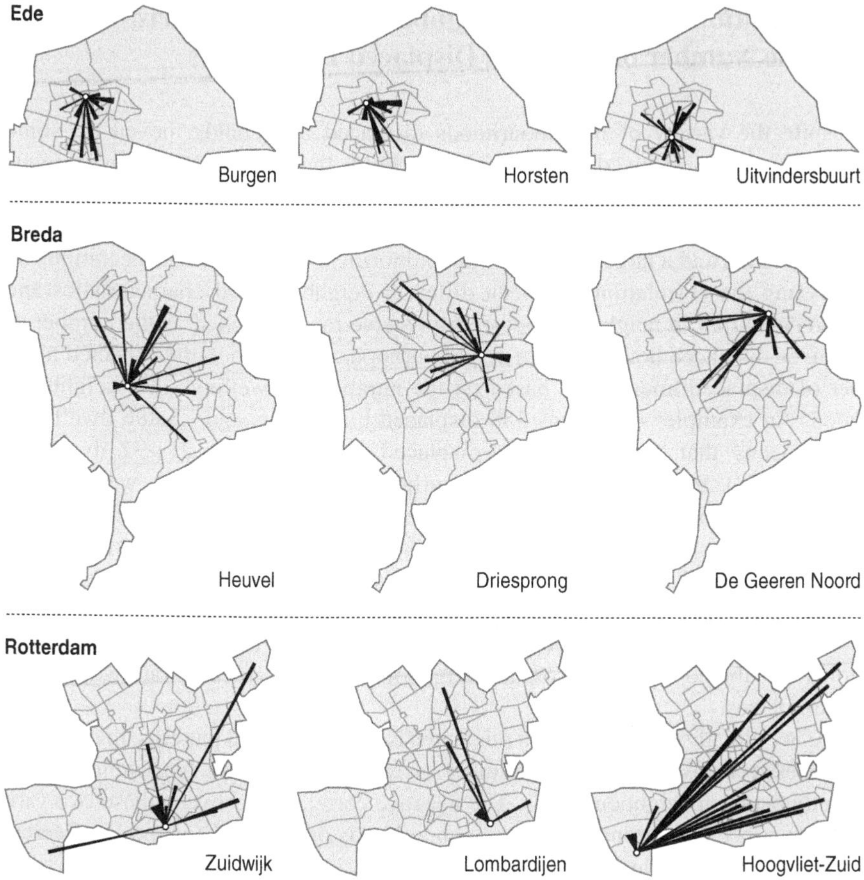

Fig. 5.1 Dispersal patterns of displaced households in Ede, Breda and Rotterdam

In contrast to Ede and Breda, we clearly see that in Rotterdam moves from the renewed neighbourhoods are commonly made to one of the adjacent neighbourhoods, and that most residents stay close to their old neighbourhood. Only in the case of Hoogvliet-Zuid, the dispersal pattern is rather diffuse, with sizeable flows to more distant neighbourhoods. The reason for that is probably the same as for Heuvel in Breda: a large proportion of the displaced households have managed to move within the neighbourhood (or to the adjacent Hoogvliet-Noord), so there were few moves made to other adjacent neighbourhoods. The small proportion that moved further away probably felt less attached to the area of origin.

Hence, the second hypothesis – displaced households move to nearby neighbourhoods – can be confirmed in most cases, with the exception of Heuvel (Breda) and Hoogvliet-Zuid (Rotterdam). But in those neighbourhoods a sizable number of households has moved within the neighbourhood, indicating that moving to nearby places is quite common for displaced households.

The Relationship Between Neighbourhood Characteristics and the Number of Received Displaced Households

Despite the variety of neighbourhoods displaced households moved to, some neighbourhoods received many more households than others. Based on previous research we expect that these neighbourhoods are located in close proximity to the restructuring projects, have a large inexpensive housing stock, a low socioeconomic status, and a large share of ethnic minorities. We test these expectations by analysing the correlations between different neighbourhood characteristics and the *receive rate* in neighbourhoods. The receive rate is defined as the number of received displaced households in neighbourhoods compared to the expected number of displaced households based on the number of dwellings in a neighbourhood. An example: Breda has 358 displaced households and 75,886 dwellings. This means that we expect one displaced household per 211.97 dwellings (75,886/358). In Fellenoord, a neighbourhood with 895 dwellings, we therefore expect that 895/211.97 = 4.22 displaced households would have settled there. In reality three displaced households moved to Fellenoord. The receive rate is therefore 3/4.22 = 0.71. A receive rate under 1 means that fewer displaced households settled than expected, while a receive rate over 1 means that more displaced households settled than expected. It would be expected that, if displaced households distributed equally across all neighbourhoods, the receive rate would be 1 for all places.

As we already concluded from our analysis of the dispersal patterns, the relationship between distance and the number of received displaced households differs greatly between neighbourhoods. The negative correlation between these two variables is especially strong for the neighbourhoods of Ede and for the De Geeren-Noord in Breda (Table 5.3). That the correlations are somewhat lower in Rotterdam is not surprising as displaced households have moved out of a wide variety of neighbourhoods. Less than a third has moved out of one of the top three neighbourhoods (Table 5.2c). For Heuvel (Breda) and Hoogvliet-Zuid (Rotterdam), the correlation between distance and moving rate is very small. Apparently, the dispersal pattern is less predictable in these two cases where a large proportion of movers stayed within the neighbourhood (see previous section). When displaced households move out of the neighbourhood (the other seven cases) there is a clear tendency to move to nearby areas. This underlines our conclusion in the previous section about the second hypothesis. Displaced households tend to move to nearby neighbourhoods, at least in most cases.

Our third hypothesis stated that displaced residents would move to neighbourhoods with an inexpensive housing stock. Inexpensive neighbourhoods are defined as neighbourhoods with a low average house value and a large proportion of social rented dwellings. We expected that displaced residents mostly move to neighbourhoods with a relatively low average house value since these residents only have a small budget to spend on their housing. The correlation between the average house

Table 5.3 Correlations between neighbourhood characteristics and receive rates in neighbourhoods in Breda, Ede and Rotterdam

	Breda	Ede	Rotterdam
	(48 n'hoods)	(54 n'hoods)	(59 n'hoods)
Distance De Burgen	X	−0.47	X
Distance De Horsten	X	−0.46	X
Distance Uitvindersbuurt	X	−0.51	X
Distance Heuvel	0.03	X	X
Distance De Geeren-Noord	−0.49	X	X
Distance Brabant Park	−0.36	X	X
Distance Hoogvliet-Zuid	X	X	−0.11
Distance Zuidwijk	X	X	−0.27
Distance Lombardijen	X	X	−0.30
% Social rented dwellings	0.72	0.82	0.64
Average house value € 1,000	−0.52	−0.60	−0.25
Average income per income recipient € 1,000	−0.54	−0.39	−0.37
Number of social welfare recipients per 1,000 residents	0.64	0.77	0.55
% Ethnic minorities	0.75	0.84	0.40

Source: WonenBreburg, Woonstede, Maaskoepel, CBS Statline, Buurtmonitor Breda, Buurtmonitor Ede, Buurtmonitor Rotterdam
Neighbourhoods with under 100 residents are not included in the analyses
The restructured neighbourhoods, neighbourhoods with a leaver rate over 1 and over 60 displaced households, are not included in the analyses

value and receive rate is indeed negative in all three cities, although relatively strong in Ede and Breda and relatively weak in Rotterdam.

We also expected that displaced residents would move within the social rented sector since they lived in dwellings within this sector before and will often stay dependent on this subsidized form of housing. At the neighbourhood level, we expect that most displaced households will move to neighbourhoods with large numbers of socially rented dwellings. The correlation between the proportion of social dwellings in the neighbourhood and the receive rate is strong and positive in all cities. Hence, the third hypothesis that displaced households move to neighbourhoods with a relatively inexpensive housing stock is confirmed. The extent to which displaced households have moved to neighbourhoods with an inexpensive housing stock differs however considerably between cities.

Fourth, we hypothesize that displaced households move to neighbourhoods with a low socioeconomic status. To measure the socioeconomic status of a neighbourhood we used two indicators: the average income for those in receipt of some means of payment either through work, or benefits of pension and the number of social welfare recipients. As expected, there is a positive correlation between a low average income and the receive rate in neighbourhoods. This relationship is clearly strongest in Breda. The receive rate is also positively related to a high number of social welfare recipients in all cities. In Ede and Breda this relationship is however stronger than in Rotterdam. Nevertheless, the hypothesis that displaced households move to neighbourhoods with a low socioeconomic status can be confirmed for all cities.

In line with our fifth hypothesis, displaced households move to neighbourhoods with a relatively large share of ethnic minorities. The table shows once again that this is true across all cities, but that the correlation is much stronger in Breda and Ede than in Rotterdam. Again, we can confirm the hypothesis. An explanation for the weaker correlations between neighbourhood characteristics and the receive rate in Rotterdam is that there are many more neighbourhoods available with a large inexpensive housing stock, low socioeconomic status, and large share of ethnic minorities. In Breda and Ede fewer neighbourhoods have these characteristics and as a result displaced households are more restricted in their neighbourhood choices. Since displaced households are less dispersed over different neighbourhoods in Breda and Ede it would be expected that the correlation between the receive rate and neighbourhood characteristics is stronger.

Comparing Restructured Neighbourhoods, Receiving Neighbourhoods and Other Neighbourhoods

Whether displaced households move to similar neighbourhoods or not can be examined by a comparison of the characteristics of three types of neighbourhoods: (1) neighbourhoods that received many displaced households; (2) restructured neighbourhoods; and (3) neighbourhoods that did not receive many displaced households (all other neighbourhoods). We define restructured neighbourhoods as neighbourhoods where more households are displaced than could be expected on the basis of the number of dwellings. In order to prevent that neighbourhoods with very small numbers of displaced households being labelled as restructured, we only include neighbourhoods in this category when at least 60 households were *forced* to move. Receiving neighbourhoods are defined as neighbourhoods that are not labelled as restructured neighbourhoods and which have a receive rate (see the discussion above) over 1 and where over 20 displaced households settled. Those neighbourhoods that do not fall into either of these two categories were defined in the 'all other neighbourhoods' category.

Table 5.4 shows a comparison between the characteristics of restructured, receiving and other neighbourhoods in all three cities. In Breda and Ede the restructured neighbourhoods are characterized by the highest proportions of social rented dwellings, ethnic minorities, social welfare recipients, and the lowest average house values and lowest average income. This finding is important as it shows that despite the restructuring policy carried out here; these neighbourhoods still seem to belong to the category of most distressed areas.

In general, the receiving neighbourhoods have more positive scores, although the scores are not equally positive across all cities. Whilst the scores for Breda and

Table 5.4 Characteristics of restructured, receiving, and other neighbourhoods in Breda, Ede and Rotterdam

	Breda			Ede			Rotterdam		
	Restructured	Receiving	Other	Restructured	Receiving	Other	Restructured	Receiving	Other
Average values	3	–2	–46	–3	–8	–46	–12	–6	–53
% Social rented dwellings	60.4	48.2	22.9	45	41.9	14.5	66	76.7	40
Average house value € 1,000	149,7	174,0	283,3	175,3	203,6	337,1	130,9	128,6	172,7
% Single family dwellings	46.3	66.9	70.5	60.5	59.8	85	26.5	12.8	31.5
Income per income recipient € 1,000	15.3	17.5	20	15.7	16.8	19.6	16.3	15.7	18.8
Social welfare per 1,000 households	98.7	66	37.6	106	60.5	13.9	155.8	193.7	97.6
% Ethnic minorities	22.3	18.5	7.9	31.7	12.1	2.6	41.4	49.7	19.6
Distance Brabant Park (km)		2.2	3.7						
Distance De Geeren-Noord (km)		2	4.2						
Distance Heuvel (km)		5.1	3.6						
Distance De Burgen (km)					1.9	4.8			
Distance De Horsten (km)					2	4.8			
Distance Uitvindersbuurt (km)					1.3	5.1			
Distance Hoogvliet-Zuid (km)								11.1	11.3
Distance Zuidwijk (km)								4.8	6.1
Distance Lombardijen (km)								4.9	6.5

Source: CBS Statline, Buurtmonitor Breda, Buurtmonitor Ede, Buurtmonitor Rotterdam, WonenBreburg, Woonstede, Maaskoepel
Neighbourhoods with under 100 residents are excluded from the analyses

Ede allow us to confirm the hypothesis that displaced households move to somewhat better-off neighbourhoods, in Rotterdam we have to reject this hypothesis as displaced households move to worse-off neighbourhoods. For all three cities it holds that restructuring and receiving neighbourhoods are similar and clearly different to the neighbourhoods in the other neighbourhood category. These other neighbourhoods are characterised by a high average income, few social welfare recipients, a high average house value and a large proportion of single family dwellings. The step upwards in the neighbourhood hierarchy that displaced households experience in Breda and Ede is thus limited.

A possible explanation for the differences between outcomes for Ede and Breda on the one hand and Rotterdam on the other is that displaced households in Rotterdam are more restricted by the allocation system. In Rotterdam the priority status is not valid when a household applies for a single family dwelling, which is not the case for Ede, at least for those with a long length of residence (7 years or more). The option model in Breda also does not restrict moves into a single family dwelling.

An alternative explanation is that restructuring is a much more recent phenomenon in the medium sized cities such as Breda and Ede. In these cities restructuring is now targeting neighbourhoods at the bottom of the local neighbourhood hierarchy, whereas in large cities these neighbourhoods have already undergone improvement by the urban renewal processes of the 1970s and 1980s. While these neighbourhoods are still amongst the worst of the city, the current focus of urban restructuring is on neighbourhoods that are not at the bottom of the neighbourhood hierarchy. As such the chance to move to a worse neighbourhood is bigger in Rotterdam than in the other two cities.

Conclusion and Discussion

Two questions were raised in this chapter. First, we asked: *How can neighbourhoods to which displaced households move be characterized?* Our results show that despite the wide variety of neighbourhoods to which displaced households move, there is a tendency for households to concentrate in neighbourhoods with specific characteristics. These neighbourhoods are, in general, near to the restructured neighbourhoods, consist of an inexpensive housing stock, have a low average socio-economic status, and a large share of ethnic minorities. Only in two (out of nine) cases of displacement mobility do we find no support that displaced households move over short distances to nearby neighbourhoods. However, both of these cases have a very large proportion of displaced household moved *within* their neighbourhoods of origin. This strengthens our hypothesis that displaced households move over short distances. Furthermore, we noted that the relationship between the receive rate and neighbourhood characteristics is considerably weaker in Rotterdam than in the medium sized cities. This may be due to the greater choices that displaced households have in Rotterdam: many more neighbourhoods have a suitable housing stock than in the cities of Breda or Ede. As a result, the effects of displacement cannot be seen separated from the structure of the local housing market.

The second question we addressed was: *How do the neighbourhoods to which many displaced households move, differ from their neighbourhood of origin?* In all three cities we observe that restructured and receiving neighbourhoods are relatively similar. However, whilst we find that displaced residents in Breda and Ede move to neighbourhoods that are generally classified as being better (less social rented dwellings, higher average house value, more single-family dwellings, higher average income, less social welfare recipients, less minorities), those displaced households moving within Rotterdam tend to move into neighbourhoods that are generally classified to be worse. We suggest that this is a consequence of the nature of the restructuring that is taking place in these cities: the neighbourhoods currently undergoing restructuring in Rotterdam are not as bad as those in Breda and Ede. The urban renewal process has been running for a longer period of time in Rotterdam, so that the weakest neighbourhoods have already been restructured. In Breda and Ede the current focus is on the weakest neighbourhoods, which implies that a move to another neighbourhood almost automatically means an upward move.

The current re-concentration of displaced households in rather similar neighbourhoods can have negative effects for these neighbourhoods. Previous research has shown that concentrations of disadvantaged residents are related to problems such as increased insecurity in the neighbourhood, criminality and tensions between residents, decreased social cohesion, fewer opportunities for social mobility and a slow integration of minorities. Since displaced residents are often relatively disadvantaged, their arrival would worsen the concentration of disadvantaged residents in the destination neighbourhoods and the problems related to it. The impact of the increase of problems may be linearly related to the increase in disadvantaged residents, or it may change when certain thresholds are passed (Galster et al. 2000). When this assumption holds, the arrival of displaced residents may cause a rapid increase of problems.

The re-concentration of displaced households does however not need to have negative effects. Negative effects may not occur since the total numbers of displaced households that settle in specific neighbourhoods are small in comparison with the total population of the neighbourhood. Furthermore, the increase of problems in neighbourhoods may not be directly related to the *number* of displaced residents that settle in that neighbourhood but more to the *type* of displaced residents: the arrival of a few multi-problem families may have a much more severe effect than the arrival of a relatively large number of regular families (Kleinhans and Varady 2011). Further research will need to reveal the possible link between problems in the neighbourhood and the inflow of displaced households.

Although the re-concentration of displaced households does not necessarily imply that problems are displaced as well, the re-concentration of displaced households implies that mixing – and its assumed positive effects – does not take place on a city-wide scale. Not many residents move to neighbourhoods with a considerably higher status and earlier research findings (Bolt et al. 2009) suggest that it is especially the small group of households with a relatively high income amongst the displaced that manages to move upwards in the neighbourhood hierarchy. Desegregation will only take place when the moving behaviour of displaced households alters. In other words: based on our current results we can conclude that displaced residents often move to areas that have comparable characteristics with their previous neighbourhoods. Re-concentration in such neighbourhoods is a more apt term than urban desegregation for the process we observe.

The re-concentration of displaced residents in disadvantaged neighbourhoods means that the policy of urban restructuring, which frequently aims to produce mixed neighbourhoods, cannot be seen as an automatic success. While the restructuring process results in a greater degree of social mix in the restructured neighbourhoods those neighbourhoods that receive the majority of displaced residents become more segregated. New concentrations of poor households occur in those areas that are not restructured. In order to get rid of these concentrations the process of urban restructuring would need to be extended to the receiving neighbourhoods. However, it has to be accepted that restructuring neighbourhoods in this manner will not automatically solve the problems for disadvantaged individuals: when all neighbourhoods have been restructured there will be no affordable rented houses left and this can be detrimental for a wide range of groups trying to access the urban housing market, including poor minority ethnic groups and young families. Policy makers should therefore ask themselves whether they are interested in tackling the concentrations of poverty or some of the structural causes behind individual disadvantage.

Further research will need to reveal what criteria displaced residents use to judge whether a neighbourhood is a good place for them to live and how they use their resources (both economic and cultural) to suffice their preferences. It may be that some of the aspects of neighbourhoods that are labelled as problematic are in fact desirable for displaced residents (see for instance Bauder 2002). Whereas negative effects of a concentration of low-income residents have been identified in many studies, displaced households may prefer to live in such a neighbourhood because of the wide availability of support networks. Apart from the preferences of displaced residents, the restrictions they experience can also affect their choices. When displaced residents for example feel a strong pressure to find a dwelling as soon as possible or have problems to understand the relocation procedures, they may choose for dwellings and neighbourhoods they actually do not prefer (Manley and Van Ham 2011). All in all, the current choices of displaced households result in re-concentration. When policy makers aim to develop mixing policies that do not result in re-concentration it seems therefore worth the effort to take a closer look at the decision making process of displaced households.

References

Andersen, H. S. (2002). Can deprived housing areas be revitalised? Efforts against segregation and neighbourhood decay in Denmark and Europe. *Urban Studies, 39*(4), 767–790.

Andersen, H. T., & Van Kempen, R. (2003). New trends in urban policies in Europe: Evidence from the Netherlands and Denmark. *Cities, 20*(2), 77–86.

Atkinson, R., & Kintrea, K. (2000). Owner-occupation, social mix and neighbourhood impacts. *Policy & Politics, 28*(1), 93–108.

Bauder, H. (2002). Neighbourhood effects and cultural exclusion. *Urban Studies, 39*(1), 85–93.
Bolt, G., & Van Kempen, R. (2010). Dispersal patterns of households who are forced to move: Desegregation by demolition: A case study of Dutch cities. *Housing Studies, 25*(2), 159–180.
Bolt, G., Van Kempen, R., & Van Weesep, J. (2009). After urban restructuring: Relocations and segregation in Dutch cities. *Tijdschrift voor Economische en Sociale Geografie, 100*(4), 502–518.
Brooks, F., Zugazaga, C., Wolk, J., & Adams, M. A. (2005). Resident perceptions of housing, neighbourhood, and economic conditions after relocation from public housing undergoing HOPE VI redevelopment. *Research on Social Work Practice, 15*(6), 481–490.
Clampet-Lundquist, S. (2004). HOPE VI relocation: Moving to new neighbourhoods and building new ties. *Housing Policy Debate, 15*(2), 415–447.
Dekker, K., & Bolt, G. (2005). Social cohesion in post-war estates in the Netherlands: Differences between socioeconomic and ethnic groups. *Urban Studies, 42*(13), 2447–2470.
Dekker, K., & Van Kempen, R. (2004). Large housing estates in Europe: Current situation and developments. *Tijdschrift voor Economische en Sociale Geografie, 95*(5), 570–577.
Dietz, R. D., & Haurin, D. R. (2003). The social and private micro-level consequences of home-ownership. *Journal of Urban Economics, 54*(3), 401–450.
Dipasquale, D., & Glaeser, E. L. (1999). Incentives and social capital: Are homeowners better citizens? *Journal of Urban Economics, 45*(2), 354–384.
Freeman, L. (2000). Minority housing segregation: A test of three perspectives. *Journal of Urban Affairs, 22*(1), 15–35.
Friedrichs, J. (1998). Do poor neighbourhoods make their residents poorer? Context effects of poverty neighbourhoods on residents. In H. J. Andress (Ed.), *Empirical poverty research in a comparative perspective* (pp. 77–99). Aldershot: Ashgate.
Friedrichs, J., & Blasius, J. (2009). Attitudes of owners and renters in a deprived neighbourhood. *European Journal of Housing Policy, 9*(4), 435–455.
Galster, G. (1983). Empirical evidence on cross-tenure differences in house maintenance and conditions. *Land Economics, 59*(1), 107–113.
Galster, G. C. (1999). The evolving challenges of fair housing since 1968: Open housing, integration, and the reduction of ghettoization. *Cityscape: A Journal of Policy Development and Research, 4*(3), 123–138.
Galster, C. G., Quercia, R. G., & Cortes, A. (2000). Identifying neighbourhood thresholds. *Housing Policy Debate, 11*(3), 701–732.
Galster, G., Andersson, R., Musterd, S., & Kauppinen, T. M. (2008). Does neighborhood income mix affect earnings of adults? New evidence from Sweden. *Journal of Urban Economics, 63*(3), 858–870.
Galster, G., Andersson, R., & Musterd, S. (2010). Who is affected by neighbourhood income mix? Gender, age, family, employment and income differences. *Urban Studies, 47*(14), 2915–2944.
Gijsberts, M., & Dagevos, J. (2007). The socio-cultural integration of ethnic minorities in The Netherlands: Identifying neighbourhood effects on multiple integration outcomes. *Housing Studies, 22*(5), 805–831.
Goetz, E. G. (2002). Forced relocation vs. voluntary mobility: The effects of dispersal programmes on households. *Housing Studies, 17*(1), 107–123.
Graham, E., Manley, D., Hiscock, R., Boyle, P., & Doherty, J. (2009). Mixing housing tenures: Is it good for social well-being? *Urban Studies, 46*(1), 139–165.
Hartung, J. M., & Henig, J. R. (1997). Housing vouchers and certificates as a vehicle for deconcentrating the poor. Evidence from the Washington, D.C., metropolitan area. *Urban Affairs Review, 32*(3), 403–419.
Joseph, M. L., Chaskin, R. J., & Webber, H. S. (2007). The theoretical basis for addressing poverty through mixed-income development. *Urban Affairs Review, 42*(3), 369–409.
Kingsley, G. T., Johnson, J., & Pettit, K. L. S. (2003). Patterns of section 8 relocation in the HOPE VI program. *Journal of Urban Affairs, 25*(4), 427–447.
Kintrea, K. (2007). Policies and programmes for disadvantaged neighbourhoods: Recent English experience. *Housing Studies, 22*(2), 261–282.

Kleinhans, R. (2003). Displaced but still moving upwards in the housing career? Implications of forced residential relocation in the Netherlands. *Housing Studies, 18*(4), 473–499.
Kleinhans, R., & Van der Laan Bouma-Doff, W. (2008). On priority and progress: Forced residential relocation and housing chances in Haaglanden, the Netherlands. *Housing Studies, 23*(4), 565–578.
Kleinhans, R., & Varady, D. (2011). Moving out and going down? A review of recent evidence on negative spillover effects of housing restructuring programmes in the United States and the Netherlands. *International Journal of Housing Policy, 11*(2), 155–174.
Kleinhans, R., Priemus, H., & Engbersen, G. (2007). Understanding social capital in recently restructured urban neighbourhoods: Two case studies in Rotterdam. *Urban Studies, 44*(5/6), 1069–1091.
Krysan, M., & Farley, R. (2002). The residential preferences of blacks: Do they explain persistent segregation? *Social Forces, 80*(3), 937–980.
Laurence, J. (2011). The effect of ethnic diversity and community disadvantage on social cohesion: A multi-level analysis of social capital and interethnic relations in UK communities. *European Sociological Review, 27*(1), 70–89.
Leventhal, T., & Brooks-Gunn, J. (2000). The neighborhoods they live in: The effects of neighborhood residence on child and adolescent outcomes. *Psychological Bulletin, 126*(2), 309–337.
Macintyre, S., MacDonald, L., & Ellaway, A. (2008). Do poorer people have poorer access to local resources and facilities? The distribution of local resources by area deprivation in Glasgow, Scotland. *Social Science & Medicine, 67*(6), 900–914.
Manley, D., & Van Ham, M. (2011). Choice-based letting, ethnicity and segregation in England. *Urban Studies, 48*(14), 1–19.
Manzo, L. C., Kleit, R. G., & Couch, D. (2008). "Moving three times is like having you house on fire once": The experience of place and impending displacement among public housing residents. *Urban Studies, 45*(9), 1855–1878.
Ministry VROM. (1997). *Nota Stedelijke Vernieuwing*. Den Haag: Ministerie van VROM.
Ministry VROM. (2000). *Mensen Wensen Wonen. Wonen in de 21ste eeuw*. Den Haag: Ministerie van VROM.
Ministry VROM. (2007). *Actieplan Krachtwijken: van aandachtswijk naar krachtwijk*. Den Haag: Ministerie van VROM.
Ministry VROM. (2008). *Stedenbeleid vanaf 2010*. Den Haag: Ministerie van VROM.
Musterd, S., & Andersson, R. (2006). Employment, social mobility and neighbourhood effects: The case of Sweden. *International Journal of Urban and Regional Research, 30*(1), 120–140.
Musterd, S., Andersson, R., Galster, G., & Kauppinen, T. (2008). Are immigrants' earnings influenced by the characteristics of their neighbors? *Environment and Planning A, 40*(4), 785–805.
Oakley, D., & Burchfield, K. (2009). Out of the projects, still in the hood: The spatial constraints on public-housing residents' relocation in Chicago. *Journal of Urban Affairs, 31*(5), 589–614.
Oberwittler, D. (2007). The effects of neighbourhood poverty on adolescent problem behaviours: A multi-level analysis differentiated by gender and ethnicity. *Housing Studies, 22*(5), 781–803.
Pendall, R. (2000). Why voucher and certificate users live in distressed neighborhoods. *Housing Policy Debate, 11*(4), 881–910.
Permentier, M., Van Ham, M., & Bolt, G. (2009). Neighbourhood reputation and the intention to leave the neighbourhood. *Environment and Planning A, 41*, 2162–2180.
Phillips, D. (1998). Black minority ethnic concentration, segregation and dispersal in Britain. *Urban Studies, 35*(10), 1681–1702.
Popkin, S. J., Levy, D. K., Harris, L. E., Comey, J., & Cunningham, M. K. (2004). The HOPE VI program: What about the residents? *Housing Policy Debate, 15*(2), 385–413.
Putnam, R. D. (2007). E pluribus unum: Diversity and community in the twenty-first century. The 2006 Johan Skytte prize lecture. *Scandinavian Political Studies, 30*(2), 137–174.
Rubenstein, J. M. (1988). Relocation of families for public improvement projects: Lessons from Baltimore. *Journal of the American Planning Association, 54*(2), 185–196.
Sampson, J. (2009). Disparity and diversity in the contemporary city: Social (dis)order revisited. *The British Journal of Sociology, 60*(1), 1–38.

Sampson, R. J., & Groves, W. B. (1989). Community structure and crime: Testing social-disorganization theory. *The American Journal of Sociology, 94*(4), 774–802.

Sampson, J., Raudenbush, S. W., & Earls, F. (1997). Neighbourhoods and violent crime: A multilevel study of collective efficacy. *Science, 277*(5328), 918–924.

Scarborough, B. K., Like-Haislip, T. Z., Novak, K. J., Lucas, W. L., & Alarid, L. F. (2010). Assessing the relationship between individual characteristics, neighbourhood context, and fear of crime. *Journal of Criminal Justice, 38*(4), 819–826.

Sirgy, M. J., & Cornwell, T. (2002). How neighborhood features affect quality of life. *Social Indicators Research, 59*(1), 79–114.

Slob, A., Bolt, G., & Van Kempen, R. (2008). *Na de sloop. Waterbedeffecten van gebiedsgericht stedelijk beleid.* Den Haag: NICIS Institute.

Swaroop, S., & Morenoff, J. D. (2006). Building community: The neighborhood context of social organization. *Social Forces, 84*(3), 1665–1695.

Trudeau, D. (2006). The persistence of segregation in Buffalo, New York: Comer vs. Cisneros and geographies of relocation decisions among low-income black households. *Urban Geography, 27*(1), 20–44.

Uitermark, J. (2003). 'Social mixing' and the management of disadvantaged neighbourhoods: The Dutch policy of urban restructuring revisited. *Urban Studies, 40*(3), 531–549.

Van Beckhoven, E., & Van Kempen, R. (2003). Social effects of urban restructuring: A case study in Amsterdam and Utrecht, the Netherlands. *Housing Studies, 18*(6), 853–875.

Van der Laan Bouma-Doff, W. (2007). Confined contact: Residential segregation and ethnic bridges in the Netherlands. *Urban Studies, 44*(5/6), 997–1017.

Van Ham, M., & Clark, W. A. V. (2009). Neighbourhood mobility in context: Household moves and changing neighbourhoods in the Netherlands. *Environment and Planning A, 41*(6), 1442–1459.

Van Ham, M., & Manley, D. (2010). The effect of neighbourhood housing tenure mix on labour market outcomes: A longitudinal investigation of neighbourhood effects. *Journal of Economic Geography, 10*(2), 257–282.

Van Kempen, R., & Bolt, G. (2009). Social cohesion, social mix, and urban policy in the Netherlands. *Journal of Housing and the Built Environment, 24*(4), 457–475.

Van Kempen, R., & Bolt, G. (2012). Social consequences of residential segregation and mixed neighborhoods. In D. Clapham, W.A.V. Clark, & K. Gibb (Eds.), The *SAGE Handbook of housing studies* pp. 439–460. Chapter 23.

Varady, D. P., & Walker, C. C. (2000). Vouchering out distressed subsidized developments: Does moving lead to improvements in housing and neighbourhood conditions? *Housing Policy Debate, 11*(1), 115–162.

Varady, D. P., Walker, C. C., & Wang, X. (2001). Voucher recipient achievement of improved housing conditions in the US: Do moving distance and relocation services matter? *Urban Studies, 38*(8), 1273–1304.

Vervoort, M., Flap, H., & Dagevos, J. (2010). The ethnic composition of the neighbourhood and ethnic minorities' social contacts: Three unresolved issues. *European Sociological Review, 27*(5), 586–605.

Wassenberg, F. (2004). Large social housing estates: From stigma to demolition? *Journal of Housing and the Built Environment, 19*(3), 223–232.

Webster, C., MacDonald, R., & Simpson, M. (2006). Predicting criminality? Risk factors, neighbourhood influence and distance. *Youth Justice, 6*(1), 7–22.

Wilson, W. J. (1987). *The truly disadvantaged: The inner city, the underclass, and public policy.* Chicago: Chicago University Press.

Wilson, W. J. (1996). *When work disappears: The world of the new urban poor.* New York: Knopf.

Wilson, J. Q., & Kelling, G. (1982). The police and neighborhood safety: Broken windows. *Atlantic, 127*, 29–38.

Wyant, B. R. (2008). Multilevel impacts of perceptions of crime risk on fear of crime: Isolating endogenous impacts. *Journal of Research in Crime and Delinquency, 45*(1), 39–64.

Chapter 6
The Effects of Neighbourhood Regeneration on the Neighbourhood Hierarchy of the City: A Case Study in Sweden

Åsa Bråmå

Introduction

Problems of residential segregation are often tackled by area-based policies aiming to solve the problems by interventions in those neighbourhoods that suffer from the negative effects of segregation. These so called 'deprived' neighbourhoods, characterised by a concentration of socioeconomically weak households, often suffer from problems related to high unemployment rates, high benefit dependency rates, social problems and poor health among residents. The geographical context is often large housing estates built in the Post-war era, located in the periphery of the cities, and dominated by public rented housing.

The rationale for area-based interventions is usually that the spatial concentration of marginalised households in these neighbourhoods has negative effects on the life chances of the residents. Several studies have found support for such 'neighbourhood effects' (for a review, see for example Galster 2007), and a number of different mechanisms seems to be involved, such as lack of positive role models for young people, lack of social capital (social network connections to people with resources) and stigmatisation effects, i.e. a spill over of the bad reputation of the neighbourhoods on their residents (Andersson and Musterd 2005; Musterd and Andersson 2005).

The interventions usually involve either social or physical measures, or a combination of these approaches. In the former case, the aim of the intervention is primarily to 'lift' the neighbourhood by 'lifting' existing residents, i.e. reducing poverty and benefit dependency rates, raising employment rates, improving health etc. The interventions usually also have a strong focus on community involvement (Wallace 2001; Blackman 2006; Andersson 2006; Andersson et al. 2010). The aim of interventions focused on physical measures is typically to achieve a more socially mixed population

Å. Bråmå (✉)
Centrum för kommunstrategiska studier, Linköpings universitet, 601 74 Norrköping, Sweden
e-mail: asa.brama@liu.se

M. van Ham et al. (eds.), *Understanding Neighbourhood Dynamics: New Insights for Neighbourhood Effects Research*, DOI 10.1007/978-94-007-4854-5_6,

by changing the housing stock of the neighbourhood. The underlying principle is that the introduction of a greater mix of housing types and tenure types, through selective demolition, construction of new housing, tenure conversion or sale of public housing to private landlords, will bring new groups of residents to the neighbourhood and/or prevent existing residents from moving out when their economic circumstances improve (van Kempen and Priemus 1999; Musterd and Andersson 2005; Kearns and Mason 2007).

Area-based policies have been criticised, on (at least) two grounds. Firstly, and this critique concerns mainly social mix policies, it has been argued that the interventions will not benefit existing residents, as they will be displaced to other neighbourhoods, as a result of demolition, conversion or rent increases (Musterd and Ostendorf 2005; Lees 2008; Davidson and Lees 2010; Walks and Maaranen 2008). The other line of critique focuses on the potential – or lack of potential – of area-based policies in actually reducing residential segregation. It is argued that if the intervention succeeds in 'lifting' the targeted neighbourhood, there is an evident risk that this will only result in a relocation of the problems of spatially concentrated deprivation to another neighbourhood (Andersson and Bråmå 2004; Andersson 2006; Andersson et al. 2010).

This chapter investigates the population dynamics in a city when one of its most deprived neighbourhoods is subject to a very extensive regeneration. It describes the effects of the regeneration on the population the neighbourhood itself, and the effects on other neighbourhoods. And more importantly, it describes the population dynamics behind these effects.

In Sweden, neighbourhoods that can be regarded as deprived or distressed generally also have high concentrations of ethnic minorities. Earlier research has shown that the deprived, immigrant-dense neighbourhoods of Swedish cities act as ports of entry to the local housing market for newly arrived immigrants and other groups with limited economic and social resources (Bråmå 2006). An important question is therefore what happens to this port-of-entry function after neighbourhood regeneration. Is the role of "port of entry" simply shifted to another neighbourhood or distributed over a larger number of neighbourhoods? Gaining a better understanding of these changes is crucial for understanding processes of segregation.

The case study neighbourhood, Navestad/Ringdansen, is a large housing estate in Norrköping, a city with about 130,000 inhabitants located 170 km southwest of Stockholm. Around the year 2000, the estate was subject to a very extensive physical renovation, including an 'ecological conversion' of the housing stock (described below). Before the regeneration, Navestad/Ringdansen was in many ways a typical example of a deprived neighbourhood, in the Swedish context, with a combination of ethnic minority concentration and social deprivation. Built during the first half of the 1970s, it had problems early on with low attractiveness, and the subsequent in-migration of groups with limited social and economic resources, such as newly arrived immigrants and Swedish households with social problems. The reputation as 'Norrköping's worst neighbourhood' persisted through the years despite frequent efforts to change the situation through (smaller-scale) physical renovations and various social projects involving the residents. So the question is, has this large-scale regeneration of the estate finally managed to lift the neighbourhood from its position at the bottom of the local neighbourhood hierarchy? And if so, has this been achieved at the expense of other neighbourhoods in the city?

The availability of longitudinal, individual-level, geocoded data (the GeoSweden database, described below) makes this one of few studies that can actually study the population dynamics before, during and after the regeneration, in terms of mobility and in situ change. I will, firstly, describe the effects of the regeneration on the population composition of the estate itself – whether the regeneration has managed to change the character of social deprivation and immigrant concentration of the neighbourhood, and if so, how this change has come about. This involves investigations both of changes in the population characteristics of the neighbourhood that have been the result of migration to and from the estate and of changes among residents who have stayed put on the estate. Secondly, and more importantly, I will describe how the regeneration has affected other neighbourhoods in the city. This is done mainly by comparing Navestad/Ringdansen's position in the neighbourhood hierarchy, in different respects, with that of other neighbourhoods in the city, before and after the regeneration. As will become apparent, the regeneration has affected the neighbouring district, Hageby, negatively. Thus, thirdly, I will describe the population dynamics that have resulted in this reordering of the neighbourhood hierarchy.

Earlier Research on Displacement Effects of Neighbourhood Regeneration

The frequent use of area-based interventions has attracted a lot of attention from researchers and city officials interested in evaluating the effects of the policies. The evaluations are often concentrated on the direct effects of the regeneration policy on the areas themselves, often showing positive effects soon after the regeneration but a more negative picture when some years have passed, and new decay and new social downgrading have again become manifest (Musterd and Ostendorf 2005). However, the impacts of neighbourhood regeneration on other parts of the city has not gained as much attention. There is of course an awareness of the fact that the regeneration of one neighbourhood can have negative effects on other neighbourhoods, but there is still a lack of knowledge as to what other neighbourhoods are affected and what the underlying mechanisms are.

In the discussion on side effects of neighbourhood regeneration, though, two interrelated problems are regularly mentioned. One is the spill over (or replacement) effect, i.e. the emergence of new deprived neighbourhoods as deprivation is removed or alleviated in the targeted neighbourhood (McGregor and McConnachie 1995; Hall 1997). The other is displacement, which generally refers to the (involuntary) movement of residents of the targeted neighbourhood to other parts of the city, as a result of demolitions or rent increases (see for example Andersson and Musterd 2005). These problems are generally believed to be related; displacement often affects the most vulnerable and deprived households, and the general belief seems to be that they 'bring their problems with them' when they move to another neighbourhood, so that their destination then becomes the new neighbourhood of deprivation (Andersson and Musterd 2005).

Musterd and Ostendorf (2005) present a more thorough investigation of displacement effects following neighbourhood restructuring, in their study of the restructuring of Bijlmermeer in Amsterdam. They found that although displacement was not very extensive, it affected those in a weak position in the labour and housing markets. The displaced found accommodation in other parts of Amsterdam, often with a high proportion of rented housing and frequently near the areas of restructuring. The result was, for the city, a 'zero sum game', where the social upgrading of the restructured area was counterbalanced by a social downgrading of the areas where the movers had settled.

Problems of displacement have otherwise mostly been the concern of researchers studying processes of gentrification. Here, a more developed understanding of different forms of displacement exists, and several studies have also been presented that endeavour to measure the extent of displacement (see for example Atkinson 2002). Following Marcuse's influential classification (Marcuse 2010; see also Slater 2009), there are four major forms of displacement, here translated to the context of neighbourhood regeneration:

1. Direct last-resident displacement: Only the last resident living in a dwelling prior to the regeneration is counted as replaced. The reasons behind the displacement might be physical (e.g. demolition and/or a reduction in the number of dwellings) or economic (e.g. rent increase or tenure conversion).
2. Chain displacement: Includes previous occupants of a dwelling who have moved at an earlier stage in the regeneration process, e.g. when plans about the regeneration became known.
3. Exclusionary displacement: Affects residents who would otherwise have moved in to the neighbourhood but who can no longer access housing there, for physical or economic reasons.
4. Displacement pressure: When the transformation of the neighbourhood makes residents no longer 'feel at home', making their leaving the neighbourhood only a matter of time.

Though the focus in the classification and gentrification research in general, is mainly concentrated on the displaced residents and their situation, the typology is highly relevant for issues related to macro-level effects of neighbourhood change in general. The notion of exclusionary displacement is particularly interesting, as it relates to effects that have to do with the spatial relocation of the systemic properties inherent in the position at the bottom of the neighbourhood hierarchy.

The population dynamics of a city can be viewed as a complex system – a system of neighbourhoods interconnected by flows of people (migration) and of information (see for example Byrne 1998; also Blackman 2006). One important distinguishing feature of such a system is that the elements of the system are interconnected so that changes in one part of the system will often have unintended effects in other parts of the system, and the chain of effects will often be far-reaching, in time and space. Neighbourhoods at the bottom of the neighbourhood hierarchy have certain characteristics that distinguish them from other, more attractive neighbourhoods – characteristics that have to do with their role in the city system (for a similar approach, see Robson et al. 2008). Perhaps the most distinguishing characteristic is the fact that they tend to function as 'regulators' in the housing market. These neighbourhoods are the last to be filled when housing demand increases in the city, and the first to have vacancies when housing demand falls. As such, they tend to be the ones that provide housing to households with limited choice, such as poor and otherwise marginalised groups. If an intervention in a neighbourhood at the bottom of the neighbourhood hierarchy succeeds in 'lifting' the neighbourhood, this will mean that the role as regulator and 'last resort' will be transferred somewhere else, and this can either be to *one* other neighbourhood, that will then replace the regenerated neighbourhood at the bottom, or to a group of neighbourhoods, each taking on a smaller part of that role.[1] Insofar as neighbourhood regeneration only results in the upgrading of one neighbourhood at the expense of another, direct displacement of the most marginalised households might not be the most influential factor. Instead, it might be the exclusionary displacement of those who would otherwise have taken up residence there but are redirected to other neighbourhoods.

Findings from gentrification research are probably less useful when it comes to the question of the effects on the population composition of neighbourhood regeneration in the targeted neighbourhoods. Although the boundaries between gentrification research and anti-segregation research are beginning to blur, especially concerning the interest in social mix strategies (see for instance Walks and Maaranen 2008), gentrification processes generally affect older, more established neighbourhoods in attractive inner city locations, i.e. neighbourhoods that prior to gentrification have a rather stable, although low income character. And more importantly, the gentrification process typically involves a rapid change in the population composition of the neighbourhood, as high-income households move in and force the original working class, low income population to leave. The main problem seems to be the inevitability of the process; once started there seems to be no 'half-way stops' in the process that enable the neighbourhood to maintain a mix of original and new residents (Lees et al. 2008).

Deprived neighbourhoods, on the other hand, very often have problems of instability, high turnover, and are involved in negative processes causing steadily worsening conditions ('spirals of decline'). In the Swedish context, the neighbourhoods affected are usually large housing estates situated in less favourable locations, usually on the outskirts of the city (Andersson and Bråmå 2004; Bråmå and Andersson 2005). The challenge here, i.e. what the policies aim to do, is primarily to bring about a halt to the negative development, and perhaps, in the best of circumstances, also to initiate positive spirals that might lift the neighbourhood from the absolute bottom of the neighbourhood hierarchy.

[1] This is a very simplified case. In reality, the city will probably consist of several geographical and/or sectorial sub-systems, all with its own neighbourhood hierarchy.

The Case Study Neighbourhood: Navestad/Ringdansen in Norrköping

The case study area of this study is a large housing estate situated in Norrköping, Sweden. Norrköping is, by Swedish measures, a medium-sized city with about 130,000 inhabitants, situated 170 km southwest of Stockholm. Historically of the major industrial cities in the country, it was hit hard by the crisis in the manufacturing industries during the 1960s and 1970s, and is now slowly recovering and adapting to the new conditions of the post-industrial society.

The estate in question, Navestad/Ringdansen, is situated about 4.5 km south of the city centre (see Fig. 6.1). It is owned and maintained by the municipal housing company, Hyresbostäder. Navestad, as it was called before the regeneration, was built 1969–73, as part of the national 'Million Homes Programme', when one million dwellings were constructed in Sweden during a 10-year period (1965–74) in order to deal with an out dated housing stock and a severe housing shortage in the larger cities in the wake of extensive urbanisation. By the time the construction of Navestad was finished, however, the housing shortage in Norrköping had already been transformed into a housing surplus (Hyresbostäder, *Ringdansen ger dig möjligheter*, *Projektbeskrivning för kv Ringdansen i Norrköping*, both documents can be found at http://www.ringdansen.se).

As with many large housing estates built during the Million Programme, problems of low attractiveness and a bad reputation have followed the estate from the very beginning. For Navestad, the low attractiveness was mainly due to the unconventional architecture of the estate, in combination with the peripheral location. In its original form, the estate consisted of two massive housing blocks built from prefabricated concrete elements, each consisting of two circular houses of varying height, one placed inside the other, with an inner passage between them, a park at the centre, and a street running outside each ring (see Fig. 6.2).

Low attractiveness and a housing surplus meant that most households with the means to choose avoided Navestad, and the estate became the home of groups with limited resources, such as immigrants and families with social problems. Ever since – or until the regeneration of the estate at least – Navestad has been 'the last resort' in the Norrköping housing market for households who cannot find housing elsewhere. Its role as 'regulator' in the housing market is illustrated by the fact that vacancies have been a constant problem. According to the municipal housing company, the estate was only fully occupied once during the 1974–2000 period, and that happened during the economic boom at the end of the 1980s (Hyresbostäder, *Ringdansen ger dig möjligheter*, http://www.ringdansen.se).

As is often the case in 'problematic' neighbourhoods, different efforts to improve the situation on the estate have succeeded each other through the years. These projects have involved improvements of the outdoor environment, conversions of individual flats from the standard three rooms and kitchen to larger and smaller dwellings, renovation of public and private service facilities, and various social and economic projects involving the residents. In the early 1990s, immediately before the physical restructuring of the estate, several projects were running in parallel, mainly aiming

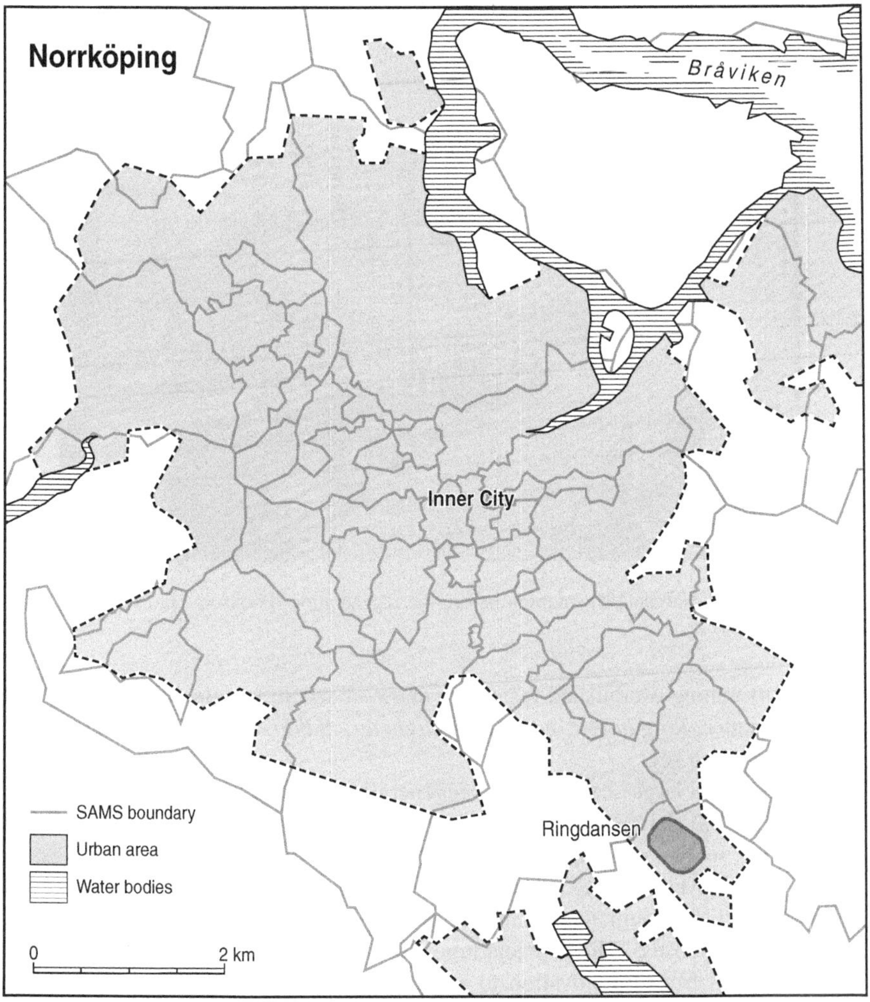

Fig. 6.1 The location of Ringdansen in Norrköping (Source: Map by author. Map objects from Statistics Sweden 2003 (SAMS areas) and GSD-Röda kartan, Lantmäteriverket 1997 (other map objects). Used with permission)

to combat the worsening social situation on the estate. The reasons for the acute crisis were many, but the severe economic recession that had hit Sweden was part of the picture, as was a large in-migration of refugees to Norrköping, mainly from former Yugoslavia. Because of the large number of empty flats in Navestad, parts of the estate were then used as a refugee reception unit,[2] and that had created

[2] The use of part of the estate as refugee reception unit began in 1992 and was ended in mid 1995. At most, the reception unit occupied 71 flats on the estate (in 1993).

Fig. 6.2 Parts of Navestad/Ringdansen before the regeneration (Photo: © Hyresbostäder. Used with permission)

discomfort among established residents, many of whom had decided to move out (Hyresbostäder, *Ringdansen ger dig möjligheter*; *Bakgrund,* both found at http://www.ringdansen.se).

The idea of a large-scale physical regeneration of the estate was born in 1996, when the social democratic government decided to issue grants for ecological conversions in the existing housing stock. The following year, the Navestad/Ringdansen conversion project was granted a substantial sum from the government grants (though the municipality and the housing company took on an even larger share of the expenses). The physical regeneration began early in 2000 and finished in 2003. Apart from a renovation to an ecologically sustainable estate, including conversions of energy systems and water and waste management, the regeneration also involved the demolition of substantial parts of the large circular houses, lowering parts of the buildings and opening up the massive circles, as well as refurbishments of the outside of the buildings with plaster and new colouring (see Fig. 6.3). The regeneration resulted in a decrease in the number of dwellings from about 1,600 in 1998 to just over 900 in 2003 (*Fakta*, http://www.ringdansen.se). The regeneration did not involve any changes in the tenure structure of the estate, although there had been plans early on in the project of converting part of the housing stock to tenant-owner cooperatives. These plans were abandoned when the project received lower governmental grants than expected (or hoped for; Lövgren 2002).[3] As part of the

[3] One of the houses on the estate is now (2011) being converted into owner-occupied terraced housing (a total of eight dwellings).

Fig. 6.3 Parts of Navestad/Ringdansen after the regeneration (Photo: Åsa Bråmå)

sustainability scheme, electricity, water and heating are now paid for separately by each tenant based on actual consumption. Thus, although the regeneration has meant a general increase of rents, the tenants have better opportunities to influence their housing expenditures.

The aim of the regeneration project was stated in rather ambitious terms: "…to bring about an overall renewal of the estate, involving the residents in a process of change aiming to create an architecturally attractive residential area that is socially, culturally, economically and ecologically sustainable." (*Bakgrund*, http://www.ringdansen.se). Early on, the residents were involved in the planning of the regeneration. Working-groups were formed with the tenants, in order to get their opinions on inward and outward architecture, and other issues related to the future design of the estate. Apart from this more practical purpose, tenant involvement was also seen as a means to strengthen the engagement for the estate among residents and to strengthen the sense of community in the neighbourhood (*Bakgrund*, http://www.ringdansen.se).

Apart from that, the social aims of the project were not directly linked to the physical renovation of the estate, but were to be achieved through the social projects that had been initiated before the physical regeneration and were still running – projects such as adult education and resident involvement in various cooperatives. The overall impression created by the social strategy of the regeneration is that a social change was to be achieved mainly by improving the socioeconomic situation of existing tenants and strengthening their engagement with the neighbourhood, so that they would not move out even though their improved situation might enable them to do so. However, there is an inherent conflict between the focus on tenant involvement and the rather extensive reduction in the number of dwellings that was also part of the regeneration plan already from the beginning. Even given the large number of vacancies on the estate, a reduction of the number of dwellings by more than 40% would inevitably lead to displacement of old residents. One tenant is reported to have been rather shocked when the first regeneration plans were made public, and she saw that "My house is gone!" (Lövgren 2002, p. 156). The ecological character of the physical renovation also suggests a wish to attract totally new groups of tenants to the estate.

Following the regeneration, the name of the estate (as used by the municipal housing company at least) was changed from Navestad to Ringdansen. Ringdansen is, and has always been, the name of the actual estate, though before the regeneration it was usually referred to by the name of the city district where it is situated, Navestad. Though I have not found any official documents confirming this, the adoption of a 'new' name was likely to be part of a deliberate strategy aiming to eliminate the last associations with the 'old' estate, and all the negative images linked to the name Navestad. In order to avoid further confusion, I will use the name Ringdansen refer to the estate in the following.

Data

The analysis of population dynamics generally requires the use of longitudinal data that makes it possible to keep track of individuals through time and space. The data used here is a subset of the GeoSweden database, which is a longitudinal dataset with annual demographic, socioeconomic and geographic information on all individuals who have resided in Sweden between 1990 and 2008. The subset used here includes individuals who were living in Norrköping sometime between 1994 and 2008. The analysis focuses mainly on four points in time, two reflecting the situation before the regeneration of Ringdansen, 1994 and 1998, and two that capture the situation after the regeneration, 2004 and 2008.

Data on the geographical location of the individuals each year is essential for analysis both of the macro-level development of spatial units such as neighbourhoods and cities and of migration flows between spatial units. In GeoSweden the geographical location of individuals is available both as 100×100 m grid coordinates and as a neighbourhood (SAMS) code.[4] Unfortunately, the neighbourhood code was not a very good means of distinguishing the Ringdansen estate, since the SAMS

[4] The neighbourhood codes in GeoSweden are based on the so called SAMS area division (Small Area Market Statistics), constructed and maintained by Statistics Sweden. The area division covers the whole country and divides it into discreet, non-overlapping geographical areas that are 'as homogeneous as possible' with respect to the character of the housing stock (type, construction period, tenure). Thus, the SAMS units capture the notion of neighbourhood rather well. The average number of residents per SAMS is just under 1,000, though for Norrköping it is a bit higher, around 1,500. For more information on the GeoSweden database, see Bråmå (2006).

area covers a much larger area (see Fig. 6.1) and additional, mostly owner-occupied, housing has been built in the area since the construction of SAMS area division. Therefore, coordinates were used to extract Ringdansen from the area and construct a neighbourhood comprising only the estate. All analyses were made using this modified neighbourhood division.

The Population of Ringdansen Before and After the Regeneration

I will start with a comparison of the population composition of Ringdansen before and after the regeneration. In order to, as far as possible, analyse the long-term effects of the regeneration I have chosen to compare the situation at two points in time not immediately before or after the regeneration. The most up-to-date data available in GeoSweden as of now (July 2011) is for 2008. At the end of 2008, approximately 4 years had passed since the regeneration was completed. 1994 is roughly 4 years before the restructuring project was initiated. The character of the population in 1994 and 2008 is described using a set of demographic and socioeconomic indicators in Table 6.1. For each year, the corresponding figures for the whole municipality of Norrköping is also shown.

A first thing to note is that the demolition of 691 dwellings in Ringdansen did result in a substantial reduction in the number of residents on the estate, as feared by some tenants (Lövgren 2002). In actual figures it meant a reduction of about 1,000, or approximately one-third of the population, from just under 2,800 in 1994 to about 1,800 in 2008. The demographic profile of the neighbourhood changed in several ways, all indicating a 'normalisation' of the population: While women were underrepresented in 1994, there is an overrepresentation of women in 2008. The population is slightly older, with a lower percentage of children and a higher percentage of old people, although Ringdansen still has a younger age profile than Norrköping municipality as a whole. The proportion of first and second generation immigrants is significantly lower in 2008, but Ringdansen is still to be considered an 'immigrant-dense' neighbourhood. And although the percentage of singles increased in Norrköping between 1994 and 2008, Ringdansen still has an overrepresentation of singles of about four percentage points above the municipality figure.

Figures describing the socioeconomic profile of the residents before and after the regeneration reveal a substantial improvement. The change in level of education of the Ringdansen population roughly mirrors that of the municipality as a whole, though there is still an overrepresentation of persons with low education and an underrepresentation of the highly educated in the Ringdansen population. Employment rates, welfare dependency rates and incomes all indicate considerable improvements in the socioeconomic situation of the population, although the situation in Ringdansen is still far below the level of Norrköping as a whole.

Table 6.1 Demographic and socioeconomic indicators for Ringdansen and Norrköping municipality in 1994 and 2008

	1994		2008	
	Ringdansen	Norrköping	Ringdansen	Norrköping
All residents				
Total number	2,782	123,231	1,743	127,670
% female	49	51	52	50.5
% aged 0–19	34.3	24.7	29	23.8
% aged 65+	9.2	17.8	15	17.4
% with foreign background	67.2	15.1	57.3	19.3
% born abroad	54.3	12	43.5	14.3
% new refugees[a]	18.6	1.8	6.1	1.1
Residents aged 20–64				
Total number	1,574	70,858	976	74,976
% singles	34.2	30.4	38.8	35.1
% single parents	7.7	6.6	10	7.3
% with low education	50.9	30	37.1	18.2
% with high education	7.5	20	16.1	31.2
% employed	28.7	69.7	44.6	73.8
% on social benefits	51.9	14	33.7	8.2
Wage income, median[b]	0	128,900	32,850	226,800
% in lowest quintile	61.4	20	47.1	20
% in highest quintile	3.2	20	4.7	20
Disposable income, median[b]	81,800	115,900	135,050	191,900
% in lowest quintile	49.4	20	35.3	20
% in highest quintile	5.3	20	4	20

Source: GeoSweden, Institute for Housing and Urban Research, Uppsala University
[a]Immigrants from major refugee-sending countries (Bosnia, Yugoslavia, Syria, Somalia and Iraq) with less than 4 years in Sweden
[b]Income in Swedish Krona

The relation between neighbourhood deprivation and instability is far from straightforward. High turnover rates is not a phenomenon found exclusively in deprived neighbourhoods, and far from all deprived neighbourhoods have high turnover rates. In Table 6.2, a comparison is made of turnover rates in Ringdansen and Norrköping before (1994–95) and after (2007–08) the regeneration.[5] Although a persistent problem in the past, high turnover rates were not a problem in Ringdansen in 1994–95. Somewhat surprisingly, the turnover rates are only slightly higher than the municipality average. Given the socioeconomic profile of the population in 2004, this is perhaps not to be interpreted as a positive sign. Instead, it suggests

[5] Stability is here defined as the percentage of the population of a neighbourhood (SAMS area) in time period 1 still living there in time period 2, out-migration rate is the percentage of the population in time 1 that has moved out, and in-migration rate is the percentage of the population in time period 2 that has living there already in time period 1.

Table 6.2 Population turnover in Ringdansen and Norrköping municipality 1994–1995 and 2007–2008

		Stability	Outmigration rate	Inmigration rate
1994/95	Ringdansen	85.7	13.6	13.2
	Norrköping	87.8	11.1	11.4
2007/08	Ringdansen	79.1	18.8	21.5
	Norrköping	86.3	12.6	13.4

Source: GeoSweden, Institute for Housing and Urban Research, Uppsala University

lock-in problems among residents, i.e. limited opportunities to 'escape' to 'better' neighbourhoods. The turnover rates are higher in 2007–08, though by no means high in comparison to what has been found in deprived neighbourhoods in other Swedish cities (see for instance Andersson and Bråmå 2004).

Through its history Ringdansen has been one of the most 'immigrant-dense' neighbourhoods in Norrköping, with large concentrations of labour immigrants during the 1970s and refugees during more recent years. Figure 6.4 shows the distribution over neighbourhoods in 1994 and 2008 of immigrants from five major refugee-sending countries who had lived less than 4 years in Sweden. In 1994, Ringdansen was *the* major reception area in Norrköping for new immigrants from these countries, with 517 persons living there, which is the same as 23% of this immigrant category, or 19% of the population of Ringdansen. One obvious explanation to this extreme situation is the fact that part of the estate was used as a refugee reception unit, although asylum seekers not granted visas are not included in the figures shown here. Evidently, many decided to stay on in Ringdansen when they had been granted permission to stay in Sweden.

In 2008, the function of port of entry for new refugees is shared much more evenly between neighbourhoods, and Ringdansen has only the fourth largest number of new refugees (108 persons). It is also obvious from Fig. 6.4 that the number of refugees arriving in Norrköping during this latter period was much lower, which naturally makes it much easier to accomplish a more even distribution. It should be noted, however, that three of the five neighbourhoods found at the top of the list in 2008 are situated in Hageby, the city district located immediately to the north of Ringdansen.

Ringdansen's Position in the Neighbourhood Hierarchy Before and After the Regeneration

In this section, I compare the position of Ringdansen in the neighbourhood hierarchy of Norrköping before and after the regeneration, using indicators that are commonly used to measure different aspects of socioeconomic deprivation. This illustrates not only the effects of the restructuring on the estate itself, but also the effects on other neighbourhoods in the city. In order to capture both relative and absolute changes,

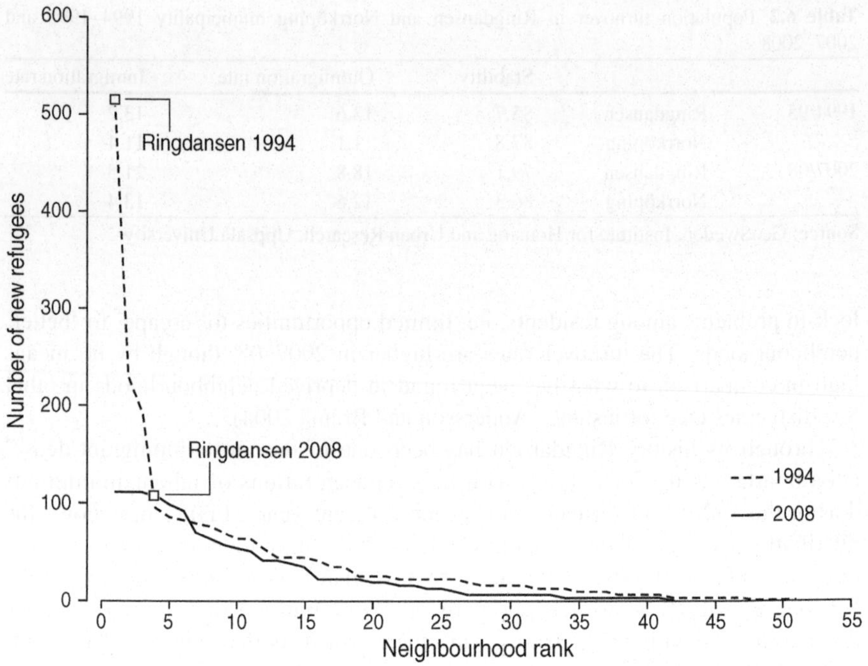

Fig. 6.4 Distribution of new refugees over neighbourhoods in 1994 and 2008. Immigrants from five major refugee-sending countries (Bosnia, Yugoslavia, Syria, Somalia and Iraq) with less than 4 years in Sweden (Source: GeoSweden, Institute for Housing and Urban Research, Uppsala University)

i.e. changes in ranking and changes in the underlying values, the neighbourhood hierarchy is illustrated using index values. The value for a specific neighbourhood is divided by the corresponding value for the whole municipality, thus giving a measure also of the distance of the value of a particular neighbourhood from the municipality average, which has index value 1.0. Finally, the situation at four points in time, 1994, 1998, 2004 and 2008 is compared.

First, changes in employment rates (Fig. 6.5). Note that only the 'worst' end of the hierarchy is shown, i.e. neighbourhoods with index values below 1.0 in this case. As is obvious from the diagram, employment rates in Ringdansen were exceptionally low in the years before the physical restructuring, with a large gap to the neighbourhood with the second worst situation, Marielund, another large housing estate located northwest of the city centre. After the regeneration, Ringdansen is only third from the bottom since two other neighbourhoods (both situated in the neighbouring Hageby district) have lower employment rates, though the distance from the bottom to the city average is smaller.

In terms of ranking, the development in benefit dependency rates has been similar (Fig. 6.6), with Ringdansen rising from the absolute bottom in 1994 and 1998 to

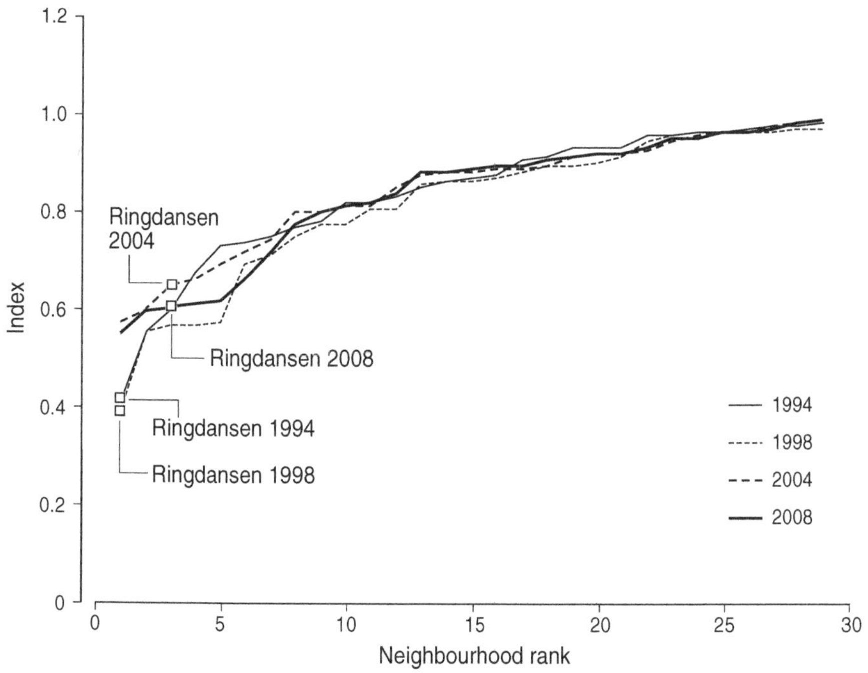

Fig. 6.5 Percentage employed. Distributions of neighbourhood index values relative to municipality average (Ringdansen marked with large symbols). Note: Only neighbourhoods with index values below the municipality average (1.0) are shown (Source: GeoSweden, Institute for Housing and Urban Research, Uppsala University)

third position in 2004 and fourth in 2008 (rising in this context of course means lower index values). Here, however, the index values reveal that when it comes to the distance from the city average the situation is actually worse in 2004 and 2008 than in 1998. The situation might have improved in Ringdansen, but so has the situation in Norrköping as a whole, and the gap is still substantial.

Index values for median disposable income (Fig. 6.7) are much more even among neighbourhoods, reflecting the distributing effects of the Swedish welfare state, but the difference between development in terms of ranking and development relative to the city average are apparent also here. Even though Ringdansen has managed to climb in the neighbourhood hierarchy after the regeneration, the distance to the city average is basically the same in 2008 as in 1994.

The development for the education measure, percentage with low education (less than 10 years), shows the same tendency (Fig. 6.8), but Ringdansen's rise in the hierarchy has happened a bit later, between 2004 and 2008, and is mainly due to the fact that the percentage with low education has increased in other neighbourhoods.

To conclude this section, then, the regeneration of Ringdansen has indeed managed to raise the neighbourhood from its 1994 and 1998 position as Norrköping's most deprived neighbourhood. In terms of ranking, the estate has managed to climb

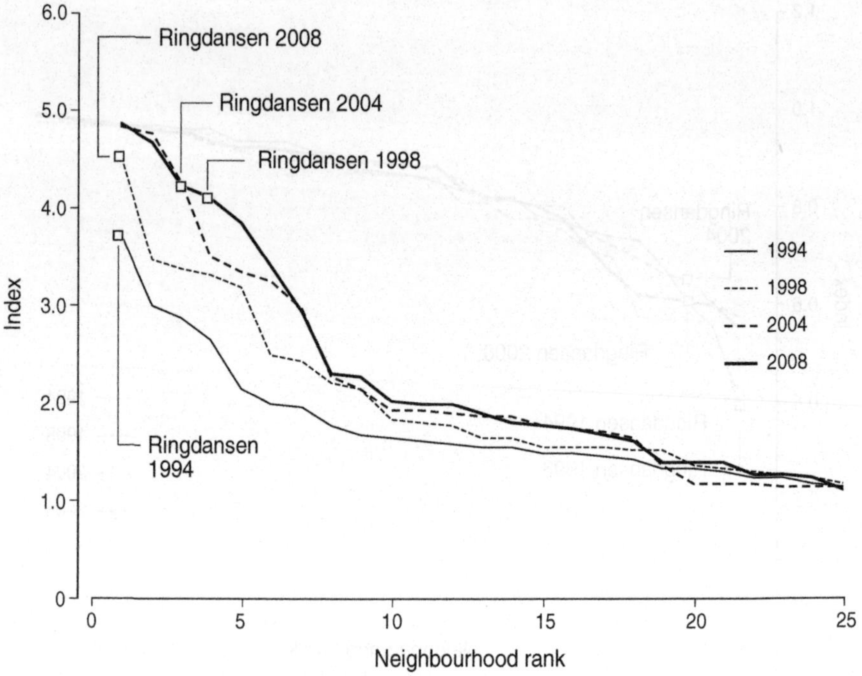

Fig. 6.6 Percentage on social benefits. Distributions of neighbourhood index values relative to municipality average (Ringdansen marked with large symbols). Note: Only neighbourhoods with index values above the municipality average (1.0) are shown (Source: GeoSweden, Institute for Housing and Urban Research, Uppsala University)

a couple of notches on the neighbourhood hierarchy ladder. In real terms, though, it is not so much that Ringdansen is in a much better position relative to the situation in Norrköping as a whole than it was before the regeneration, but rather that other neighbourhoods have joined Ringdansen at the bottom. In that respect, there has been a spread of the role as most deprived neighbourhood over more neighbourhoods. Although this was not shown in the diagrams, most of these neighbourhoods are located in the neighbouring district of Hageby. But it is not one and the same neighbourhood in Hageby that is found at the bottom for all measured variables. Instead, this varies somewhat between indicators. Hageby is also a larger district than Navestad, containing owner-occupied as well as rented housing,[6] and it is only the rental dominated parts that have been affected. In essence, this means that the regeneration of Ringdansen seems to have succeeded in 'spreading the burden' somewhat over more neighbourhoods, both spatially and in terms of dimension of deprivation. But even so, the distance from the neighbourhoods at bottom (including Ringdansen) to the city average is just as large as before, or in some cases larger.

[6] The most affected neighbourhoods in Hageby are the northern, western and central parts, all dominated by public or private rental housing.

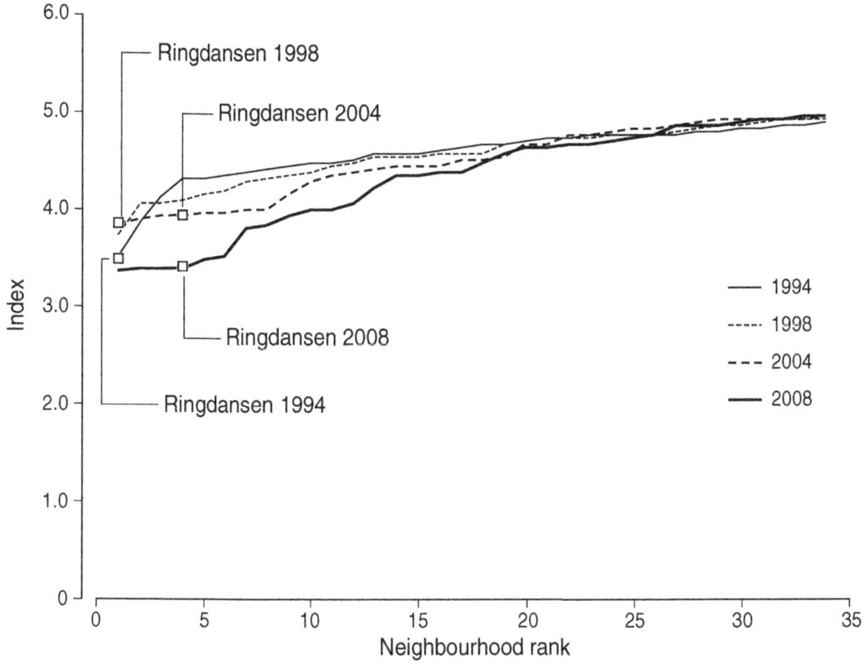

Fig. 6.7 Disposable income (median). Distributions of neighbourhood index values relative to municipality average (Ringdansen marked with large symbols). Note: Only neighbourhoods with index values below the municipality average (1.0) are shown (Source: GeoSweden, Institute for Housing and Urban Research, Uppsala University)

The Dynamics Behind the Change

So far, this account has focused mainly on comparisons of 'snapshots' of the population composition of Ringdansen and other neighbourhoods at different points in time. This section addresses the question of the dynamics behind the improved situation in Ringdansen and the worsening situation in parts of Hageby? If results from earlier studies of similar cases of neighbourhood regeneration are an indication, this might be explained by a process of out-migration of the most vulnerable segments of the Ringdansen population to Hageby. Has this really been the case? In order to investigate this I have analysed the selectivity and the directions of the migration flows to and from Ringdansen during three periods – the period covering the actual regeneration (1998–2004) but also the 4-year periods immediately before (1994–1998) and after (2004–2008) the intervention.

First, comparisons are made of the demographic and socioeconomic profiles of in-movers, out-movers and 'stayers' during each period.[7] In the case of the out-movers,

[7] Out-movers are those individuals who were living in Ringdansen at the end of the first year of the period but who had left the estate by the end of the last year of the period, and in-movers are those who have moved in between the same points in time. 'Stayers' are residents who were living on the estate at both points in time.

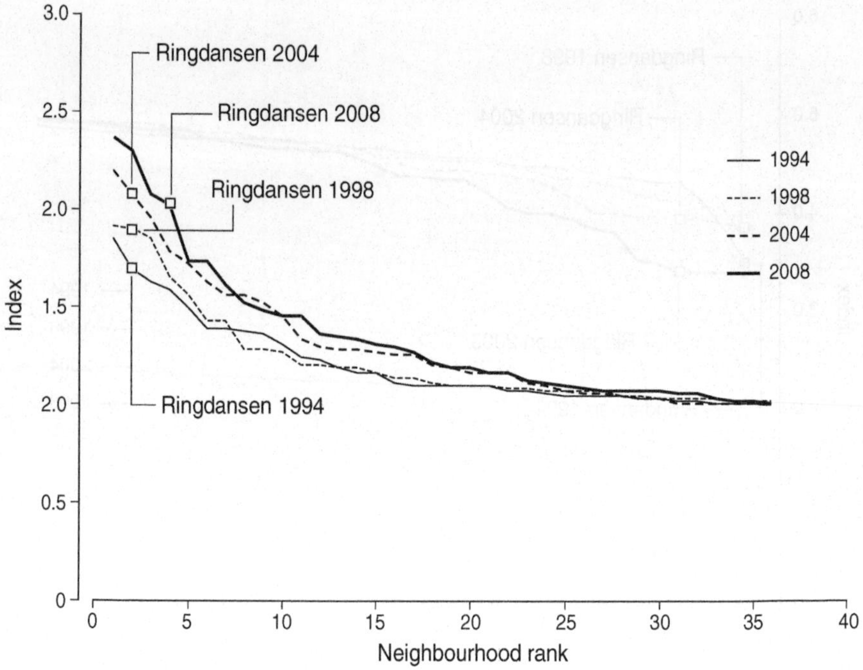

Fig. 6.8 Percentage with low education. Distributions of neighbourhood index values relative to municipality average (Ringdansen marked with large symbols). Note: Only neighbourhoods with index values above the municipality average (1.0) are shown (Source: GeoSweden, Institute for Housing and Urban Research, Uppsala University)

a comparison is made based on the situation before the move, while the comparison of in-movers and stayers refers to the situation after the move. This also makes it possible to track the changes that have occurred among the stayers between the beginning and end of each period.

The figures for the first period (see Table 6.3) reveal that the loss of population associated with the regeneration actually began already before 1998. Between 1994 and 1998 almost half of the population moved out (1,371 of 2,782), and the in-movers were much fewer, only 592. More detailed analyses of annual population figures (not shown here) reveal that the major loss of population occurred during the last 2 years of the period, i.e. after the plans of the regeneration had been revealed. Apparently, some residents decided to leave the estate already at this stage. In terms of demography, the out-movers are younger than the stayers and have an overrepresentation of men. The overall share of ethnic minorities is about the same as that among the stayers, but the percentage of newly arrived immigrants is substantially larger.

An earlier study on the dynamics of deprived neighbourhoods in Stockholm has shown that neighbourhoods at the bottom of the neighbourhood hierarchy tend to display a characteristic pattern of selective migration, where out-movers are more well-off than both in-movers and stayers, and the stayers, in turn, are more well-off than in-movers (Andersson and Bråmå 2004) Initially observed by Friedrichs (1991)

Table 6.3 Demographic and socioeconomic indicators for stayers, out-movers and in-movers to Ringdansen 1994–1998

	1994		1998	
	Stayers	Out-movers	Stayers	In-movers
All residents	1,321	1,371	1,321	592
% female	50.3	47.8	50.3	47.3
% aged 0–19	32.4	38.4	26.6	28.5
% aged 65+	11.1	3.4	15	8.1
% with foreign background	68.1	68.6	68.1	79.9
% born abroad	54.1	55.8	54.1	73.1
% new refugees[a]	14.8	23	0	24.7
Residents aged 20–64	747	797	772	375
% singles	30.8	36.5	29.5	39.7
% single parents	7.8	8.1	8.4	6.4
% with low education	56.2	45.3	51	52.8
% with high education	6.3	8.9	6.2	9.3
% employed	32.3	25.5	32.6	14.7
% on social benefits	48.2	54.5	52.7	78.9
Wage income, median[b]	0	0	0	0
% in lowest quintile	59.7	62.6	55.6	76.5
% in highest quintile	4.7	1.6	3.5	0.8
Disposable income, median[b]	88,000	72,200	95,600	82,900
% in lowest quintile	43.5	55.3	39.5	53.6
% in highest quintile	5.1	5.6	5.3	4.3

Source: GeoSweden, Institute for Housing and Urban Research, Uppsala University
[a]Immigrants from major refugee-sending countries (Bosnia, Yugoslavia, Syria, Somalia and Iraq) with less than 4 years in Sweden
[b]Income in Swedish Krona

in German cities, the phenomenon has been referred to as 'middle-class leakage' or 'those who get on get out' (Bailey and Livingston 2008). A comparison of the socio-economic status of out-movers and stayers during this first period shows that the out-movers cannot be described in these terms. Compared to the stayers, the out-movers had lower employment rate, higher benefit dependency rate and a slightly more pronounced low-income character. But the differences are not as large as to conclude that the out-movers constituted *the* weakest segment of the Ringdansen population.

It is also clear, however, that the in-movers who replaced them were not better off. On the contrary, most socioeconomic indicators show that the in-movers constituted an even weaker group, with a very low employment rate and a very high benefit dependency rate. The demographic profile of the in-movers is rather similar to that of the out-movers, with a large share of singles and an overrepresentation of men. About 80 % have foreign background, and one out of four is a new immigrant from one of the major refugee-sending countries.

There were some changes also among the stayers during the period. Apart from the fact that the stayer cohort obviously got older, and those who could be considered new refugees in 1994 had spent another 4 years in Sweden (and in Ringdansen), thus no longer qualifying for that label in 1998, the level of education improved slightly, as did incomes, especially in terms of the share belonging to the lowest quintile. At the same time, though, the benefit dependency rate increased slightly, but whether this is the result of a worsening situation among some individuals or a cohort effect is impossible to say from these results only.[8]

All in all, the figures for the 1994–1998 period strongly reflect Ringdansen's function as 'first stop in Sweden' for new immigrants; a large part of the dynamics seems to consist of the replacement of an older refugee cohort by a more recent one. The fact that part of the estate was used to host asylum seekers has of course a large role in this, but as the refugee reception unit was closed already in mid 1995, the second-order effects, in terms of the large number of vacancies that this resulted in, directly through the closing of the reception unit and indirectly through the negative reputation the reception unit had brought on the estate, were perhaps more important during this period than the settlement in Ringdansen of refugees from the reception unit who were subsequently granted residence permits.

The loss of population continued during the actual regeneration period, 1998–2004 (Table 6.4), mainly as a result of the reduction in the number of dwellings. The differences between the stayers and the out-movers at the beginning of the period were relatively small. The most significant differences are found in the age profiles, where the out-movers were younger, and the level of education, where out-movers on average were better educated, though this is probably related to the age composition, given that younger people generally have a higher education than older people. Furthermore, a larger share of the out-movers were born in Sweden, and benefit dependency rates were slightly higher among out-movers. But just as during the previous period, the differences are not so large as to suggest that the regeneration resulted in a displacement of particularly weak groups.

The regeneration of the estate seems to have managed to attract more well-off groups. The situation among in-movers between 1998 and 2004 were stronger than that of the stayers in terms of incomes, benefit dependency rates and education. There were also a lower share of first and second generation immigrants, of women and of persons aged 20–64 among in-movers. But the situation among stayers was also considerably improved during the period, resulting in a higher employment rate, higher incomes, a lower benefit dependency rate and on average higher education. Thus, the improvement in the socioeconomic profile of the Ringdansen population that happened during the regeneration seems not primarily to have been a result of displacement of the weakest residents, but rather the result of, on the one hand, in-migration of more well-off groups, and on the other, an improvement among sitting tenants. To discern which of these two effects that has been driving the change can

[8] While changes among the whole cohort of stayers are rather easy to track, changes among residents aged 20–64 can be due both to individual changes and to the transition that takes place in the age cohort, as older members are replaced by younger. More detailed analyses than the ones given here would be needed in order to distinguish between these effects.

Table 6.4 Demographic and socioeconomic indicators for stayers, out-movers and in-movers to Ringdansen 1998–2004

	1998		2004	
	Stayers	Out-movers	Stayers	In-movers
All residents	758	1,178	758	625
% female	50.5	48.1	50.5	53.6
% aged 0–19	28.9	37.9	22.2	20.2
% aged 65+	14.1	3.8	22	12.8
% with foreign background	74.9	74.1	74.9	31.4
% born abroad	60	54.8	60	26.2
% new refugees[a]	7.8	6.8	0	4
Residents aged 20–64	432	686	423	419
% singles	30.8	32.8	30.5	47.3
% single parents	8.4	7.7	8.1	12.4
% with low education	60.8	46	50.6	32.5
% with high education	4.4	9	5.9	18.1
% employed	28	25.5	47	46.1
% on social benefits	56.3	64.7	36.6	26.5
Wage income, median[b]	0	0	39,600	41,800
% in lowest quintile	64.4	61.2	45.6	40.8
% in highest quintile	2.8	2.5	3.3	7.4
Disposable income, median[b]	93,250	91,100	124,000	126,200
% in lowest quintile	43.1	45.2	35.9	31
% in highest quintile	6.5	4.2	4	7.4

Source: GeoSweden, Institute for Housing and Urban Research, Uppsala University
[a]Immigrants from major refugee-sending countries (Bosnia, Yugoslavia, Syria, Somalia and Iraq) with less than 4 years in Sweden
[b]Income in Swedish Krona

be rather difficult, as it has to do with the magnitude of the changes due to migration versus the changes among stayers and the size of the mover and stayer groups. In this case, though, the changes among stayers and the changes due to migration have tended to go in the same direction for most variables.

The 4 year period after the regeneration (2004–2008) saw an increase in the Ringdansen population again, from 1,503 to 1,743 residents, and this was mainly due to positive net migration of about 200 persons (see Table 6.5). It also saw a slight increase in the presence of ethnic minorities again, as the share of first and second generation immigrants, and the share of newly arrived refugees among in-movers was higher than among out-movers. But even so, the in-migration flow tended to have a larger share of native Swedes than the stayer cohort also in this period. In demographic terms, the mover groups continued to distinguish themselves from the stayers by being younger and more male and singles dominated.

As for the socioeconomic selectivity, the population dynamics during this period display a pattern more in line with the 'middle class leakage' model. The out-movers were better off than the stayers in terms of education, employment rate, benefit dependency rate and most income measures (the exception being a slightly higher share in the lowest disposable income quintile). Also, the stayers were more well-off than

Table 6.5 Demographic and socioeconomic indicators for stayers, out-movers and in-movers to Ringdansen 2004–2008

	2004		2008	
	Stayers	Out-movers	Stayers	In-movers
All residents	793	627	793	832
% female	53.1	50.7	53.1	50.5
% aged 0–19	25.1	34.3	20.7	26.9
% aged 65+	18.5	5.1	23.6	8.9
% with foreign background	63.1	48.2	63.1	52.3
% born abroad	47.5	34.8	47.5	44.5
% new refugees[a]	1.3	2.6	0	13
Residents aged 20–64	447	380	442	534
% singles	35.6	42.1	33.7	43.1
% single parents	10.7	10.1	10	10.1
% with low education	48.3	33.4	42.1	33
% with high education	8.7	15.8	10.2	21
% employed	44.7	48.9	52	38.4
% on social benefits	34.7	28.2	27.1	39.1
Wage income, median[b]	21,200	54,300	85,600	1,200
% in lowest quintile	47	38.4	41.4	51.9
% in highest quintile	3.4	7.6	4.1	5.2
Disposable income, median[b]	123,200	128,450	144,850	127,200
% in lowest quintile	33.3	33.9	28.3	41.2
% in highest quintile	3.8	8.2	2	5.6

Source: GeoSweden, Institute for Housing and Urban Research, Uppsala University
[a]Immigrants from major refugee-sending countries (Bosnia, Yugoslavia, Syria, Somalia and Iraq) with less than 4 years in Sweden
[b]Income in Swedish Krona

the in-movers in terms of employment rate, benefit dependency rate and median incomes. In terms of incomes, though, the in-movers were a more varied group, with higher shares both in the lowest and the highest income quintiles than the stayers.

Thus, trend brought about by the regeneration of attracting more well-off groups to Ringdansen seems not to have lasted very long. Though the situation is much better now than before the regeneration, the estate still seems vulnerable to external 'disturbances', such as fluctuations in the number of refugees arriving in Norrköping.[9] At the end of the period (in 2008), Ringdansen seems to be balancing between following the path of improvement set out by the regeneration, or falling back to something similar to the old position at the bottom of the neighbourhood hierarchy – but with one crucial difference: Ringdansen is no longer *the* 'sink estate' of Norrköping. It has been joined at the bottom by other neighbourhoods, mainly neighbourhoods in the adjacent district, Hageby.

[9] The number of refugees arriving in Norrköping, and in Sweden at large, increased again in the mid 00s, after a period of about 10 years of much lower numbers.

The analysis of selective migration to and from Ringdansen has already indicated that the worsening situation in other neighbourhoods, mainly parts of Hageby, has not been the result of displacement from Ringdansen to these neighbourhoods. During the last investigated period, the out-movers were actually socioeconomically stronger than the stayers, and during the two preceding periods, the socioeconomic situation among out-movers was not that much worse than that among stayers as to indicate that there had been a displacement of the most vulnerable segment of the Ringdansen population to other neighbourhoods. But an investigation of the destinations of the out-movers can reveal more.

Figure 6.9 shows a map of the destinations of out-movers from Ringdansen who moved to other neighbourhoods within Norrköping. The size of the 'pies' illustrate the total number of out-movers to each neighbourhood during the three periods while the 'slices' shows the period of the moves. The map reveals that the largest out-flows have indeed been directed towards Hageby. But the flows to the neighbourhoods that have taken Ringdansen's place at the bottom of the neighbourhood hierarchy (the northern, western and central parts of Hageby) were actually much smaller than the flow to southern Hageby, which has not been hit as hard.[10] Another reason for the worsening situation in parts of Hageby might be a drain of more well-off residents from these neighbourhoods to Ringdansen. Figure 6.10 shows prior residence of in-movers to Ringdansen during the three periods. But the map reveals that this explanation seems even more unlikely. The in-movers to Ringdansen came from all parts of Norrköping, with the largest flow also in this case from the southern part of Hageby.

So, what has caused the worsening situation in parts of Hageby? In order to shed some light on this, I have analysed the effects of in-migration from Ringdansen to Hageby and the effects from in-migration from other sources. Table 6.6 shows the socioeconomic profile of the Hageby district population in 2008 (first column) compared with that of the Hageby population when in-movers from Ringdansen are excluded (second column) and when other in-movers are excluded (third column). As expected, the figures reveal only a minor direct influence from in-migration from Ringdansen. Instead, the large effects come from in-migration of socioeconomically weak groups from other prior addresses, including other parts of Sweden and other countries. Had it not been for this in-migration, the situation in Hageby would have been considerably better, at least in terms of employment rate, benefit dependency rate and income levels.

Thus, the deteriorating situation in Hageby seems primarily to be the result not of direct displacement of socioeconomically weak residents from Ringdansen, but of exclusionary displacement of vulnerable households that would probably have ended up in Ringdansen, had it not been for the regeneration of the estate and the subsequent rent increases there.

[10] The SAMS areas do not reflect the city districts very well here. The southernmost part of the SAMS area immediately north of Ringdansen is actually part of the Navestad district. Though I have not investigated this in details, it is likely that a large part of the out-migration from Ringdansen had this neighbourhood (called Atrium) as destination.

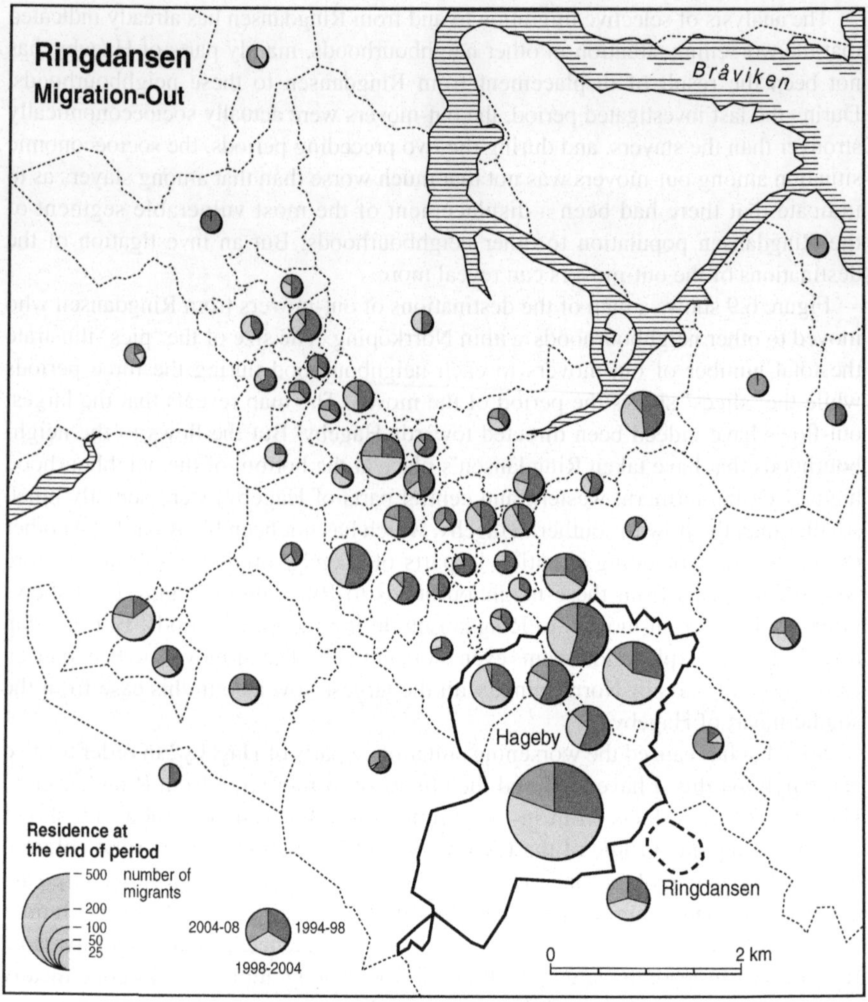

Fig. 6.9 Destinations of out-movers from Ringdansen during the three periods (Source: Map by author. Map objects from Statistics Sweden 2003 (SAMS areas) and GSD-Röda kartan, Lantmäteriverket 1997 (other map objects). Used with permission)

Conclusions

Insofar as the situation about 4 years after the conclusion of the regeneration can reveal the long-term effects, the regeneration seems to have resulted in a substantial improvement, in absolute terms, of the socioeconomic profile of the Ringdansen population. This has been achieved partly by in-migration of more well-off residents and partly by an improvement among stayers on the estate, though, contrary to results of earlier research, not by out-migration of the most vulnerable segments of the Ringdansen population.

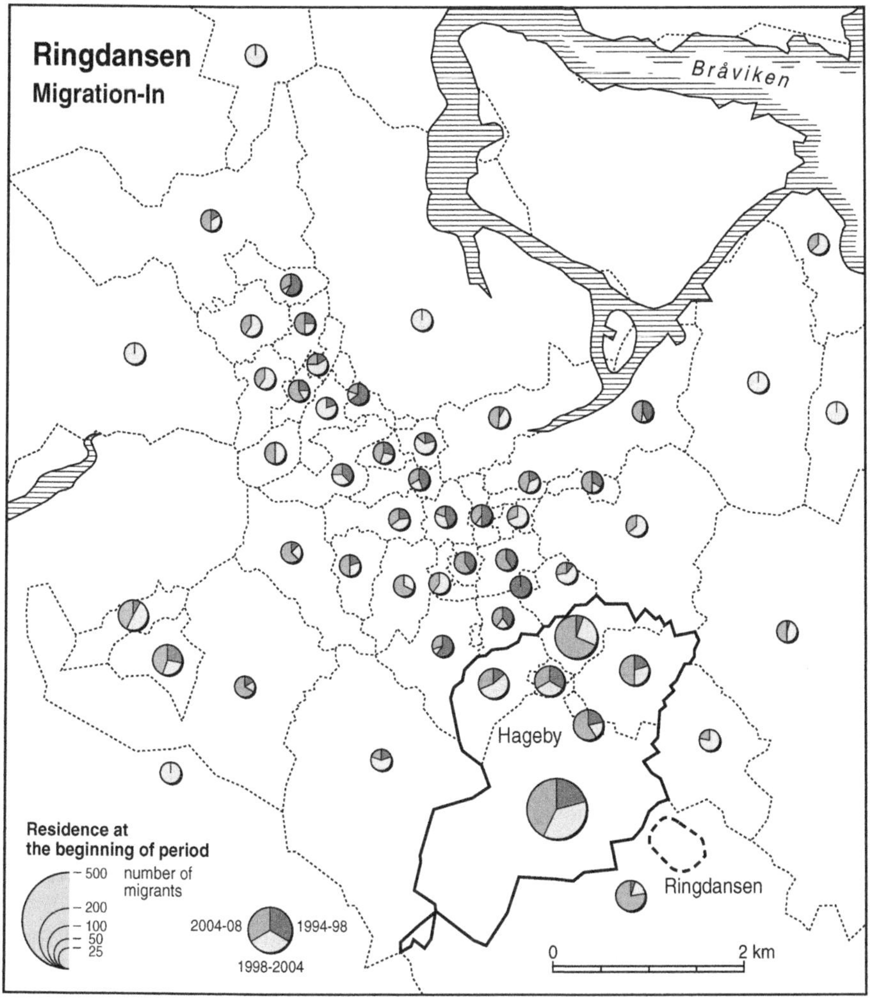

Fig. 6.10 Prior residence of in-movers to Ringdansen during the three periods (Source: Map by author. Map objects from Statistics Sweden 2003 (SAMS areas) and GSD-Röda kartan, Lantmäteriverket 1997 (other map objects). Used with permission)

The regeneration has also managed to raise Ringdansen in the neighbourhood hierarchy, from its position at the absolute bottom before the regeneration to around third or fourth from the bottom after the regeneration, depending on which indicator is used. In relative terms, though, the gap between the socioeconomic situation of the Ringdansen population and the municipality average has not changed much. Thus, what has happened is not so much that the relative position of Ringdansen has improved but that other neighbourhoods have joined Ringdansen at the bottom. In that sense, the regeneration seems to have resulted in a dispersion of spatially concentrated deprivation over a larger geographical area.

Table 6.6 The effects of in-migration from Ringdansen and other in-migration on the socioeconomic situation in Hageby district in 2008. Figures for residents aged 20–64 in 2008

	All residents	Excluding in-movers from Ringdansen	Excluding other in-movers
Total number	5,716	5,425	2,820
% with low education	34.0	33.6	34.9
% employed	53.3	53.4	59.8
% on social benefits	26.8	26.8	18.5
Wage income[a]	94,400	94,200	140,500
Disposable income[a]	149,250	150,200	162,500

Source: GeoSweden, Institute for Housing and Urban Research, Uppsala University
[a]Median Swedish Krona

However, most of the neighbourhoods that have taken over Ringdansen's place at the bottom of the hierarchy in different respects are located in the neighbouring city district, Hageby. The worsening situation in the rental-dominated parts of Hageby has mainly been the result of processes similar to what in gentrification research is referred to as exclusionary displacement. The rent increase following the regeneration of Ringdansen has resulted in a redirection of migration flows consisting of the most vulnerable groups, such as newly arrived refugees, away from Ringdansen towards other destinations, mainly Hageby.

But why Hageby? Unfortunately, I have no satisfactory answer to that. As earlier research has shown, spill over or displacement effects often hit neighbouring areas. It would have been easier to understand, had it been the result of direct displacement of the most vulnerable groups of the Ringdansen population, but this clearly was not the case here. What I do know is that the neighbourhoods affected could be found near the bottom of the hierarchy already before the regeneration of Ringdansen. But the same is true also of other neighbourhoods that seem not to have been affected negatively. This is clearly an issue where more research is needed.

Nevertheless, the study presented here illustrates very clearly the need for a systems approach to the study of the population dynamics of neighbourhoods and cities. The development in one specific neighbourhood can never be fully understood by focusing only on that neighbourhood. What happens in one neighbourhood will always be dependent on the development in other parts of the city and in the surrounding world. The key to an understanding lies in identifying the role, or function, of the neighbourhood in the city system, and the character and direction of the migration flows to and from the neighbourhood is of fundamental importance in this. There is a strong interdependence between the neighbourhoods of the city, and especially neighbourhoods that serve, or potentially can serve, the same function in the 'population dynamic system' that constitutes the city. Although generally considered part of the problem of deprived neighbourhoods, these neighbourhoods serve an important function in the housing market by offering housing to those with the weakest position in the labour and housing markets. Where these groups end up after neighbourhood regeneration will more or less decide whether the regeneration of one neighbourhood will result in a re-emergence of old patterns, a reshuffling of the neighbourhood hierarchy, or an actual decrease in levels of segregation.

References

Andersson, R. (2006). 'Breaking segregation' – rhetorical construct of effective policy? The case of the metropolitan development initiative in Sweden. *Urban Studies, 43*(1), 78–799.

Andersson, R., & Bråmå, Å. (2004). Selective migration in Swedish distressed neighbourhoods: Can area-based urban policies counteract segregation processes? *Housing Studies, 19*(4), 517–539.

Andersson, R., & Musterd, S. (2005). Area-based policies: A critical appraisal. *Tijdshcrift voor Economische en Sociale Geografie, 96*(4), 377–389.

Andersson, R., Bråmå, Å., & Holmqvist, E. (2010). Counteracting segregation: Swedish policies and experiences. *Housing Studies, 25*(2), 237–256.

Atkinson, R. (2002). *Does gentrification help or harm urban neighbourhoods? An assessment of the evidence-base in the context of the new urban agenda.* Bristol: ESRC Centre for Neighbourhood Research.

Bailey, N., & Livingston, M. (2008). Selective migration and neighbourhood deprivation: Evidence from 2001 census migration data for England and Scotland. *Urban Studies, 45*(4), 943–961.

Blackman, T. (2006). *Placing health: Neighbourhood renewal, health improvement and complexity.* Bristol: Policy Press.

Bråmå, Å. (2006). *Studies in the dynamics of residential segregation* (Geografiska regionstudier no. 67). Uppsala: Department of Social and Economic Geography, Uppsala University. Available at: http://urn.kb.se/resolve?urn=urn:nbn:se:uu:diva-6336

Bråmå, Å., & Andersson, R. (2005). Who leaves Sweden's large housing estates? In R. van Kempen, K. Dekker, S. Hall, & I. Tosics (Eds.), *Restructuring large housing estates in Europe* (pp. 169–192). Bristol: Policy Press.

Byrne, D. (1998). *Complexity theory and the social sciences. An introduction.* London: Routledge.

Davidson, M., & Lees, L. (2010). New-built gentrification: Its histories, trajectories, and critical geographies. *Population, Space and Place, 16*(5), 395–411.

Friedrichs, J. (1991). Middle-class leakage in large new housing estates: Empirical findings and policy implications. *Journal of Architectural and Planning Research, 8*(4), 287–295.

Galster, G. (2007). Should policy makers strive for neighborhood social mix? An analysis of the western European evidence base. *Housing Studies, 22*(4), 523–545.

Hall, P. (1997). Regeneration policies for peripheral housing estates: Inward- and outward-looking approaches. *Urban Studies, 34*(5–6), 873–890.

Kearns, A., & Mason, P. (2007). Mixed tenure communities and neighbourhood quality. *Housing Studies, 22*(5), 661–691.

Lees, L. (2008). Gentrification and social mixing: Towards an inclusive urban renaissance? *Urban Studies, 45*(12), 2449–2470.

Lees, L., Slater, T., & Wyly, E. (2008). *Gentrification.* New York: Routledge.

Lövgren, S. (2002). *Att skapa ett framtidens folk. Governmentality och miljödiskurs i modern svensk bostadspolitik: miljonprogramsområdet Navestad* (Linköping studies in Arts and Sciences, no. 259). Linköping: The Tema Institute, Linköping University.

Marcuse, P. (2010). Abandonment, gentrification and displacement: The linkages in New York city. In L. Lees, T. Slater, & E. Wyly (Eds.), *The gentrification reader* (pp. 333–347). London: Routledge.

McGregor, A., & McConnachie, M. (1995). Social exclusion, urban regeneration and economic reintegration. *Urban Studies, 32*(10), 1587–1600.
Musterd, S., & Andersson, R. (2005). Housing mix, social mix and social opportunities. *Urban Affairs Review, 40*(6), 761–790.
Musterd, S., & Ostendorf, W. (2005). On physical determinism and displacement effects. In R. van Kempen, K. Dekker, S. Hall, & I. Tosics (Eds.), *Restructuring large housing estates in Europe* (pp. 149–168). Bristol: Policy Press.
Robson, B., Lymperopoulou, K., & Rae, A. (2008). People on the move: Exploring the functional roles of deprived neighbourhoods. *Environment and Planning A, 40*(11), 2693–2714.
Slater, T. (2009). Missing Marcuse: On gentrification and displacement. *City, 13*(2 & 3), 292–311.
van Kempen, R., & Priemus, H. (1999). Undivided cities in the Netherlands: Present situation and political rhetoric. *Housing Studies, 14*(5), 641–657.
Walks, R. A., & Maaranen, R. (2008). Gentrification, social mix, and social polarization: Testing the linkages in large Canadian cities. *Urban Geography, 29*(4), 293–326.
Wallace, M. (2001). A new approach to neighbourhood renewal in England. *Urban Studies, 38*(12), 2163–2166.

Chapter 7
Neighbourhood Social Capital and Residential Mobility

Beate Völker, Gerald Mollenhorst, and Veronique Schutjens

Introduction: The Increase of Neighbourhood Studies and Studies in Social Capital

During the last decades many new technologies have been developed that enable people to build and maintain contacts across large geographical distances. In the media, but also among scientists it has been argued that geographical distances therefore do not matter anymore for social relationships – social networks are liberated from geographical boundaries (see e.g. Wellman 1979; Collins and Wellman 2010). After all, the internet allows direct and inexpensive communication across long distances. In line with this, the importance of the locale for people's life and wellbeing has been questioned. Interestingly, and maybe as a counterpart to this assumption, which is made by politicians, journalists and scientists as well, we can observe a revival of scientific studies investigating the role of the direct living environment for all kinds of individual behaviour and attitudes. For example, neighbourhood characteristics are studied as a condition for an individuals' satisfaction with life (Lee and Guest 1983), career prospects (Wilson 1996), and individual health (e.g., Kawachi and Berkman 2003; Mohnen et al. 2011). In addition, there has been a host of studies that inquire into the influence of neighbourhood conditions on deviant behaviour and crime (e.g. see the work of Sampson et al. 1997; Sampson et al. 1999). This research builds upon the seminal studies by Shaw and McKay (1942), who were among the first to show that structural characteristics of neighbourhoods are associated

B. Völker (✉) • G. Mollenhorst
Faculty of Social and Behavioural Sciences, Sociology, Utrecht University, P.O. Box 80140, 3508 TC Utrecht, The Netherlands
e-mail: B.Volker@uu.nl; G.W.Mollenhorst@uu.nl

V. Schutjens
Faculty of Geosciences, Utrecht University, P. O. Box 80.115, 3508 TC Utrecht, The Netherlands
e-mail: V.A.J.M.Schutjens@uu.nl

M. van Ham et al. (eds.), *Understanding Neighbourhood Dynamics: New Insights for Neighbourhood Effects Research*, DOI 10.1007/978-94-007-4854-5_7,

with other social phenomena in these neighbourhoods. They developed the influential theory of social disorganization and argued that, in particular, three structural neighbourhood conditions are associated with high crime rates. These conditions are a high ethnically mixed population, high residential turnover, and poverty. Succeeding generations of researchers who studied neighbourhood effects consequently controlled for these structural conditions in neighbourhoods (see for example Sampson and Groves 1989; Sampson and Raudenbush 1999; Smith et al. 2000; Markowitz et al. 2001; Morenoff et al. 2001).

Next to the increase in neighbourhood studies, in both sociology and political sciences the research on social capital has grown enormously. This is not only due to the usefulness of the notion of social capital for the explanation of individual behaviour, but also because the idea of social capital is relatively broad, allowing for different interpretations and, consequently, measurements. Note that there are two general streams of social capital research: social capital at the micro level, which is directed to the resourcefulness of an individual's relationships, and social capital at the macro level, where the focus is on the resourcefulness of a collective, such as an organization, a school or a neighbourhood.

Social capital research at the micro level is mostly employed by sociologists and focuses on the actual relationships and the network an individual has. Dimensions of micro level social capital are the number of people in someone's network, their willingness to help in case of need, and their capability to do so (Bourdieu 1980; Burt 1992; Lin 2001). The main idea is that those with better social capital will be better able to realize their goals.

Among political scientists and (urban) geographers a more communitarian, collective approach to social capital is more common (see Moore et al. 2005). Influenced by the work of Robert Putnam, such as *Making Democracy Work* (1993) and *Bowling Alone* (2000), these scholars conceive social capital often as a feature of larger entities, or of corporate actors, like states, regions or municipalities. In Putnam's view, social capital is indicated by general trust, norms of reciprocity and especially by memberships of voluntary organizations. In his 1993 book Putnam makes a case for the economic and social welfare of the North of Italy and the impoverishment of the South of Italy as flowing from the presence and absence, respectively, of a regional tradition of organizational involvement. Cohesive networks at the collective level and in particular so-called bridging ties that interconnect people from different strands and, finally, different communities enhance general trust and cooperation.[1] Using these lateral ties to each other, citizens can force local politicians and bureaucrats to act according to the interests of the citizens.

Both the micro and macro social capital perspectives developed relatively independently from each other and in different fields of the social sciences (sociology and political science respectively, see Halpern 2005 for an overview). They do not

[1] Note that in his most recent work Putnam (2007) argues that diversity, in particular ethnic diversity enhances distrust and what he calls the 'turtle' effect, i.e. refraining from all kinds of participation and lower trust in all others, also in co-ethnics.

contradict each other but, rather, are complementary. Yet, it should be noted that the view on social capital at the macro level differs from the micro perspective in the sense that at the macro level, individual investments are not always necessary and returns have collective good characteristics. While the focus of the micro level perspective on social capital is on an individual's actions and behaviours, the focus of macro level social capital is on collective actions or collective good consumption. This latter view entails that people benefit not only from accessing or using relationships – ties are not always necessary to enjoy benefits – but there are collective goods available in certain groups of people which can be accessed merely via membership to that group. For example, one can benefit from the attention neighbours pay when they watch the streets, houses and each other's children in a neighbourhood, without having direct ties to these neighbours. So, *macro level social capital* is a public-good which can be accessed by all members of a community and of which all members can benefit. People are presumed to be better off and hence also healthier when they live in communities with higher levels of macro level social capital – even when they themselves do not have many actual social ties to others.

In this contribution, we focus on macro level social capital on the level of neighbourhoods. An example of macro level social capital referring to the context of local neighbourhoods was given by Coleman (1990). He stated that in neighbourhoods with high social capital it is 'possible for women to walk freely outside at night'. It is not necessary to have individual relationships – micro level social capital – to benefit from these macro conditions. Coleman cited social capital as a collective good because it is a resource that cannot be easily exchanged, or saved, and because investment is not a necessary condition for enjoying the benefits of that type of good.

The idea of macro level social capital has been applied in many fields and in particular in connection to the neighbourhood studies on health. Although results are mixed, possibly due to variations in measurements of social capital and sizes of the neighbourhoods investigated in the different studies, most studies show a positive effect of neighbourhood social capital on an individual's health. The implicit argument in these studies is that the more social capital present in the neighbourhood, the better inhabitants' health. The opposite has not been studied yet: how does a dramatic lack or decrease in social capital influence people's health and behaviour? Do people take action aiming at improving their situation? In other words, do people plan to leave their neighbourhood if they experience a lack or – maybe even more important, a decrease of social capital in their neighbourhood? Furthermore, do they realize their intentions and actually leave the neighbourhood as soon as possible? In this chapter we want to inquire into the consequences of a lack of, or declining social capital in neighbourhoods. Our research question is straightforward:

> *Does the amount of neighbourhood social capital and its change between 2002 – 2006 affect an individual's intention to leave the neighbourhood as well as an individual's actual moving behaviour?*

We are not the first to study whether there is a relation between social capital and the intention to stay or leave the neighbourhood. Kleinhans (2009) also studied this, but in his study neighbourhood social capital was measured at the individual level and not treated as a phenomenon on the collective level. In addition, he only investigated two neighbourhoods which had been subject to restructuration in the city of Rotterdam. As a consequence, his study reveals little about the general effects of social capital at the neighbourhood level. Moreover, the cross-sectional investigation of the neighbourhoods did not enable the measurement of social capital change.

Indeed, not only changes in social capital also the question whether social capital matters at all is hard to study with a cross-sectional approach. The lack of social capital can be a consequence of the intention to move, rather than its cause. One can argue in both directions: people plan to move and therefore stop investing in the neighbourhood community, or, there is a lack of social capital which causes people to look for a friendlier place to live. In our study, a large national representative sample is employed which includes 75% of all Dutch neighbourhoods. From this data, social capital is measured by help of an ecometric procedure (see below, Sect. 4) on the level of the neighbourhood. Lastly, we have two points of measurement in 2002 and in 2006 which allow for studying dynamics in neighbourhood social capital and its consequences for moving intentions and moving behaviour.

The remainder of this chapter is organized in five sections. In the next section we briefly review the literature on moving and moving intentions. In Sect. 3 we formulate our hypotheses based on arguments from a cost-benefit scheme, e.g. cost of moving are lower for people who have many resources. Therefore, they might react more easily to a decline in social capital in their neighbourhood. Section 4 presents our data and measurements used and sketches the ecometric approach which we used to measure social capital reliably on the neighbourhood level. Section 5 presents the results, and finally, Sect. 6 concludes and discusses our findings and their implications for housing and neighbourhood policies.

What Do We Know About Why People (Want to) Move to Other Neighbourhoods?

Moving is costly, even if it can improve one's living conditions, for example if one moves to a better house or neighbourhood. People do not move without a strong reason. This is not only due to the financial costs involved, but also because of the time and energy which have to be spent during the search and selection process (Sjaastad 1962). Moreover, when one decides to move over a large distance, the actual move may destroy local social ties.[2] Hence moving is not only costly in a financial way, it is also costly from a social point of view: existing ties might become difficult to maintain and new ties need to be established. What is known in general on why people move – or want to move?

---

[2] On the website 'bowlingalone.com', named after Putnam's (2000) book, it is mentioned that every ten minutes of commuting reduces all forms of social capital by 10%.

Conditions that stimulate moving do not differ markedly from the general conditions which stimulate other individual action. The housing market literature identifies three main factors which explain the intentions to move and actual moving behaviour: preferences, resources, and opportunities or constraints (Musterd and Van Kempen 2007; van Ham 2012). Personal preferences are of course important, since individual aspirations and ambitions are strong drivers for all kinds of intentions and actions; in our case also of housing demands and actual moving behaviour. However, the intention to move is a necessary but not a sufficient condition for the actual move (see the pioneering work of Rossi 1980 [1955]).

Resources refer to the extent to which the individual preferences can be realised, which of course strongly depends on the financial resources of the household. But resources can also be social or related to the knowledge of the market opportunities. Both preferences and resources are not stable, but change over time as they are strongly affected by changes in the individual or household situation. Recently, based on an empirical study on stages in the migration process of young German adults leaving the city, Kley and Mulder (2010) showed that resources matter in particular for turning moving aspirations into reality. Finally, opportunities and constraints reflect the availability of housing alternatives within and outside the neighbourhood (Mulder 1993). The supply of attractive and affordable dwellings in a favourable area may literally give birth to the idea of moving quickly, even if there is not much wrong with the current dwelling (South and Crowder 1997).

According to classic choice-oriented studies on housing mobility, a specific threshold has to be passed before one considers a move: this was frequently characterized as a certain level of residential 'stress' (Wolpert 1965; Brown and Moore 1970). Although the word 'stress' nowadays is associated with something negative, here it means a larger difference between the current housing situation and the set of housing aspirations. Common coping strategies for this type of stress are changing the attitude on the current dwelling or changing ones aspirations (Deane 1990; Van der Land and Doff 2010; Coulter et al. 2011).

The causes of residential stress (or a large gap between actual and preferred housing situation) can be caused by both individual and contextual conditions. From the (individual) life-course approach to the housing market behaviour, we learn that housing needs and aspirations change according to a number of incisive events in the life course of individuals, reflecting both personal preferences and available resources. For instance, changes in household composition, such as having children, divorce, or even children leaving the parental home, are powerful triggers of moving intentions and behaviour (see Clark and Dieleman 1996). Also starting vocational training or university education, getting a new job, an increase or decline of household income, or changing job conditions (such as the possibility to work part-time or from home), may change satisfaction with the current housing situation and even fuel new ambitions with respect to housing standards.

Contextual factors (dwelling or neighbourhood characteristics) may also be a cause of residential stress for households and individuals, leading to many people desiring a move, and finally also people actually moving to other dwellings or even areas (van Ham and Feijten 2008; van Ham and Clark 2009). Dwelling characteristics (or changes therein) may lead to moving intentions or moving behaviour. This includes, for instance, an urgent need to renovate, which may be a cause for individuals considering an alternative dwelling especially if the costs involved are high. Neighbourhood characteristics, such as the quality of the living environment, and especially a noticeable change in this quality, is among the most important conditions for residential stress, and, ultimately, residential mobility. South and Crowder (1997) argue that neighbourhood changes can involve physical as well as social aspects. For example, changing zoning regulations, disappearing shopping centres or green areas, incisive neighbourhood restructuring plans or the building of a new highway close to the neighbourhood – leading to noise and the demolition of original physical structures – is obviously rather unattractive for many inhabitants. Social neighbourhood changes, stemming from the influx of new population groups and out-migration of original inhabitants, both lead to a changing population composition in terms of age, income levels and ethnicity and often also to lower local social interaction and contacts for the people who stay (Livingstone et al. 2010). These neighbourhood changes, and especially the resulting growing discomfort with the neighbourhood, may have consequences for both moving intentions and actual moves. For example, Andersen (2008) concluded from a study in Danish deprived areas that neighbourhood dissatisfaction significantly increases inhabitants' plans to leave the neighbourhood.

Feijten and Van Ham (2009) showed that neighbourhood inhabitants' propensity to actually move out the neighbourhood is related to the social composition of the neighbourhood: high levels of local population turnover and in-migration of non-western ethnic minorities stimulate individual moving intentions. Although it seems plausible that moving plans and actual moves mounts with dissatisfaction with the living environment (Kearns and Parkes 2005; Clark and Huang 2003), the recent literature is quite ambiguous about the effect of (changing) social neighbourhood characteristics on moving intentions and behaviour. In contrast to the literature above, Kley and Mulder (2010) argue that satisfaction with local conditions hardly influences actual moving behaviour, especially in studies that take into account factors of relocation decision making process. Evidence of the opposite is presented by Musterd and Van Kempen (2007), who find that, controlled for other individual aspects, neighbourhood residents with strong local contacts are less inclined to turn aspirations to move towards another neighbourhood into reality.

As discussed above moving intention and behaviour rests on a strong interplay between preferences, resources and opportunities, in other words, between contextual and individual causes of residential stress. On the one hand, a pleasant and safe living environment may offset the urge of households with young children to move to a larger house elsewhere. Furthermore, as the share of non-western ethnic minorities in neighbourhoods is greater, native Dutch residents are more likely to move to another neighbourhood than ethnic minorities (Schaake et al. 2010). On the other hand, for many people the threefold path from residential stress to moving intention to actually moving house and improving their housing situation is not straightforward. Not only can many low income households not afford to turn their housing aspirations into practice, the ones among them that do move, often only take small steps up the housing ladder or even downward, or choose neighbourhoods at similar level or only slightly higher in the neighbourhood hierarchy (Musterd and Van Kempen 2007; Kendig 1990).

According to Lyons and Lowery (1989) strong place attachment prevents people from moving. Findings from investigations into place attachment are, however, not consistent: Livingstone and colleagues (2010) conclude from interviews that place attachment does not influence moving behaviour. "[P]eople valued their local connections and social networks but they would improve their material or environmental circumstances if the opportunity arose. ... Attachment .... does not appear to be the factor discouraging mobility" (Livingstone et al. 2010, p. 425).

In summary, the intention to move is driven by the interdependency of people's preferences, resources and market opportunities/constraints (see Glaeser et al. 2008 for a dynamic model explanation of housing markets, predicting that markets are largely local). Changes in life events such as household composition or work influence preferences and resources as well.

It is striking that studies that take into account the neighbourhood context as a possible determinant of moving intentions and behaviour tend to have three major limitations. First, a static stance is taken, relating the neighbourhood situation from a specific point in time to later residential mobility events. Second, the indicators for neighbourhood characteristics are frequently based on demographic statistics and not on resident's evaluation of their environment (Rabe and Taylor 2010). Third and finally, in most studies on residential mobility, neighbourhood community and social capital are not taken into account, nor are changes in these measures both of which might influence people's inclination to move.

Hypotheses: When Will People (Want to) Move?

As stated above, we study the influence of neighbourhood social capital on people's moving intention and behaviour. Social capital at the macro level can be understood as the degree to which neighbourhood residents in general have friendly relationships with each other and assume that they can ask each other for help (see e.g. Mohnen et al. 2011). This will enhance the feelings of belonging and community and we expect that moving intentions will be discouraged if this type of social capital is perceived being high, maybe even if the dwelling does not meet the household's current requirements or desires. Our argument is that these relationships enhance feelings of attachment to the neighbourhood and will cause people to stay. Maybe, even if the neighbourhood conditions have changed in terms of facilities, people will not quickly leave because they feel so much 'at home'.

We furthermore expect that social capital will not only influence the intention to move. Also, actual moving will be stimulated by decline in social capital. Based on that reasoning, our two general hypotheses reads:

1a) *If there is more social capital in a neighbourhood, people are less likely to have the intention to move.*

1b) *If there is more social capital in a neighbourhood, people are less likely to move.*

It goes without saying that we expect this influence of neighbourhood social capital on moving intentions while controlling for other conditions which influence moving, such as neighbourhood composition and average income level.

As stated in the previous section, an individual's resources are among the most important conditions required to realize a move. If an individual does not have the means to afford a move, simply nothing will happen. However, given individual income, it is plausible to expect that people wish to leave a low income neighbourhood and actually do so if possible. Hence, our hypotheses read:

2a) *If average income in a neighbourhood is low, moving intentions are higher.*
2b) *If average income in a neighbourhood is low, people more often leave the neighbourhood.*

In addition, we assume that a change in neighbourhood social capital also influences moving intentions and actual behaviour. In particular, we expect that a decrease in neighbourhood social capital leads to an increase in residents' moving intentions. Our third hypotheses read

3a) *If social capital declined in a neighbourhood, people will have more intentions to move.*
3b) *If social capital declined in a neighbourhood, people move more often.*

Data, Measurements, and Analytical Strategy

Data

This study used data from the 'Dutch housing demand survey', a survey that has been conducted every 2 years since 1998. It inquires many aspects of people's dwelling and residential environment. We have used the waves from 2002 to 2006, because in these waves the postal codes of the respondents were included and a period of 4 years is sufficient to measure some neighbourhood changes. Neighbourhood areas in these data are delineated on the basis of 4-digit postcode units. These areas comprise between 1 and 8 km^2 with on average 2,500–3,000 addresses (http://statline.cbs.nl/statweb/) and about 4,000 residents. About 75% of all neighbourhoods at this scale in the Netherlands are represented in the data.

The Dutch housing demand survey data are representative for the whole Dutch population aged 18 or over. Interviews took about 40 min on average, and the response rate is about 56–60%, with slight variations between waves. Information on micro level social capital as well as on some relevant household characteristics was not collected from every respondent, but only from the 'core-household' members. By definition, adult family (such as elderly parents) or children living in a particular household do not belong to the core-household. The final sample size employed for this study was 63,334 respondents from all over the Netherlands.

Measurement of Individual Level Variables

We use two dependent variables in this study. The first dependent variable is the intention to move out of the neighbourhood. Respondents were asked to indicate the extent to which they agreed with the statement "If possible, I will move out of this neighbourhood". In response, the residents could choose to fully agree, agree, disagree and fully disagree with this statement. The second dependent variable indicates whether or not the respondent moved to another neighbourhood between 2004 and 2006.

A number of independent variables on the individual level were included in the analyses as controls: *Sex*, coded as a dummy variable with males as 0; *age*, measured in years and centered on the average (47.6 years); and *ethnic background* (Native Dutch, Western immigrant, Non-Western immigrant). *Social status was measured using two indicators:* education and income. *Education* was measured as the 'highest school degree achieved so far' at the time of questioning. We used a 5-point scale ranging from 1 (primary school or less) to 5 (university degree). *Income* was measured as the log of the 'equivalent monthly household income'. This variable took into account all kinds of household level income including social benefits, pensions, and salaries. It was calculated by accounting for the costs of having children and the benefits of sharing a household (Siermann et al.2004). We also controlled for having a *paid job*, measured as a dummy variable. It has been shown in several neighbourhood studies that home ownership matters for a number of outcomes. Owners, in contrast to renters, usually invest more in the physical and social order in the neighbourhood (see Dipasquale and Glaeser 1999). To account for this difference we controlled for *housing tenure* by making a difference between 'owner', and 'renter'. *Household composition* was also included by differentiating between single person households, couples with/without children, one parent families and households where people lived together who are not family members. Finally, the '*years of residence*' that the respondent had lived in their current place of living were included. This was measured by the question: "How long have you been living on this address?". Table 7.1 presents the descriptive statistic of variables on individual level, and additionally variables on the neighbourhood level.

Measurement of Neighbourhood Level Variables

'*Neighbourhood social capital*' was measured at the level of the individual by combining three questions which ask about contacts among neighbours:

- whether people in the neighbourhood know each other;
- whether neighbours are friendly to each other;
- whether there is a friendly and sociable atmosphere in the neighbourhood.

Response categories were 'totally agree', 'agree', 'neutral', 'don't agree', and 'totally don't agree' using a scoring system of 1–5. For the analyses, the respondent

Table 7.1 Descriptive statistics of variables in the analyses

	Percentage	Min	Max	Mean	Standard deviation	N
Neighbourhood characteristics						
Social capital (ecometrics)						
2002		−0.68	0.46	0	0.16	3,434
2006		−0.62	0.40	0	0.13	3,420
Change 2002–2006		−0.48	0.59	0	0.14	3,189
Mean income (log)		7.47	12.24	10.33	0.43	3,489
Ethnic composition						3,495
Native Dutch	87.8					
Western immigrants	6.6					
Non-western immigrants	5.5					
Mean # years of residence		0	77	15.62	8.17	3,424
Individual characteristics						
Sex						
Male (0)	47.2					64,005
Female (1)	52.8					
Age		18	103	47.55	18.65	64,005
Level of education		1	5	3.42	1.32	63,668
Ethnicity						
Native	82.4					64,005
Western immigrant	8					
Non-western immigrant	9.6					
Income (log)		3.4	15.79	10.29	0.81	63,878
Household composition						
Single person household	27.1					
Couple without children	27.8					
Couple with child(ren)	36.2					
One-parent family	7.6					
Non-family household	1.4					64,005
Paid job (≥1 h)						
No (0)	41.6					64,005
Yes (1)	58.4					
Housing tenure[a]						
Renter	47.2					64,005
Homeowner	52.8					
Years of residence		0	99	14.42	11.95	64,005
Intention to move to another neighbourhood:						
If possible, I will move out of this neighbourhood[b]		1	5	2.29	1.06	64,005
Fully disagree (1)	20.7					
Disagree (2)	51.6					
Neutral (3)	8.6					
Agree (4)	15.4					
Fully agree (5)	3.4					

(continued)

Table 7.1 (continued)

	Percentage	Min	Max	Mean	Standard deviation	N
Moved to another neighbourhood between 2004 and 2006						
No (0)	89.1					
Yes (1)	10.9					64,005

Source: Dutch Housing Demand Survey, 2002 and 2006
[a]We imputed missing values on this variable (12.6%) using the variable that indicated the neighbourhood and three variables on the urgency to move to another house
[b]We imputed missing values on this variable (13.1%) using a variable that indicated the intention to move within the next 2 years

categories were recoded in such a way that higher values indicate more social capital. For the aggregation of our measurements to the level of neighbourhoods we applied the ecometric procedure developed by Raudenbush and Sampson (1999) which accounts for the nesting of social capital items within individuals while including the neighbourhood level in the analysis (see also Mujahid et al. 2007). We elaborate on this procedure in the next section.

Often, generalized trust in neighbours is used as a proxy for social capital. Our study measures social capital via indicators of the quality of neighbourhood relations, which we consider as an improvement. Generalized trust is not necessarily related to contacts. Other neighbourhood variables include average (log) income, average length of residence in the neighbourhood and ethnic composition at the neighbourhood level. Just like the neighbourhood social capital variables, also these variables have been aggregated from the information provided by the individual respondents in the Dutch Housing Demand Survey. We note that in part of these research neighbourhoods only a small number of residents have been interviewed, which negatively affects the reliability of these variables. We therefore conducted several additional analyses in which we excluded the cases for which the neighbourhood indicators were based on less than 10 respondents and also while excluding the cases for which the neighbourhood indicators were based on less than 15 respondents. Because these additional analyses yielded similar results as when all cases are included, we report on the results from the initial analyses using all cases. In total we analysed moving intentions and actual moves of 63,334 respondents in 3,495 neighbourhoods. Table 7.1 provides summary statistics on the key variables.

The Measurement of Social Capital at the Neighbourhood Level

To estimate neighbourhood social capital, information provided by individual residents has to be aggregated to the neighbourhood level. A straightforward procedure would be to calculate the mean (or the standard deviation) of the items measured at the individual level for each neighbourhood. This procedure has a number of problems. First, variables measuring neighbourhood social capital are based on individual perceptions which can be expected to be systematically influenced by the characteristics of the respondents. For example, women, said to be more emphatic, might report more often that people in the neighbourhood are very helpful and friendly. Younger people often do not have many actual contacts in the neighbourhood and might therefore perceive no neighbourhood community at all. Second, the reliability of the aggregated measurement differs among neighbourhoods because of the different numbers of respondents per neighbourhood. Third, the items measuring social capital are not independent of each other but nested within respondents; that is, answers from one item are likely to be associated with answers from another item. Hence, an approach is needed which accounts for individual differences in response to certain items, for differences in the number of respondents on which estimations are based, and for interdependency among the items that measure neighbourhood social capital. The ecometric procedure developed by Raudenbush and Sampson (1999; see also Mujahid et al. 2007) fulfils these requirements and overcomes the shortcomings of simple aggregation of individual characteristics. This method accounts for the nesting of social capital items within individuals while including the neighbourhood level in the analysis, which results in a three-level model: neighbourhoods, individuals, and items measuring social capital.

We adjusted for four individual characteristics that can be expected to influence the perception of neighbourhood social capital: sex, age, education, and having a non-Western origin. In the first step of the analysis, neighbourhood social capital was estimated by a three-level model, with neighbourhood, individuals and items of social capital as separate levels. The residuals of the neighbourhood social capital measurement – the part that could not be attributed to response patterns arising from individual characteristics – constituted the social capital indicator for the final analyses where the hypotheses were tested. In this second step, the ecometric-based social capital measurement was used as an independent variable in a two-level logistic model with the intention to leave the neighbourhood as binary dependent variable, as well as in the model of having moved between 2004 and 2006.

The average reliability of our ecometric-based neighbourhood social capital measurement was 0.66. The interpretation of this reliability coefficient is similar to a Cronbach's alpha in psychometrics scale analysis, although the values are usually somewhat lower than those of psychometric scales. Values above 0.60 are considered to be adequate (Cohen 1988). The correlation at the neighbourhood level between an aggregated social capital measure and the ecometric-based collective efficacy measure was 0.88.

Results

Table 7.2 presents the results of the analyses on the intention to move out of the neighbourhood. We estimated seven models. Model 1 shows the influence of social capital: in neighbourhoods with little social capital, people are more inclined to move. Model 2 adds the changes in social capital between 2002 and 2006 to the

Table 7.2 Multilevel ordered logit models on the intention to move to another neighbourhood (2006, log odds ratio)

	Model 1	Model 2	Model 3	Model 4	Model 5	Model 6	Model 7
Neighbourhood characteristics							
Social capital 2002	−1.09***	−1.74***			−1.10***	−1.15***	−0.97***
Increase in social capital		−1.62***			−1.25***	−1.29***	−1.18***
Mean income (log)				−0.47***		−0.35***	−0.01
Mean # years of residence (× 10 years)				−0.15***		−0.09***	0.03†
Ethnic composition							
Proportion western immigrants				0.02		−0.28*	−0.34**
Proportion non-western immigrants				1.44***		0.74***	0.46***
Individual characteristics							
Sex			−0.09***		−0.09***		−0.09***
Age			−0.03***		−0.03***		−0.03***
Ethnicity (reference = native)							
Western immigrant			0.08**		0.05*		0.07**
Non-western immigrant			0.11***		0.03		0.00
Level of education			0.09***		0.08***		0.08***
Paid job			−0.00		0.00		0.00
Income (log)			−0.02*		−0.03*		−0.02*
Household composition (reference = single)							
Couple without children			0.13***		0.16***		0.16***
Couple with child(ren)			0.14***		0.20***		0.20***
One-parent family			0.27***		0.29***		0.29***
Non-family household			−0.20**		−0.19**		−0.20**
Housing tenure (reference = renter)							
Home owner			−1.04***		−0.99***		−0.99***
# Years of residence (× 10 years)			0.07***		0.08***		0.08***
Cut-point 1	−1.28	−1.27	−1.82	−6.37	−1.80	−5.04	−1.92

(continued)

Table 7.2 (continued)

	Model 1	Model 2	Model 3	Model 4	Model 5	Model 6	Model 7
Cut-point 2	1.07	1.09	0.84	–4.00	0.86	–2.67	0.73
Cut-point 3	1.57	1.59	1.41	–3.50	1.43	–2.17	1.30
Cut-point 4	3.47	3.48	3.41	–1.61	3.42	–0.28	3.30
# Respondents	63,334	63,286	63,543	63,919	62,832	63,283	62,832
# Neighbourhoods	3,232	3,189	3,487	3,418	3,186	3,186	3,186
Log likelihood	–80811	–80531	–76222	–81325	–75226	–80424	–75209
Neighbourhood-level variance	0.07***	0.04***	0.05***	0.05***	0.02***	0.02***	0.02***

Source: Dutch Housing Demand Survey, 2002 and 2006; † $p < 0.10$, * $p < 0.05$, ** $p < 0.01$, *** $p < 0.001$.

equation. Clearly, in neighbourhoods with low social capital people are more inclined to have moving intentions. In addition, if social capital has declined within 4 years, people also want to move out of the neighbourhood.

Model 3 adds individual characteristics to the analysis. In particular men, younger people and people who have not a Dutch background have more moving intentions. Interestingly, there is also a positive influence of education: higher educated people also want to leave the neighbourhood more often. Income has no effect in this model. Furthermore, compared to single person households, couples and families with children are clearly more inclined to move. Non family households are an exception here: they are least likely to have moving intentions, compared to singles. Finally, home owners compared to renters are also much less inclined to have moving intentions. In model 4, the neighbourhood indicators are included in the model. The model shows that residential turnover, measured by the average years of residence, and aggregated income both affect moving intentions in the expected direction: high residential fluctuation and low average income stimulate the intention to leave the neighbourhood. Furthermore, also the social composition in terms of ethnicity matters: if there is a high proportion of non-western migrants in a neighbourhood, individuals have more often the intention to move. Model 5 combines social capital with the individual characteristics. The coefficients are rather stable, with the exception of ethnicity.

Model 6 shows effects of all neighbourhood conditions, including social capital. Outcomes are robust, if compared with the fourth model.

Model 7, finally, includes all variables at the individual and the neighbourhood level. Importantly, the influence of social capital is in all models robust and coefficients do not change much. Model 7 does show however that neighbourhood income does not matter anymore if it is considered together with individual income. Individual income has a weak negative effect. Hence, it is not so much the poverty of the neighbourhood, but rather the poverty of the individual with affects his or her intentions to move. This finding is somewhat counterintuitive with the finding on education: again, the higher educated report more often the intention to move. Also ethnic background of the individual shows an effect: compared to the Dutch, western migrants are more inclined to move out of the neighbourhood. Note however, that the association between the proportion of non-western foreigners in the neighbourhood and moving intentions is considerably mediated by social capital: the coefficient decreases for more than 50% if it is controlled for social capital in the analysis (compare model 4 with model 6 and 7). Indicators concerning sex, age, household composition and ownership are unchanged compared to previous models.

In summary, individual characteristics as well as neighbourhood conditions influence an individual's intention to move out of the neighbourhood. Male respondents as well as people with a higher education are more inclined to move. Interestingly, those with a lower income are also more inclined to move, but the effect is small. Western migrants are more willing to move than non-migrants and so are younger people. Probably, the latter finding is related to the life events which occur relatively often at a younger age, such as first job, marriage, and getting a child. Also, the findings with regard to household composition are interesting: Couples, with or without children, but especially one-parent families are more inclined to leave the neighbourhood than people living in non-family households. Similar as already found in previous studies, home ownership makes people less likely to express an intention to move out of the neighbourhood.

In the next step of the analysis we investigate actual moving behaviour. The sequence of models in Table 7.3 is as follows: model 8 starts with controlling only for social capital, and model 9 includes changes in social capital. Model 10 shows the effects of individual characteristics and model 11 those of the neighbourhood indicators. Model 12 and 13 combine social capital with individual and neighbourhood conditions respectively. Model 14 is the final model including all conditions. Importantly, and in line with our previous results we found an influence of social capital on actual moving behaviour. People moved more often between 2004 and 2006, if they lived in a neighbourhood with low social capital in 2002. The less social capital in the neighbourhood and the more decrease in social capital, the more people did move. Income on the neighbourhood level has no importance here. Furthermore and not clearly in line with the expectation is that higher residential stability seems to incline moving behaviour in this model. Moving behaviour is also positively associated with the proportion of non-western foreigners in the neighbourhood: more foreigners stimulate moving behaviour, independent of a person's own ethnic background. And similar to the findings on moving intentions, also here we find that the association between the proportion of non-western foreigners in the neighbourhood and actual moving behaviour is considerably mediated by the level of social capital in the neighbourhood. Moreover, we found that for moving behaviour, it does not matter whether an individual is Dutch or not. Similar to the findings on moving intentions, we find that higher educated are more among those who have moved, but now we also find that the same holds for people with higher income. The latter finding shows that for actual moving, own resources become more important than for the intention to move. However, having a paid job seems to be a (weak) incentive to stay. Single persons and non-family households are those who move most often. These findings are rather unexpected: People living together with a partner and/or with children are more inclined to move out of the neighbourhood, but are less likely to have done so between 2004 and 2006. In summary, hypotheses 1a/b and 3a/b are confirmed, hypotheses 2a and b are not.

Most important however, are our findings with regard to collective social capital: it is intriguing that there is evidence for another stimulant of moving intentions and behaviour.

Conclusion

In this contribution, we showed that social capital affects intentions to move to another neighbourhood as well as actual behaviour with regard to neighbourhood exit. People who live in low social capital areas are more likely to have an intention to move and they actually do so accordingly. This is important as it demonstrates that social capital matters to individuals when they move and is an important factor

Table 7.3 Multilevel logit models on having moved to another neighbourhood between 2004 and 2006 (log odds ratio)

	Model 8	Model 9	Model 10	Model 11	Model 12	Model13	Model14
Neighbourhood characteristics[a]							
Social capital 2002	−1.47***	−1.75***			−1.10***	−1.63***	−1.02***
Increase in social capital 2002–2006		−0.60***			−0.31*	−0.54***	−0.26†
Mean income (log)				−0.22**		−0.06	−0.10
Mean # years of residence (× 10 years)				0.00		0.09*	0.21***
Ethnic composition							
Proportion western immigrants				0.43†		−0.07	−0.02
Proportion non-western immigrants				1.38***		0.38*	0.58***
Individual characteristics[b]							
Sex			0.19***		0.20***		0.20***
Age			−0.05***		−0.05***		−0.06***
Ethnicity (reference = native)							
Western immigrant			0.17***		0.03		0.03
Non-western immigrant			0.24***		0.01		−0.01
Level of education			0.05***		0.06***		0.06***
Paid job			−0.24***		−0.18***		−0.18***
Income (log)			0.46***		0.45***		0.46***
Household composition (reference = single)							
Couple without children			−0.22***		−0.08*		−0.09*
Couple with child(ren)			−1.59***		−1.47***		−1.48***
One-parent family			−1.17***		−1.08***		−1.09***
Non-family household			0.20*		0.20*		0.19*
Housing tenure (reference = renter)							
Homeowner			−0.37***		−0.28***		−0.28***
Intercept	−2.46***	−2.47***	−6.56***	−0.20	−6.84***	−1.99*	−6.23***
# Respondents	62,406	62,330	63,543	62,865	61,908	62,326	61,907

(continued)

Table 7.3 (continued)

	Model 8	Model 9	Model 10	Model 11	Model 12	Model13	Model14
# Neighbourhoods	3,266	3,225	3,487	3,410	3,221	3,222	3,221
Wald Chi2	232.82	263.17	4693.63	128.40	4227.48	266.44	4207.27
Rho	0.08	0.08	0.05	0.09	0.06	0.09	0.07

Source: Dutch Housing Demand Survey, 2002 and 2006; † $p < 0.10$, * $p < 0.05$, ** $p < 0.01$, *** $p < 0.001$.
[a]Neighbourhood characteristics apply:
– to the neighbourhood in which the respondent lived in 2006, if he/she did not move to another neighbourhood between 2004 and 2006
– to the neighbourhood in which the respondent lived in 2004, if he/she did move to another neighbourhood between 2004 and 2006
[b]Individual characteristics apply to the situation in 2006

in determining desires and behaviours, along with personal resources and market opportunities. To get a better understanding of the interactions between intentions, behaviours and social capital, future work should inquire more deeply into the conditions which cause social capital in neighbourhoods to change. For example, next to the option of leaving the neighbourhood ('exit', cf. Hirschman 1970), there might also be people who choose to change something and help to increase social capital, while staying ('voice'). Staying in a neighbourhood and investing in social capital, might be an option for people who cannot afford moving or who believe that it is possible to change the neighbourhood. In future research, it should also be sorted out, whether people deliberately stay and how they differ from those who leave. In addition, we did not investigate whether people moved to a neighbourhood with more social capital. So far, we only know that a low level of social capital stimulates moving.

However, our research is not completely in line with what would be expected from other neighbourhood studies on individual behaviour. For instance, we did not find evidence supporting neighbourhood poverty as a driving force for moving intentions or behaviours. Individual income seems much more important. While lower income groups have more often an intention to move, people from higher income groups actually move more often. Education appears to stimulate both moving intention and behaviour. The effects of residential stability are not as expected: high residential turnover does stimulate moving intentions but seems to hamper individual moving. This finding deserves more attention and additional analyses.

Interestingly, ethnic background matters most on the neighbourhood level. Independent of an individual's own ethnic background, the proportion of foreigners in a neighbourhood, in particular non-western foreigners stimulates moving intentions as well as moving behaviour. We note however, that although these effects remain significant, these are substantially mediated by the level of social capital in the neighbourhood.

In this study, we restricted ourselves to arguments and analyses on general effects of our conditions specified. Future research should also develop arguments on interaction effects. For example, the influence of social capital on moving intention might depend on a number of other neighbourhood conditions as well as on characteristics of the individual. If a person is poor, effects of social capital – as another resource, next to money – might be stronger. One also would like to know how people from different ethnic backgrounds are affected in their moving intentions and behaviour by social capital.

Our study has added to the literature on moving in several ways. We were able to show evidence for another condition for this type of behaviour using longitudinal data from a large national representative data set. We also added to the literature on macro level social capital, while showing that this type of social capital matters for neighbourhood stability. For policymakers, it might be important to know that social capital binds people to their neighbourhoods, and that a decline in social capital enhances moving intentions and behaviour. Future research therefore should also more deeply inquire into the conditions under which neighbourhood social capital is created.

References

Andersen, H. S. (2008). Why do residents want to leave deprived neighborhoods? The importance of residents' subjective evaluations of their neighborhood and its reputation. *Journal of Housing and the Built Environment, 23*(2), 79–101.

Bourdieu, P. (1980). Le capital social. *Actes de la recherche en sciences sociales, 31*, 2–3.

Brown, L. A., & Moore, E. G. (1970). The intra-urban migration process: A perspective. *Geografiska Annaler, 52B*, 1–13.

Burt, R. S. (1992). *Structural holes: The social structure of competition*. Cambridge: Harvard University Press.

Clark, W. A. V., & Dieleman, F. M. (1996). *Households and housing: Choice and outcomes in the housing market*. New Brunswick: Canter for Urban Policy Research.

Clark, W. A. V., & Huang, Y. (2003). The life course and residential mobility in British housing markets. *Environment and Planning A, 35*(2), 323–339.

Cohen, J. (1988). *Statistical power analysis for the behavioural sciences*. Mahwah: Lawrence Erlbaum Associates.

Coleman, J. S. (1990). *Foundations of social theory*. Cambridge: Bellknap Press.

Collins, J. L., & Wellman, B. (2010). Small town in the internet society: Chapleau is no longer an island. *American Behavioral Scientist, 53*(9), 1344–1366.

Coulter, R., van Ham, M., & Feijten, P. (2011). *Partner (dis)agreement on moving desires and the subsequent moving behaviour of couples*. IZA discussion paper no. 5612. www.iza.org

Deane, G. D. (1990). Mobility and adjustments: Paths to the resolution of residential stress. *Demography, 27*(1), 65–79.

DiPasquale, D., & Glaeser, E. (1999). Incentives and social capital: Do homeowners make better citizens? *Journal of Urban Economics, 45*(2), 354–384.

Feijten, P., & van Ham, M. (2009). Neighbourhood change… reason to leave? *Urban Studies, 46*(10), 2103–2122.

Glaeser, E. L., Gyourko, J., & Saiz, A. (2008). Housing supply and housing bubbles. *Journal of Urban Economics, 64* (2), 198–217.

Halpern, D. (2005). *Social capital*. Cambridge: Polity Press.

Hirschman, A. O. (1970). *Exit, voice and loyalty. Responses to decline in firms, organizations and states*. Cambridge/Massachusetts/London: Harvard University Press.

Kawachi, I., & Berkman, L. (2003). *Neighborhoods and health*. Oxford: Oxford University Press.

Kearns, A., & Parkes, A. (2005). Living in and leaving poor neighborhood conditions. In J. Friedrichs, G. C. Galster, & S. Musterd (Eds.), *Life in poverty neighborhoods* (pp. 31–56). London: Routledge.

Kendig, H. L. (1990). A life course perspective on housing attainment. In D. Myers (Ed.), *Housing demography: Linking demographic structure and housing markets* (pp. 133–156). Madison: The University of Wisconsin Press.

Kleinhans, R. (2009). Does social capital affect resident's prospensity to move from restructured neighborhoods? *Housing Studies, 24*(5), 629–651.

Kley, S. A., & Mulder, C. H. (2010). Considering, planning, and realizing migration in early adulthood. The influence of life-course events and perceived opportunities on leaving the city in Germany. *Journal of Housing and the Built Environment, 25*(1), 73–94.

Lee, B. A., & Guest, A. (1983). Determinants of neighborhood satisfaction: A metropolitan-level analysis. *The Sociological Quarterly, 24*(2), 287–303.

Lin, N. (2001). Reputation and social capital: The rational basis for social exchange. In N. Lin (Ed.), *Social capital. A theory of social structure and action* (pp. 143–164). Cambridge: Cambridge University Press.

Livingstone, M., Bailey, N., & Kearns, A. (2010). Neighbourhood attachment in deprived areas: Evidence from the north of England. *Journal of Housing and the Built Environment, 25*(4), 409–427.

Lyons, W. E., & Lowery, D. (1989). Citizen responses to dissatisfaction in urban communities. *Journal of Politics, 51*(4), 841–868.
Markowitz, F. E., Bellair, P. E., Liska, A. E., & Liu, J. H. (2001). Extending social disorganization theory: Modeling the relationships between cohesion, disorder, and fear. *Criminology, 39*(2), 293–320.
Mohnen, S., Groenewegen, P., Völker, B., & Flap, H. (2011). Neighborhood social capital and individual health. *Social Science & Medicine, 72*(5), 660–667.
Moore, S., Sheila, A., Hawed, P., & Haines, V. A. (2005). The privileging of communitarian ideas: Citation practices and the translation of social capital into public health research. *American Journal of Public Health, 95*(8), 1330–1337.
Morenoff, J. D., Sampson, R., & Raudenbush, S. W. (2001). Neighborhood inequality, collective efficacy and the spatial dynamics of urban violence. *Criminology, 39*(3), 17–559.
Mujahid, M. S., Diez-Roux, A. V., Morenoff, J. D., & Raghunathan, T. (2007). Assessing the measurement properties of neighborhood scales: From psychometrics to ecometrics. *American Journal of Epidemiology, 165*(8), 858–867.
Mulder, C. H. (1993). *Migration dynamics: A life course approach*. Amsterdam: Thesis Publishers.
Musterd, S., & van Kempen, R. (2007). Trapped or on the springboard? Housing careers in large housing estates in European cities. *Journal of Urban Affairs, 29*(3), 311–329.
Putnam, R. D. (1993). *Making democracy work. Civic traditions in modern Italy*. Princeton: Princeton University Press.
Putnam, R. D. (2000). *Bowling alone. The collapse and revival of civic America*. New York: Simon & Schuster.
Putnam, R. D. (2007). *E Pluribus Unum*: Diversity and community in the twenty-first century – The 2006 Johan Skytte prize lecture. *Scandinavian Political Studies, 30*(2), 137–174.
Rabe, B., & Taylor, M. (2010). Residential mobility, quality of neighborhood and life course events. *Journal of the Royal Statistical Society A, 173*(3), 531–555.
Raudenbush, S., & Sampson, R. (1999). Ecometrics: Towards a science of assessing ecological settings, with application to the systematic observations of neighbourhoods. *Sociological Methodology, 29*(1), 1–41.
Rossi, P. H. (1980 [1955]). *Why families move*. Beverly Hills/London: Sage.
Sampson, R., & Groves, W. B. (1989). Community structure and crime. Testing social-disorganization theory. *The American Journal of Sociology, 94*(4), 774–802.
Sampson, R. J., & Raudenbush, S. W. (1999). Systematic social observation of public spaces: A new look at disorder in urban neighborhoods. *The American Journal of Sociology, 105*(3), 603–651.
Sampson, R. J., Raudenbush, S. W., & Earls, F. (1997). Neighborhoods and violent crime: A multilevel study of collective efficacy. *Science, 277*(5328), 918–924.
Sampson, R., Morenoff, J. D., & Earls, F. (1999). Beyond social capital: Spatial dynamics of collective efficacy for children. *American Sociological Review, 64*(5), 633–660.
Schaake, K., Burgers, J., & Mulder, C. H. (2010). Ethnicity at the individual and neighborhood level as an explanation for moving out of the neighborhood. *Population Research and Policy Review, 29*(4), 593–608.
Shaw, C., & McKay, H. (1942). *Juvenile delinquency and urban areas*. Chicago: University of Chicago Press.
Siermann, C., Van Teeffelen, P., & Urlings, L. (2004). *Equivalentiefactoren*. The Hague: Statistics Netherlands.
Sjaastad, L. A. (1962). The costs and returns of human migration. *Journal of Political Economy, 70*(1), 80–93.
Smith, W. R., Frazee, S. G., & Davison, E. L. (2000). Furthering the integration of routineactivity and social disorganization theories: Small units of analysis and the study of street robbery as a diffusion process. *Criminology, 38*(2), 489–524.
South, S. J., & Crowder, K. D. (1997). Escaping distressed neighborhoods: Individual, community and metropolitan influences. *The American Journal of Sociology, 102*(4), 1040–1084.

Van der Land, M., & Doff, W. (2010). Voice, exit and efficacy: Dealing with perceived neighborhood decline without moving out. *Journal of Housing and the Built Environment, 25*(4), 429–445.
Van Ham, M. (2012). Housing behaviour. In D. Clapham, W. A. V. Clark & K. Gibb (Eds.), *Handbook of housing studies*. Chapter 4. London: Sage.
Van Ham, M., & Clark, W. A. V. (2009). Neighborhood mobility in context: Household moves and changing neighborhoods in the Netherlands. *Environment and Planning A, 41*(6), 1442–1459.
Van Ham, M., & Feijten, P. (2008). Who wants to leave the neighborhood? The effect of being different from the neighborhood population on wishes to move. *Environment and Planning A, 40*(5), 1151–1170.
Wellman, B. (1979). The community question. The intimate networks of east Yorkers. *The American Journal of Sociology, 85*(5), 1201–1231.
Wilson, W. J. (1996). *When work disappears. The world of the new urban poor*. New York: Alfred Knopf.
Wolpert, J. (1965). Behavioral aspects of the decision to migrate. *Papers in Regional Science, 15*(1), 159–169.

Chapter 8
Neighbourhood Reputations, Moving Behaviour and Neighbourhood Dynamics

Matthieu Permentier

Introduction

> "A bad reputation haunts a neighbourhood"
> "Reputation still bothers problem neighbourhoods"
> "Neighbourhoods visibly improved, but do potential residents see that?"
> (Headlines from newspaper articles in national newspapers, AD 2008 and Trouw 2007)

Over the last few years, an increasing amount of attention has been paid to the role that neighbourhood reputations have in our understanding of neighbourhood dynamics. There are several reasons behind this development. First, a considerable amount of academic research has emerged that suggests that living in deprived or stigmatised neighbourhoods might have negative consequences for its residents (the so-called neighbourhood effect) (Galster 2011). Not only is it thought that resident's well-being and self-image is affected by the neighbourhoods' reputation, but also that different social outcomes (social participation, gaining and keeping employment) are negatively impacted by the negative reputation of neighbourhoods (Wacquant 1993; Wilson 1996). For instance, it is believed that jobs are not offered to residents because of the stigma of the neighbourhood in which they reside. Potential employers perceive the stigma as is an indicator of the workers' values and norms. Second, certain neighbourhoods are thought to be in low demand owing to, among other factors, their external reputation. Many professionals consider this to be a problem, because these unpopular neighbourhoods receive a disproportionate inflow of deprived residents which, in turn, is believed to exacerbate the number and intensity of the neighbourhood's problems. Furthermore, the longevity of negative neighbourhood perceptions can hamper regeneration efforts. Many regeneration projects,

M. Permentier (✉)
The Netherlands Institute of Social Research/SCP,
P.O. Box 16164, 2500 BD The Hague, The Netherlands
e-mail: m.permentier@scp.nl

M. van Ham et al. (eds.), *Understanding Neighbourhood Dynamics: New Insights for Neighbourhood Effects Research*, DOI 10.1007/978-94-007-4854-5_8,

at least in Northwestern Europe, target middle and high-income groups. These projects are seen as a potential solution to the assumed neighbourhood effects: by introducing a socio-economic mix the impact of the neighbourhood on the life-chances of its residents should be reduced. However exactly these income groups may be reluctant to buy dwellings in a neighbourhood with a poor reputation. As a result, the creation of genuinely socially mixed neighbourhoods is unlikely to occur.

A third theme where neighbourhood reputations could be important relates to selective mobility. Neighbourhoods with poor reputations may experience a selective inflow of residents which in turn may lead to a further decline of the neighbourhood because only those with the least means end up entering neighbourhoods with the poorest reputations. Reputation is not only thought to affect the inflow of residents into a neighbourhood. It is equally likely that the outflow of residents from a neighbourhood will be highly selective as well. As a result specific groups of individuals may be removed from neighbourhoods with the poorest reputations, reproducing the factors that lead to the poorest reputation in the first place. Leaving the neighbourhood would thus not only be affected by whether or not residents are satisfied with their neighbourhood, but also by how they think that other city residents assess their neighbourhood: the perceived external reputation of the neighbourhood.

Before discussing the subject any further, it is important to determine how the term "neighbourhood reputation" will be used in this chapter. Reputation "refers to the meaning and esteem that residents and other involved parties attribute to a neighbourhood. Reputation also refers to the relatively stable image a neighbourhood has among city residents and to its' place in the urban neighbourhood hierarchy" (Hortulanus 1995, p. 42: author's translation from Dutch). The self-image of people is strongly affected by the way they believe others see and think of them and the groups they themselves belong to (Goffman 1963; Mead 1934; Ridgeway 2006). Repeatedly, studies have found an effect of negative neighbourhood reputations on the self-image of residents of neighbourhoods with poor reputations (Bush et al. 2001; Hastings and Dean 2003; Taylor 1998; Wacquant 1993). The impact of the neighbourhood's reputation on the self has to be placed in a context in which neighbourhoods function increasingly as status symbols. The place where one lives is a reflection of one's position in society and one's preferences (Bourdieu 1984; Forrest and Kearns 2001). If people believe that their status suffers as a consequence of belonging to a specific group (such as through living in a certain neighbourhood) they are likely to try to disassociate themselves from that group. Thus, those living in neighbourhoods with a poor (perceived) reputation can therefore be expected to be more likely to have the intention to leave their neighbourhood than people living in neighbourhoods with a good reputation.

In this chapter I study moving intentions rather than actual moves. Actual mobility behaviour only occurs when there are no restrictions or constraints preventing an intention from being realised. By focusing on actual moving behaviour, all those people who have the intention to leave their neighbourhood, but are unable to do so because of housing market constraints and the direct and indirect monetary and non-monetary costs involved in moving would be missed. Studying moving intentions provides a direct insight in how neighbourhood reputations affect mobility decisions (van Ham and Feijten 2008).

At present there is relatively little knowledge about whether and how neighbourhood reputations impact the (size of the) in- and out- flow of neighbourhood residents. In the context of this chapter, I therefore specifically focus on the impact of neighbourhood reputations on people's intentions to move. The underlying mechanisms of moving intentions (what aspects of the neighbourhood trigger residents to leave?) will give us insight into processes of neighbourhood sorting and will lead to important cues for the success of urban renewal projects. If perceived reputation triggers moving intentions, improving the neighbourhood satisfaction of residents will most likely be insufficient to transform deprived neighbourhoods into attractive places to live. To be successful, neighbourhoods should also have a good – or at least not a bad – reputation.

Definition of Reputation

Walter Firey reported in 1945 that, besides functional, social, and economic dimensions, neighbourhoods also have a symbolic and sentimental dimension. Firey's example of Beacon Hill (Boston) shows that certain neighbourhoods have a certain reputation among both residents inside and outside the neighbourhood and that the neighbourhood stands as a symbol for certain values. The concept of neighbourhood reputation consists of several elements.

First, and in line with other authors, I argue that the collective shared view is an important feature of the concept of reputation: the individual view of only one or a few people does not constitute a reputation. A reputation is an image shared by a significant number of individuals. Consequently, the same neighbourhood can have multiple reputations: certain groups (with different socio-demographic characteristics) may see a neighbourhood as a highly-impoverished no-go area, whereas others would assess the same neighbourhood as a place full of potential (Suttles 1968). Second, reputations are thought to differ between residents and non-residents (Arthurson 2001; Hastings and Dean 2003; Murie et al. 2003). The internal reputation, that is the reputation held among the residents of a neighbourhood, is often thought to be rated higher than the external reputation, the reputation among other city residents. An internal reputation will generally consist of a more detailed view based on the physical and social attributes of the neighbourhood than is possible for most external people. Residents often employ a micro hierarchy of areas within a neighbourhood of 'good' and 'bad' parts (Wakefield and McMullan 2005). The external reputation is based on less information and less personal experience than the internal reputation. The external reputation consists of simplified images shaped by exaggerated differences between neighbourhoods (Suttles 1972). Third, the reputation of a neighbourhood contains a stratification element: the reputation reflects the individual status of the residents. In other words: the neighbourhood can be used as an indicator and a symbol of residents' socio-cultural and/or socio-economic position in society and their preferences (Bourdieu 1984; Warner 1960). "So pervasive is this effect that residential location has frequently been used as one of the measures of an individual's position in the local prestige hierarchy" (Congalton 1969). The urban population assesses neighbourhoods and their residential groups in a relative manner, through which each neighbourhood is seen as with respect to other neighbourhoods. This positioning leads to a hierarchy in which different neighbourhoods are ranked both internally and externally (Suttles 1972).

This chapter adopts the definition of reputation proposed by Hortulanus (1995, p. 42; and see discussion above), because it incorporates most of the previously-discussed elements. In contrast with the concept of stigma, reputation is more neutral: Stigma indicates an anomaly, something that society considers unacceptable (Harvey 2001). Reputation, on the other hand, can have both positive and negative connotations.

Neighbourhood Reputations and Neighbourhood Effects

Before we deal with the main topic of this chapter, the relationship between neighbourhood reputations, neighbourhood dynamics and selective mobility, it is useful to discuss the role that neighbourhood reputations play in the neighbourhood effects debate. Neighbourhood reputations are not only thought to impact on how neighbourhoods develop (by influencing residential mobility patterns of residents), but also on the lives of people who live in notorious neighbourhoods.

In the literature on neighbourhood effects, there is a strong belief amongst proponents of the argument that the neighbourhood context plays an important role in a wide variety of social and economic outcomes for residents. These so-called neighbourhood effects are thought to occur in (mostly deprived) neighbourhoods where low-income groups and immigrants are concentrated (see for reviews on the neighbourhood effects discussion Dietz 2002; Ellen and Turner 1997; Friedrichs 1998; Galster 2005; Leventhal and Brooks-Gunn 2000; Sampson et al. 2002; van Ham et al. 2011). There is an ongoing debate about the extent of the neighbourhood effects and in which contexts for what groups these are most likely to occur (see for example van Ham and Manley 2010). In debates on the effect of the neighbourhood context on the behaviour of neighbourhood residents, a lot of attention is paid to the statistical relationships between the neighbourhood context (for instance the percentage of low-income households or percentage of ethnic minorities) and individual outcomes. Theories on the most widely discussed neighbourhood effects, such as socialisation, and social network theories, put social networks in neighbourhoods as the prime mechanism underlying neighbourhood effects. More recently, the role of a neighbourhood's reputation as an alternative mechanism that impacts on residents' outcomes and behaviour has been recognised (Galster 2003, 2007).

Most research on this topic examines the material and psychological disadvantages of living in a neighbourhood with a poor reputation (see for example Bauder 2002; Hastings and Dean 2003). It is argued that the chances of social participation external to the neighbourhood for people residing in neighbourhoods with a poor reputation, are limited due to the bad name their neighbourhood has (Bauder 2001, 2002;

Wacquant 1993). Residents from neighbourhoods with poor reputations experience discrimination in the job market (Wilson 1996) they are unable to obtain mortgages from banks, or can only do so under disadvantageous conditions (Aalbers 2005, 2012, this volume) and people's self-esteem can be damaged by living in a notorious area (Dean and Hastings 2000; Taylor 1998; Wacquant 1993). Airey (2003) reports that long-term residents believe their personal identities are stigmatised through a negative neighbourhood reputation, which can lead to psychosocial stress (see also Dean and Hastings 2000; Wacquant 1993; Wakefield and McMullan 2005). The (perceived) reputation of the neighbourhood affects people's well-being because the neighbourhood can be a source of social status that may provide a valuable psycho-social benefit to neighbourhood residents (Kearns et al. 2000; Wacquant 1993). White (1987, p. 267) argues that the reputation of neighbourhoods is of increasing importance to residents: "Neighbourhood can be an important way of maintaining status in a mobile society. (…) Increasingly community itself, along with the neighbourhood, is something consciously purchased through a market, a bundle of goods that comes with residence".

To understand the full scope of the effects of stigmatisation of neighbourhoods based on a poor neighbourhood reputation on residents lives requires an understanding of the role of neighbourhood reputation in the sorting process of (different) households into different neighbourhoods. In the rest of this chapter, I focus on how neighbourhood reputations might play a role in this process, by both focusing on the relationship between reputations and the outflow of residents and the inflow of residents in different neighbourhoods. This knowledge can improve our understanding of migration flows and how neighbourhoods change might be related to the reputations of these neighbourhoods.

Neighbourhood Reputation and Migration Flows

Neighbourhood Reputations and Inflow

In this chapter the relationship between neighbourhood reputations and mobility out of the neighbourhood is central. However, to understand selective mobility and neighbourhood dynamics one must also pay attention to the settling process of people into different neighbourhoods. In the literature there is some knowledge on neighbourhood reputations and the inflow of groups into neighbourhoods. The decision not to move and relocate into certain urban neighbourhoods with a negative reputation among non-residents is one of the more well-known studied mechanisms. A good example of this from the American literature (Clark 1991) is the process of white avoidance whereby white residents searching for a new residential neighbourhood will avoid those neighbourhoods that have high proportions of non-white residents. This process has been found to exert a significant influence on the racial composition of urban neighbourhoods. Developing on ideas of Schelling (1969, 1971), Clark carried out different studies (1991, 1992) that have shown the preference of white Americans for predominantly white neighbourhood and the impact of this preference on racial composition of neighbourhoods. Another example comes from the literature around blocking strategies. Based on the reputation of (bad) neighbourhoods, institutions may develop strategies to deal with such neighbourhoods and their residents. A prime example, again from the American literature, relates to the process whereby actors try to prevent certain groups from stigmatised neighbourhoods entering highly regarded up-market urban neighbourhoods, thus avoiding changes in the neighbourhood composition (Wyly 2002). Much discussion surrounds realtors who serve as gatekeepers, seeking to 'preserve' white neighbourhoods from an influx of people from stigmatised (Afro-American) areas by steering individuals from these areas to certain other parts of the city (Galster and Godfrey 2005).

Neighbourhood Reputations and Outflow

Neighbourhood (dis)satisfaction is often reported as one of the key predictors of moving intentions (Clark and Ledwith 2006; Lee et al. 1994; Lu 1998). According to Speare's classical study (1974) residential satisfaction is a significant predictor of moving even when controlling for socio-demographic characteristics of the residents. Besides the assessment of the neighbourhood by residents themselves, the assessments of the neighbourhood by other city residents can also play a role in shaping people's intention to leave their neighbourhood. Mead (1934) has argued that the self-image of people is influenced by the way they perceive that others think of them and the group that they belong to (see also Festinger 1954; Goffman 1963). Living in a neighbourhood with a poorly perceived reputation can have a negative effect on the self-image of individuals, even when they themselves are generally satisfied with their neighbourhood. Ultimately, ideas about how outsiders see a neighbourhood may lead to people's intention to leave the neighbourhood.

Although neighbourhood reputations are likely to have a substantial impact on residential mobility (Semyonov and Kraus 1982) and the dynamics of neighbourhoods, the literature on residential mobility seldom includes the neighbourhood's reputation as an explanatory variable. This is surprising, since many academics stress the function that the residential address has as an indicator of the social status of an individual (Coleman and Neugarten 1972; Firey 1945; Forrest and Kearns 2001; Suttles 1972). The neighbourhood is more than just the location of the dwelling: it represents a consumable good, symbolising an individual's prestige (Bourdieu 1984). Moving to a neighbourhood with a better reputation can improve a person's individual status and self-image and consequently their general well-being.

Tsfati and Cohen (2003) investigated the link between residential mobility and neighbourhood reputation across a number of towns in Israel. Including neighbourhood perception in their model, they found that the way residents perceive the image of their town (among externals) has an independent effect on their thinking about residential mobility over and above the effect of satisfaction with the living conditions. The reasoning behind this is that the self-image of people is strongly affected by the way they believe others see them and the groups they belong to. When an individual believes that their status suffers from membership to a certain group, they will try to disassociate themselves from that group. Of course, that is not possible when someone is stigmatised on the basis of an ascribed characteristic (such as gender and race). However, when an individual feels that they are stigmatised on the basis of place of residence, there is the possibility to disassociate from fellow residents by moving out of the neighbourhood.

The study by Tsfati and Cohen (2003) does not deal with the fact that people are not randomly sorted into towns but select themselves according their preferences and resources. People who find the reputation of their town very important are less likely to decide to live in a town with a poor reputation. It can be expected that this mechanism of self-selection decreases the effect of perceived reputation on moving intentions. Self-selection can affect moving intentions in two ways. First, the degree of choice people had in selecting their dwelling and neighbourhood is likely to have an impact on moving intentions. It can be argued that individuals who perceived a high degree of choice when they selected their neighbourhood are less likely to want to leave the neighbourhood compared to individuals who were more limited in their choice set. It should be noted that people with little choice may still be less likely to express an intention to move as a result of a poor neighbourhood reputation due to the difficulty of improving their situation in the housing market (see Festinger 1957 on cognitive dissonance reduction). Second, people who are very status-conscious are likely to have already selected themselves into a neighbourhood with a good reputation which positively reflects on their self-image (see De Jong and Fawcett 1981). Those less affected by status considerations are also less likely to select a neighbourhood based on its reputation. There is, therefore a complex set of interactions between neighbourhood reputation and individual satisfaction which are multidirectional.

Investigating Neighbourhood Reputations and Moving Intentions

To investigate the relationship between neighbourhood reputations and moving intentions we used individual-level data from our own survey, which was specifically designed to understand this relationship. The survey was carried out in the spring of 2006, in the city of Utrecht in the Netherlands. Utrecht is a compact city with 281,011 residents (GBA City of Utrecht 2006), and it has a diverse range of neighbourhoods in terms of population composition. Compared with the two largest cities in the Netherlands (Amsterdam and Rotterdam), the relatively large proportion of medium and highly-educated residents in Utrecht is striking (in 2004: 69.4%, Rotterdam: 47%; and Amsterdam, 56.4%). Utrecht has a large university and graduates find the city centre and surrounding neighbourhoods to be attractive residential environments. Partly as a result of the university connection, the city has a high percentage of residents under the age of 25. Compared with the other three cities, Utrecht has a low percentage of non-Western immigrants; 23.8% in 2006 compared

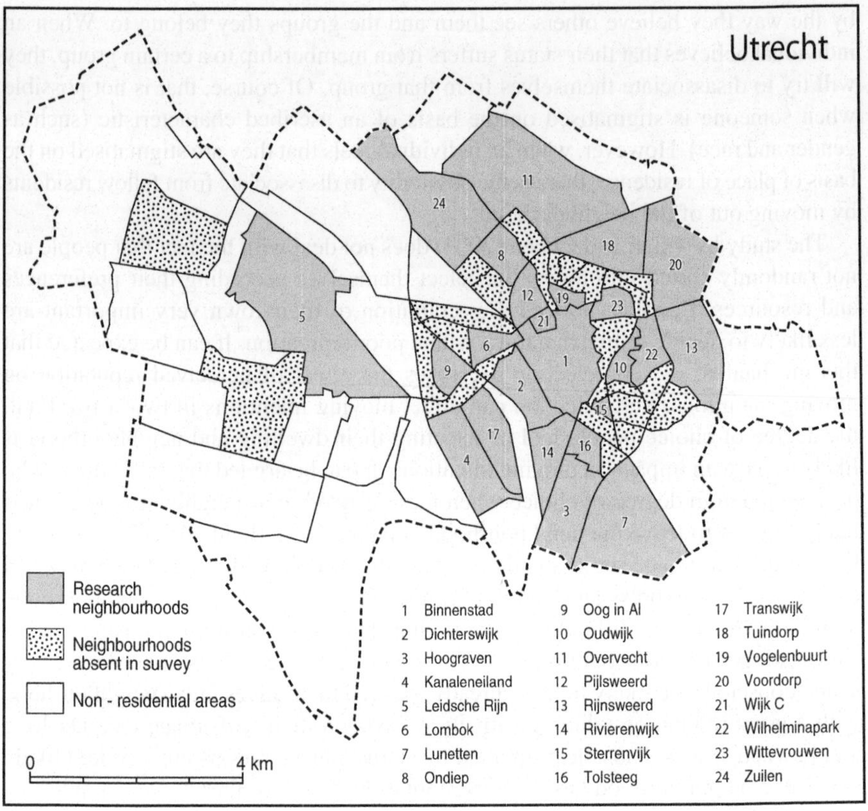

Fig. 8.1 Research neighbourhoods in the City of Utrecht

with 34.3% in Amsterdam, 35.4% in Rotterdam, and 32.2% in The Hague (GBA City of Utrecht 2006; O+S Amsterdam 2006). The segregation index of non-Western immigrants is similar to that of the three other cities; Utrecht, 37.4; Amsterdam, 36.3; Rotterdam, 38.5; The Hague, 46.1 (Bolt et al. 2006).

The survey data provides information on individual and household characteristics, including information on housing, the perceived reputation of the neighbourhood, general satisfaction with the area, and moving intentions. The survey was carried out using a random sample of addresses in 24 Utrecht neighbourhoods (see Fig. 8.1). These neighbourhoods consist of 69% of the total Utrecht population. The neighbourhoods were selected on the basis of a small telephone survey. In each sampled household, either the head of the household or his/her partner was asked to fill out a questionnaire. Both the distribution and collection of questionnaires took place in person. The neighbourhood Kanaleneiland – with the worst reputation in the city – was over-sampled because in future research we want to focus on this particular area. Because of the oversampling we weighted the data.

For the analysis we selected all respondents between 18 and 94 years old, excluding people living in institutions. We also excluded cases with missing information on key variables. This selection resulted in a sample of 1,339 respondents. Since residents are likely to define their neighbourhood-borders in different ways, we did not pre-define neighbourhoods in our questionnaire. Respondents decided what to consider as their neighbourhood. According to several authors (Lee et al. 1994; Lu 1998) using pre-defined neighbourhoods would probably lead to a distortion of the empirical findings.

Summary statistics for the dependent and independent variables of the models are given in Table 8.1. We constructed a binary dependent variable 'intention to move out of the neighbourhood' by combining two survey questions (a) "Do you plan to move within the next 2 years?" (b) "Are you planning to move within the neighbourhood?". Respondents who answered the first question with 'yes' and the second question with 'no' were considered to have the intention to leave the neighbourhood (1) while all others were considered not to have the intention to leave (0). According to this definition, 299 respondents (22.3 %) had the intention to leave their neighbourhood. Since the dependent variable was binary we used logistic regression models. Because individual respondents are clustered in neighbourhoods we used cluster correction to correct for potential bias in the standard errors of some coefficients. Perceived reputation of the neighbourhood is measured by using the survey question: "Please indicate on a 5-point scale (very negative to very positive), how you think that other city residents assess the reputation of your neighbourhood".

As well as reputation we also included several other independent variables in the model: neighbourhood satisfaction, different individual and family background characteristics, choice variables for dwelling and neighbourhood and neighbourhood characteristics and neighbourhood attachment.

Neighbourhood Reputation and Moving Intentions

Table 8.2 presents the results of six stepwise logistic regressions, estimating an individual's intention to leave the neighbourhood. Model 1 includes the main individual level characteristics. Age is negatively associated with intentions to leave the neighbourhood: the older people are the lower the likelihood that they intent to leave their neighbourhood. Wealthier households are more likely to leave a neighbourhood than poorer households. People who are dissatisfied with their dwelling are more likely to express the intention to leave compared to people who are satisfied.

In model 2, neighbourhood characteristics are included, and they appear to have a limited impact on the intention to move out of the neighbourhood. In model 3 we introduce the perceived neighbourhood reputation as an explanatory variable of moving intentions. As expected, those who hold a positive perception of the reputation of their neighbourhood are less likely to express an intention to move than people who perceive the reputation of their neighbourhood to be negative. After controlling for perceived neighbourhood reputation the effect of the ethnic composition of the

Table 8.1 Variable summary statistics of the weighted data (N = 1,339)

	N (%)	Mean (S.d.)	Min./Max.
Intention to leave neighbourhood (dependent)	299 (22.3)		
Female	709 (54.1)		
Age		44.35 (14.81)	19–94
Household type			
Single person household	364 (27.2)		
Single parent household	74 (5.5)		
Couple	436 (32.6)		
Couple with children	385 (28.7)		
Other[a]	80 (6.0)		
Ethnicity[b]			
Belonging to ethnic minority	166 (12.4)		
Not belonging to ethnic minority	1,173 (87.6)		
Level of education[c]			
Low	284 (21.2)		
Middle	374 (28.0)		
High	681 (50.8)		
Unemployed[d]	429 (32.1)		
Monthly household income (*€100)		22.33 (9.58)	1.8–38
Owner-occupant	783 (58.5)		
Dwelling satisfaction		7.55 (1.40)	1–10
Persons/per room-ratio		0.60 (0.30)	0.1–2
Flat/apartment	399 (28.8)		
Length of residency			
Living in neighbourhood 0–3 years	362 (27.0)		
Living in neighbourhood 4–7 years	322 (24.1)		
Living in neighbourhood 8–16 years	325 (24.3)		
Living in neighbourhood 17 years and over	330 (24.6)		
NBH Percentage ethnic minorities[e]		27.37 (17.67)	5.35–73.43
NBH Average household income (year)		28.47 (5.12)	23.3–45.0
NBH Crime rates		112.87 (30.55)	13.7–174.9
NBH Housing density		3,212.88 (1047.29)	928–5,546
Perceived neighbourhood reputation		3.2 (1.0)	1–5
Current dwelling first choice	974 (72.8)		
Current neighbourhood first choice	371 (27.8)		
Sensitivity to social neighbourhood status		0	–3.4 – 2.7
Sensitivity to general social status		0	–2.7 – 4.1
Neighbourhood satisfaction		6.99 (1.52)	1 – 10
Neighbourhood attachment (emotional)		0	–2.5 – 1.8
Most friends live in neighbourhood	102 (7.6)		

(continued)

Table 8.1 (continued)

	N (%)	Mean (S.d.)	Min./Max.
Family lives in neighbourhood	313 (23.4)		
Contact with neighbours	1,038 (77.6)		
Member of neighbourhood committee	127 (9.5)		

[a]For example, households with cohabiting grandparents

[b]Ethnic minorities are defined as people who categorise themselves as member of an ethnic group from Africa, Asia; Latin America; Turkey; Surinam or the Dutch Antilles

[c]Defined as the respondent's highest completed level of education (low = primary education + lower vocational training; middle = secondary education/high school, middle vocational training; high = higher vocational training + university)

[d]Individuals whose main activity is working part-time or full-time are categorised 'employed'. Others, including students are categorised 'unemployed'

[e]Defined as share of people in the neighbourhood born in, or with at least one parent born in: Africa, Asia, Latin America, Turkey, Surinam or the Dutch Antilles

neighbourhood is no longer significant. This indicates that neighbourhood characteristics only have an indirect effect on an individual's intention to move through perceived neighbourhood reputation. Other findings by Permentier and colleagues (2011) already suggested that ethnic composition is a significant and strong predictor of perceived reputation.

In model 4 we introduce a set of variables that control for selection effects. These variables measure three important aspects from the theoretical literature. The first variable measures the amount of choice the individual perceived they had in the selection of their neighbourhood and dwelling. The second variables measures an individual's sensitivity to the reputation of their neighbourhood and the third variable measures the sensitivity of an individual to status in general. By including these variables we control the effect of perceived reputation as found in model 3 for self-selection into neighbourhoods linked to neighbourhood reputation and status. As expected, individuals who moved into their dwelling and neighbourhood of choice are less likely to express an intention to move out of their neighbourhood than people who experienced less choice. The results also show that people who are sensitive to the status of neighbourhoods are far more likely to express the intention to leave their neighbourhood than people who are not sensitive to neighbourhood status. Sensitivity to general social status, on the other hand, does not appear to be relevant as it has no significant independent impact on the intention to leave.

It may be expected that a neighbourhood with a poorly perceived reputation affects moving intentions of individuals who are sensitive to social status of neighbourhoods in general. The introduction of an interaction term between perceived neighbourhood reputation and sensitivity to neighbourhood social status did not yield any significant results (results not shown). This result shows that when considering a move out of the neighbourhood, the perceived reputation is important for residents regardless of their sensitivity to social status. This is a finding that needs further investigation. For instance, this result could demonstrate that the effect we found for perceived reputation is merely one dimension of neighbourhood satisfaction?

Table 8.2 Logistic regression of the intention to leave the neighbourhood (N = 1,339)

	Model 1			Model 2		
	B	S.E.	EXP(B)	B	S.E.	**EXP(B)**
Constant	0.729	0.586		0.595	1.022	
Female (ref = male)	–0.057	0.195	0.944	–0.049	0.201	0.952
Age	–0.027	0.007***	0.974	–0.024	0.007***	0.976
Household type (ref = single)						
Single parent household	0.348	0.346	1.416	0.237	0.312	1.268
Couple	0.094	0.363	1.099	–0.042	0.350	0.959
Couple with children	–0.754	0.526	0.471	–1.012	0.486**	0.363
Other	0.008	0.239	1.008	0.127	0.248	1.135
Belonging to ethnic minority (ref = no)	–0.189	0.306	0.827	–0.474	0.303	0.622
Level of education (ref = low)						
Middle education	–0.077	0.165	0.926	–0.052	0.174	0.950
High education	0.334	0.247	1.397	0.548	0.272**	1.729
Unemployed (ref = employed)	0.066	0.207	1.068	0.059	0.215	1.060
Household income	0.034	0.016**	1.035	0.041	0.017**	1.042
Owner-occupant (ref = renter)	–0.277	0.179	0.758	–0.228	0.187	0.796
Dwelling satisfaction	–0.273	0.061***	0.761	–0.245	0.061***	0.783
Person/room ratio	0.409	0.351	1.505	0.725	0.342**	2.065
Flat/apartment (ref = other)	0.184	0.256	1.202	–0.114	0.263	0.892
Length of residency (ref = <4)						
4–7 years	0.483	0.258*	1.621	0.417	0.260	1.518
8–16 years	0.408	0.262	1.504	0.464	0.261*	1.590
17 and more	0.210	0.450	1.234	0.210	0.482	1.234
NBH percentage ethnic minorities				0.018	0.005***	1.018
NBH average household income				–0.027	0.021	0.974
NBH crime rates				0.001	0.003	1.001
NBH housing density				0.000	0.000	1.000
Perceived neighbourhood reputation						

Current dwelling first choice (ref = other)						
Current neighbourhood first choice (ref = other)						
Sensitivity to social neighbourhood status						
Sensitivity to general social status						
Neighbourhood satisfaction						
Neighbourhood attachment (emotional)						
Most friends live in neighbourhood (ref = no)						
Family lives in neighbourhood (ref = no)						
Contact with neighbours (ref = no)						
Member of neighbourhood committee (ref = no)						
Log-likelihood	–653.430			–638.880		
Improvement (wald)	331.470	p = 0.000		28.030	p = 0.000	
Nagelkerke R-Square	0.127			0.157		
Initial	–711.330					
	Model 3			Model 4		
	B	S.E.	EXP(B)	B	S.E.	EXP(B)
Constant	0.888	1.022		0.555	1.1	
Female (ref = male)	–0.040	0.205	0.961			
Age	–0.023	0.007***	0.977	–0.012	0.244	0.988
Household type (ref = single)				–0.02	0.006***	0.98
Single parent household	0.260	0.373	1.300			
Couple	–0.092	0.343	0.912	0.262	0.386	1.299
Couple with children	–1.038	0.459**	0.354	–0.072	0.357	0.931
Other	0.177	0.276	1.193	–1.012	0.473**	0.363
Belonging to ethnic minority (ref = no)	–0.334	0.305	0.716	0.138	0.231	1.148
Level of education (ref = low)				–0.476	0.392	0.621
Middle education	–0.053	0.165	0.948			
High education	0.520	0.290*	1.682	–0.17	0.167	0.844

(continued)

Table 8.2 (continued)

	Model 3			Model 4		
	B	S.E.	EXP(B)	B	S.E.	EXP(B)
Unemployed (ref = employed)	0.076	0.225	1.079	0.457	0.298	1.579
Household income	0.043	0.017**	1.044	0.097	0.212	1.102
Owner-occupant (ref = renter)	−0.156	0.203	0.855	0.041	0.018**	1.042
Dwelling satisfaction	−0.225	0.065***	0.800	−0.127	0.21	0.881
Person/room ratio	0.714	0.334**	2.041	−0.166	0.066**	0.847
Flat/apartment (ref = other)	−0.034	0.280	0.966	0.716	0.348**	2.045
Length of residency (ref = <4)				−0.06	0.23	0.942
4–7 years	0.347	0.274	1.416			
8–16 years	0.434	0.265	1.543	0.407	0.279	1.503
17 and more	0.161	0.465	1.175	0.485	0.266*	1.625
NBH percentage ethnic minorities	0.009	0.006	1.009	0.226	0.428	1.253
NBH average household income	0.005	0.018	1.005	0.008	0.006	1.008
NBH crime rates	0.000	0.003	1.000	0.007	0.019	1.007
NBH housing density	0.000	0.000	1.000	0.001	0.003	1.001
Perceived neighbourhood reputation	−0.501	0.096***	0.606	0	0	1
Current dwelling first choice (ref = other)				−0.486	0.083***	0.615
Current neighbourhood first choice (ref = other)				−0.467	0.236**	0.627
Sensitivity to social neighbourhood status				−0.504	0.277*	0.604
Sensitivity to general social status				0.158	0.056***	1.171
Neighbourhood satisfaction				0.173	0.178	1.188
Neighbourhood attachment (emotional)						
Most friends live in neighbourhood (ref = no)						
Family lives in neighbourhood (ref = no)						
Contact with neighbours (ref = no)						
Member of neighbourhood committee (ref = no)						

Log-likelihood	−624.750					
Improvement (wald)	27.390	p=0.000		−612.87		
Nagelkerke R-Square	0.185			29.44	p=0.000	
Initial				0.209		
	Model 5			Model 6		
	B	S.E.	EXP(B)	B	S.E.	EXP(B)
Constant	0.88	1.169		−1.074	1.671	
Female (ref=male)	−0.007	0.242	0.993	0.031	0.254	1.032
Age	−0.021	0.007***	0.979	−0.017	0.007***	0.984
Household type (ref=single)						
Single parent household	0.224	0.39	1.25	0.163	0.348	1.177
Couple	−0.095	0.354	0.909	−0.192	0.339	0.825
Couple with children	−0.998	0.486**	0.369	−0.895	0.457*	0.408
Other	0.158	0.24	1.171	0.043	0.273	1.044
Belonging to ethnic minority (ref=no)	−0.456	0.409	0.634	−0.293	0.392	0.746
Level of education (ref=low)						
Middle education	−0.146	0.174	0.864	−0.188	0.19	0.829
High education	0.503	0.307	1.653	0.554	0.373	1.741
Unemployed (ref=employed)	0.081	0.208	1.084	0.074	0.19	1.076
Household income	0.042	0.018**	1.043	0.047	0.018**	1.048
Owner-occupant (ref=renter)	−0.126	0.209	0.882	−0.073	0.198	0.929
Dwelling satisfaction	−0.097	0.09	0.908	−0.1	0.084	0.904
Person/room ratio	0.72	0.335**	2.055	0.857	0.389**	2.356
Flat/apartment (ref=other)	−0.043	0.216	0.958	−0.091	0.237	0.913
Length of residency (ref=<4)						
4–7 years	0.449	0.285	1.566	0.438	0.296	1.55
8–16 years	0.551	0.264**	1.736	0.646	0.286**	1.907
17 and more	0.27	0.428	1.309	0.437	0.394	1.547

(continued)

Table 8.2 (continued)

	Model 5			Model 6		
	B	S.E.	EXP(B)	B	S.E.	EXP(B)
NBH percentage ethnic minorities	0.006	0.005	1.006	0.005	0.005	1.005
NBH average household income	0.014	0.022	1.014	0.017	0.03	1.017
NBH crime rates	0.001	0.003	1.001	0.002	0.003	1.002
NBH housing density	0	0	1	0	0	1
Perceived neighbourhood reputation	−0.375	0.108***	0.687	−0.298	0.110***	0.742
Current dwelling first choice (ref = other)	−0.452	0.249*	0.637	−0.158	0.268	0.853
Current neighbourhood first choice (ref = other)	−0.424	0.283	0.654	−0.307	0.253	0.736
Sensitivity to social neighbourhood status	0.143	0.056***	1.154	0.173	0.074**	1.188
Sensitivity to general social status	0.143	0.167	1.153	0.158	0.172	1.172
Neighbourhood satisfaction	−0.212	0.097**	0.809	−0.052	0.09	0.95
Neighbourhood attachment (emotional)				−0.521	0.130***	0.594
Most friends live in neighbourhood (ref = no)				−0.863	0.456*	0.422
Family lives in neighbourhood (ref = no)				0.201	0.325	1.223
Contact with neighbours (ref = no)				−0.497	0.193***	0.608
Member of neighbourhood committee (ref = no)				−0.141	0.277	0.869
Log-likelihood						
Improvement (wald)	−607.14			−586.51		
Nagelkerke R-Square	4.79	p = 0.029		32.01	p = 0.000	
Initial	0.22			0.26		

This table has been previously published as Table 3 in: Permentier et al. (2009, p. 2172–2173), *= $p < 0.10$, **= $p < 0.05$, ***= $p < 0.01$

There are a number of reasons why this might not be the case. First of all the magnitude of the correlations (between neighbourhood satisfaction and perceived reputation) does not indicate a high risk of multicollinearity and confirms that the concept of perceived neighbourhood reputation truly differs from the concept of neighbourhood satisfaction. If perceived reputation were merely one dimension of neighbourhood satisfaction then multicollinearity would be expected. Second, although controlling for neighbourhood satisfaction has a clear impact on the effect of perceived neighbourhood reputation this latter variable is still highly significant. This is shown in model 5, where introducing satisfaction with the neighbourhood decreases the effect of reputation, but does not eliminate the impact of reputation on moving intentions. The latter effect remains even after introducing several variables that indicate a person's attachment (both emotional and social) with the neighbourhood (model 6). Most spectacularly, after including neighbourhood attachment, also the effect of neighbourhood satisfaction disappears. This indicates that satisfaction is likely to be channelled through the emotional neighbourhood attachment variable: residents who feel attached to the neighbourhood are also the ones most satisfied with their neighbourhood. Again, the effect of the perceived neighbourhood reputation on moving intention drops a little, but remains significant. This result is important, as it shows that the concept of perceived neighbourhood reputation as conceptualised in this chapter is a useful addition to more established explanations of residential mobility.

Discussion

While it has been acknowledged that, in the present network-society, the daily life of individuals is no longer wholly centred in their area of residence, the neighbourhood continues to play an important role in their lives (Wellman 1996; Kearns and Parkinson 2001; Blokland 2003). One attribute of the neighbourhood that has attracted recent interest is its' reputation. This rise in interest is related in part to the need among policymakers to understand what type of neighbourhoods make successful living environments, what types do not (and why), and what type of neighbourhoods are most likely to acquire negative reputations. Through a survey of neighbourhoods in Utrecht in the Netherlands, it was shown that a negative perception increases the chance that residents will express an intention to leave the neighbourhood. The results show that even though a person might be satisfied, or was even initially attached to their neighbourhood, an intention to move can develop if that neighbourhood acquires a negative reputation.

These results are important, because they give insight into not only the mechanisms responsible for changes in the socio-spatial structure of the urban landscape, but also the stability of urban neighbourhoods. We know for example that people who perceive their neighbourhood's reputation to be negative express an intention to leave their area. If those intentions are translated into actual moves by selective groups of residents (for example by better off households), then the dynamics of neighbourhoods are influenced by the neighbourhood's reputation. Selective groups would leave (and probably enter) specific types of neighbourhoods based on (among other things) the perceived reputation of the neighbourhood. In this way, reputation is an influencing factor of the socio-spatial structure of cities. Changing the underlying causes of the perceived reputation of a neighbourhood could result in more affluent residents expressing an intention to stay, thus creating a more sustainable neighbourhood with a greater diversity of residents. Successful regeneration is however not just about the current residents, but also about making neighbourhoods attractive for other city residents (see below).

There are, therefore, a number of issues relating to neighbourhood reputations that need to be further explored. Although this chapter has shown us insights into the relationship between neighbourhood reputations and residential mobility intentions, some points needs further consideration. Below I identify four aspects that deserve greater attention if the ways in which neighbourhoods are constructed are to be better understood. First more attention should be paid to what type of residents are most likely to be influenced by poor neighbourhood reputations. Equally another unknown issue concerns whether the social status of neighbourhoods is equally important to all, or are certain groups (for example high income groups) more sensitive than other (low- and middle income) groups? If such differences occur, then it is to be expected that reputations will contribute to the selective mobility out of certain neighbourhoods (and to neighbourhood changes).

Second, longitudinal data that follows over time and can trace not only which neighbourhoods they leave, but also the neighbourhoods they enter. Research on how neighbourhood reputations affect the neighbourhood choice of residents is not well understood not well developed. Such research could provide us with a more complete picture of how reputations not only influence what neighbourhoods people leave, but also what type of neighbourhoods they avoid as a consequence of those neighbourhood's reputations. This will increase our understanding of the effects of neighbourhood reputations on the dynamics of neighbourhoods, and can help to develop a more comprehensive understanding of how reputations play a role in the future developments of neighbourhoods.

Third, considering the issue of the inflow of individuals into various neighbourhoods we need more information about how neighbourhood regeneration projects are influenced by the notorious name of neighbourhoods. Some of the regeneration efforts are introduced to improve the socio-economic status and reputation of neighbourhoods. However we know from several studies (for example Hastings and Dean 2003) that changing the reputation (and by result, changing the inflow and outflow of residents) can be a complicated matter. Nevertheless, urban professionals have introduced various policies targeted at improving reputations. These policies may consist, for example, of improving the physical appearance of a neighbourhood and changing its social composition by introducing a social mix or even by utilising marketing instruments, such as the branding of neighbourhoods and changing the official name of the neighbourhood (for example see the rebranding the Gorbals, Glasgow in Scotland as Hutchinsontown in conjunction with a large scale urban regeneration project). The lack of evidence of the success of dealing with negative reputations through urban regeneration indicates that reputations are not easily changed and that labels do not simply alter even after intensive physical renewal (see for instance Meen 2012). In this regard, a systematic study that investigates to what extent these policy efforts have been successful in improving these reputations of residential areas is inadequate. What is needed is a study that follows the perception of neighbourhoods by residents and non-residents over time (before and after an intervention) to ascertain whether these policy approaches are effective.

Finally, future work should focus more on how neighbourhood reputations influence not only the selection mechanisms into different neighbourhoods along with how neighbourhood reputations can affect the social outcomes of neighbourhood residents such as getting a job. It would be of interest to investigate whether a poor neighbourhood reputation may affect the willingness of employers to hire people from infamous areas. But even more so whether the reputation has a detrimental effect on neighbourhood contacts and area cohesion. For example a notorious reputation could create distrust between neighbourhood residents. The distrust may decrease social ties within the neighbourhood, preventing people to share information on for instance jobs and education. In turn because of a lack of transfer of social capital between residents the potential of upward social mobility of the neighbourhood residents might be affected by the reputation of the neighbourhood. Similarly research should focus on the effect of reputations on residents' networks outside the neighbourhoods. Wacquant (1993) suggested that living in 'bad' neighbourhoods hamper ties with people outside of the neighbourhood. It would be instructive to study whether this is true and, if true, whether the social networks (and the transfer of capital) of stigmatized residents is more limited compared to residents who live in better neighbourhoods.

Acknowledgements This chapter is based on my Ph.D. thesis: Reputation, neighbourhoods and behaviour (Permentier 2009).

References

Aalbers, M. (2005). Who's afraid of red, yellow and green? Redlining in Rotterdam. *Geoforum, 36*(5), 562–580.

Aalbers, M. (2012). How do mortgage lenders influence neighbourhood dynamics? Redlining and predatory lending. In M. van Ham, D. Manley, N. Bailey, L. Simpson, & D. Maclennan (Eds.), *Understanding neighbourhood dynamics: New insights for neighbourhood effects research* (pp. xx–xx). Dordrecht: Springer.

AD. (2008). *Hotspots. Zichtbaar verbeterde wijken, maar zien potentiële bewoners dat? – Imago zit probleembuurten nog flink dwars* [Hotspots. Neighbourhoods visibly improved, but do potential residents see that? Reputation still bothers problem neighbourhoods]. AD, January 17, 2008.

Airey, L. (2003). 'Nae as nice as scheme as it used to be': Lay accounts of neighbourhood incivilities and well-being. *Health & Place, 9*(2), 129–137.

Arthurson, K. (2001). Achieving social justice in estate regeneration: The impact of physical image construction. *Housing Studies, 16*(6), 807–826.

Bauder, H. (2001). You're good with your hands, why don't you become an auto mechanic': Neighborhood context, institutions and career development. *International Journal of Urban and Regional Research, 25*(3), 593–608.

Bauder, H. (2002). Neighbourhood effects and cultural exclusion. *Urban Studies, 39*(1), 85–93.
Blokland, T. (2003). *Urban bonds. Social relationships in an inner city neighbourhood.* Cambridge: Polity Press.
Bolt, G., van Ham, M., & van Kempen, R. (2006). Allochtonen op de woningmarkt. ruimtelijke Segregatie en verhuisdynamiek [Immigrants on the housing market. Spatial segregation and migration dynamics]. In F. van Tubergen & I. Maas (Eds.), *Allochtonen in Nederland in international perspectief* [Immigrants in the Netherlands from an international perspective]. Amsterdam: Amsterdam University Press.
Bourdieu, P. (1984). *Distinction: A social critique of the judgment of taste.* Cambridge: Harvard University Press.
Bush, J., Moffatt, S., & Dunn, C. (2001). 'Even the birds round here cough': Stigma, air pollution and health in Teesside. *Health & Place, 7*(1), 47–56.
Clark, W. A. V. (1991). Residential preferences and neighborhood racial segregation: A test of the Schelling segregation model. *Demography, 28*(1), 1–19.
Clark, W. A. V. (1992). Residential preferences and residential choices in a multiethnic context. *Demography, 29*(3), 451–466.
Clark, W. A. V., & Ledwith, V. (2006). Mobility, housing stress, and neighborhood contexts: Evidence from Los Angeles. *Environment and Planning A, 38*(6), 1077–1093.
Coleman, R. P., & Neugarten, B. L. (1972). *Social status in the city.* San Francisco: Jossey-Bass.
Congalton, A. A. (1969). *Status and prestige in Australia.* Melbourne: Cheshire.
De Jong, G. F., & Fawcett, J. (1981). Motivations for migration: An assessment and value-expectancy research model. In G. F. De Jong & R. W. Gardner (Eds.), *Migration decision making: Multidisciplinary approaches to microlevel studies in developed and developing countries.* New York: Pergamon Press.
Dean, J., & Hastings, A. (2000). *Challenging images. Housing estates, stigma and regeneration.* Bristol: The Policy Press and Joseph Rowntree Foundation.
Dietz, R. (2002). The estimation of neighbourhood effects in the social sciences. An interdisciplinary approach. *Social Science Research, 31*(4), 539–575.
Ellen, I. G., & Turner, M. A. (1997). Does neighbourhood matter? Assessing recent evidence. *Housing Policy Debate, 8*(4), 833–866.
Festinger, L. (1954). A theory of social comparison processes. *Human Relations, 7*(2), 117–140.
Festinger, L. (1957). *A theory of cognitive dissonance.* Stanford: Stanford University Press.
Firey, W. (1945). Sentiment and symbolism as ecological variables. *American Sociological Review, 10*(2), 140–148.
Forrest, R., & Kearns, A. (2001). Social cohesion, social capital and the neighbourhood. *Urban Studies, 38*(12), 2125–2143.
Friedrichs, J. (1998). Do poor neighborhoods make their residents poorer? In H. Andress (Ed.), *Empirical poverty research in a comparative perspective.* Hants: Ashgate.
Galster, G. (2003). Investigating behavioural impacts of poor neighbourhoods: Towards new data and analytical strategies. *Housing Studies, 18*(6), 893–914.
Galster, G. (2005). *Neighborhood mix, social opportunities, and the policy challenges of an increasingly diverse Amsterdam.* Amsterdam: AMIDSt.
Galster, G. (2007). Should policy makers strive for neighborhood social mix? An analysis of the Western European evidence base. *Housing Studies, 22*(4), 523–545.
Galster, G. (2011). The mechanism(s) of neighbourhood effects. Theory, evidence, and policy implications. In M. van Ham et al. (Eds.), *Neighbourhood effects research: New perspectives.* Dordrecht: Springer.
Galster, G., & Godfrey, E. (2005). By words and deeds: Racial steering by real estate agents in the U.S. in 2000. *Journal of the American Planning Association, 71*(3), 251–268.
GBA City of Utrecht. (2006). *Buurtmonitor.* Available at http://utrecht.buurtmonitor.nl/. Accessed February 20, 2006.
Goffman, E. (1963). *Stigma: Notes on the management of spoiled identity.* New York: Prentice Hall.
Harvey, R. D. (2001). Individual differences in the phenomenological impact of social stigma. *Journal of Social Psychology, 141*(2), 174–189.

Hastings, A., & Dean, J. (2003). Challenging images: Tackling stigma through estate regeneration. *Policy & Politics, 31*(2), 171–184.

Hortulanus, R. P. (1995). *Stadsbuurten – bewoners en beheerders in buurten met uiteenlopende reputaties* [Urban neighbourhoods – residents and managers in neighbourhoods with diverging reputations]. Den Haag: VUGA.

Kearns, A., & Parkinson, M. (2001). The significance of neighbourhood. *Urban Studies, 38*(12), 2103–2110.

Kearns, A., Hiscock, R., Ellaway, A., & Macintyre, S. (2000). 'Beyond four walls', The psycho-social benefits of home: Evidence from West Central Scotland. *Housing Studies, 15*(3), 387–410.

Lee, B. A., Oropesa, R. S., & Kanan, J. W. (1994). Neighborhood context and residential mobility. *Demography, 31*(2), 249–270.

Leventhal, T., & Brooks-Gunn, J. (2000). The neighbourhoods they live in: The effects of neighbourhood residence on child and adolescent outcomes. *Psychological Bulletin, 126*(2), 309–337.

Lu, M. (1998). Analyzing migration decisionmaking: Relationships between residential satisfaction, mobility intentions, and moving behavior. *Environment and Planning A, 30*(8), 1473–1495.

Mead, G. H. (1934 [1967]). *Mind, self, and society: From the standpoint of a social behaviorist.* Chicago/London: University of Chicago Press.

Meen, G. (2012). The causes of long-term urban and neighbourhood change. In M. van Ham, D. Manley, N. Bailey, L. Simpson, & D. Maclennan (Eds.), *Understanding neighbourhood dynamics: New insights for neighbourhood effects research.* Dordrecht: Springer.

Murie, A., Knorr-Siedow, T., & Van Kempen, R. (2003). *Large estates in Europe. General developments and theoretical backgrounds. Restate report 1. Restructuring large-scale housing estates in European cities: Good practices and new visions for sustainable neighbourhoods and estates.* Utrecht: URU.

O+S Amsterdam. (2006). *Amsterdam in cijfers.* Available at http://www.os.amsterdam.nl/feitenen-cijfers/amsterdamincijfers2006. Accessed March 30, 2006).

Permentier, M. (2009). *Reputation, neighbourhoods and behaviour.* Utrecht: KNAG/Faculteit Geowetenschappen.

Permentier, M., van Ham, M., & Bolt, G. (2009). Neighbourhood reputation and the intention to leave the neighbourhood. *Environment and Planning A, 41*(9), 2162–2180.

Permentier, M., Bolt, G., & Van Ham, M. (2011). Determinants of neighbourhood satisfaction and perceived neighbourhood reputation. *Urban Studies, 48*(5), 977–996.

Ridgeway, C. L. (2006). Status construction theory. In P. J. Burke (Ed.), *Contemporary social psychological theories.* Stanford: Stanford University Press.

Sampson, R. J., Morenoff, J. D., & Gannon-Rowley, T. (2002). Assessing 'neighborhood effects': Social processes and new directions in research. *Annual Review of Sociology, 28*, 443–478.

Schelling, T. (1969). Models of segregation. *The American Economic Review, 59*(2), 488–493.

Schelling, T. (1971). Dynamic models of segregation. *Journal of Mathematical Society, 1*(2), 143–186.

Semyonov, M., & Kraus, V. (1982). The social hierarchies of communities and neighborhoods. *Social Science Quarterly, 63*(4), 780–789.

Speare, A. (1974). Residential satisfaction as an intervening variable in residential mobility. *Demography, 11*(2), 173–188.

Suttles, G. D. (1968). *The social order of the slum. Ethnicity and territory in the inner city.* Chicago/London: The University of Chicago Press.

Suttles, G. D. (1972). *The social construction of communities.* Chicago/London: The University of Chicago Press.

Taylor, M. (1998). Combating the social exclusion of housing estates. *Housing Studies, 13*(6), 819–832.

Trouw. (2007). *Slecht imago blijft de wijk achtervolgen* [Bad reputation haunts a neighbourhood], Trouw, July 30, 2007.

Tsfati, Y., & Cohen, J. (2003). On the effect of the 'third-person effect': Perceived influence of media coverage and residential mobility intentions. *Journal of Communication, 53*(4), 711–727.

van Ham, M., & Feijten, P. (2008). Who wants to leave the neighbourhood? The effects of being different from the neighbourhood population on wishes to move. *Environment and Planning A, 40*(5), 1151–1170.

van Ham, M., & Manley, D. (2010). The effect of neighbourhood housing tenure mix on labour market outcomes: A longitudinal investigation of neighbourhood effects. *Journal of Economic Geography, 10*(2), 257–282.

van Ham, M., Manley, D., Bailey, N., Simpson, L., & Maclennan, D. (Eds.). (2011). *Neighbourhood effects research: New perspectives*. Dordrecht: Springer.

Wacquant, L. J. D. (1993). Urban outcasts: Stigma and division in the black American ghetto and the French periphery. *International Journal of Urban and Regional Research, 17*(3), 366–383.

Wakefield, S., & McMullan, C. (2005). Healing in places of decline: (Re)imaging everyday landscapes in Hamilton, Ontario. *Health & Place, 11*(4), 299–312.

Warner, W. L. (1960). *Social class in America: A manual of procedure for the measurement of social status*. New York: Harper & Row.

Wellman, B. (1996). Are personal communities local? A Dumptarian reconsideration. *Social Networks, 18*, 347–540.

White, M. (1987). *American neighbourhoods and residential differentiation*. New York: Sage Foundation.

Wilson, W. J. (1996). *When work disappears*. Chicago: The University of Chicago Press.

Wyly, E. K. (2002). Mortgaged metropolis: Evolving urban geographies of residential lending. *Urban Geography, 23*(1), 3–30.

Chapter 9
The Components of Socioeconomic Neighbourhood Change: An Analysis of School Census Data at Varying Spatial Scales in England

Stephen Jivraj

Introduction

Over time, neighbourhoods will change in terms of the socioeconomic composition of the people that reside within them. Components of socioeconomic area change include migration, in situ status change and natural change. Measurement of the combined effect of these components at the neighbourhood level is often problematic because of inconsistencies in socioeconomic indicators and geographical scales of analysis between time points. In the UK, studies have overcome these challenges by tracking neighbourhood change over time using cross sectional census data (Dorling et al. 2007; Norman 2010). However, these studies are not able to unpack the component mechanisms that drive neighbourhood change because this requires individual level longitudinal data. It has been suggested that residential mobility between neighbourhoods will widen socioeconomic inequalities as affluent households choose to move away from deprived neighbourhoods leaving poor households trapped in these locations (Bailey and Livingston 2007; Cheshire et al. 2003; Cole et al. 2007; Meen et al. 2005). There has been little evidence that has tested this effect and even less showing how residential mobility compares with other components of socioeconomic neighbourhood change.

This chapter measures the change in the concentration of low-income primary school aged pupils at the neighbourhood level using the English School Census. Low-income is measured using the Free School Meal (FSM) status of a pupil which is widely used in educational research as an indicator of low socioeconomic status (Hobbs and Vignoles 2010; Styles 2008). The longitudinal nature of the School Census allows one to decompose the effect of socioeconomic neighbourhood change

S. Jivraj (✉)
Cathie Marsh Centre for Census and Survey Research (CCSR), School of Social Sciences, University of Manchester, Humanities Bridgeford Street, Manchester M13 9PL, UK
e-mail: stephen.jivraj@manchester.ac.uk

M. van Ham et al. (eds.), *Understanding Neighbourhood Dynamics: New Insights for Neighbourhood Effects Research*, DOI 10.1007/978-94-007-4854-5_9,

into the net effect of internal migration within England (residential mobility), entry and exit to and from the primary school system (school turnover), late entry and early exit to and from the primary school system (a proxy for international migration), and improved and declined socioeconomic status of those who do not move (in situ change). The analysis is conducted at different spatial scales of a neighbourhood using administrative and data boundaries. Change in the concentration of low-income pupils due to each component is measured at Local Authority District, Statistical Ward, Lower Super Output Area and Output Area levels. Data at each spatial scale was compared using deciles of areas using the Townsend deprivation index.[1]

The aim of this chapter is two-fold. First, to set in context the impact of residential mobility compared with other components of socioeconomic neighbourhood change. Second, to determine whether the components have varying effects at different spatial scales. The chapter begins by exploring existing evidence that has assessed the components of neighbourhood socioeconomic change. The following section outlines the geographical levels of analysis in this study and discusses why the effect of residential mobility and other components of area change might be different at varying spatial scales reviewing the modifiable area unit problem. The fourth section describes the School Census data. The fifth section explains how the measures used to test the effect of each component of socioeconomic neighbourhood change are calculated. The penultimate section presents research findings and the final section provides conclusions.

Theory and Evidence of Socioeconomic Neighbourhood Change

Residential mobility is only one component of neighbourhood socioeconomic change. The population of a neighbourhood could change as it remains in situ. For example, as the general economic conditions improve more people might move from unemployment to employment without moving home. Demographic changes are also important although they tend to take much longer to have an effect. For example, if lower income households are disproportionately having more children the individual poverty rate for all people will rise. Moreover, if disproportionate numbers of poor people die within a neighbourhood the overall poverty rate will fall. There are very few studies which attempt to quantify these components of socioeconomic area change at any spatial scale (Lupton and Power 2006). This is because it requires longitudinal data, preferably at the individual level so the different forces of change can be isolated and measured directly. This section will explore a small number of studies which have measured socioeconomic neighbourhood change by component mechanism.

---

[1] The Townsend Index was devised by Townsend et al. (1988) to provide a material measure of deprivation and disadvantage. The index is based on four census variables unemployment, non-car ownership, non-home ownership, and household overcrowding.

Strait (2006) uses 1990 and 2000 US Census data for census tracts in LA County to compare the effect on poverty concentration of residential mobility and in situ status change. He finds that the overall poverty rate increased in LA County from 14 to 17% during the decade and that the poor were more spatially concentrated in poor neighbourhoods. In general, there was a greater effect of compositional change (in situ change) than redistributive forces (residential mobility). However, both increased the exposure of poor people to poor neighbourhoods. Strait (2006) concedes that he may underestimate the effect of residential mobility because it is measured indirectly using cross-sectional data at two time points. A direct approach to measuring the effect of residential mobility on the concentration of poverty has been conducted by Rosenbaum (1995). She has analysed a survey dataset of households in New York City sub-boroughs which was conducted at 3 year intervals (1978–81, 1981–84 and 1984–87) to disentangle the competing mechanisms of poverty concentration. The results indicate that poverty-shifts (in situ change) account for 90% of the total increase in poverty in the New York City sub-boroughs. However, selective migration also reinforces the continued decline in high-poverty areas, while sustaining the economic vitality of low-poverty areas.

Cooke (2010) takes a similar approach using the US Panel Study of Income Dynamics. The sample of this longitudinal survey is too small to analyse the movement of individuals within particular neighbourhoods but it is possible to aggregate the data into neighbourhood typologies. He uses data from 1989 to 2005 to monitor changes in poverty concentration in urban core, inner-ring and outer-ring neighbourhoods. The results show that poverty rose steadily between 1989 and 1997 in the urban core and inner-ring neighbourhoods. There was a sharp drop during 1997–2001 and a steady rise again up to 2005. The poverty rate remained fairly constant in outer-ring neighbourhoods throughout the whole period. The changes in poverty concentration in the urban core and inner-ring neighbourhoods were largely driven by in situ change. During the 1990s more people were falling into poverty than were climbing out which led to a higher poverty rate. Residential mobility had the same effect because there was greater out-migration of non-poor relative to poor persons. However, between 1997 and 2001 the effect of migration continued to increase the concentration of poverty but a greater effect of more people climbing out of poverty than falling into poverty reduced the overall poverty concentration.

Bailey (2012) finds a comparable result in a more complete analysis of the components of socioeconomic neighbourhood change in Scotland. He uses the Scottish Longitudinal Study (SLS) to compare four processes which impact on the concentration of people aged 25–64 by educational attainment, social class and employment status between 1991 and 2001. The processes examined are internal migration (residential mobility), natural change (deaths only), in situ change and ageing (exit by 55–64 and entry by 15–24). The analysis is conducted for Continuous Areas Through Time (CATT). These areas vary widely in population size but have an average population of 500. Bailey finds that internal migration was the only component which increased the segregation of working age people for each measure of socioeconomic status. However, the effect was small and insubstantial when compared with the largest net effect which was in situ change. In situ change acted to reduce segregation between CATTs for each socioeconomic measure. The effect of ageing increased segregation by employment status but reduced segregation by educational attainment and social class. Natural change, measured only by the effect of deaths, increased segregation by low social class and decreased segregation by educational attainment, employment status and high social class.

Spatial Scales of Analysis

The effect of residential mobility on the change in the concentration of low-income pupils is likely to vary between different spatial scales because certain families are more likely to move over longer distances and across larger administrative boundaries than others. For example, Finney and Simpson (2008) have shown that migrant individuals are more likely to move longer distances if they are white, younger, not employed, highly qualified and with no dependent children. These characteristics are often associated with the different motivations for longer and shorter distance moves. In the economic migration literature, movement between larger administrative boundaries is often associated with labour market changes (Boheim and Taylor 2002) whereas localised movement between smaller spatial scales is often associated with housing aspirations and family (dis)unification (De Jong and Graefe 2008). Therefore, the varying level of selectivity of migration between larger and smaller geographical scales is likely to result in a different effect on area socioeconomic change.

The modifiable area unit problem (MAUP) refers to the issue that occurs when inferences are different when the same data are analysed at varying spatial scales (Manley et al. 2006; Schuurman et al. 2007). For example, much of the variation in an outcome of interest at one spatial scale can be lost when data is aggregated to a higher spatial scale. This will affect the inference for area change components that sum to an aggregate total, notably, the number of pupils that change their low-income status but do not move between neighbourhoods (in situ change). Schuurman and colleagues (2007) tested the effect of MAUP for spatial health inequalities at three geographical scales in Vancouver, Canada using a census deprivation index. They suggest that researchers should use the smallest geographical scale available as deprivation indices are susceptible to spatial granularity. This refers to the ability of smaller spatial units to capture greater geographical variation in the outcome of interest.

Another component of MAUP is the artificial nature of boundaries placed on data. It is suggested that larger spatial inequalities will be observed when data boundaries reflect socioeconomic homogeneity (Manley et al. 2006; Stafford et al. 2008). However, Stafford and colleagues (2008) find that varying the definitions of neighbourhood based on administrative or homogenous data boundaries does not have substantive effects on the measurement of spatial health inequalities. Their study was limited to neighbourhoods in London and therefore comparison for the whole of the country might yield different results.

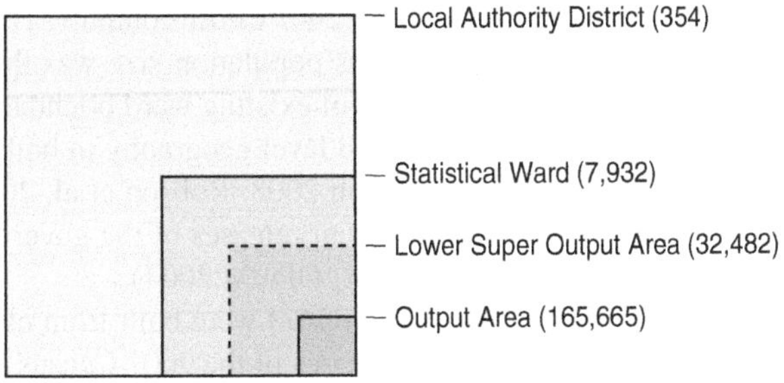

Fig. 9.1 English administrative and data boundaries

The inclusion of the postcode of each individual pupil in the School Census allows enormous geographical flexibility for neighbourhood change analyses. Figure 9.1 shows selected scales of administrative and data boundaries in England that are used in this study. The highest scale is Local Authority Districts (LADs). These boundaries are unlikely to reflect neighbourhoods due to the large variation in their population size. However, analysis is conducted at this level to contextualise results at neighbourhood scales. LADs include, London Boroughs, Non-Metropolitan Districts, Metropolitan Districts and Unitary Authorities. The London Boroughs, Non-Metropolitan Districts and Metropolitan Districts were initially established by the 1974 two-tier administrative structure of counties and districts. Following further Local Government Organisation in the 1990s a number of Unitary Authorities were established. The London Boroughs, Metropolitan Districts and Unitary Authorities are responsible for all areas of local government whereas the Non-Metropolitan Districts have split responsibilities with their respective County Council. In England, there were 354 LADs before the 2009 Local Government Reorganisation. These LADs will be referred to as districts henceforth.

In England, the next lower building block of administrative geography is Electoral Wards which are used to elect local government councillors for districts. These boundaries frequently change to reflect eligible voters and are created largely on the basis of population size. However, features such as roads, railways and rivers are considered as well as community identity (ONS 2010). In 2003, the Office for National Statistics (ONS) introduced Statistical Wards to minimise the analytical impact of boundary changes. They reflect the Electoral Wards as at May 2003, but for 28 local authorities they also included boundary changes that were not operational until June 2004. Therefore, for any given year Statistical Wards in some local authorities were different to the statutory Electoral Wards because of the varying time lags between promulgation and operation dates of boundary changes (ONS 2009a). There are 7,932 English Statistical Wards used in this study which will be referred to as wards henceforth.

Lower Super Output Areas (LSOAs) are a geographical hierarchy designed by ONS to improve the reporting of small area statistics. Unlike wards, LSOAs are of consistent size (approximately 1,500 people) across the country and will not be subjected to regular boundary change. The 32,482 LSOAs in England were built from groups of Output Areas (see below) and constrained by the boundaries of the

2003 Statistical Wards used for 2001 Census outputs. They do not necessarily reflect socioeconomic homogeneity as population size was the only determinant of their creation within the constraints of existing ward boundaries. LSOAs have been used extensively as a neighbourhood level geography in both academic and government research (Bailey and Livingston 2008; Robson et al. 2008). They were used as the geographical unit for most recent releases of the government's Indices of Multiple Deprivation (CLG 2008b, 2011; ODPM 2004).

2001 Census Output Areas (OAs) were built from clusters of adjacent unit postcodes and reflect the characteristics of the 2001 Census data. They were designed to have similar population sizes and be as socially homogenous as possible (based on tenure of household and dwelling type). They have approximately regular shapes and tended to be constrained by obvious boundaries such as major roads. The OAs were required to have a specified minimum size to ensure the confidentiality of data (ONS 2007). In England and Wales, 2001 Census OAs are based on postcodes as at Census Day and fit within the boundaries of 2003 Statistical Wards. If a postcode straddled a ward boundary, it was split between two or more OAs. The minimum OA size is 40 resident households and 100 resident persons but the ONS recommended size was larger at 125 households. In total there are 165,665 OAs in England.

School Census Data

This chapter uses data from the School Census collected during the period 2002–2007. The School Census records details of all state school pupils in England and is derived from an electronic administrative form completed by each school (Machin et al. 2006). The School Census has been collected since 2002 in January of each year and since 2006 has been supplemented with two smaller collections in the summer and autumn. Only data from the annual January School Census is used in this study. There are similar School Censuses collected in Wales, Scotland and Northern Ireland. However, there has been no attempt to link data between each constituent country to date.

Completion of the School Census is a statutory requirement for all state maintained primary, secondary and special schools under section 537A of the Education Act 1996 (Harland and Stillwell 2007). It is collated in England by the Department for Education (DfE) through Local Education Authorities. The School Census includes information about individual school pupils including their home postcode and free school meal eligibility. The inclusion of a unique pupil number in the School Census allows data to be matched between academic years. A change in the postcode of a pupil's matched record can indicate residential mobility and a change in the FSM status can indicate socioeconomic status change.

The School Census does not include information about school aged[2] children that do not attend state establishments. This is problematic for generalisation to the wider

[2] Compulsory school age ranges from 5 to 16 years in the UK.

school aged population because while the proportion of children not in state schools is about 8% for England as a whole, it varies between districts (ONS 2004). Comparison of mid-year population estimates produced by ONS and stocks of pupils included in the School Census show that for a small number of districts the latter includes a considerably lower number of school aged residents (e.g. Kensington and Chelsea, Barnet, Richmond upon Thames). This is explained by the high proportion of children living in these areas attending independent schools (ONS 2009b).

The proportion of school aged children not attending state schools appears to be lower for primary school pupils (age 5–10) compared with secondary school pupils (age 11–15) when comparing the School Census data with the ONS mid-year population estimates. For this reason and an apparent over recording of local residential moves at age 11, when all pupils transfer from a primary to secondary school and are required to provide contact details for their new school, the analysis in this chapter is restricted to primary aged pupils. Simpson et al. (2010) have shown it is unlikely that a higher rate of pupils move at age 11 because this is not shown in comparable data from the 2001 Census. However, they find it difficult to determine whether the over recording of residential moves at age 11 is a result of a child's parent not reporting a house move until asked to provide new contact details or a result of data entry errors. Data entry errors will be more likely at age 11 because the secondary school will be required to enter address information for all pupils rather than those that have registered a different address. Nonetheless, from analysis not reported here, the restriction of analysis to primary school aged pupils does not substantially alter the findings in this chapter for the effect of residential mobility on the change in the concentration of low-income pupils.

In order to test the effect of the various components of socioeconomic neighbourhood change, the FSM indicator recorded in the School Census was used to disaggregate pupils at each spatial scale. The indicator provides a binary measure of low-income (claimant or non-claimant) recorded each year a pupil is in the School Census. Some authors argue that FSM is limited as a measure of socioeconomic status because its binary nature does not allow one to distinguish between different levels of deprivation (DfES 2006; Hobbs and Vignoles 2007). Nonetheless, FSM status has been used widely as a proxy measure of low socioeconomic status in educational research (Hobbs and Vignoles 2007; Machin et al. 2006; Styles 2008). To be eligible for FSM, a child must be living in a household claiming a means-tested income benefit (Hobbs and Vignoles 2010). Hobbs and Vignoles (2010) found that the vast majority of pupils claiming FSM live in low-income families, but not all pupils living in low-income families claim FSM. This is because not all low-income families are eligible or are unwilling to claim the means-tested benefits which allow them to access FSM for their children.

Aggregate data for FSM status is strongly correlated with other deprivation measures at every spatial scale used in this study. Table 9.1 shows the relationship between the ranks of areas ordered by the percentage of pupils claiming FSM and the Townsend deprivation index score. The Spearman's rank correlation coefficients indicate there is a strong positive relationship between the relative positions of areas for the two measures at every spatial scale. The relationship is strongest at district

Table 9.1 Spearman's rank correlation coefficient of relationship between rank of areas by % Free School Meal pupils and Townsend deprivation index score

Scale	Deprivation score
District	0.923
Ward	0.881
LSOA	0.884
OA	0.739

Source: Calculated from School Census, 2002–2007 and 2001 Census, CAS tables

level and weakest at OA level. This may reflect the different time points when the data was collected for each measure. The School Census data is averaged between 2002 and 2007 whereas the Census data was collected in 2001. There is likely to be a greater level of change at the smallest spatial scales where, for example, a construction of the new housing development might have a large change in the socioeconomic composition of an OA. The lower level of association at the OA level might also reflect the absence of primary aged pupils in some neighbourhoods which will therefore have a zero FSM rate. However, the Townsend index uses data for all people and an OA which has no primary age pupils, and therefore 0% with low-income, might be relatively deprived.

A pupil's parent has to verify their eligibility for FSM status using appropriate documentation which is reviewed by their Local Education Authority on a rolling basis. Should a pupil's parent cease claiming the means-tested benefit which makes their child eligible for FSM status they will become ineligible for FSM. A pupil's parent is also required to reapply for FSM status when they move school. The outcome of this process should result in no pupils claiming FSM that are not eligible. However, it does mean that some pupils that are eligible will not claim FSM status. This could be a result of unwillingness to claim due to stigma at school or lack of knowledge of eligibility (Plewis and Kallis 2008; Styles 2008). Hobbs and Vignoles (2010) analysis of the Family Resources Survey shows that about 11% of pupils that are eligible for FSM do not claim.

A variable was created for this study, which took into account whether a pupil's FSM status changed over each 1 year period between 2002–03 and 2006–07 where two consecutive School Censuses were merged. Pupils were categorised into four groups: (1) Those with FSM status at the start and end of a 1 year period; (2) those that did not have FSM status at the start and end of a 1 year period; (3) those with FSM status at the start but not at the end of a 1 year period (improved), and; (4) those that did not have FSM status at the start but did at the end of a 1 year period (declined).

Table 9.2 shows the proportion of primary school aged pupils by each category for each 1 year period between 2002–03 and 2006–07. The proportion of pupils in each category remained fairly constant over time. There were a lower proportion of pupils claiming FSM at the start and end of a 1 year period in later years. This reflects findings from the British Household Panel Survey which suggest the proportion of low-income households has fallen during the period 1991–2007 with the largest reductions for families with children since 2001 (DWP 2009).

Table 9.2 Free School Meal status at start and end of 1 year periods

%	2002–03	2003–04	2004–05	2005–06	2006–07
FSM	15.20	15.40	15.40	14.60	14.20
Non-FSM	78.90	79.00	79.00	79.50	80.00
Improve	3.30	2.70	3.10	3.50	3.00
Decline	2.70	2.90	2.40	2.40	2.80
Total	2,921,342	2,885,737	2,863,447	2,830,071	2,797,135

Source: Calculated from School Census, 2002–2007

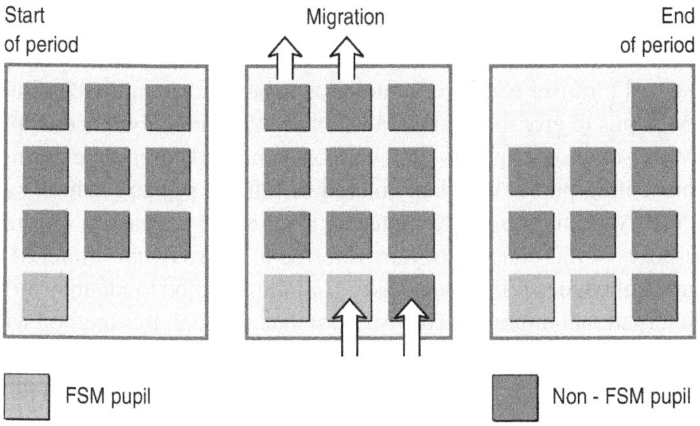

Fig. 9.2 Example effect of residential mobility on neighbourhood change

Measures of the Components of Socioeconomic Area Change

The change in the concentration of low-income pupils as a result of each component from the district to output area scale was measured as follows. The components analysed are residential mobility, school turnover, international migration, and in situ socioeconomic status change. These are comprehensive in the sense that they together constitute all the change in the concentration of low-income pupils. Each component is presented as its net impact on the concentration of low-income pupils. A small net impact may be the result of large changes for each component.

The change in the concentration of low-income pupils due to *residential mobility* was derived by comparing the percentage of low-income pupils at the start of each 1 year period with the end of the period by only allocating residentially mobile pupils into destination neighbourhoods. Residential mobility refers to pupils who moved address within England and is isolated from international migration. Figure 9.2 represents the effect of residential mobility during a 1 year period for an example neighbourhood. At the start of the period the neighbourhood had ten pupils including one that had FSM status which means the concentration of low-income pupils was 10%. During a 1 year period one FSM pupil moved in, one non-FSM pupil moved in, and two non-FSM pupils moved out. The percentage of low-income pupils was therefore 20% at the end of the 1 year period. This means the absolute change in the concentration of low-income pupils was +10 percentage points in this area during the period when only taking into account residential mobility.

Pupils that were in their last year of primary school at the start of a 1 year period and pupils that were in their first year of primary school at the end of a 1 year period were identified as school leavers and school starters to calculate a measure of *school turnover*. These pupils were disaggregated by their FSM status which was only measured once as they were only present at either the start or end of a 1 year period. A measure of net change of those that entered and left the primary school system was calculated by low-income status (just as the effect of residential mobility was measured) and then added to the pupil population by FSM status at the start of each 1 year period. The result was then used to calculate a percentage of low-income pupils had only school turnover occurred, which was subtracted from the baseline percentage of FSM pupils to give the change in the concentration of low-income pupils.

There were some other pupils that were only in the dataset once during a 1 year period representing pupils who had entered or left the primary school system at a non-compulsory primary age (i.e. entering after age 5 or leaving before age 11). For the purposes of this chapter they are referred to as proxy *international migrants*. Simpson and colleagues (2010) have used a similar method to identify this group of pupils as international migrants. They suggest that although this method will capture the vast majority of school age international migration it will include some pupils transferring between state and independent schooling as well as pupils moving between countries within the UK.

The rate of late starting and early leaving pupils was about 1% nationally which is more than twice the rate of primary school aged immigrants and emigrants measured over a similar time period using estimates from the International Passenger Survey for the UK. The International Passenger Survey estimates are subject to large sampling error as a result of the small sample size and only record international migrants who are enter or leave the UK for at least 12 months (Boden and Rees 2010; Hatton 2005). Nonetheless, the measure of international migration as measured by the School Census is likely to overestimate the number of immigrants and emigrants and therefore should be treated with caution when used to identify these individuals.

The net effect by FSM status for pupils that entered and left at a non-compulsory school age (proxy international migration) was added to the pupil population at the start of each 1 year period in the same way the effect of school turnover was calculated.

The final individual component of neighbourhood change measured was *in situ change* in socioeconomic status. This refers to the pupils that changed their FSM status but did not move between neighbourhoods. The effect of in situ status change was measured by the net change of pupils that improved and declined their socioeconomic status over each 1 year period. The net effect was then added to the population at the start of a 1 year period to give a measure of the number of pupils disaggregated by FSM status at the end of a 1 year period. This was used to calculate the percentage of low-income pupils had only in situ change occurred. This was subtracted from the percentage before net in situ change was added to give a change in the concentration of low-income pupils.

Almost a quarter of pupils that changed their socioeconomic status over an average 1 year period also moved within England during the same period. The effect of this type of change was isolated from residential mobility and in situ change so as not to distort either effect. It is not unexpected that residential mobility and socioeconomic status change would occur at the same time. For example, if a parent begins or ends a relationship this is likely to prompt a move and a change in socioeconomic status as might starting or ending employment. The net effect of this component was calculated in the same way as the effect of residential mobility was measured.

The average percentage point change of FSM pupils for each component between 2002–03 and 2006–07 is used for the rest of the analysis in this chapter and is referred to as the change in concentration of low-income pupils. An average was taken to simplify the analysis but also to take account of change over a longer period of time than 1 year. Given that the impact of each component on area change is isolated from other effects, the percentage of FSM pupils at the end of the average 1 year period does not refer to the actual percentage of FSM pupils but the percentage if only one of the components of change had occurred.

Change in the Concentration of Low-Income Pupils by Component of Change and Neighbourhood Scale

Local Authority Districts

Figure 9.3 shows the number of pupils by low-income status at the start of an average 1-year period between 2002–03 and 2006–07 (shown by shaded bars) and the average annual percentage point change of low-income pupils for each 1-year period between 2002–03 and 2006–07 (shown by shaded lines) for all primary aged pupils by each spatial scale. Figure 9.3a shows that the more deprived deciles of districts using the Townsend index included a greater number of pupils than less deprived districts. The poorest 20% of districts included over a third of the total pupil population between 2002 and 2006 (54% of FSM pupils and 30% of non-FSM pupils).

The component responsible for the greatest level of change in the concentration of low-income pupils in districts was in situ change. In situ change decreased the concentration of low-income pupils in each decile of districts. The greatest change was in the most deprived decile where this component decreased the concentration of low-income pupils by 0.5 percentage points. This is a result of more pupils improving their income status than declining their income status which has the effect of improving the socioeconomic status, which as already mentioned was a general trend in Britain during this period.

The effect of pupils changing their FSM status and moving at the same time also decreased the concentration of low-income pupils in all deciles of districts. This is a result of more pupils that moved and changed their FSM status improving rather than declining their socioeconomic status. The decreased concentration of low-income

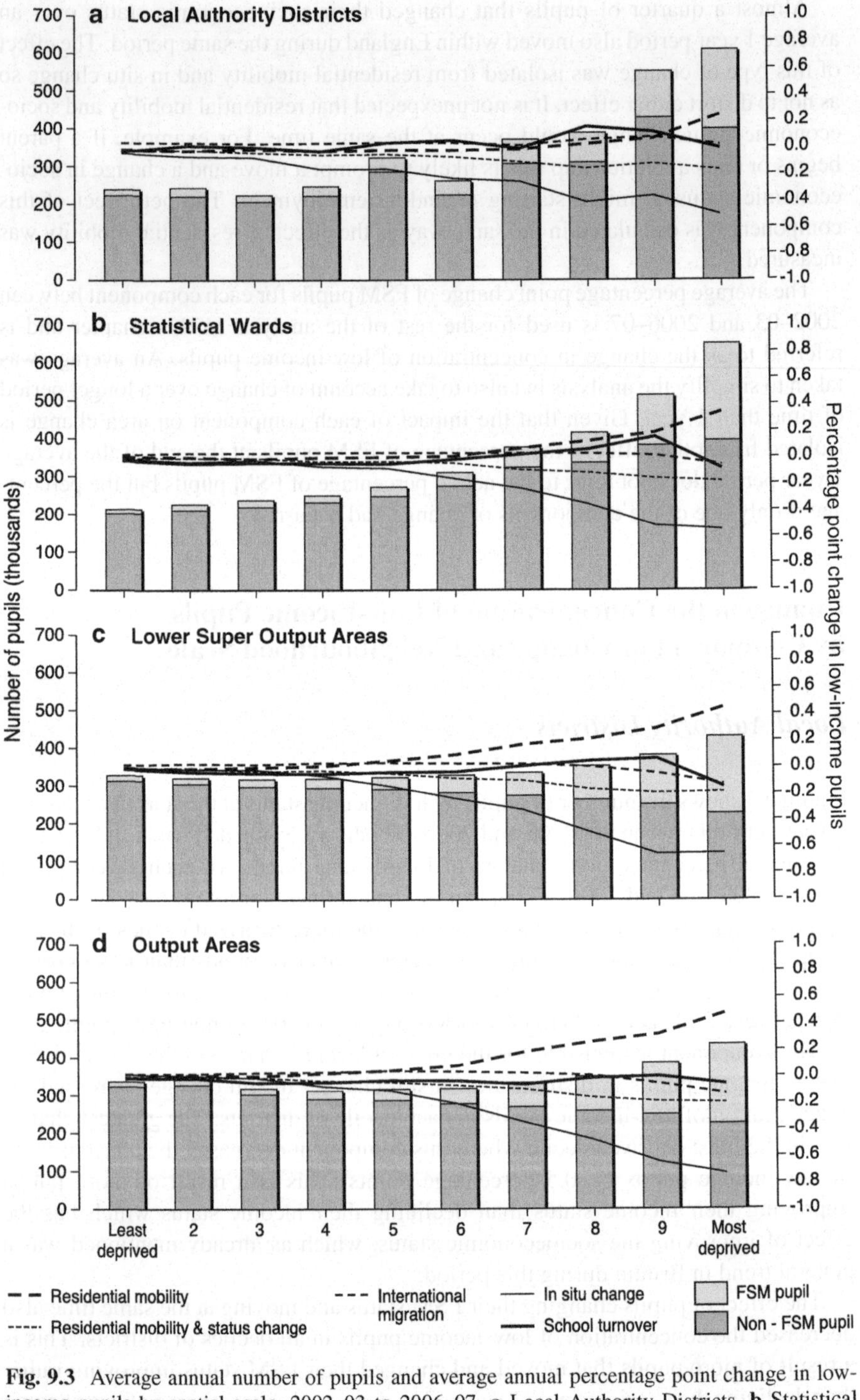

Fig. 9.3 Average annual number of pupils and average annual percentage point change in low-income pupils by spatial scale, 2002–03 to 2006–07. **a** Local Authority Districts, **b** Statistical Wards, **c** Lower Super Output Areas, **d** Output Areas (Source: Calculated from School Census, 2002–2007)

pupils due to this component was greatest in the most deprived decile of districts where it decreased the concentration of low-income pupils by almost 0.2 percentage points. Examining the gross flows of pupils (not shown), more pupils improved their FSM status and moved away than declined their FSM status and moved in. Moreover, fewer pupils declined their FSM status and moved away than improved their FSM status and moved in. Overall, this had the effect of disproportionately increasing the non-FSM population and decreasing the FSM population in the more deprived compared with less deprived districts when only taking into account this component.

The impact of residential mobility was also greatest in the most deprived districts. However, this component increased the concentration of low-income pupils in the most deprived decile of districts by 0.2 percentage points. The increased concentration of low-income pupils in the most deprived districts could be the result of three different migration dynamics. Firstly, if FSM pupils were moving into an area and non-FSM pupils were moving out there would be a greater concentration of low-income pupils in that area. Secondly, if FSM pupils were moving in and non-FSM pupils were moving in, but FSM pupils were moving in at a faster rate the concentration of low-income pupils would rise. Thirdly, if FSM pupils were moving out of an area and non-FSM pupils were moving out, but non-FSM pupils were moving out at a faster rate the concentration of low-income pupils in the area would rise. By comparing the net migration rates by FSM status the dynamic that is responsible for the change in the concentration of low-income pupils can be uncovered.

Figure 9.4 shows this further analysis. Figure 9.4a shows that the net internal migration rates for districts were outward for FSM pupils and non-FSM pupils in the most deprived decile of districts. However, there was a greater net outflow of non-FSM pupils compared with FSM pupils for districts in this decile. This results in the increased concentration of low-income pupils in these areas. The effect of school turnover and international migration was marginal at the district level as well as every other spatial scale analysed. Therefore, their effects are not discussed in detail in this section.

Census Statistical Wards

Figure 9.3b shows that for wards there was a similar relationship as for districts between the Townsend deprivation deciles and each component of change in the concentration of low-income pupils. There were also higher numbers of pupils living in the most deprived wards compared with the less deprived wards as there were in districts. This is because less deprived wards and districts tend to be located in rural areas and have smaller populations compared with deprived wards and districts which tend to be located in metropolitan areas and have much larger populations.

In the most deprived deciles of wards the change in the concentration of low-income pupils was greatest. As with districts, the in situ change component had the largest effect. In the most deprived decile of wards, in situ change decreased the concentration of low-income pupils by almost 0.6 percentage points. This is the equivalent of

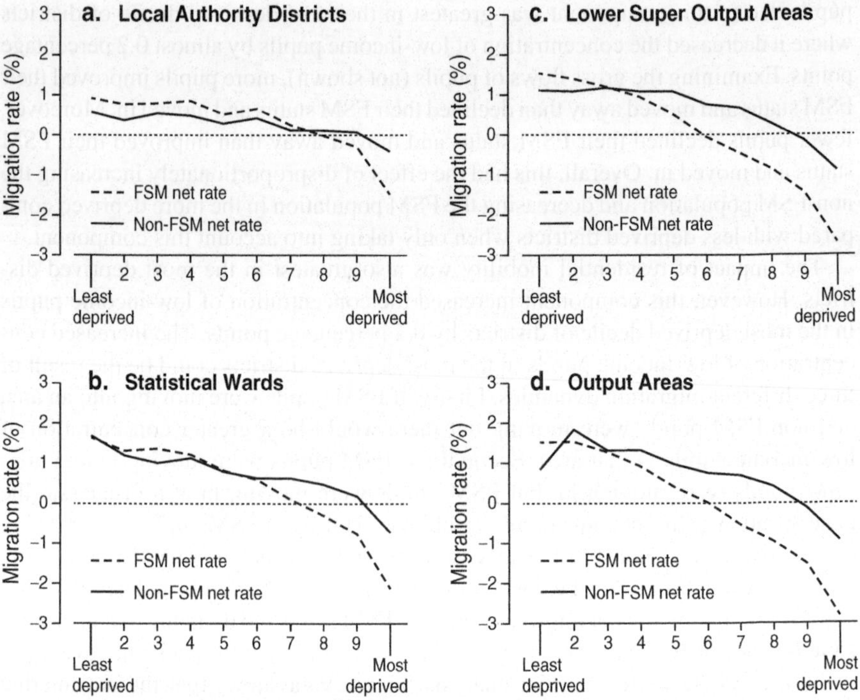

Fig. 9.4 Average annual net migration rate by FSM status and spatial scale, 2002–03 to 2006–07. **a** Local Authority Districts, **b** Statistical Wards, **c** Lower Super Output Areas, **d** Output Areas. Notes: the relative difference between FSM and non-FSM net migration rates indicates the effect on the change in the concentration of low-income pupils shown in Fig. 9.2. A lower net migration rate (positive or negative) of FSM pupils compared with non-FSM pupils indicates increased concentration of low-income pupils (Source: Calculated from School Census, 2002–2007)

five more FSM pupils improving their income status than declining their income status in an average ward in the most deprived decile. The effect of pupils changing their FSM status and moving was very similar at the ward level as at the district level. In the most deprived decile of wards, this component decreased the concentration of low-income pupils by almost 0.2 percentage points.

The second largest component of change was the effect of residential mobility which increased the concentration of low-income pupils in the most deprived decile of wards by 0.3 percentage points. The effect of residential mobility had a gradually larger increase in the concentration of low-income pupils from the seventh to the most deprived decile of wards. This was unlike the effect at district level which only had a noticeable effect in the most deprived decile.

Figure 9.4b shows that increased concentration of low-income pupils in the most deprived deciles of wards was a result of net outward movement by non-FSM pupils and net in migration of FSM pupils. There was an exception in the most deprived decile of wards which had net outward movement for both socioeconomic groups. However, the net out migration rate was higher for non-FSM pupils.

Lower Level Super Output Areas

Figure 9.3c shows that the total number of pupils was much more evenly distributed across deciles of LSOAs using the Townsend deprivation index than wards or districts. This is because LSOAs were designed using the 2001 Census output to create even sized population areas. As expected, there was a much higher proportion of low-income pupils in the more deprived LSOAs compared with the least deprived. Almost 50% of pupils living in the most deprived decile of LSOAs had low-income status compared with 2% in the least deprived decile of LSOAs.

The diverging effect of in situ change and residential mobility was even greater in LSOAs by decile of deprivation than wards or districts. In the 40% most deprived LSOAs, in situ change decreased the concentration of low-income pupils by 0.5 percentage points with the effect strongest in those most deprived LSOAs. The effect of residential mobility was also more severe than for wards or districts increasing the concentration of low-income pupils in the four most deprived deciles of LSOAs by at least 0.2 percentage points. Figure 9.4c shows that this was a result of net outward movement by non-FSM pupils together with lower net outward movement or net inward movement of FSM pupils.

Output Areas

The effect of each component of change in the concentration of low-income pupils was very similar for OAs and LSOAs by deprivation deciles. The distribution of the pupil population was also much more even for OAs compared with wards and districts. There was also a much higher proportion of low-income pupils in the more deprived OAs compared with the less deprived OAs. The only difference in OAs compared with LSOAs is that the negative impact of in situ change and the positive effect of residential mobility on the concentration of low-income pupils were both slightly more severe. This indicates the effect of spatial granularity by highlighting the greater variation in neighbourhood change at the finest geographical scale.

Table 9.3 shows the spatial granularity of the low-income percentage point change in the 20% most deprived areas from district to output area level. The effect of residential mobility, in situ change and residential mobility combined with FSM status change were all greatest at the OA scale. The effect of school turnover and international migration were fairly negligible at each spatial scale.

Conclusion

This chapter has uniquely analysed the component mechanisms of socioeconomic neighbourhood change using data from the School Census in England during 2002–2007. Change in the concentration of primary school aged low-income pupils indicated by FSM status was measured at varying neighbourhood scales. The components

Table 9.3 Percentage point change in concentration of low-income pupils due to each component in 20% most deprived neighbourhoods, 2002–03 to 2006–07

Component of socioeconomic area change	District	Ward	LSOA	OA
Residential mobility	0.15	0.26	0.37	0.40
In situ FSM status change	−0.44	−0.53	−0.65	−0.69
Residential mobility and FSM status change	−0.15	−0.17	−0.19	−0.19
School turnover	0.05	0.03	−0.04	−0.03
International migration	0.05	−0.02	−0.08	−0.09

Source: Calculated from School Census, 2002–2007

measured which contribute to overall change in the concentration of low-income pupils were residential mobility, in situ status change, school turnover and international migration. In situ status change had the greatest effect which supports the findings from similar studies which have decomposed the component mechanisms of socioeconomic area change (Bailey 2012; Cooke 2010; Rosenbaum 1995; Strait 2006). In situ change, which refers to pupils improving or declining their income status without moving, decreased the concentration of low-income pupils at each neighbourhood scale. This is a result of a national trend of fewer pupils claiming FSM in the later years of the period 2002–2007.

Moreover, decreased concentration of low-income pupils as a result of in situ change was greatest in the most deprived neighbourhoods. This might reflect a greater level of intervention to improve socioeconomic conditions in the most deprived neighbourhoods in England during this period. The Neighbourhood Renewal Fund (NRF) (subsequently renamed Working Neighbourhoods Fund) has financed a number of spatially-targeted programmes that aim to improve socioeconomic outcomes in the poorest neighbourhoods relative to the national average (CLG 2010). Although the NRF programmes have only covered a small proportion of deprived neighbourhoods in England the model of spatial targeting has been used in non-NRF local authority areas through Local Area Agreements (CLG 2008a).

The effect of residential mobility on change in the concentration of low-income pupils was also greatest in the most deprived neighbourhoods at each spatial scale. Although the effect was not as strong as in-situ change it increased the concentration of low-income pupils in these areas. In the most deprived decile of areas, this was a result of greater net outward movement of non-FSM pupils compared with FSM pupils. This supports existing theories about residential mobility for deprived areas that presuppose those most able to move away will be more likely to do so. Poor households, however, will find it more difficult to escape the most deprived neighbourhoods because even if they move they will not have the resources to move to less deprived neighbourhoods.

The effect of residential mobility was isolated from socioeconomic neighbourhood change due to pupils changing their income status and moving within England at the same time. The latter component reduced the concentration of low-income pupils in the poorest neighbourhoods. It completely counterbalanced the isolated effect of residential mobility in the 20% most deprived areas at the district level and halved the effect at the ward, LSOA and OA levels. These two separate components should be added together and considered as the overall effect of residential mobility. The effect of both in-situ change and overall residential mobility were moderately accentuated at smaller neighbourhood scales which supports findings that variation in outcomes are more pronounced at finer geographical levels (Schuurman et al. 2007). Nonetheless, the substantive findings did not alter at varying spatial scales. The patterns were most consistent between the spatial scales which have been previously used as neighbourhood level geography including, wards, LSOAs and OAs. The findings at the OA level should be treated with some caution as there are a substantial number of these neighbourhoods which contain zero or very few primary school aged pupils. Therefore, a measure of change in the concentration of low-income pupils is not as reliable at this scale. Moreover, the effect of the other components of change in the concentration of low-income pupils including school turnover and international migration were relatively small in all deciles of neighbourhoods by deprivation status and at each spatial scale.

The data used in this chapter refers to a period of sustained national economic growth. This is reflected by the decline in the percentage of pupils claiming FSM during this time. Since 2007, the UK economy has experienced a severe contraction and unsurprisingly the claimant rate for FSM has risen (DfE N.d.). Therefore, the change in the concentration of low-income pupils is likely to have reversed and this will probably impact on deprived areas most heavily. Cooke (2010) found that socioeconomic area change in the poorest neighbourhoods tends to be more responsive to national economic conditions driven largely by in situ status change. However, he found that the effect of residential mobility remains consistent despite being much smaller. This suggests that local policy makers could reverse or at least temper the effects of residential mobility during times of national economic growth and contraction through attempts to make deprived neighbourhoods more attractive places to live.

The effect of component mechanisms of socioeconomic change could be measured in the current UK context using more recent data from the School Census as well as nationally representative longitudinal surveys. The Understanding Society survey provides an annual track of people's lives including whether they move within the UK. Data is available since 2009 and is incorporated with data from the British Household Panel Survey for 1991–2009. This data could be used to measure individual level change in income and how it impacts on neighbourhood change when measured as in situ change and as a result of residential mobility. Income would have fewer limitations as a measure of socioeconomic status than a proxy measure like FSM status.

In summary, the findings from this study contribute to our understanding of neighbourhood socioeconomic change. They suggest it is important to consider the component mechanisms of change because they can operate in different directions. The net effect during the period 2002–2007 has decreased the concentration of low-income pupils with the effect greatest in the most deprived neighbourhoods. This is driven by pupils changing their income status and not moving residence.

Acknowledgements The author would like to thank Paul Norman for permission to reproduce Fig. 9.1. I would also like to thank Mark Brown and Nissa Finney for their diligent supervision of my Ph.D. thesis on which this chapter is based. Finally, I am grateful to the Department for Education for access to the School Census.

References

Bailey, N. (2012). *How spatial segregation changes over time: sorting out the sorting processes.* Environment and Planning A, 44(3), 705–722.

Bailey, N., & Livingston, M. (2007). *Population turnover and area deprivation*. Bristol: Policy Press.

Bailey, N., & Livingston, M. (2008). Selective migration and neighbourhood deprivation: Evidence from 2001 census migration data for England and Scotland. *Urban Studies, 45*(4), 943–961.

Boden, P., & Rees, P. (2010). Using administrative data to improve the estimation of immigration to local areas in England. *Journal of the Royal Statistical Society: Series A (Statistics in Society), 173*(4), 707–731.

Boheim, R., & Taylor, M. P. (2002). Tied down or room to move? Investigating the relationships between housing tenure, employment status and residential mobility in Britain. *Scottish Journal of Political Economy, 49*(4), 369–392.

Cheshire, P., Monastiriotis, V., & Sheppard, S. (2003). Income inequality and residential segregation: Labour market sorting and the demand for positional goods. In R. L. Martin & P. S. Morrison (Eds.), *Geographies of labour market inequality* (pp. 83–109). London: Routledge.

CLG. (2008a). *Assessing neighbourhood-level data for target setting*. London: Department for Communities and Local Government.

CLG. (2008b). *The English indices of deprivation 2007*. London: Department for Communities and Local Government.

CLG. (2010). *Evaluation of the national strategy for neighbourhood renewal final report*. London: Department for Communities and Local Government.

CLG. (2011). *The English indices of deprivation 2010*. London: Department for Communities and Local Government.

Cole, I., Lawless, P., Manning, J., & Wilson, I. (2007). *The moving escalator? Patterns of residential mobility in new deal for communities area.* Research report 32. London: Department for Communities and Local Government.

Cooke, T. (2010). Residential mobility of the poor and the growth of poverty in inner-ring suburbs. *Urban Geography, 31*(2), 179–193.

De Jong, G. F., & Graefe, D. R. (2008). Family life course transitions and the economic consequences of internal migration. *Population, Space and Place, 14*(4), 267–282.

DfE. (N.d.). *Statistical first releases*. [Online] (Updated June 9, 2011). Available at: http://www.education.gov.uk/rsgateway/DB/SFR/index.shtml. Accessed 15 June 2011.

DfES. (2006). *Ethnicity and education: The evidence on minority ethnic pupils aged 5–16*. London: Department for Education and Skills.

Dorling, D., Rigby, J., Wheeler, B., Ballas, D., Thomas, B., Fahmy, E., Gordon, D., & Lupton, R. (2007). *Poverty, wealth and place in Britain, 1968 to 2005*. Bristol: Policy Press.

DWP. (2009). *Low-income dynamics 1991-2007 (Great Britain)*. London: Department for Work and Pensions.

Finney, N., & Simpson, L. (2008). Internal migration and ethnic groups: Evidence for Britain from the 2001 census. *Population, Space and Place, 14*(2), 63–83.

Harland, K., & Stillwell, J. (2007). *Using the PLASC data to identify patterns of commuting to school, residential migration and movement between schools in Leeds*. Working paper 07/03. Leeds: School of Geography, University of Leeds.

Hatton, T. J. (2005). Explaining trends in UK immigration. *Journal of Population Economics, 18*(4), 719–740.

Hobbs, G., & Vignoles, A. (2007). *Is free school meal status a valid proxy for socio-economic status (in schools research)?* CEEDP 84. London: Centre for the Economics of Education, School of Economics and Political Science.
Hobbs, G., & Vignoles, A. (2010). Is children's free school meal 'eligibility' a good proxy for family income? *British Educational Research Journal, 36*(4), 673–690.
Lupton, R., & Power, A. (2006). *What we know about neighbourhood change: A literature review.* CASEreport 27. London: Centre for the Analysis of Social Exclusion, School of Economics and Political Science.
Machin, S., Telhaj, S., & Wilson, J. (2006). *The mobility of English school children.* CEEDP 67. London: Centre for the Economics of Education, School of Economics and Political Science.
Manley, D., Flowerdew, R., & Steel, D. (2006). Scales, levels and processes: Studying spatial patterns of British census variables. *Computers, Environment and Urban Systems, 30*(2), 143–160.
Meen, G., Gibb, K., Goody, J., McGrath, T., & Mackinnon, J. (2005). *Economic segregation in England: Causes, consequences and policy.* Bristol: Policy Press.
Norman, P. (2010). Identifying change over time in small area socio-economic deprivation. *Applied Spatial Analysis and Policy, 3*(2–3), 107–138.
ODPM. (2004). *The English indices of deprivation 2004 (revised).* London: Office of the Deputy Prime Minister.
ONS. (2004). Pupils and teachers: By type of school, 2002/03. Regional Trends, 38. [Online] (Updated March 31, 2004) Available at: http://www.ons.gov.uk/ons/rel/regional-trends/regional-trends/index.html. Accessed 27 July 2012.
ONS. (2007). *Census geography.* [Online] (Updated October 30, 2007) Available at: http://www.statistics.gov.uk/geography/census_geog.asp#oa. Accessed 27 May 2010.
ONS. (2009a). *Electoral wards/divisions.* [Online] (Updated June 25, 2009). Available at: http://www.statistics.gov.uk/geography/electoral_wards.asp. Accessed 27 May 2010.
ONS. (2009b). *Use of school census data to improve population and migration statistics.* Titchfield: Office for National Statistics.
ONS. (2010). *Boundary changes.* [Online] (Updated May 28, 2010). Available at: http://www.statistics.gov.uk/geography/boundary_changes.asp. Accessed 4 August 2010.
Plewis, I., & Kallis, C. (2008). *Changing economic circumstances in childhood and their effects on subsequent educational and other outcomes.* Working paper No 49. London: Department for Work and Pensions.
Robson, B., Lymperopoulou, K., & Rae, A. (2008). People on the move: Exploring the functional roles of deprived neighbourhoods. *Environment and Planning A, 40*, 2693–2714.
Rosenbaum, E. (1995). The making of a ghetto: Spatially concentrated poverty in New York city in the 1980s. *Population Research and Policy Review, 14*(1), 1–27.
Schuurman, N., Bell, N., Dunn, J. R., & Oliver, L. (2007). Deprivation indices, population health and geography: An evaluation of the spatial effectiveness of indices at multiple scales. *Journal of Urban Health, 84*(4), 591–603.
Simpson, L., Marquis, N., & Jivraj, S. (2010). International and internal migration measured from the school census in England. *Population Trends, 140*, 106–124.
Stafford, M., Duke-Williams, O., & Shelton, N. (2008). Small area inequalities in health: Are we underestimating them? *Social Science & Medicine, 67*(6), 891–899.
Strait, J. B. (2006). Poverty concentration in the prismatic metropolis: The impact of compositional and redistributive forces within Los Angeles, California, 1990-2000. *Journal of Urban Affairs, 28*(1), 71–94.
Styles, B. (2008). Moving on from free school meals: National census data can describe the socio-economic background of the intake of each school England. *Educational Research, 50*(1), 41–53.
Townsend, P., Phillimore, P., & Beattie, A. (1988). *Health and deprivation: Inequalities and the north.* London: Croom Helm.

Chapter 10
How Ethnic Mix Changes: Typologising Neighbourhood Population Dynamics of Ethnic Groups

Nissa Finney

Introduction

The image of the black ghetto is perhaps the most pervasive representation of undesirable neighbourhoods in western societies (Wacquant 2008; Peach 1996; Slater and Anderson 2012). Although this negative image was somewhat re-framed in Britain during the 1980s and 1990s through the lens of multiculturalism's celebration of diversity, the first decade of the twenty-first century has seen a return to concern about ethnic difference, ethnic conflict and ethnic residential segregation. Two ways in which researchers have responded, in an attempt to understand the contemporary meanings of ethnically diverse neighbourhoods, are by examining the population dynamics of neighbourhoods and how the diversity of neighbourhoods affects their residents.

The stereotyping of areas on the basis of race or ethnicity does not recognise the dynamism of neighbourhoods; that neighbourhoods are in flux, places of coming and going. The make-up of a neighbourhood's population, in terms of ethnicity (or any other social marker), is determined by ongoing demographic processes of births, deaths, in-migration and out-migration. In Britain, these processes are producing more ethnic mixing residentially (Finney and Simpson 2009a). Questioning the meaning of an area's ethnic character has ushered in research on the impacts diverse neighbourhoods have on their residents; whether there are social advantages or disadvantages from living in ethnically diverse areas; whether there are neighbourhood effects of diverse areas (e.g. Putnam 2007; Bécares et al. 2009; Taylor et al. 2010).

N. Finney (✉)
Cathie Marsh Centre for Census and Survey Research (CCSR), School of Social Sciences, University of Manchester, Humanities Bridgeford Street, Manchester M13 9PL, UK
e-mail: nissa.finney@manchester.ac.uk

M. van Ham et al. (eds.), *Understanding Neighbourhood Dynamics: New Insights for Neighbourhood Effects Research*, DOI 10.1007/978-94-007-4854-5_10,

This chapter contributes to the literature concerned with the processes and impacts of changes in the ethnic composition of neighbourhoods by examining neighbourhoods in terms of their demographic functions. Rather than focusing on the static composition of an area, the chapter suggests that neighbourhoods can be thought about in terms of their population change, and the mechanisms of that change. It is argued that a focus on population dynamics is a helpful approach for understanding the contemporary meaning of neighbourhood ethnic mix.

The chapter begins with a review of literature on neighbourhood population dynamics of ethnic groups and effects of diverse neighbourhoods. The approach and data used in the analyses are then outlined. The findings are presented in two sections. The first describes the population dynamics of Britain's neighbourhoods for White, Caribbean, African, Indian, Pakistani, Bangladeshi, Chinese and Other ethnic groups. The second provides an approach for categorising neighbourhoods according to their combination of White and ethnic minority population dynamics.

Dynamic Diverse Neighbourhoods

Demographic Components of Neighbourhood Population Change

Demographic studies of neighbourhood population change are concerned with understanding how the components of change – births, deaths, in-migration and out-migration – together contribute to population change of an area. The contributions of each component are dependent on the age structure of the population: births will be proportionately greater where there are more young adults of reproductive ages; deaths will be proportionately greater where there are more elderly adults. A number of themes can be identified in demographic studies of area change: the relation between components of population change; changes, or transitions, in the demographic function of places over time; linked to this, the demographic role of urban and rural areas; and typologising places according to their demographic change.

Studies of the roles of natural change and migration in local population change have highlighted, for Britain's population as a whole, the dominance of (internal) migration in altering a neighbourhood's population size and composition (Rees et al. 1996). Nevertheless, the natural and migration components of change are intertwined. For example, if the urban core loses population to peripheral areas through migration, the peripheral areas gain young populations and grow through natural increase until young populations move again from the peripheral areas leaving an ageing population and natural decrease (Webb 1963). Population change reflecting this demographic pattern has been found in Britain: "the natural change component has usually been operating in the same direction and has thus reinforced rather than offset the effect of migration developments – as indeed would be expected, given that young couples about to start a family form a major element in outward migration from city cores" (Champion 1987, p. 395). Champion (1987) found that rural areas tended to experience net migration gain and natural decrease.

Considerable attention has been paid in this field to sub-national areas' changing demographic functions and how this relates to urban-ness. One of the most widely cited theories, which focuses on the migration component of population change, is Zelinsky's (1971) idea of 'mobility transitions'. This suggested there would be transitions from 'rural to rural' migration, to 'rural to urban' migration, to 'urban to urban' migration. Since the middle of the twentieth century patterns of counter-urbanisation – 'urban to rural' migration – have been identified in much of the developed world (e.g. Champion 1989; Frey 2006; Plane et al. 2005). Recent studies have revealed, however, that there may be once again urban population gain due to migration (re-urbanisation), particularly for young people. Migration flows are not as unidirectional as traditional theories suggest and may not be a step-wise progression of moves up or down the urban hierarchy (Champion et al. 2007; Plane et al. 2005; Dennett and Stillwell 2009).

Plane, Henrie and Perry (2005) used the concept of an urban hierarchy to explore patterns of natural change and migration. They showed that, for the USA, natural change is the most important component of population change for the country as a whole and for each type of area on a categorisation of urban hierarchy with the exception of the least urban. They found that younger urban populations – resulting from the young populations migrating to the most urban areas – had highest natural growth (excess births over deaths).

A common characteristic of these demographic studies is an attempt to identify what characteristics of places are associated with certain types of population change. In population studies more broadly, the construction of area typologies has become a sophisticated field. Vickers and Rees (2007), for example, used 2001 Census data at neighbourhood level for the UK to identify areas with similar demographic, socio-economic and environmental characteristics. Relatively few studies have attempted to typologise areas on the basis of population change. Dennett and Stillwell's (Dennett and Stillwell 2009) national geodemographic area classification for Britain based on the characteristics of migrants and migration flows is an exception. Others have attempted to classify places and population change on the basis of the relationship between demographic components of change (natural change). It is these studies that are most closely aligned to the aims of this chapter. Webb (1963) made use of 1921 and 1931 Census data for England and Wales to examine the drivers of population change and their geographies. He proposed an eight category typology of population change based on the balance of natural change and net migration. This approach is developed by Morrill (1995) who draws together the relationships between migration, births, deaths, ages and type of area to produce a typology of population change. He demonstrated, using net migration estimates and US Census data, that the typology accurately reflected population change in the counties of Oregon and Washington in the 1980s. Morrill brought together concepts of demographic and mobility transitions, life-stage and urban-ness. He theorised that the type of population change of an area depends on whether the population of that area is growing or declining and at what rate, the age structure of the population, the rates of natural increase and migration, and the type of area in terms of urban-ness and economic development. In particular, he distinguished between the age of

Table 10.1 Ethnic group age structures and main period of arrival in Britain

Ethnic group	% GB population aged 15–40 2001	% GB population aged 60+ 2001	Main period of arrival in Britain
White	35.0	22.0	Pre-1900
Caribbean	44.5	16.1	1955–1964
African	53.1	4.0	Since 1991
Indian	46.3	10.1	1965–1974
Pakistani	47.1	6.5	1965–1979
Bangladeshi	47.9	5.8	1980–1988
Chinese	53.8	7.6	Since 1991
Other	44.8	5.1	–

Finney and Simpson (2009b)

migrants: young people are found to be moving out of urban areas with declining populations and low natural increase, and those with high natural increase but where there is economic decline. They move into areas of economic resurgence and population growth. In contrast, older people migrate to areas of average population growth and natural increase but with high levels of amenities.

As Morrill's (1995) study indicates, the dynamics of neighbourhood population change are complicated and determined by many contextual factors. It has long been acknowledged that the population dynamics of a neighbourhood "may be interrupted by new trends, particular to the place, which start and re-direct demographic processes" (Webb 1963, p. 142). A place is unlikely to have a consistent, single demographic role or a simple stepwise sequence of demographic change because of the complex overlapping of generations in any place, places acting in more ways than one, and with broader changes in migration (e.g. re-urbanisation) and fertility patterns (e.g. low levels of fertility resulting in fewer births than deaths and population decline, as identified in the second demographic transition, see van de Kaa 1987).

Neighbourhood Demographic Change for Ethnic Groups

This chapter aims to contribute to debate about the demographic function of neighbourhoods by examining how population dynamics of ethnic groups vary within and between areas. Does an area play the same demographic role for all ethnic groups? Little work has examined neighbourhood demographic change for ethnic groups but differences in the components of population change can be expected because of the differing age structures of ethnic groups in Britain, the minority ethnic populations having a youthful age structure compared to a mature, ageing White population (Table 10.1). Indeed, natural change is a larger contributor to population growth than migration for minority groups, in most districts of Britain (Finney and Simpson 2009b; Finney 2010). Natural change is particularly important for South Asian populations, whilst populations of recent immigrant groups (Chinese and African) continue to grow primarily through (im)migration.

Although minority ethnic group populations in Britain are growing more through natural change than migration, it is migration that redistributes the population. In early theories of minority integration migration was theorised as a sequence of 'invasion and succession' which would see a gradual out-movement of immigrants from settlement areas, with areas passing through racial transition as the majority were replaced by minorities who themselves were replaced by new immigrants (Duncan and Duncan 1957; Gordon 1964). In the UK, some case studies explored these theories for immigrant populations such as Jews in London and Manchester (Newman 1985; Valins 2003) and Irish in major cities such as London, Manchester, Birmingham and Glasgow (MacRaild 1999; Busteed et al. 1992; Busteed 2000; Neal 2000). Whilst some dispersal was evident, clustering remained an important characteristic of immigrant-origin populations, disrupting the 'straight line' theories of spatial and social integration, and bringing discussion about 'good segregation' and 'bad segregation' (Peach 1996).

It was not until the availability of UK census data on ethnicity that large scale studies explored ethnic group population change (Peach 1996; Champion 1996). More recently the debate has been renewed, partly in response to the political context and increased interest in ethnic integration (see Kalra and Kapoor 2009; Flint and Robinson 2008) and partly as a result of calls for a more dynamic approach to ethnic integration research (Simpson et al. 2008; Simpson 2007). Analysis of ethnic group migration using census data has consistently shown similarities across ethnic groups in both the characteristics of migrants and the geographies of their migration (Finney and Simpson 2008; Simpson and Finney 2009; Stillwell and Hussain 2010; Simon 2010). Within Britain, White and minority groups are moving away from concentrations of minority population; away from urban centres (Simpson and Finney 2009; Stillwell and Hussain 2010; Simon 2010).

The migrants from concentrations of minority population have specific characteristics which are similar in each ethnic group; they tend to be older adults and families, suburbanising and in higher occupational classes (Finney 2011; Catney and Simpson 2010). The social gradient of moves from urban settlement areas that is consistent across ethnic groups suggests 'affluent flight' rather than racially motivated migration (Catney and Simpson 2010).

Effects of Diverse Neighbourhoods

There are reasons to theorise that the population dynamics of ethnic groups in a neighbourhood can affect the experiences of its residents. Two fields of neighbourhood effects research are relevant for this theorisation. First, work that has asked how the ethnic diversity of a neighbourhood affects its residents in terms of, for example, perceptions of social cohesion, experiences of crime and health outcomes. Second, the field concerned with social disorganisation which encompasses the potential effect that population change in a neighbourhood has on the lives of its residents.

Perhaps the most influential neighbourhood effects debate concerned with ethnic diversity has been around diversity's relation to social capital, stimulated by the work of Putnam (2007). This study found greater ethnic diversity to be associated with less neighbourhood trust, the argument being that ethnic grouping is a social marker defining individuals' belonging, and trust is greater within rather than between social groups. Counterarguments have been made and questions raised about the causal pathways of the associations between social capital (or cohesion) and diversity, such as the role of inter-group contact (e.g. Laurence 2011; Letki 2008; Hooghe et al. 2009) and whether it is deprivation rather than diversity that is having the effect (Laurence and Heath 2008; Forrest and Kearns 1999).

Studies on the effects of diverse neighbourhoods have extended their focus beyond impact on social capital or cohesion. For example, Bécares et al. (2009) have examined the effect of ethnic diversity of neighbourhood of residence on health outcomes. They found that living in areas of high co-ethnic density had a buffering effect on negative health outcomes. In other words, mechanisms are operating such that living with people of the same ethnicity has a protective health effect. Taylor et al. (2010) examined the contention that people living in ethnically diverse areas perceive higher levels of anti-social behaviour and found evidence to the contrary. Both Bécares et al. (2009) and Taylor et al. (2010) conclude that material conditions of the neighbourhood, particularly the level of deprivation, are more important determinants of perceptions of crime and health outcomes than neighbourhood ethnic diversity.

A second body of neighbourhood effects research of relevance for this chapter is that which engages with theories of social disorganisation (Raudenbush and Sampson 2004). The basic premise here is that disorganised communities are less socially cohesive. One aspect of disorganisation is said to be neighbourhood population instability. Although this work has tended to focus on crime (or perceptions of crime) resulting from neighbourhoods with unstable populations, an argument can also be made about community cohesion and ethnic relations. For example, if there is greater residential instability it might be hypothesised that there is less feeling of neighbourhood belonging and, furthermore, if that instability is resulting in increased ethnic diversity, a greater erosion of community feeling. Using the Citizenship Survey, Laurence and Heath (2008) found that population turnover did not have a significant effect on perceptions of community cohesion in a neighbourhood but the in-migration of large numbers of non-white immigrants negatively affected cohesion. In addition, migration to and from an area may be affected by the diversity of the area in that people may be more or less attracted to areas of certain ethnic make-up (van Ham and Feijten 2008).

Data and Methods

A Demographic Typology of Population Dynamics

In order to describe the population dynamics for ethnic groups in Britain's neighbourhoods and provide an approach for conceptualising and operationalising these population dynamics, this chapter develops a typology of population dynamics.

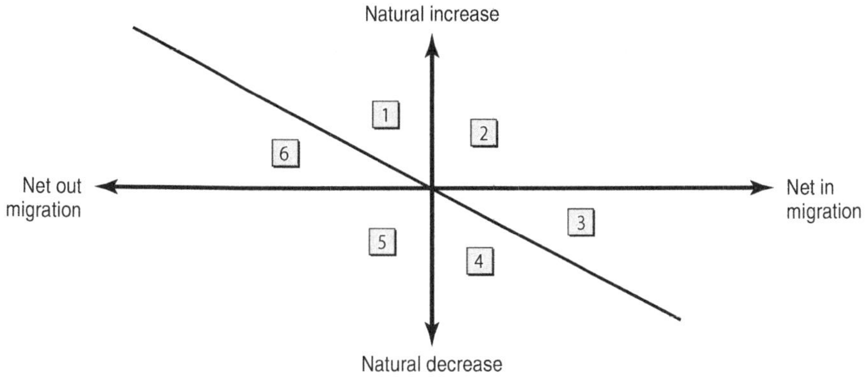

Typology category	Typology category title	Demographic indicators of population dynamics 1 Population increase or decrease	2 Natural gain or loss	3 Net migration gain or loss
1	Growth: family building & migration loss	Increase	Natural gain	Net migration loss
2	Growth: family building & migration gain	Increase	Natural gain	Net migration gain
3	Growth: ageing loss & migration gain	Increase	Natural loss	Net migration gain
4	Decline: ageing loss & migration gain	Decrease	Natural loss	Net migration gain
5	Decline: ageing loss & migration loss	Decrease	Natural loss	Net migration loss
6	Decline: family building & migration loss	Decrease	Natural gain	Net migration loss

Fig. 10.1 Demographic typology of population dynamics (Adapted from Webb 1963)

The typology, which will henceforth be referred to as the Demographic Typology of Population Dynamics, is summarised in Fig. 10.1. The starting point for this typology was the work of Webb (1963) who examined the relationship between migration and natural change for sub-national areas of England and Wales in the 1920s.

The Demographic Typology of Population Dynamics characterises the relationship between natural change and migration and can be applied to ethnic groups in neighbourhoods. Each of the six categories of the typology provides a summary of three demographic indicators of population change for the population, place and time period of interest:

1. Population increase or decrease;
2. Natural gain (more births than deaths) or natural loss (more deaths than births);
3. Net migration gain (more in-migrants than out-migrants) or net migration loss (more out-migrants than in-migrants).

These three indicators are depicted by the axes in Fig. 10.1. To the right of the diagonal represents population increase and to the left represents population decrease; above the horizontal represents natural increase and below represents natural decrease; to the right of the vertical axis represents net migration gain and to the left represents net migration loss. Thus, the typology has six categories that uniquely combine these three indicators.

A neighbourhood that has natural gain can be considered to be a place where people are having children, where they are building families (and thus, there are more births in the area than there are deaths). To give more interpretative meaning to the titles of the Demographic Typology of Population Dynamics categories, natural increase is referred to as 'Family Building'. A neighbourhood that has natural loss can be considered to be a place where there is an ageing population structure i.e. there are relatively high proportions of older adults and elderly people. Death rates increase with age (excluding infants) and the occurrence of more deaths than births in a neighbourhood (natural loss) is likely to be, therefore, a result of an ageing population. In the titles of the Demographic Typology of Population Dynamics categories, natural loss is therefore referred to as 'Ageing Loss'.

The advantage of using this typology rather than, for example, a measure of migration alone, is that it captures all the demographic components of population change in a neighbourhood and the relative importance of these components. It thereby provides a categorical depiction of the demographic function of the neighbourhood and allows us to compare how this varies for population sub-groups, in this case ethnic groups.

Data

This chapter uses original estimates of components of population change – births, deaths and net migration – for ethnic groups in wards in Britain for the decade 1991–2001. Although the UK censuses provide migration data for ethnic groups and sub-national areas (see Finney and Simpson 2008 for a review), these data are for the 1 year before each census only, while birth and death registrations in the UK do not record ethnic group. This research developed well established demographic techniques for decomposing population change for application to ethnic groups, small areas and the data available in the UK.

The estimates of components of population change used, as their base population, estimates that take into account changes in the population base, ethnic group categories and small area boundaries between 1991 and 2001 (Sabater and Simpson 2007).

Births and deaths were estimated for ethnic groups in each ward then subtracted from the decade population change to give local net migration as a residual. The estimates provide population also broken down by single year of age and sex, though this detail is not used here.

The resultant dataset of components of population change is particularly original in its estimation of the age structure of the net impact of migration over a decade with emigration included. Such information is not available directly from the UK censuses. The method also has the advantage of being applicable at all geographical scales. A disadvantage of the method, however, is that it provides statistics of net migration; details of inflows, outflows, origins and destinations are lacking. For further details of the estimation procedures see Finney and Simpson (2009b) or Finney (2010). The ethnic group components of population change estimates for wards and districts of Britain are available from the UK Data Archive.

Defining Ethnic Groups

The components of population change estimates categorise people into ethnic groups based on their responses to the 1991 and 2001 census questions on ethnic group. Eight ethnic group categories are used in this chapter. These eight categories are the most robust over the inter-censal decade (see Sabater and Simpson 2007). There is much debate about the meaning of the census ethnic group categories, and the extent to which they successfully capture the ethnic diversity of Britain (for example see Aspinall 2000). There is considerable heterogeneity within the ethnic groups captured by the census and they can in no way provide an essential character for a set of people nor full explanations for differing experiences. However, ethnic group information can be viewed as a useful indicator of certain individual and group characteristics. In this chapter ethnic categories are used to approximate groups who differ in terms of their ancestral (im)migration history, their colour, their religion, and their customs and traditions. Particular age structures and levels of education and wealth are also associated with different ethnic groups. For a demographic analysis such as this, ethnic difference in age structure are particularly important. Table 10.1 summarises the age structure of the eight ethnic groups. While around a third (35%) of the White population are aged between 15 and 40, closer to half of the population of the non-White ethnic groups falls into this young age category. This is a result of immigration history: immigrants arriving in Britain over the last few decades were predominantly in their 20s and 30s and are only now entering older age.

Defining Neighbourhoods

The neighbourhood analysis in this chapter is based on wards. Wards are electoral divisions represented by councillors in local government. There are 8,797 wards in Britain with an average population (in 2001) of just under 6,000. Ward populations range from 995 to 35,767 (standard deviation of 4,114). The maps in Figs. 10.2

and 10.4 display results for local authority districts. Districts are aggregations of wards; they are administrative units with an average population in 2001 of 140,746, ranging from 2,138 (Isles of Scilly) to 984,642 (Birmingham) (standard deviation 95,506). There are 408 districts in Britain. This chapter distinguishes London, Metropolitan areas, and other urban and rural areas.

Population Dynamics of Ethnic Groups

This section examines how the ethnic group populations of neighbourhoods changed in the 1990s using the Demographic Typology of Population Dynamics (Fig. 10.1). Table 10.2 displays the frequency of each Demographic Typology of Population Dynamics category for each of the eight ethnic groups and minorities (non-White groups) taken as a whole. If the proportion of wards with population growth (categories 1–3) is compared with the proportion whose population declined (categories 4–6) there are clear ethnic differences: in 90% of wards the ethnic minority population grew in the 1990s whereas this was the case for the White population in 54% of Britain's wards.

A key difference between the minority and White population dynamics is in the proportion of areas experiencing ageing loss (more deaths than births). This is the case for the White population in over 50% of wards whereas very few wards were characterised by ageing loss in the 1990s for the non-White (minority) population. This difference is expected given the older age structure of the White population (Table 10.1).

In two-thirds of the wards with White natural loss there was also net in-migration (categories 3 and 4). This suggests that White migration is replacing the ageing White population in almost a third of Britain's wards. By far the most common population dynamic for each of the minority ethnic groups was growth due to migration combined with family building (category 2). This accounted for population change for the minority population taken as a whole in more than three quarters of Britain's wards.

In summary, Table 10.2 presents a number of important messages. First, the population of each ethnic group grew in the majority of wards. For the non-White groups, most wards experienced net in-migration and family building together (the case for the White population in a fifth of wards). In the minority of wards with population decline, this was mainly due to out-migration for all ethnic groups. In a third of wards White in-migration replaced loss of an ageing population. Very few wards were characterised by natural decline in the 1990s for the non-White ethnic groups.

Let us turn now to consider where the areas of each type of population change are located. This is presented as a map for each of four broad ethnic groups in Fig. 10.2. The ethnic groups have been collapsed to these four broad categories on the basis of similarities in their immigration histories and age structures (see Table 10.1) and in the frequency and spatial distribution of Demographic Typology of Population Dynamics categories across wards.

Table 10.2 Frequency of Demographic Typology of Population Dynamics categories, by ethnic group (percentages of wards in Britain)

	White	Minority	Caribbean	African	Indian	Pakistani	Bangladeshi	Chinese	Other
1. Growth: family building and migration loss	6.8	13.3	4.8	4.6	8.3	7.7	6.2	5.7	13.8
2. Growth: family building and migration gain	20.5	77.3	37.8	65.2	62.4	70.0	74.7	66.6	80.2
3. Growth: ageing loss and migration gain	26.1	0.1	21.6	11.0	6.0	9.9	4.0	3.8	0.1
4. Decline: ageing loss and migration gain	9.0	0.0	0.5	0.1	0.1	0.1	0.1	0.1	0.0
5. Decline: ageing loss and migration loss	15.0	0.0	7.9	2.6	1.1	0.8	0.9	0.6	0.0
6. Decline: family building and migration loss	22.6	9.2	27.4	16.4	22.1	11.4	14.1	23.2	5.8

Source: CCSR Components of Population Change Estimates (1991–2001), Wards of Britain

Fig. 10.2 Geographical distribution of demographic typology of population dynamics categories, by broad ethnic group (Source: Census 2001, Local Authority Boundaries)

The areas of White population decline due to migration (shaded black and dark grey) are urban centres of London, Birmingham, South Wales, Glasgow and northern English cities. Districts with White population decline due to ageing loss are in the peripheries of urban regions, particularly the North West and North East of England and Scotland. Migration gain together with family building characterises White population change in districts bordering urban centres, particularly in South and South East England. Migration gain with ageing loss characterises White population change in rural districts of Britain. White family building is the predominant population dynamic for Whites in South East England, in the ring of districts peripheral to greater London. These patterns of population change reflect recognised processes of decentralisation, migration to the South East and rural ageing loss.

However, the recognised patterns that characterise population dynamics for the majority ethnic population are not replicated for other ethnic groups. Migration gain with family building characterises population change throughout the country, including in London, for the African/Chinese/Other and South Asian groups. The Caribbean population in London and the South East also grew predominantly as a result of net in-migration with family building. For Caribbeans, population loss due to migration outweighed gains from family building in districts across the rest of England and Wales.

What the maps in Fig. 10.2 suggest is that a neighbourhood can have different demographic functions for different ethnic groups. This is confirmed by an examination of population dynamics for areas categorised by urban-ness. Figure 10.3 presents the frequency of Demographic Typology of Population Dynamics categories for wards of varying urban-ness, by ethnic group. Inner London wards are characterised by population growth due to migration and family building of all groups, with migration gain dominant for the African/Chinese group and family building dominant for the South Asian group. Net out-migration resulted in loss of the White population in almost 40% of Inner London wards and loss of Caribbean population in half of Inner London wards. In Outer London, growth due to migration dominates for the non-White groups whilst the White population declined in four-fifths of wards due to migration loss. With increasing rural-ness, the proportion of wards losing White and Caribbean population (due to migration) declines as the impact of net in-migration grows. For the African/Chinese and South Asian groups the proportion of wards experiencing population loss (due to migration) remains around 10% for metropolitan, mixed and rural areas. A further feature of Fig. 10.3 is notable: in three quarters of rural wards White population was gained where there was a combination of ageing loss and migration gain.

Characterising Neighbourhood Ethnic Group Population Dynamics

The results have so far presented population dynamics for ethnic groups separately, showing ethnic difference in the relations and relative importance of natural change and migration, and in the geographies of population dynamics. This section turns to

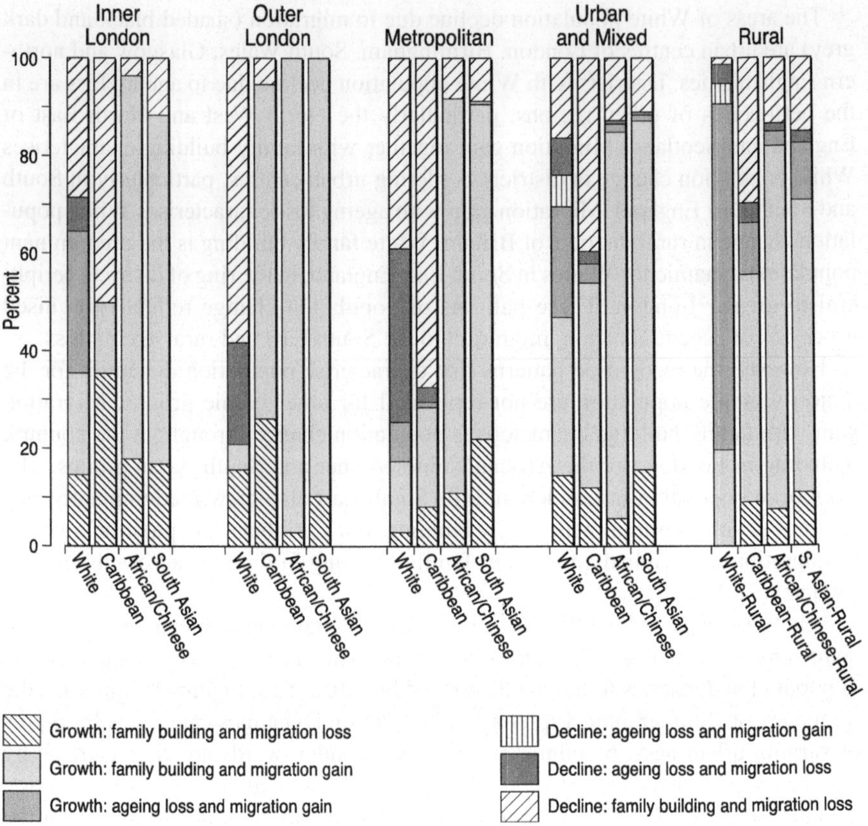

Fig. 10.3 Frequency of demographic typology of population dynamics categories for wards of varying urban-ness, by ethnic group (Source: CCSR Components of Population Change Estimates (1991–2001), Wards of Britain)

compare directly the dynamics of ethnic groups within areas. Population dynamics of the White population are compared with those of the minority (non-White) population. The minority population, made up of all the non-White groups discussed above, is heterogeneous in terms of its demographics. However, Table 10.2 and Figs. 10.2 and 10.3 illustrate that the types and spatial distribution of the Demographic Typology of Population Dynamics categories are more similar between minority groups than between those groups and the White group. The results for the minority ethnic group as a whole cannot be generalised to each ethnic group but rather indicate the population dynamics for populations whose origins are in immigration to Britain over the last 60 years.

The method used to compare wards in terms of their White and minority population dynamics is a straightforward one. All the potential combinations (permutations) of the six Demographic Typology of Population Dynamics categories for the White population with the six categories for the minority population were listed and the frequency of the occurrence of each for wards in Britain was calculated. In total there are 30 potential combinations (permutations) of White and minority population dynamics.[1] However, 70% of wards in Britain fall into five combinations of white and minority population dynamics. These five combinations of white and minority population dynamics can be summarised into four categories (plus a residual 'Other' category), as shown in Table 10.3: Family growth/White migration loss, Attractor (with demographic momentum), Replacement (White loss, minority gain) and Multi-ethnic growth.

Ethnic group population dynamics category 1, 'Family Growth/White migration loss', contains areas where there was family building (natural increase) for Whites and non-Whites. In most of these wards family building was reinforced by migration gain of the minority population and counteracted by migration loss of the White population. Category 2, 'Attractor (with demographic momentum)', represents wards where the predominant mechanism of population change for both White and non-White groups was migration gain, accompanied by ageing loss of the White population and family building of the minority population. Category 3, 'Replacement (White loss, minority gain)', represents wards where the White population declined due to migration loss and ageing loss and the minority population grew due to migration gain and family building. Category 4, 'Multi-ethnic growth', represents wards where both the White and minority populations grew through migration and family building.

The categories of ethnic group population dynamics reveal whether wards play the same or different demographic functions for the White and minority populations. Around a quarter of Britain's wards were, in the 1990s, operating the same natural change function – family building – for Whites and minorities (category 1; Family Growth/White Migration Loss). A similar proportion were operating the same migration function – net in-migration – for Whites and minorities (category 2; Attractor). A further 10% of wards were operating the same migration and natural change functions, growth in both cases, for Whites and minorities (category 4; Multi-ethnic growth). This suggests ethnic similarities in what is considered to be a desirable neighbourhood to migrate to or in which to build a family. In a further 10% of wards opposing population dynamics were seen for the White and minority populations: Migration loss and ageing loss of Whites with migration gain and family building of minorities (category 3; Replacement).

Figure 10.4 shows the geographical distribution of the four categories of ethnic group population dynamics. It shows that the Family Growth/White Migration Loss and Multi-ethnic Growth areas are over-represented in the peripheries of large urban centres and Attractor areas are over-represented in rural parts of Britain. There is no clear geography to Replacement areas, though they are all in urban districts.

[1] The number of permutations for six categories and two ethnic groups is calculated as: 6!/(6–2!) = 720/24 = 30.

Table 10.3 Categories of ethnic group population dynamics

	Ethnic group population dynamics category	White population dynamic	Minority population dynamic	Demographic function	% of GB wards
1.	Family growth/white migration loss	Family building/migration loss	Family building/migration loss Family building/migration gain	Same natural change function for Whites and minorities	23.3
2.	Attractor (with demographic momentum)	Ageing loss/migration gain	Family building/migration gain	Same migration function for Whites and minorities	27.2
3.	Replacement (white loss, minority gain)	Ageing loss/migration loss	Family building/migration gain	Opposite demographic functions for Whites and minorities	9.1
4.	Multi-ethnic growth	Family building/migration gain	Family building/migration gain	Same demographic functions for Whites and minorities	10.9
5.	Other				29.5

Source: CCSR Components of Population Change Estimates (1991–2001), Wards of Britain

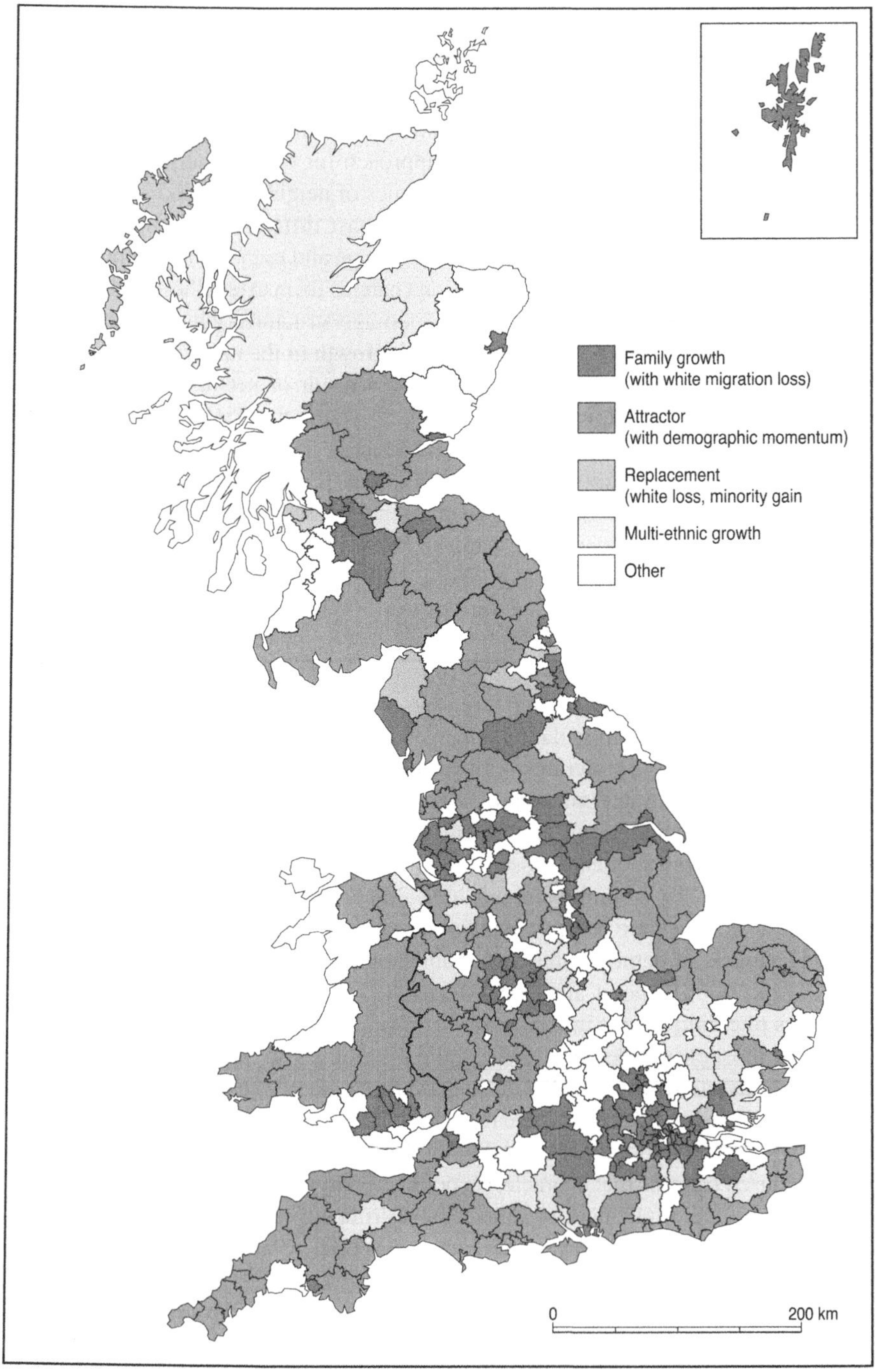

Fig. 10.4 Geographical distribution of categories of ethnic group population dynamics (Source: CCSR Components of Population Change Estimates (1991–2001), Ward level categorisation applied to districts of Britain. 2001 Census)

Discussion

This chapter has used estimates of components of population change for the 1990s to analyse the population dynamics of ethnic groups in neighbourhoods, and their geographical patterns; and to provide an approach for conceptualising and operationalising the ethnic group population dynamics of neighbourhoods.

It is clear from the analyses that ethnic groups have different population dynamics in terms of the relative importance of natural change and migration, and the relation between these two components of population change. To an extent these ethnic differences can be interpreted in terms of the group age structures which are related to their immigration histories. So, the population growth in the majority of wards that is found for each ethnic group was primarily a result of net in-migration for all groups apart from Pakistani and Bangladeshi, for whom the growth was mainly due to family building (natural increase). This is expected given the young age structures of these South Asian populations. For the same reason, very few wards were characterised by ageing loss (natural decline) in the 1990s for the non-White ethnic groups. More than three quarters of wards in Britain experienced migration gain and family building together for the non-White ethnic groups (the case for the White population in a fifth of wards). In a third of wards White in-migration replaced loss of an ageing White population.

Given these results, it seems necessary to pay attention to distinctions in ethnic group population change so that area-based policies can be based on fuller understandings of area population change and its demographic underpinnings. Certainly, differing age structures between ethnic groups play an important role in shaping their population dynamics locally. However, it is not necessarily the case that as minority populations mature in terms of age structure their family and housing choices will replicate those of the majority. Convergence may be sensibly expected in mortality (if improvements in health, health care and life expectancy are assumed to benefit ethnic groups equally) but not necessarily in fertility or migration. Existing models of demographic and mobility transitions (Champion 1987; Webb 1963; Frey 2006; Plane et al. 2005; Morrill 1995) do not capture the population dynamics of ethnic groups in contemporary Britain.

This is most clearly demonstrated by the differences in geographical patterns of population dynamics for the White and minority populations. The geographical patterns of White population change reflect recognised processes of decentralisation, migration to the South East and rural natural loss of ageing populations. However, the recognised patterns that characterise population dynamics for the majority ethnic population are not replicated for other ethnic groups. For example, migration gain together with family building characterises White population change in areas bordering urban centres, particularly in South and South East England whereas for the non-White groups (with the exception of the Caribbean who experienced widespread out migration), family building and migration gain characterised population change throughout the country. More generally, the urban-rural distinction is clear for the White population but not so much for minority groups.

This chapter has suggested that neighbourhood ethnic group population dynamics can be summarised into four categories, which account for dynamics of population change in 70% of Britain's wards. The categories of ethnic group population dynamics are Family Growth/White Migration Loss, Attractor, Replacement and Multi-ethnic Growth. The categorisation demonstrates that a neighbourhood can have the same or different demographic functions for different ethnic groups; it can predominantly operate a single demographic function or multiple demographic functions for its sub-populations.

'Family Growth/White Migration Loss' wards are those where there was family building (natural increase) for Whites and non-Whites accompanied in most cases by net out-migration of the White population. 'Multi-ethnic Growth' wards are those in which the White and minority population are growing through net in-migration and natural growth. Family Growth and Multi-ethnic Growth wards are over-represented in areas peripheral to large urban centres (particularly London and Birmingham). 'Attractor' wards are those where the predominant mechanism of population change was net in-migration, accompanied by natural loss of the White population and family building of the non-White population. Attractor districts are over-represented in rural areas.

Attractor and Multi-ethnic Growth wards – where the main force of population change is growth either through White and minority in-migration (Attractor), or in-migration and natural growth (Multi-ethnic Growth) – account for population dynamics in 40% of wards in Britain. These rural and urban-periphery neighbourhoods can be described as having singular demographic functions, and planners can respond to population change common across ethnic groups. The extent that ward population dynamics in these neighbourhoods are largely ethnically indistinct suggests ethnic similarities in area choice for the residentially mobile, and people starting families.

In 10% of Britain's wards the mechanism of population change is a combination of White loss (through migration and ageing) and minority growth (through migration and family building). These 'Replacement' neighbourhoods, which are in urban areas, are having to respond to different dynamics of different sectors of the population. The same is true for 'Family Growth/White Migration Loss' neighbourhoods, at least in terms of migration: White are moving out and minorities are moving in.

This chapter does not provide any insight into residential and family choices that produce the population dynamics observed. Although dispersal of minority ethnic groups from the urban areas in which they are concentrated has been observed (Simpson and Finney 2009; Stillwell and Hussain 2010; Simon 2010), it is not clear whether minority families will remain in urban centres or follow the patterns of suburbanisation and counterurbanisation which have so consistently characterised population change of the White population. Certainly, there are reasons for minority families to remain close to ethnic or cultural centres (Peach 1996) and the migration decisions of minority young adults may well be different from those of their White peers (Finney 2011). If suburbanisation of minority populations does not follow that of Whites, this is not necessarily an indication of lack of ethnic integration. Diverse urban neighbourhoods may be playing an important role demographically and socially for Britain's maturing minority populations.

A clear extension of this chapter would be to analyse the Demographic Typology of Population Dynamics alongside data on community cohesion to test for evidence of neighbourhood effects of ethnic group population dynamics. It could be proposed, in accordance with disorganisation theory (Raudenbush and Sampson 2004) that, for example, Replacement districts would be of concern in terms community cohesion due to the population dynamics most dramatically resulting in change in ethnic composition, namely an increase in diversity. It is possible to assess this assertion by combining the Demographic Typology of Population Dynamics with data about cohesion such as the Citizenship Survey in England and Wales. The extent to which lower levels of cohesion indicators are to do with residents observing ethnically differentiated population change and interpreting this as problematic would be difficult to establish. However, investigation of whether it is diversity, population instability, both or neither that affect community cohesion would be an interesting avenue for further research.

This chapter has demonstrated the complexities of neighbourhood ethnic group population change and has identified the key types of population dynamics for each ethnic group and their geographies. It has provided an approach for conceptualising and operationalising neighbourhood ethnic group population change and demonstrated that the categorisation is interpretable in terms of urban change and migration patterns, and may be useful in understanding perceptions of cohesion, given that these may be affected more by local population change than by static measures of segregation. Using a categorisation of the ethnic group dynamics of neighbourhoods as an alternative to static measures of ethnic composition may provide alternative and more nuanced understandings of the effects of diverse neighbourhoods.

Acknowledgements The boundary data used in the maps in Figs. 10.2 and 10.4 come from the UK Census. Census output is Crown copyright and is reproduced with the permission of the Controller of HMSO and the Queen's Printer for Scotland. This research was sponsored by the Economic and Social Research Council through the Understanding Population Trends and Processes (UPTAP) programme, grant RES-163-27-0011. I am extremely grateful for the support, financial and otherwise, provided by the UPTAP initiative. I am grateful to the editors for helpful comments on earlier versions of this chapter.

References

Aspinall, P. (2000). The challenges of measuring the ethno-cultural diversity of Britain in the new millennium. *Policy and Politics, 28*(1), 109–118.

Bécares, L., Nazroo, J., & Stafford, M. (2009). The buffering effects of ethnic density on experienced racism and health. *Health & Place, 15*(3), 670–678.

Busteed, M. (2000). Little islands of Erin: Irish settlement and identity in mid-nineteenth century Manchester. In D. M. MacRaild (Ed.), *The great famine and beyond: Irish migrants in Britain in the nineteenth and twentieth centuries* (pp. 94–127). Dublin: Irish Academic Press.

Busteed, M., Hodgson, R., & Kennedy, T. (1992). The myth and reality of Irish migrants in mid-19th century Manchester: A preliminary study. In P. O'Sullivan (Ed.), *The Irish in the new communities* (pp. 26–51). Leicester: Leicester University Press.

Catney, G., & Simpson, L. (2010). Settlement area migration in England and Wales: Assessing evidence for a social gradient. *Transactions of the Institute of British Geographers, 35*(4), 571–584.

Champion, A. G. (1987). Recent changes in the pace of population deconcentration in Britain. *Geoforum, 18*(4), 379–401.

Champion, A. (1989). *Counterurbanisation: The changing pace and nature of population deconcentration*. London: Edward Arnold.

Champion, T. (1996). Internal migration and ethnicity in Britain. In P. Ratcliffe (Ed.), *Ethnicity in the 1991 census* (Social geography and ethnicity in Britain: Geographical spread, spatial concentration and internal migration, Vol. 3, pp. 135–173). London: ONS/HMSO.

Champion, T., Coombes, M., Raybould, S., & Wymer, C. (2007). *Population movement and the socio-economic complexion of communities*. York: Joseph Rowntree Foundation.

Dennett, A., & Stillwell, J. (2009). Internal migration in Britain, 2000-01, examined through an area classification framework. *Population, Space and Place, 16*(6), 517–538.

Duncan, O. D., & Duncan, B. (1957). *The negro population of Chicago*. Chicago: University of Chicago Press.

Finney, N. (2010). Ethnic group population change and integration: A demographic approach to small area ethnic geographies. In J. Stillwell & M. van Ham (Eds.), *Understanding population trends and processes* (Ethnicity and integration, Vol. 3, pp. 27–45). Dordrecht: Springer.

Finney, N. (2011). Understanding ethnic differences in migration of young adults within Britain from a lifecourse perspective. *Transactions of the Institute of British Geographers, 36*(3), 455–470.

Finney, N., & Simpson, L. (2008). Internal migration and ethnic groups: Evidence for Britain from the 2001 census. *Population, Space and Place, 14*(2), 63–83.

Finney, N., & Simpson, L. (2009a). *Sleepwalking to segregation? Challenging myths of race and migration*. Bristol: The Policy Press.

Finney, N., & Simpson, L. (2009b). Population dynamics: The roles of natural change and migration in producing the ethnic mosaic. *Journal of Ethnic and Migration Studies, 35*(9), 1479–1496.

Flint, J., & Robinson, D. (Eds.). (2008). *Community cohesion in crisis? New dimensions of diversity and difference*. Bristol: Policy Press.

Forrest, R., & Kearns, A. (1999). *Joined-up places? Social cohesion and neighbourhood regeneration*. York: Joseph Rowntree Foundation.

Frey, W. (2006). *Diversity spreads out: Metropolitan shifts in Hispanic, Asian, and black populations since 2000* (Living cities census series). Washington, DC: The Brookings Institute.

Gordon, M. M. (1964). *Assimilation in American life: The role of race, religion, and national origins*. Oxford: Oxford University Press.

Hooghe, M., Reeskends, T., Stolle, D., & Trappers, A. (2009). Ethnic diversity and generalized trust in Europe. *Comparative Political Studies, 42*(2), 198–223.

Kalra, V., & Kapoor, N. (2009). Interrogating segregation, integration and the community cohesion agenda. *Journal of Ethnic and Migration Studies, 35*(9), 1397–1415.

Laurence, J. (2011). The effect of ethnic diversity and community disadvantage on social cohesion: Multi-level analysis of social capital and interethnic relations in UK communities. *European Sociological Review, 27*(1), 70–89.

Laurence, J., & Heath, A. (2008). *Predictors of community cohesion: Multi-level modelling of the 2005 citizenship survey*. London: CLG.

Letki, N. (2008). Does diversity erode social cohesion. Social capital and race in British neighbourhoods. *Political Studies, 56*(1), 99–126.

MacRaild, D. M. (1999). *Irish migrants in modern Britain, 1750–1922*. Basingstoke: Macmillan.

Morrill, R. L. (1995). Aging in places, age specific migration and natural decrease. *The Annals of Regional Science, 29*(1), 41–66.

Neal, F. (2000). The foundations of the Irish settlement in Newcastle upon Tyne: The evidence in the 1851 census. In D. M. MacRaild (Ed.), *The great famine and beyond: Irish migrants in Britain in the nineteenth and twentieth centuries* (pp. 71–93). Dublin: Irish Academic Press.

Newman, D. (1985). Integration and ethnic spatial concentration: The changing distribution of the Anglo-Jewish community. *Transactions of the Institute of British Geographers, 10*(3), 360–376.

Peach, C. (1996). Good segregation, bad segregation. *Planning Perspectives, 11*(4), 1–20.

Plane, D. A., Henrie, C. J., & Perry, M. J. (2005). Migration up and down the urban hierarchy and across the life course. *PNAS, 102*(43), 15313–15318.

Putnam, R. (2007). *E Pluribus Unum:* Diversity and community in the twenty-first century – The 2006 Johan Skytte prize lecture. *Scandinavian Political Studies, 30*(2), 137–174.

Raudenbush, S. W., & Sampson, R. J. (2004). Seeing disorder: Neighbourhood stigma and the social construction of "broken windows". *Social Psychology Quarterly, 67*(4), 319–342.

Rees, P., Durham, H., & Kupizzewski, M. (1996). *Internal migration and regional population dynamics in Europe: United Kingdom case study*. Council of Europe University of Leeds, Department of Geography. University of Leeds, Department of Geography Working Paper 96/20. Available at: http://www.geog.leeds.ac.uk/fileadmin/downloads/school/research/wpapers/96-20.pdf. Accessed Aug 2012.

Sabater, A., & Simpson, L. (2007). *Correcting the census: A consistent time series of ethnic group, age, sex for small areas in England and Wales, 1991-2001*. CCSR working Paper 2007–2011. Available at: http://www.ccsr.ac.uk/publications/working/2007-11.pdf. Accessed Aug 2012.

Simon, A. (2010). Do ethnic groups migrate towards areas of high concentrations of their own groups within England and Wales? In J. Stillwell & M. van Ham (Eds.), *Understanding population trends and processes* (Ethnicity and integration, Vol. 3, pp. 133–151). Dordrecht: Springer.

Simpson, L. (2007). Ghettos of the mind: The empirical behaviour of indices of segregation and diversity. *Journal of the Royal Statistical Society: Series A (Statistics in Society), 170*(2), 405–424.

Simpson, L., & Finney, N. (2009). Spatial patterns of internal migration: Evidence for ethnic groups in Britain. *Population, Space and Place, 15*(1), 37–56.

Simpson, L., Gavalas, V., & Finney, N. (2008). Population dynamics in ethnically diverse towns: The long-term implications of immigration. *Urban Studies, 45*(1), 163–184.

Slater, T., & Anderson, N. (2012). The reputational Ghetto: Territorial stigmatisation in St. Paul's, Bristol. *Transactions of the Institute of British Geographers, 37*.

Stillwell, J., & Hussain, S. (2010). Ethnic internal migration in England and Wales: Spatial analysis using a district classification framework. In J. Stillwell & M. van Ham (Eds.), *Understanding population trends and processes: Vol. 3. Ethnicity and integration* (Chapter 6). Dordrecht: Springer.

Taylor, J., Twigg, L., & Mohan, J. (2010). Investigating perceptions of antisocial behaviour and ethnic heterogeneity in the British crime survey. *Transactions of the Institute of British Geographers, 35*(1), 59–75.

Valins, O. (2003). Stubborn identities and the construction of socio-spatial boundaries ultra-Orthodox Jews living in contemporary Britain. *Transactions of the Institute of British Geographers, 28*(2), 158–175.

van de Kaa, D. J. (1987). Europe's second demographic transition. *Population Bulletin, 42*(1), 1–59.

van Ham, M., & Feijten, P. (2008). Who wants to leave the neighbourhood? The effect of being different from the neighbourhood population on wishes to move. *Environment and Planning A, 40*(5), 1151–1170.

Vickers, D. W., & Rees, P. H. (2007). *Creating the national statistics 2001 output area classification*. Series: Journal of the Royal Statistical Society. *A*59.

Wacquant, L. (2008). *Urban outcasts: A comparative sociology of advanced marginality*. Cambridge: Polity Press.

Webb, J. W. (1963). The natural and migrational components of population changes in England and Wales, 1921-1931. *Economic Geography, 39*(2), 130–148.

Zelinsky, W. (1971). The hypothesis of the mobility transition. *Geographical Review, 61*(2), 219–249.

Chapter 11
Testing the Racial Proxy Hypothesis: What Is It That Residents Don't Like About Their Neighbourhood?

Karien Dekker

Introduction

Studies investigating neighbourhood effects aim to find out to what extent individual outcomes can be explained by individual level characteristics (such as level of education), or by neighbourhood characteristics. This approach is part of the general interest among urban geographers, sociologists and social psychologists to connect influences and outcomes at the macro and micro level and understand how these impact people's lives, with the 'Coleman Boat' as the most famous and graphically clear example (Coleman 1990). The Coleman Boat shows how a macro level phenomena influences individual level behaviours, which also then lead to a macro level effects. Neighbourhood effect studies focus on a wide variety of outcomes, such as health (Galster 2010), moving patterns (Hedman and van Ham 2011), occupational mobility (van Ham and Manley 2010), and income (Andersson et al. 2007). Many of these studies find associations between living in an area with a concentration of low-income and/or non-Western ethnic minorities and individual behaviour and attitudes. Some of these studies claim to have found causal effects of neighbourhood characteristics on individual outcomes, but these are heavily debated.

Despite an increasing interest in neighbourhood effects, many questions remain unanswered. First, most studies use a few indicators of the neighbourhood context, focusing mostly on a neighbourhood's social demographic characteristics, limiting our understanding of how the neighbourhoods are experienced by the residents themselves. Second, most studies are limited to a single time point (Sampson and Groves 1989; Sampson et al. 2005), and it remains unclear if generalisations to other points in

K. Dekker (✉)
Faculty of Social Sciences, Sociology, Utrecht University,
P.O. Box 80140, 3508 TC Utrecht, The Netherlands
e-mail: kariendekker@telfort.nl

M. van Ham et al. (eds.), *Understanding Neighbourhood Dynamics: New Insights for Neighbourhood Effects Research*, DOI 10.1007/978-94-007-4854-5_11,

time can be made. Third, it is usually unclear which kind of neighbourhood deprivation is studied. Deprivation can be defined in terms of low income (Madanipour 1998) but is sometimes confused with concentrations of ethnic groups. Yet, as Musterd (2005) points out, segregation levels of low-income households tend to be lower than segregation levels of ethnic minorities in the Netherlands. Ethnic minorities are concentrated in certain parts of the city more than low-income households, which indicates that more caution in the differential effects of concentration of low-income households and ethnic minorities is needed.

The discussion on neighbourhood effects is highly policy-relevant, as in many Western countries including the Netherlands, the UK and the USA (see Dekker and Varady 2011; Kearns and Mason 2007) current and past urban renewal policies aim to create neighbourhoods in which people have opportunities, and where satisfaction with the neighbourhood is high (VROM-raad 2002; VROM 2000, 2004, 2007). Through improving housing, education, work, integration and safety the government aims to create equal opportunity and satisfaction. In the Dutch context, the 'Special Measures Regarding the Big Cities Problems' (informally labelled 'the Rotterdam Law', see www.rijksoverheid.nl) enables cities to specify areas with high unemployment and high shares of low income households as 'Opportunity Zones'. These zones receive extra funding and can be subject to special measures, such as preventing any more low-income households from moving in[1] (Ministry of Justice 2005). Again, a connection is made between certain neighbourhood characteristics (unemployment, low incomes) and problems, all with the aim to create neighbourhoods with higher levels of satisfaction. Implicitly the government thereby confirms the connection between a low social-economic status[2] of a neighbourhood (with high shares of non-Western ethnic minorities[3] in the Netherlands, because concentrations of non-Western ethnic minority populations is even higher), the existence of problems, and low satisfaction rates.

The aim of this chapter is to add to the scientific and policy discussion, and increase our understanding about what causes neighbourhood satisfaction. Residential satisfaction is a key factor in explaining selective in- and out-migrations. The degree of residential satisfaction with their neighbourhood provides an indication of the factors that may affect the decision to stay in a neighbourhood or leave, or maybe to move within it to a dwelling that better satisfies their needs. Satisfaction of current

[1] The acceptance of the 'Rotterdam Law' resulted in large-scale protest because the implicit racial connotation to it. The law allows cities to select low-income households (among them many non-Western ethnic minorities) and refuse them as new residents of deprived neighbourhoods.

[2] Low socio-economic status can be measured in terms of income. In 2010 the average standardized income was €17,000 for a household from a non-Western ethnic minority background, and €24,000 for a household from Dutch origin (CBS, 2010).

[3] According to the Dutch Statistical Office non-Western ethnic minorities are citizens that were born in Asia (excl. Japan and Indonesia), Africa, Turkey, or South America. Also citizens with at least one parent that was born in one of these countries is registered as a non-Western ethnic minority.

neighbourhood residents may also spread over the city, the neighbourhood then gains a better reputation which may attract new residents (Permentier 2012, this volume). Satisfaction with the current neighbourhood lies at the roots of the desire to move or stay, after which preferences, possibilities and constraints influence if and where people move. This is to say, not all residents are capable or willing to move out in the case of dissatisfaction, some may stay. A better understanding of satisfaction is therefore at the core of our understanding of selective migration in and out of neighbourhoods.

There are many factors related to neighbourhood satisfaction. For instance, the ethnic composition of a neighbourhood has been linked to neighbourhood dissatisfaction, because residents (non-Western ethnic minorities, Western ethnic minorities and originally Dutch) negatively evaluate concentrations of non-Western ethnic minorities. However, more recent work has suggested that the ethnic composition acts as a proxy for concentrations of individuals with lower socio-economic achievements and the problems associated with low socio-economic status. If this is true then not the ethnic composition, but the socio-economic composition and associated problems are negatively perceived. Ethnicity then acts as a proxy for low socio-economic status (see for instance Harris 2001). Nevertheless, some recent studies find that the concentration of ethnic minorities and low income households causes dissatisfaction among residents (Bolt et al. 2008; van der Laan Bouma-Doff 2007; Feijten and van Ham 2009; Baum et al. 2009). Few studies point out that area type and subjective neighbourhood attributes are better predictors of neighbourhood satisfaction than objective socio-demographic characteristics (McCrea et al. 2005; Parkes, et al. 2002). Following up on those studies, and adding evidence from the current policy approach, this chapter investigates the following question: "to what extent do the ethnic composition and socio-economic composition of neighbourhoods have a net influence upon satisfaction, or is this a proxy for a negative evaluation of characteristics of the neighbourhood?"

In the first section of the analysis presented in this chapter, the neighbourhood variables most closely associated with individual neighbourhood satisfaction are investigated, using a multilevel regression model. The model is based on data from the Housing Demand Survey 1998 (WBO 1998), and the Housing Research Netherlands 2009 (WoON 2009) combined with neighbourhood data from Statistics Netherlands (CBS 1997, 2008) and the local administration (GBA 1998, 2009). Then the analysis focuses on which individual and household characteristics are closely associated with neighbourhood satisfaction. Using a range of neighbourhood contextual variables, the analysis investigates to what extent residents attach importance to the general evaluation of problems, having things in common with other residents, anti-social behaviour, and feelings of safety. Finally, interaction terms between the evaluation of neighbourhood assets and socio-demographic characteristics are included in the models. Before introducing the models constructed in the analysis, a review is presented on literature on the determinants of neighbourhood satisfaction and the ways in which preferences for certain neighbourhood compositions (ethnic, income mix) are shaped.

Background and Theoretical Assumptions

In the Netherlands, concentrations of low-income which are often also concentrations of non-Western ethnic minorities, are higher in the four big cities – Amsterdam, Rotterdam, The Hague and Utrecht – than in the medium-sized cities, which in turn have higher concentrations than the smaller-sized cities (Bolt et al. 2008). In total, 11 % of the Dutch population are non-Western ethnic minorities (with at least one parent that was born abroad (Statistics Netherlands 2011)). One percent of the total Dutch population is from the Netherlands Antilles, 2 % from Suriname, 2 % from Morocco and 2 % from Turkey.

Relatively large shares of these ethnic minority groups live in social housing in the large cities in the Western part of the Netherlands, and in the (former) industrial areas in the East (textile industries) and South (coalmines) (Zorlu and Latten 2009). The most segregated groups are the Moroccans and Turks, whereas Surinamese and Antilleans tend to be less segregated. Up to the end of the 1990s residential segregation used to be higher in Rotterdam and The Hague, and lower in Utrecht and Amsterdam. Nowadays, however, Rotterdam has similar segregation levels than Amsterdam and Utrecht, where segregation has remained stable over the last decade. In Utrecht and Amsterdam concentrations of ethnic minorities in the old neighbourhoods around the city centre never really occurred because of the competition in the housing market from young well-educated households (Bolt and Van Kempen 2002). Segregation levels in The Hague remain high, although they declined in the 1990s.

The share of ethnic minority households strongly correlates with the share of low-income households in a neighbourhood, although ethnic minorities are more concentrated in certain parts of the areas than low-income groups. As Musterd (2005) shows, segregation levels of all ethnic minority groups in the Netherlands tend to be similar to Black Caribbean groups in Birmingham and London (United Kingdom), but lower than the segregation levels of Bangladeshi and Pakistani groups in London, Birmingham and Oldham. Within the Netherlands, the Turks and Moroccans are more segregated than the Surinamese.

Empirical and theoretical studies show that there are three frequently discussed explanations for segregation (Krysan et al. 2009). First, segregation is seen as being an outcome of racial differences in economic status. Recent analyses suggest that there is indeed some impact of economic factors (Charles 2000, 2009; Fong and Chan 2010). Second, ethnic minorities are unevenly spread over the city due to discrimination in the housing- and mortgage markets (Aalbers 2007, 2012, this volume; Williams et al. 2005). A third explanation emphasizes preferences: people tend to live in segregated areas because they have different preferences with regard to housing and neighbourhoods, or place different priorities on these in their expenditures.

The third explanation – preferences – has been the focus of much research, for example to find out what kind of neighbourhood composition people prefer, and if these are based on ethnic or on socio-economic preferences. Traditionally the focus was on the desire of White Americans to live in areas with low proportion of Black Americans (see Massey and Denton 1993; Pettigrew 1973). Before the 1990s, ethnicity was regarded as the essential element in White American housing choices. More recently, ethnicity is no longer the crux driving preferences for a predominantly white neighbourhood, rather it is the problems that White Americans associate with areas with higher shares of Afro-Americans. This includes the problems of crime, vandalism, deterioration, and declining property values (Clark 1991; Harris 2001; Krysan 2002; Krysan and Farley 2001; Krysan et al. 2009; Taub et al. 1984). The racial composition of a neighbourhood is thus a proxy for a low average social-economic status (SES) in the neighbourhood. Since people with low SES have higher chances of developing health problems, lower social capital, and more chance of becoming involved in crime than those with higher SES, deprived neighbourhoods are more frequently problematic neighbourhoods than non-deprived neighbourhoods. There are more problems in neighbourhoods with a low average SES, which may result in lower satisfaction rates among the people in the neighbourhood. Consequently, the problems are – perhaps wrongly – associated with the ethnic composition of the neighbourhood. This is what we call the racial proxy hypothesis (Harris 2001).

Alternative Mechanisms That Predict Satisfaction

It is often found that concentrations of low-income households and non-Western ethnic minorities results in lower neighbourhood satisfaction. The mechanisms behind these findings, however, remain unclear. Some research shows that the lower satisfaction rates are due to negative attitudes towards the 'other' or towards other ethnic groups (Havekes et al. 2010; Gay 2006; Branton and Jones 2005; Ihlanfeldt and Scafidi 2002). There are two theories that may help to understand what may be happening: social identity theory and group position theory (with the extension of the ethnic hierarchy theory).

The social identity theory (SIT) (Tajfel 1982) states that people tend to associate with like-minded people. Consequently, people might choose to live in neighbourhoods with many residents of their own group (either ethnic or socio-economic) because this will make them feel safe and 'at home'. Moreover, neighbourhoods with many like-minded people (in terms of ethnicity and/or income) can function as a social safety net for its residents. Thus, residents can help each other out in times of need; because of the inter-ethnic and inter-class contacts all have more means to protect themselves from harm. Last, a larger proportion of the own group implies a smaller proportion of the possibly threatening other groups. One may expect that the larger the proportion of the own group (in terms of ethnicity and/or income) in the neighbourhood, the higher individuals' level of satisfaction with the neighbourhood.

The second theory is the group position theory (Blumer 1958). The central element in this theory is that attitudes towards other ethnic groups do not spring from individual feelings, beliefs and material condition but from a collective process in which ethnic groups define and redefine other groups (Blumer 1958). Four elements which establish a sense of group position are distinguished; group identity, out-group (i.e. ethnic minorities) stereotyping, preferred group status and perceived threat.

The first is a belief about in-group superiority: the belief that an individual's in-group is naturally superior or better. Second, in-group members view out-group members as alien and different, which invokes stereotyping. Third, establishing a group position requires assumptions about claims over certain rights, such as resources, privileges and statuses, which largely are entitled to the in-group. The fourth element is the desire of the out-group to acquire these rights that are 'understood' to 'belong' to the in-group. This threatens the position of the dominant group (Blumer 1958). In a system with one dominant group it is argued that the dominant group will endeavour to maintain their dominant position by promoting social attitudes and policies which advantage themselves (Sidanius and Pratto 1999). Consequently, majority members will not be satisfied in neighbourhoods with many ethnic minority groups because of the fear of losing economic and social privileges (Blalock 1967; Oliver and Wong 2003). Ethnic minority groups would, according to this theory, prefer to live with a certain amount of their in-group because this would help them improve the economic position of their in-group.

However, not all ethnic minority groups enjoy living in concentrations of other ethnic minority groups. This may be explained by ethnic hierarchy theory, an extension of Blumer's group position theory by Hagendoorn and colleagues (1998). They state that "The evidence for the existence of consensual ethnic hierarchies consists of shared preferences for differential contact with ethnic out-groups and shared differential stereotypes" (p. 484), and which has been tested in the Netherlands, France, the US, the former Soviet Union (Hagendoorn 1995; Hagendoorn et al. 1998) and in Canada (Berry and Kalin 1979). The ethnic hierarchy theory is measured using a scale that refers to how much a person accepts another person from another ethnic group as a marriage partner, friend, neighbour or colleague. The studies found that in each country a perceived ranking of ethnic groups exists. All groups are said to prefer the in-group, and within each ethnic group there is consensus on the rank of the out-groups in the hierarchy. The ethnic hierarchy as perceived in the Netherlands indicates that the Dutch have the highest position, followed by Western ethnic minorities, and then non-Western ethnic minorities. The hierarchy is based on the degree of mastering the Dutch language and religious conviction. For instance, the literature reports that Muslims are seen as the most threatening to Dutch culture and identity (Hagendoorn 1995). Consequently, it is expected that members of the majority group prefer to live in an all majority neighbourhood, with many people in the same social class. Within this hierarchical classification, western ethnic minorities, are regarded as a slightly below the native Dutch (similar culture, usually a high socio-economic status, usually white, but some language problems), and as a result it is expected that they are more satisfied if they live with other Western ethnic minorities but also with the majority, because they are highest in the hierarchy. Non-Western ethnic minorities are at the bottom of the ethnic hierarchy due to the cultural and socio-economic distance. Consequently it can be expected that they are satisfied when they live with the group at the top of the hierarchy (majority) but they are also more satisfied than either the native Dutch or Western immigrants if they live in a neighbourhood with a high proportion of other Non-Western ethnic minorities members.

Individual Evaluations of Neighbourhood Quality

Previous research has asserted that low satisfaction in deprived neighbourhoods might be a response to the stresses of living in a low status environment, rather than to the presence of other ethnic groups. A high share of non-Western ethnic minorities and a high share of low-income households often coincide in deprived neighbourhoods; residents of ethnically diverse neighbourhoods are on average less educated, have a lower income, and are more likely to receive social benefits (Wittebrood et al. 2005). Therefore, low levels of satisfaction with the neighbourhood may derive from a more general frustration with local social problems as crime, social disorder, and physical decay that are prominent in low status neighbourhoods (Gay 2006; Branton and Jones 2005). A high prevalence of problems in the neighbourhood, such as litter in the streets, drug related problems, vandalism, crime, traffic problems, and others, correlates with negative attitudes and less satisfaction (Harris 2001). A lack of safety can be an important source of dissatisfaction: feelings of a lack of safety can generate a strong desire to move (Atkinson and Kintrea 2002).

As Sampson (2009) indicates, the perception and evaluation of problems is mediated by perceptions of the social quality of the neighbourhood. Individuals that are satisfied with the (ethnic) population composition of the neighbourhood will experience lower levels of physical disorder. More social ties and social interaction in turn leads to higher feelings of neighbourhood satisfaction (Amerigo and Aragones 1997; Andersen 2010; Dekker and Bolt 2005; Parkes et al. 2002). Individuals with more friends, acquaintances and relatives in the neighbourhood, are more satisfied with the neighbourhood. Also the feeling of having things in common with the neighbours is positively related to satisfaction (Dekker and Bolt 2005; Lee and Campbell 1999).

Data, Measures, and Method

The research question that will be answered is: "to what extent do the ethnic and socio-economic composition of neighbourhoods have a net influence upon satisfaction, or is this a proxy for a negative evaluation of characteristics of the neighbourhood?" To answer this question, two different data sources are combined.

Data

The analysis presented below uses the dataset Woning Behoefte Onderzoek (WBO 1998) and Woon Onderzoek Nederland (WoON 2009) collected by Statistics Netherlands, and the Dutch Ministry of Housing, Spatial Planning and Environment respectively. The data were gathered by means of face-to-face computer-assisted interviews. The sample was drawn in two steps, first cities and villages ('local administrations') were selected, then individuals were selected from the local administration (GBA, Gemeentelijke Basis Administratie). As is common with many sample datasets, young males and residents of highly urbanized areas are slightly underrepresented.

In contrast to most other research in the Netherlands that uses four digit postal codes as a proxy for neighbourhoods, this study uses 'neighbourhood-codes' as provided by *Statistics Netherlands*. These neighbourhood classifications have several advantages over postal codes. First, neighbourhood borders are defined by styles of architecture and time periods, representing more homogeneous areas with respect to socioeconomic composition. Second, neighbourhood codes refer to smaller geographical areas and are more likely to be perceived by residents as their own neighbourhood. However, as the borders of the neighbourhoods are defined by municipalities themselves, this classification is less uniform with respect to the size of a neighbourhood (both in number of residents and size).

Overall in the Netherlands, there are approximately 12,000 neighbourhoods[4] distributed over 458 municipalities (on average 25 neighbourhoods per municipality) (Gijsberts et al. 2010). The mean number of residents within these neighbourhoods is 1,444, but varies between 0 and 26,000. This large variation is mainly due to some outliers, as 95 % of all neighbourhoods have a population under 5,300 residents. We selected the neighbourhoods with up to 6,000 residents and excluded larger areas. The total number of cases in the 1998 analyses is 65,474 contained within 11,587 neighbourhoods. From the 2009 dataset 48,992 cases within 12,812 neighbourhoods.

Dependent Variable: Satisfaction

Satisfaction was calculated on the basis of eight items. Respondents indicated how satisfied they are with the housing environment, the built environment, the shops, parking facilities, public transport, green areas, the population and facilities for youngsters. These items refer to neighbourhood qualities that are experienced by all residents, independent of their use of the neighbourhood. Satisfaction with each item is measured on a scale from 1, which referred to high satisfaction, to 5, which referred to very low satisfaction in the 2009 dataset. In 1998 the answers were 1 (sufficient) or 2 (not sufficient). The new variable 'satisfaction' counts the times that the respondents answers that they are satisfied or very satisfied with an issue (2009) or thinks the issue is 'sufficient' (1998), with a minimum of 0 and a maximum of 8. The average score was 5.7 in 1998 and 5.8 in 2009. Descriptive statistics of the dependent variable and the neighbourhood and individual level predictors are summarized in Table 11.1.

[4] The exact number varies over the years. In 1998 there were fewer neighbourhoods identified than in 2009. This is due to the building of new neighbourhoods and sometimes splitting up bigger neighbourhoods into smaller ones.

Table 11.1 Descriptive statistics of variables in the regression models

	Range	% or mean	St. dev.
Dependent variable			
Satisfaction	0–8	5.7	2
Neighbourhood predictors			
Number of residents (*K)	0–6	2.69	1.57
% Non-Western ethnic minorities (*10)	0–8.20	0.82	1.07
% high income hh (*10)	0.5–7.20	2.07	0.91
% low income hh (*10)	1.4–9.5	3.96	0.75
Average property value (*million)	0.2–1.75	0.14	0.1
Income ratio low/high (*10)	0.02–1.52	0.25	0.18
Year of survey = 1998	0/1	57.2	
Individual predictors N = 65,474			
Men	0/1	46	
Hh with children	0/1	34.8	
Ln age	03-May	3.85	0.34
Education	01-Mar	1.94	0.73
Ethnicity			
Non-Western ethnic minority	0/1	1.8	
Western ethnicity ethnic minority	0/1	0.7	
Home owners	0/1	63.3	
Years lived in neighbourhood	0–92	14.21	12.62
Low household income	0/1	19.3	
High household income	0/1	20.6	
Satisfaction with dwelling	01-May	4.35	0.69
Single family home	0/1	68.6	
Evaluation of the neighbourhood problems	0/1	30.3	
# problems with anti-social beh	0–2	0.06	0.26
Things in common	0–5	2.13	1.23
Feels safe	01-May	4	0.084

Source: Own Calculations WBO (1998), WoON (2009), and (Statistics Netherlands (CBS 1997, 2008)

Measures of Social-Demographic Characteristics of Neighbourhoods

Information on neighbourhood characteristics is obtained from the register database "Key figures districts and neighbourhoods" of 1997 and 2008 from *Statistics Netherlands (CBS)*. The *share of ethnic minorities* in the neighbourhood was measured as the percentages of residents with at least one parent that was born in a non-Western country. The majority group members and ethnic minorities from Western countries are non-discernable in the data available. It is impossible to take into account the degree of ethnic diversity in the neighbourhood (like the entropy measure used by Andersson et al. 2007; Baum et al. 2009; Kearns and Mason 2007) because there are only two groups. The average share of ethnic minorities has risen from 4.4 % in 1997 to 11.4 % in 2008.

Next, the share of low income groups (less than €15,057/year[5] in 1997, €22,491 per year in 2008), and the share of high income groups (1998: more than €51,937/year; 2009: €69,937/year) in the neighbourhood are included in the analysis. Moreover, the ratio of low and high income households in the neighbourhood is included ((% low income households/% high income households)/10).

The average value of the property is controlled for, and was derived from local tax offices. The average value of a dwelling in the Netherlands rose from €40,724 to 210,000 between 1997 and 2009. In addition, the *number of residents* of the neighbourhood (on average 2,560 and 2,870 respectively), is also included. Various neighbourhood characteristics might be strongly correlated with each other. For example the share of ethnic minorities in a neighbourhood and the share of low-income households. However, within the dataset used here, correlation between the share of ethnic minorities and the share of low-income households is relatively low ($r=0.327$). Hence, neighbourhoods with large shares of ethnic minorities are not more likely to have large shares of low-income households. The correlation between the value of the houses and the share of high income households is relatively strong ($r=0.7$), but not too strong to include in the model (see Belsley et al. 1980 for discussion). Other measures have low correlations and can therefore be included in the modelling process.

Household-Level Demographic Characteristics

The characteristics of the respondent are also taken into consideration. A dummy variable for *gender* is included (with 1 assigned to males and a split of 47.4 and 44.1% for 1998 and 2009 respectively). Furthermore, households with children are distinguished from those without children ('children', very stable at 34.7 and 34.9%). *Age* is measured as the natural logarithm of age in years. Next, low income households (less than fl 33,275/year in 1997, € 22,491/year in 2008), and the share of high income groups (1998: more than fl 114,781/year; 2009: € 69,937/year) are included in the analysis with two dummy variables. The original variable was calculated by *Statistics Netherlands* on the basis of an extensive list of questions on income and expenses. There are no missing cases on this variable. *Educational attainment* is measured as the highest completed (or current in case of students) education, either in the Netherlands or abroad, on a scale from 1 (lower professional education or less) to 3 (higher professional education or higher). Those with another kind of education were given the mean value. *Ethnicity* is represented in two dummies: non-Western ethnic minorities (respectively 0.4 and 1% of the sample) and western ethnic minorities (respectively 0.5 and 3.7% of the sample). The reference category is the Dutch ethnic group in both cases. The number of individuals in the ethnic minority are too low to divide the ethnic minority groups more specifically according

[5] Calculated with the conversion rate of 1 €=fl 2.21 at the time of the introduction of the euro.

to country of origin. *Home-ownership* is indicated with a dummy variable, contrasting home-owners (respectively 65.8 and 60.1%) with tenants in both the social and the private sector. The number of *years* that an individual has *lived in the neighbourhood* is also taken into consideration. On average the respondents have lived for 14 years in their neighbourhood.

Housing characteristics are also taken into consideration because they may influence satisfaction with the neighbourhood. *Satisfaction with the dwelling* is measured on a 5 point scale (5=very satisfied, average score 4.34 in both datasets). A dummy variable indicates if someone lives in a *single family house* (either terraced housing, detached, or semi-detached, respectively 69.5 and 67.3 %) or in a multi-family home.

Perceived Problems, Crime, Safety, Social Quality

The *experience of social problems* in the neighbourhood is a dummy based on the respondent's answer to the question "To what extent do you experience problems with graffiti or vandalism". The variable 'problems' indicates if the respondent (sometimes) experiences problems or not. The share of respondents that (sometimes) experienced problems with graffiti or vandalism has risen from 24.0% in 1998 to 41.6% in 2009. The *feeling of a lack of safety* is a reaction to the question "how often do you feel unsafe in your neighbourhood" on a Lickert like scale from 1 (never) to 5 (often). We recoded this, so a high score means the respondent feels safe and vice versa. The missing information on this variable was recoded as the mean score. A new variable *'antisocial'* counts the times that the respondent answers that he or she (sometimes) experiences problems with the direct or other neighbours. The share of residents with problems with their neighbours has risen from 5.2% in 1998 to 6.7% in 2009. From this descriptive information, it could be concluded that there are indications that residents have more negative experiences in 2009 than in 1998. Yet, they also have more positive experiences and report more positively about the *social climate.* The evaluation of social aspects of the neighbourhood is measured using five items counting the number of times that a respondent answers "I (totally) agree" to the following statements "I have a lot of contact with my direct neighbours", "I have a lot of contact with other than my direct neighbours", "in this neighbourhood people interact pleasantly", "I live in a cohesive neighbourhood", "In this neighbourhood people hardly know each other (reversely recoded)". The new variable 'incommon' has a minimum of 0 and a maximum of 5. The average score on the indicator has risen from 1.87 in 1998 to 2.47 in 2009.

Method and Model Specification

By combining WBO (1998) and WoON (2009) data with information on the neighbourhood in which respondents reside, the data contains a two-level structure: respondents (level 1) are nested within neighbourhoods (level 2). The data are a repeated cross-sectional design with two time points. We combined the data from the two points in time into one dataset. Thus, each time a combined model for both points in time is estimated, using a dummy for the year and estimating year interaction effects. To address the research questions, multilevel regression analysis are used, which is a statistical method that is optimally suited to handle the fact that observations of respondents within the same neighbourhood are not independent (Snijders and Bosker 1999). This method allows estimating the effects of both individual level (e.g. educational attainment, interethnic contact) and neighbourhood level predictors (e.g. ethnic composition, socioeconomic status) on satisfaction with the neighbourhood simultaneously. We started our multi-level regression analysis by estimating an empty model (Table 11.2, model 0). This model only includes the intercept and shows how the total variation in satisfaction with the neighbourhood is divided between the individual and the neighbourhood level (Hox 2002). The intra-class correlation of ρ neighbourhood = .059 indicates the fraction of variance in the dependent variable (i.e. satisfaction with the neighbourhood) at the neighbourhood level. This initial analysis shows that a multilevel structure is appropriate here as the ρ value is better than 0.05 (see Snijders and Bosker 1999). The models in Table 11.2 present the outcomes from the regression with the unstandardized Bs and the standard deviation. To interpret them properly, the scale of the explanatory variables must be taken into account (Hox 2002). Unstandardized Bs above 0 refer to a higher likelihood and below 0 to a reduced likelihood of predicting the dependent variable 'satisfaction'.

Results

The Impact of Neighbourhood Characteristics on Neighbourhood Satisfaction

The results of the regression models are presented in Table 11.2. The addition of the neighbourhood variables in the regression (model 1) improves the model significantly compared to intercept only model (model 0); the −2 log likelihood reduces (the smaller the −2 log likelihood, the better the model fit). The findings in model 1 suggest that the share of non-Western ethnic minorities is negatively related to neighbourhood satisfaction. This is in line with the expectations. For the impact of the socio-economic status of the neighbourhood a more mixed picture emerges. The coefficients for the proportion of high income households in a neighbourhood suggest a positive association between higher income neighbourhoods and neighbourhood satisfaction. However, the proportion of low income households in the neighbourhood is not significant. The coefficient for the ratio of low/high income households is negative. As this ratio increases (indicating an increasing relative share of people with a low income), the likelihood that an individual will be satisfied with the neighbourhood declines when keeping the other variables constant.

Table 11.2 Multi-level regression on satisfaction with the neighbourhood model 0 and model 1 and 2

	Model 0			Model 1			Model 2		
				Neigbh. charact.			M1 + ind. charact.		
	B	SE	Sign	B	SE	Sign	B	SE	Sign
Intercept	5.600	0.010	***	−3.860	5.250		2.920	0.380	***
Neighbourhood characteristics									
# residents				0.050	0.010	***	0.060	0.010	***
% ethnic minorities				−0.160	0.030	***	−0.080	0.010	***
% high income				0.100	0.040	***	0.110	0.020	***
% low income				0.010	0.040		0.020	0.020	
Housing value				0.220	0.830		−0.031	0.130	***
Income ratio				−0.310	0.140	*	−0.270	0.080	**
Year 1998				0.000	0.000	*	−0.003	0.000	***
Individual characteristics									
Men							−0.070	0.020	***
Hh with child							0.040	0.010	
Age (ln function)							0.520	0.020	***
Education							−0.050	0.010	***
Non-Western ethnic minority							−0.310	0.110	
Western ethnic minority							0.020	0.110	
Home-owner							0.060	0.010	***
Years in the nbh							0.000	0.000	***
Low income							0.060	0.020	***
High income							0.080	0.020	
Single family dwelling							−0.360	0.010	***

(continued)

Table 11.2 (continued)

	Model 0			Model 1			Model 2		
				Neigbh. charact.			M1 + ind. charact.		
	B	SE	Sign	B	SE	Sign	B	SE	Sign
Satisfied with dwelling							0.480	0.010	***
−2 log likelihood		487925.4			370,149			326,347	
Residual		4.019			3.68			2.53	
Intercept subject variance		0.25			0.145			0.153	
ICC		0.059			0.038			0.057	
Significance		0			0			0	

Source: WBO (1998), WoON (2009), and Statistics Netherlands (1997, 2008)
*significant at 10 %; **significant at 5 %; ***significant at 1 %

The average dwelling value, measured in million Euros is not significantly related to neighbourhood satisfaction in this model. This is in line with the expectations. The size of the neighbourhood, measured using the number of residents, has a small positive impact on neighbourhood satisfaction, where larger neighbourhoods tend to have higher levels of satisfaction. A possible explanation is that larger numbers of residents also means more shops, better public transport and the like. These outcomes largely reflect the findings of previous studies.

The Impact of Socio-demographic Characteristics on Neighbourhood Satisfaction

In model 2 (Table 11.2) satisfaction is explained using individual and household characteristics in addition to the neighbourhood characteristics. The models show a remarkable change, compared with model 1, if we take individual and household characteristics into account. One of the most noticeable results is that the effect of average housing value in the neighbourhood has become an important predictor of satisfaction. Respondents who live in expensive areas are much less satisfied than those in other areas, especially those in single family dwellings, taking individual- and household characteristics into consideration. Surprisingly, residents in single family dwellings appear to be less satisfied than residents in a flat, apartment or maisonette. Both findings are probably related to higher expectations: the more you pay for something, the more you expect from it. Single family dwellings are usually more expensive than multi-family dwellings and therefore residents have higher expectations that are more easily disappointed. The indicator 'years in the neighbourhood' is significant, and the coefficient on this variable shows that individuals who have been long-term residents of the neighbourhood are slightly less likely to be satisfied.

According to model 2, men are slightly less satisfied with the neighbourhood than women. Older respondents are more satisfied than younger ones; this supports findings by Lu (1999). Non-Western ethnic minorities are equally satisfied as others.

Furthermore, higher educated people are less satisfied with their neighbourhood than lower educated people. This is in line with other research (Blokland 2005; Guest and Wierzbicki 1999). The housing variables included in the analyses account for tenure, satisfaction with the current home, and length of residence. Importantly, home-owners are slightly more satisfied with their neighbourhood than tenants, but only if one controls for satisfaction with the dwelling. Satisfaction with the dwelling is positively related to satisfaction with the neighbourhood.

Income is significant in the model: low income households are more satisfied. However, a model without satisfaction with the dwelling (not shown) indicates that the effect of income rises after controlling for satisfaction with the dwelling. This implies that satisfaction with the neighbourhood is partially explained by satisfaction with the dwelling, and that high income households are better able to satisfy their housing needs than medium and low income households. In other research it was found that that the impact of income could be either positive or negative, depending on the situation (Amerigo and Aragones 1997; Clark and Dieleman 1996).

The Impact of Subjective Neighbourhood Evaluations on Neighbourhood Satisfaction

The key question considered is whether subjective evaluations of aspects of the neighbourhood, rather than the proportion of non-Western ethnic minorities, are associated with residential satisfaction. The variables that were added to the model (model 3, Table 11.3) are:

- The number of problems experienced (including for example, vandalism, graffiti)
- Anti-social behaviour that was experienced (trouble with direct neighbours, and neighbourhood residents in general);
- The evaluation of the number of things in common (contact with direct neighbours, with other residents in general, interaction, cohesion, knowing each other), and;
- Evaluation of feelings of safety.

The variables were individually added to the model first (models 3a–3d, Table 11.3), to assess the contribution each makes to the final outcome (model 3 complete, Table 11.3). The model fit −2 log likelihood slightly improves when the separate variables are included and significantly when all four variables are included, although not as much as with the previous models. The most important finding of the separate models 3a–d is that the variable 'share of ethnic minorities' is still negatively related to neighbourhood satisfaction, but is less important. This implies that, once the single subjective evaluations of neighbourhood characteristics are included, most people still feel negative about higher shares of ethnic minorities in the neighbourhood, but the chances of negative evaluations of high shares of ethnic minorities have diminished slightly. However, including all evaluations of the neighbourhood (the complete model 3), the negative effect of the share of ethnic minorities is no longer significant. The results can be seen as supporting our theoretical specification of the effect of subjective evaluation of neighbourhood characteristics.

In all cases subjective evaluations of the neighbourhood significantly influence the dependent variable as expected, controlling for individual variables. As for more specific findings, residents' perceptions of problems and the experience of antisocial behaviour were associated with significantly lower neighbourhood satisfaction. This is in line with what others found (Galster and Hesser 1981; Gans 1967, 1968; Lansing and Zehner 1970). There were some interrelationships between these evaluation measures, but not so strong that one of the measures should be removed from the model.

As expected, the index measuring perceptions of the neighbourhood as a place for contact with direct neighbours, with other residents in general, and a place with interaction, cohesion, where people know each other, positively influences neighbourhood satisfaction. This is in line with other research (Gans 1967, 1968). Also individuals that feel safe in the neighbourhood are more satisfied than other individuals.

Table 11.3 Multi-level regression on satisfaction with the neighbourhood model 3a, b, c, d and 3 complete

	Model 3a			Model 3b			Model 3c			Model 3d			Model 3 complete		
	M2 + problems			M2 + antisocial behaviour			Model 2 + having things in common			M2 + feeling unsafe			M2 + all subjective issues		
	B		SE	B		SE	B		SE	B		SE	B		SE
Intercept	42.92	***	4.61	66.3	***	4.62	89.76	***	4.53	64.84	***	4.53	71.62	***	4.53
Neighbourhood characteristics															
# residents	0.06	***	0	0.06	***	0.01	0.06	***	0	0.06	***	0	0.06	***	0
% ethnic minorities	−0.04	***	0.01	−0.08	***	0.01	−0.05	***	0.01	−0.05	***	0.01	0		0.01
% high income	0.12	***	0.02	0.11	***	0.02	0.13	***	0.02	0.12	***	0.02	0.13	***	0.02
% low income	0		0.02	0.02		0.02	0.02		0.02	0.02		0.02	0		0.02
Housing value	−0.55	***	0.46	−0.29	**	0.14	−0.51	***	0.14	−0.25	***	0.14	−0.67	***	0.14
Income ratio	−0.21	**	0.08	−0.23	***	0.08	−0.25	***	0.08	−0.22	*	0.08	−0.14	*	0.08
Year 1998	−0.2	***	0.01	−0.3	***	0.01	−0.04	***	0.01	−0.03	***	0.01	−0.03	***	0
Individual characteristics															
Gender (ref = female)	−0.07	***	0.01	−0.07	***	0.01	−0.07	***	0.01	−0.06	***	0.01	−0.04	***	0.01
Hh with child	0.03	**	0.01	0.05	**	0.01	0.11	***	0.01	0.05	***	0.01	0.09	***	0.01
Age (ln function)	0.46	***	0.02	0.48	***	0.02	0.37	***	0.02	0.53	***	0.02	0.37	***	0.02
Education	−0.06	***	0.01	−0.07	***	0.01	−0.05	***	0.01	−0.08	***	0.01	−0.05	***	0.01
Non-Western ethnic minority	−0.22		0.1	−0.28		0.04	−0.26		0.04	−0.29		0.04	−0.2		0.04
Western ethnic minority	0.01	***	0.1	0.01	***	0.06	0	***	0.06	0	***	0.06	0	***	0.06
Home-owner	0.05	***	0.01	0.06	***	0.01	0.04	***	0.01	0.06	***	0.01	0.06	***	0.01
Years in the nbh	0	***	0	0	***	0	−0.08	***	0	0	***	0	0	***	0
Low income	0.08	***	0.02	0.07	***	0.02	0.07	***	0.02	0.06	***	0.02	0.07	***	0.02
High income	0.05	***	0.02	0.06	***	0.02	0.04	***	0.02	0.06	***	0.02	0.04	***	0.02
Single family dwelling	−0.28	***	0.01	−0.36	***	0.01	−0.31	***	0.01	−0.34	***	0.01	−0.24	***	0.01
Satisfied with dwelling	0.45	***	0.01	0.45	***	0.01	0.4	***	0.01	0.44	***	0.01	0.33	***	0.01

(continued)

Table 11.3 (continued)

	Model 3a			Model 3b			Model 3c			Model 3d			Model 3 complete		
	M2 + problems			M2 + antisocial behaviour			Model 2 + having things in common			M2 + feeling unsafe			M2 + all subjective issues		
	B		SE	B		SE	B		SE	B		SE	B		SE
Evaluation of neighbourhood															
Problems	–0.63	***	0.34										–0.52	***	0.01
Antisocial behaviour				–0.57	***	0.02							–0.43	***	0.02
Things in common							0.344	***	0				0.33	***	0
Feels safe										0.23	***	0	0.17	***	0
–2 log likelihood	323769.4			325,499			321,044			3E+06			317,640		
Residual	2.459			2.511			2.382			2.502			2.289		
Intercept subject variance	0.156			0.153			0.151			0.151			0.153		
ICC	0.06			0.057			0.06			0.057			0.063		
Significance	0			0			0			0			0		

Source: WBO (1998), WoON (2009), and Statistics Netherlands (1997, 2008)
*significant at 10%; **significant at 5%; ***significant at 1%

Interaction Effects of Experience of the Neighbourhood with Share of Ethnic Minorities

To identify which measures of neighbourhood characteristics are related to neighbourhood satisfaction in neighbourhoods with more ethnic minorities, interaction effects between the share of ethnic minorities and evaluation of characteristics of the neighbourhood were included in the models. The interaction effects in model 4 (Table 11.4) show that the main effect of the share of ethnic minorities is negative, the main effect of problems in the neighbourhood is negative, and in addition the interaction effect of the two is negative. This indicates that residents that experience problems and live in neighbourhoods with more ethnic minorities are less satisfied than those in similar neighbourhoods with fewer problems.

In neighbourhoods with more ethnic minorities it may be more difficult for residents to correct deviant behaviour because there are fewer social ties. Indeed, the experience of antisocial behaviour is negatively related to satisfaction and with the proportion of ethnic minorities. The interaction effect (model 4) is not significant, which shows that respondents that experience antisocial behaviour in neighbourhoods with a higher share of ethnic minorities are equally satisfied as those that experience less antisocial behaviour in neighbourhoods with similar shares of ethnic minorities. This is in line with the expectations (Sampson 2009). This finding suggests that negative behaviour is 'blamed' on the ethnic minorities, whereas general problems in the neighbourhood are not. It is unfortunate that a neighbourhood measure for social ties is not available, because it would be interesting to see if residents experience less antisocial behaviour in cohesive neighbourhoods (see Hipp 2010).

In the theoretical part it was stated that the perception of the neighbourhood is mediated by perceptions of the social quality of the neighbourhood (Sampson 2009). It could be the case that residents feel that the ethnic neighbourhood composition affects the formation of social ties. Models 3 indicated a negative effect of the share of ethnic minorities in the neighbourhood, and a positive effect of the feeling of having things in common on satisfaction. Model 4a shows that respondents that feel they have things in common with the other residents in the neighbourhood, are more satisfied in neighbourhoods with higher shares of ethnic minorities than residents that feel they don't have things in common. This implies that residents feel more positive in neighbourhoods with higher shares of ethnic minorities if they feel socially connected to others. This is in line with the expectations derived from the social disorganization theory (Sampson and Groves 1989).

In the theoretical part we also hypothesized that feelings of safety were positively related to satisfaction with the neighbourhood, an effect demonstrated in model 3. When an interaction effect is included there is a small positive and significant effect of feeling safe in neighbourhoods with high shares of ethnic minorities. This implies that if an individual feels safe, he or she is more positive about the neighbourhood when the proportion of ethnic minorities is higher. This finding provides more evidence that supports the ethnic proxy hypothesis.

The research question to be answered in this chapter was: "to what extent do the ethnic composition and socio-economic composition of neighbourhoods have a net influence upon satisfaction, or is this a proxy for a negative evaluation of characteristics of the neighbourhood?" It is possible to concluded that on the basis of the findings in Table 11.4, model 4a, respondents in neighbourhoods with higher shares of ethnic minorities, and those that experience problems in neighbourhoods with concentrations of ethnic minorities, are less likely to be satisfied with the neighbourhood. The second part of the research question will be answered below.

Interaction Effects of Experience of the Neighbourhood with the Relative Share of Low Income Households

The racial proxy hypothesis is not just about ethnicity, as it mainly claims that residents in neighbourhoods with a high proportion of people on lower incomes are less satisfied: the problems in the neighbourhood are due to poverty and not the result of ethnicity, according to this hypothesis. But do our respondents also make the distinction between ethnicity and socio-economic inequality? And does the income situation of the respondent influence the assessment? Model 4b tests the interaction between the evaluation of issues in the neighbourhood and the share of low income households.

Model 4b shows that the main effect of the share of low income households becomes significant if we include an interaction effect for the neighbourhood evaluations and the share of low income households in the neighbourhood. In low income neighbourhoods the number of problems and anti-social behaviour experienced, as well as the perception of having things in common with your neighbours are significant predictors of satisfaction, and so is the interaction with the proportion of lower income households. This implies that the experience of the neighbourhood matters, and that the share of low income households matters. One exception is the impact of feeling safe on satisfaction. This main effect of feeling safe is no longer significant in model 4b, but the interaction effect with feeling safe is significant. This means that not feeling safe itself, but feeling safe in a neighbourhood with many low income households influences satisfaction. The model also shows that the impact of the income of the respondent does not change now these interaction effects are included. The dissatisfied individuals in low income neighbourhoods are middle income households and not the low income households. A possible explanation may be that these middle income households would like to live in 'better' neighbourhoods, and that low income households are less concerned by living amongst other low income households.

Following the models presented in Table 11.4, it is possible to answer the second part of the research question: respondents in neighbourhoods with higher shares of low income households, and those that experience problems in neighbourhoods with concentrations of low income households, are less likely to be satisfied with the neighbourhood. This means that we cannot confirm the racial proxy hypothesis.

Table 11.4 Multi-level regression on satisfaction with the neighbourhood model 4: interaction effects evaluation *characteristics of the neighbourhood

	Model 4a			Model 4b		
	Evaluation of nbd * % ethnic minorities			Evaluation of nbd * % low income hhs		
	B	SE		B	SE	
Intercept	71.42	4.50	***	73.24	4.50	***
Neighbourhood characteristics						
# residents	0.06	0.01	***	0.06	0.01	***
% ethnic minorities	−0.21	0.03	***	0.00	0.01	*
% high income	0.13	0.02	***	0.14	0.02	***
% low income	0.01	0.02	*	−0.19	0.04	***
Housing value	−0.65	0.13	***	−0.64	0.13	***
Income ratio	−0.14	0.08	**	−0.09	0.08	
Year 1998	−0.03	0.00	***	−0.04	0.00	***
Individual characteristics						
Gender (ref=female)	−0.04	0.01	***	−0.04	0.01	***
Hh with child	0.09	0.01	***	0.09	0.01	***
Age (ln function)	0.36	0.02	***	0.36	0.02	***
Education	−0.05	0.01	***	−0.04	0.01	***
Non-Western ethnic minority	−0.20	0.04	***	−0.19	0.04	***
Western ethnic minority	0.00	0.06		0.00	0.06	
Home-owner	0.07	0.01	***	0.07	0.01	***
Years in the nbh	−0.01	0.00	***	−0.01	0.00	***
Low income	0.07	0.02	***	0.07	0.02	***
High income	0.04	0.01	***	0.04	0.01	***
Single family dwelling	−0.23	0.01	***	−0.24	0.01	***
Satisfied with dwelling	0.34	0.01	***	0.34	0.01	***
Evaluation of neighbourhood						
Problems	−0.57	0.02	***	−0.32	0.07	***

(continued)

Table 11.4 (continued)

	Model 4a			Model 4b		
	Evaluation of nbd * % ethnic minorities			Evaluation of nbd * % low income hhs		
	B	SE		B	SE	
Antisocial behaviour	–0.43	0.03	***	–0.60	0.11	***
Things in common	0.31	0.01	***	0.18	0.02	***
Feels safe	0.13	0.01	***	0.04	0.03	
Interaction effects						
Problems*% ethnic in nbh	0.06	0.01	***			
Antisocial * % ethnic in nbh	0.00	0.02				
Incommon * % ethnic	0.02	0.00	***			
Feels safe * % ethnic in nbh	0.04	0.01	***			
Problems*% low income hh in nbh				–0.05	0.02	***
Antisocial *% low income hh in nbh				0.04	0.03	*
Incommon *% low income hh in nbh				0.04	0.01	***
Feels safe *% low income hh in nbh				0.03	0.01	***
–2 log likelihood		317552.05			317572.73	
Residual		2285.00			2286.00	
Intercept subject variance		0.15			0.15	
ICC		0.06			0.06	
Significance		0.00			0.00	

Source: WBO (1998), WoON (2009), and Statistics Netherlands (1997, 2008)
*significant at 10 %; **significant at 5 %; ***significant at 1 %

Changing Effects over the Decade

The data allow us to investigate if the impact of the evaluations of the neighbourhood has changed between the two points of measurement (1998, 2009). Table 11.5 shows four models, each with an interaction term of the year of measurement and the evaluation of a neighbourhood issue.[6] The slopes in the model now refer to the year 2009 (which is the zero value of the dummy 'year') (Hox 2002). From the models 5a and 5d (Table 11.5) it can be concluded that experiencing problems and feeling unsafe has a more negative impact on satisfaction in 2009 than in 1998. From the same table (but now models 5b and 5c) it can also be concluded that experiencing antisocial behaviour as a more positive impact on satisfaction in 2009 than in 1998. Also having things in common has a (smaller) positive effect on satisfaction. Roughly, this means that people are more irritated by problems and that safety has become a more important issue in predicting satisfaction. On the other hand, residents may have become more used to antisocial behaviour and weigh feelings related to more cohesion more heavily in 2009 than in 1998.

Conclusion

The aim of this chapter was to test the racial proxy hypothesis and find out how it is related to satisfaction with the neighbourhood. The racial proxy hypothesis states that the racial (or ethnic in the European context) composition of a neighbourhood is a proxy for the socio-economic composition, which causes problems related to liveability of the neighbourhood, which in turn negatively influences the satisfaction with a neighbourhood (Clark 1991; Harris 2001; Taub et al. 1984). In order test this hypothesis, use was made of survey data from two points in time (Housing Demand Survey (WBO) 1998; Housing Research Netherlands (WoON) 2009), combined with neighbourhood data from the tax office and Statistics Netherlands. In addition to 'regular' analyses of neighbourhood satisfaction, we also included the evaluation of neighbourhood characteristics, and we compared measurements on two points in time.

The analyses here show no support for the racial proxy hypothesis. At first sight, the proportion of non-Western ethnic minorities and the proportion of low-income households in the neighbourhood seemed to be consistently related to lower satisfaction with the neighbourhood. This would mean that the hypothesis is refuted. However, the individual evaluation of neighbourhood characteristics also proved important. As would be expected, the fewer problems perceived, little anti-social behaviour, feelings of safety and commonality amongst neighbours the higher the reported level of neighbourhood satisfaction. However, when interactions of the evaluation of neighbourhood characteristics with neighbourhood composition are

[6] Adding all the interaction terms at once into one model did not work – the number of iterations became too large for the remote access connection to the data.

Table 11.5 Multi-level regression on satisfaction with the neighbourhood model 5: interaction effects evaluation * year

	Model 5a: problems * year			Model 5b: M3 antisocial * year			Model 5c: incommon problems * year			Model 5d: M3 unsafe * year		
Parameter	B		S.E.	B		S.E.	B		S.E.	B		S.E.
Intercept	87.44	***	4.81	62.75	***	4.66	76.77	***	5.84	126.59	***	10.74
Neighbourhood characteristics												
# residents	0.06	***	0.01	0.06	***	0.01	0.06	***	0.01	0.06	***	0.01
% ethnic minorities	–0.06	***	0.01	–0.07	***	0.01	–0.06	***	0.01	–0.05	***	0.01
% high income	0.11	***	0.02	0.12	***	0.02	0.13	***	0.02	0.12	***	0.02
% low income	0.01		0.02	0.02		0.02	0.02		0.02	0.02		0.02
Housing value	–0.27	**	0.14	–0.32	**	0.14	–0.49	***	0.14	–0.27	**	0.14
Income ratio	–0.19	**	0.08	–0.24	***	0.08	–0.25	***	0.08	–0.22	***	0.08
Year 1998	–0.04	***	0.00	–0.03	***	0.00	–0.04	***	0.00	–0.06	***	0.01
Individual characteristics												
Men	–0.08	***	0.01	–0.08	***	0.01	–0.08	***	0.01	–0.05	***	0.01
Hh with child	0.03	**	0.01	0.05	***	0.01	0.10	***	0.01	0.05	***	0.01
Age (ln function)	0.45	***	0.02	0.48	***	0.02	0.37	***	0.02	0.54	***	0.02
Education	–0.07	***	0.01	–0.07	***	0.01	–0.05	***	0.01	–0.08	***	0.01
Non western ethnic minority	–0.24	***	0.04	–0.29	***	0.04	–0.26	***	0.04	–0.29	***	0.04
Western ethnic minority	0.02		0.06	0.00		0.06	0.00		0.06	–0.01		0.06
Home-owner	0.06	***	0.01	0.06	***	0.01	0.05	***	0.01	0.06	***	0.01
Years in the nbh	–0.01	***	0.00	–0.01	***	0.00	–0.01	***	0.00	–0.01	***	0.00
Low income	0.08	***	0.02	0.07	***	0.02	0.07	***	0.02	0.06	***	0.02
High income	0.06	***	0.01	0.06	***	0.01	0.04	***	0.01	0.06	***	0.01
Single family dwelling	–0.26	***	0.02	–0.36	***	0.02	–0.31	***	0.02	–0.34	***	0.02
Satisfied with dwelling	0.45	***	0.01	0.45	***	0.01	0.40	***	0.01	0.45	***	0.01

Evaluation of neighbourhood												
Problems	−140.35	***	4.62									
Antisocial				44.52	***	7.45						
Incommon							6.48	***	1.74			
Safe										−15.16	***	2.42
Year*evaluation of neighbourhood												
Year * problems	0.07	***	0.00									
Year * antisocial				−0.02	***	0.00						
Year * incommon							0.00	***	0.00			
Year * safe										0.01	***	0.00
−2 log likelihood	322858.433			325462.478			321031.553			325120.591		
Residual	2.435			2.511			2.382			2.501		
Intercept (subject buurtcode)	0.150			0.153			0.151			0.153		
ICC	0.058			0.058			0.060			0.058		
Sign	0.000			0.000			0.000			0.000		
Sign	0.000			0.000			0.000			0.000		

Source: WBO (1998), WoON (2009), and Statistics Netherlands (1997, 2008)
***Significant at 1%; **Significant at 5%; *Significant at 10%

introduced a different story was uncovered. It became clear that a concentration of low income households and a concentration of ethnic minorities negatively influences satisfaction, but only when the evaluation of neighbourhood characteristics was taken into consideration. The racial proxy hypothesis cannot be confirmed. Thus, not the positive and negative assets of the neighbourhood but the actual concentration of low income households and ethnic minorities are experienced negatively by residents.

The comparison of data of 1998 and 2009 showed that the impact of neighbourhood experiences has changed. In 2009, people that experienced problems in neighbourhoods with higher proportions of ethnic minorities or low-income households are even less satisfied. This leads us to conclude that the ethnic proxy hypothesis held some merit in 1998, but is not relevant in current Dutch society. If this conclusion is valid, then it has far-reaching consequences, because it may indicate that the changes in society (more tensions between ethnic and religious groups, for example) result in new contexts in which existing insights must be tested.

As with most studies that draw on cross-sectional data, it is hard to make strong conclusions on causation as the association between the socioeconomic and ethnic composition of the neighbourhood and satisfaction may derive from selective migration patterns in and out the neighbourhood. However, our results do not provide evidence that selective migration processes are at work here. The reason is that we found no differences between high and low income residents in the effect of the ethnic and socioeconomic neighbourhood composition. Since low income households have similar reactions to different neighbourhood attributes as high income groups, we can assume that there is no selection effect.

So why does this research matter for the study of neighbourhood effects? One of the most important contributions of this research is that it shows that the impact of the neighbourhood changes over time. This makes studying neighbourhood effects more complex, because not only do exposure to a neighbourhood and neighbourhood change itself influence the neighbourhood effect (Hedman 2011), also the impact of different variables changes over time. The reason is that subjective evaluations of certain characteristics by individuals change. Or, to put it in other words, neighbourhood characteristics that were valued positively 10 years ago have lost importance and other neighbourhood characteristics now have more explanatory value. This finding advocates that a review of old neighbourhood effect studies is needed.

The research reported here shows that it is important for future urban regeneration policies to focus on ways to tackle problems in neighbourhoods, in order to enhance satisfaction. Urban policy-makers stress upon the importance of social mixing as it would increase social cohesion and interethnic contacts among neighbourhood residents and improve the liveability of the neighbourhood (See Dekker and van Kempen 2004; van Kempen and Bolt 2009). This study finds evidence for the policy assumption that lower concentrations of low income and ethnic minority households by itself results in higher satisfaction rates.

Finally, future research could give more insight into the processes that take place in ethnically and socio-economically diverse neighbourhoods. The investigation in this chapter focused on the extent to which the share of ethnic minorities and the share of low income groups influence satisfaction, and found that the experience of neighbourhood characteristics is also as important. However, less attention has been paid to how neighbourhood residents experience neighbourhood life in ethnically and socio-economically diverse neighbourhoods. It would be of interest to explore what kind of problems and conflicts residents of ethnically and socio-economically diverse neighbourhoods experience in daily life that might affect satisfaction levels. Moreover, research should focus on how explanations for neighbourhood satisfaction change over time, especially with the rising number of ethnic minorities; are the Dutch (natives and ethnic minorities) becoming more conscious of racial differences? Are the differences between the groups more often mentioned as a problem? And finally, it would be of interest to find out what people do when they are dissatisfied. Do they move out of the neighbourhood? And if so, is the migration selective in any way?

References

Aalbers, M. (2007). Place-based and race-based exclusion from mortgage loans: Evidence from three cities in the Netherlands. *Journal of Urban Affairs, 29*(1), 1–29.

Aalbers, M. (2012). How do mortgage lenders influence neighbourhood dynamics? Redlining and predatory lending. In M. van Ham, D. Manley, N. Bailey, L. Simpson, & D. Maclennan (Eds.), *Understanding neighbourhood dynamics: New insights for neighbourhood effects research*. (pp. 63–86) Dordrecht: Springer.

Amerigo, M., & Aragones, J. (1997). A theoretical and methodological approach to the study of residential satisfaction. *Journal of Environmental Psychology, 17*(1), 47–57.

Andersen, H. S. (2010). Spatial assimilation in Denmark? Why do immigrants move to and from multi-ethnic neighbourhoods? *Housing Studies, 25*(3), 281–300.

Andersson, R., Musterd, S., Galster, G., & Kauppinen, T. (2007). What mix matters? Exploring the relationships between individuals' incomes and different measures of neighbourhood context. *Housing Studies, 22*(5), 637–660.

Atkinson, R., & Kintrea, K. (2002). Area effects: What do they mean for British housing and regeneration policy? *European Journal of Housing Policy, 2*(2), 147–166.

Baum, S., Arthurson, K., & Rickson, K. (2009). Happy people in mixed-up places: The association between the degree and type of local socioeconomic mix and expressions of neighbourhood satisfaction. *Urban Studies, 47*(3), 467–485.

Belsley, D. A., Kuh, E., & Welsch, R. E. (1980). *Regression diagnostics: Identifying influential data and sources of collinearity*. New York: Wiley.

Berry, J., & Kalin, R. (1979). Reciprocity of inter-ethnic attitudes in a multicultural society. *International Journal of Intercultural Relations, 3*(1), 99–112.

Blalock, H. M. (1967). *Toward a theory of minority-group relations*. New York: Academic.

Blokland, T. (2005). *Goeie buren houden zich op d'r eigen. Buurt gemeenschap en sociale relaties in de stad*. Den Haag: Dr. Gradus Hendriks Stichting.

Blumer, H. (1958). Race prejudice as a sense of group position. *The Pacific Sociological Review, 1*(1), 3–7.

Bolt, G., & van Kempen, R. (2002). Moving up or moving down? Housing careers of Turks and Moroccans in Utrecht, the Netherlands. *Housing Studies, 17*(3), 401–422.

Bolt, G., van Kempen, R., & van Ham, M. (2008). Minority ethnic groups in the Dutch housing market: Spatial segregation, relocation dynamics and housing policy. *Urban Studies, 45*(7), 1359–1384.

Branton, R. P., & Jones, B. S. (2005). Reexamining racial attitudes: The conditional relationship between diversity and socioeconomic environment. *American Journal of Political Science, 49*(2), 359–372.

Centraal Bureau voor de Statistiek. (1997, 2008, 2010). Data retrieved June 25, 2009, from www.cbs.nl
Charles, C. Z. (2000). Neighbourhood racial composition preferences: Evidence from a multi-ethnic metropolis. *Social Problems, 47*(3), 379–407.
Charles, C. Z. (2009). *Won't you be my neighbor: Race, class, and residence*. Los Angeles: Russell Sage.
Clark, W. A. (1991). Residential preferences and neighbourhood racial segregation: A test of the Schelling segregation model. *Demography, 28*(1), 1–19.
Clark, W. A. V., & Dieleman, F. M. (1996). *Households and housing: Choice and outcomes in the housing market*. New Brunswick: Center for Urban Policy Research.
Coleman, J. S. (1990). *Foundation of social theory*. Cambridge: The Belknop Press of Harvard University Press.
Dekker, K., & Bolt, G. (2005). Social cohesion in post war estates in the Netherlands: Differences between socio-economic and ethnic groups. *Urban Studies, 42*(12), 2447–2470.
Dekker, K., & Van Kempen, R. (2004). Urban governance within the big cities policy. *Cities, 21*(2), 109–117.
Dekker, K., & Varady, D. P. (2011). A comparison of Dutch and U.S. neighbourhood regeneration planning: The similarity grows? *Urban Research and Practice, 4*(2), 123–152.
Feijten, P., & van Ham, M. (2009). Neighbourhood change … Reason to leave? *Urban Studies, 46*(10), 2103–2122. doi:10.1177/0042098009339430.
Fong, E., & Chan, E. (2010). The effect of economic standing, individual preferences, and co-ethnic resources on immigrant residential clustering. *International Migration Review, 44*(1), 111–141.
Galster, G. C. (2010). *The mechanism(s) of neighbourhood effects: Theory, evidence, and policy implications*. Fife: St Andrews University.
Galster, G., & Hesser, G. (1981). Residential satisfaction: Compositional and contextual correlates. *Environment and Behavior, 13*(6), 735–758.
Gans, H. (1967). *The Levittowners: Ways of life and politics in a new suburban community*. New York: Colombia University Press.
Gans, H. (1968). *People and plans*. New York: Basic Books.
Gay, C. (2006). Seeing difference: The effect of economic disparity on black attitudes towards Latinos. *American Journal of Political Science, 50*(4), 982–997.
Gemeentelijke Basis Administratie. (1998, 2009). *Data provided by the Centraal Bureau voor de Statistiek*.
Gijsberts, M., Vervoort, M., Havekes, E., & Dagevos, J. (2010). *Maakt de buurt verschil? de relatie tussen de etnische samenstelling van de buurt, interetnisch contact en wederzijdse beeldvorming*. Den Haag: Sociaal en Cultureel Planbureau.
Guest, A., & Wierzbicki, S. (1999). Social ties at the neighbourhood level: Two decades of GSS evidence. *Urban Affairs Review, 35*(1), 92–111.
Hagendoorn, L. (1995). Intergroup biases in multiple group systems: The perception of ethnic hierarchies. *European Review of Social Psychology, 6*(1), 199–228.
Hagendoorn, L., Drogendijk, R., Tumanov, S., & Hraba, J. (1998). Interethnic preferences and ethnic hierarchies in the former Soviet Union. *International Journal of Intercultural Relations, 22*(4), 483–503.
Harris, D. R. (2001). Why are Whites and Blacks averse to Black neighbors? *Social Science Research, 30*(1), 100–116.
Havekes, E., Dekker, K., & Coenders, M. (2010, July). *Interethnic attitudes in ethnically diverse neighbourhoods: A multigroup approach*. Paper presented at the ISA Conference, Göteborg.
Hedman, L. (2011). Measurement of neighbourhood effects. *Housing Studies, 26*(4), 501–519.
Hedman, L., & van Ham, M. (2011). The impacts of residential mobility on measurements of neighbourhood effects. In M. van Ham, D. Manley, N. Bailey, L. Simpson, & D. Maclennan (Eds.), *Neighbourhood effects research: New perspectives*. Dordrecht: Springer.
Hipp, J. R. (2010). A dynamic view of neighborhoods: The reciprocal relationship between crime and neighborhood structural characteristics. *Social Problems, 57*(2), 203–230.

Hox, J. (2002). *Multilevel analysis: Techniques and applications*. Mahwah/London: Lawrence Erlbaum.

Ihlanfeldt, K. R., & Scafidi, B. P. (2002). The neighbourhood contact hypothesis: Evidence from the multicity study of urban inequality. *Urban Studies, 39*(4), 619–641.

Kearns, A., & Mason, P. (2007). Mixed tenure communities and neighbourhood quality. *Housing Studies, 22*(5), 661–691.

Krysan, M. (2002). Whites who say they'd flee: Who are they, and why would they leave? *Demography, 39*(4), 675–696.

Krysan, M., & Farley, R. (2001). Residential preferences of blacks: Do they explain persistent segregation? *Social Forces, 80*(3), 937–980.

Krysan, M., Couper, M., Farley, R., & Forman, T. (2009). Does race matter in neighborhood preferences? Results from a video experiment. *The American Journal of Sociology, 115*(2), 527–559.

Lansing, J., & Zehner, R. (1970). *Planned residential environments*. Ann Arbor: Institute for Social Research, University of Michigan.

Lee, B. A., & Campbell, K. E. (1999). Neighbor networks of black and white Americans. In B. Wellman (Ed.), *Networks in the global village: Life in contemporary communities* (pp. 119–146). Boulder: Westview Press.

Lu, M. (1999). Determinants of residential satisfaction: Ordered logit vs. regression models. *Growth and Change, 30*(2), 264–287.

Madanipour, A. (1998). Social exclusion and space. In A. Madanipour, G. Cars, & J. Allen (Eds.), *Social exclusion in European cities: Processes, experiences and responses* (pp. 75–89). London: Jessica Kingsley.

Massey, D., & Denton, N. (1993). *American apartheid: Segregation and the making of the underclass*. Cambridge: Harvard University Press.

McCrea, R., Stimson, R., & Western, J. (2005). Testing a moderated model of satisfaction with urban living using data for Brisbane-South east Queensland, Australia. *Social Indicators Research, 72*(2), 121–152.

Ministry of Justice. (2005). *Wet bijzondere maatregelen grootstedelijke problematiek* [Law special measures big cities problems]. Ministry of Housing, Neighbourhoods and Integration: The Hague.

Musterd, S. (2005). Social and ethnic segregation in Europe: Levels, causes and effects. *Journal of Urban Affairs, 27*(3), 331–348.

Oliver, J. E., & Wong, J. (2003). Intergroup prejudice in multiethnic settings. *American Journal of Political Science, 47*(4), 567–582.

Parkes, A., Kearns, A., & Atkinson, R. (2002). What makes people dissatisfied with their neighbourhoods? *Urban Studies, 39*(13), 2413–2438.

Permentier, M. (2012). Neighbourhood reputations, moving behaviour and neighbourhood dynamics. In M. van Ham, D. Manley, N. Bailey, L. Simpson, & D. Maclennan (Eds.), *Understanding neighbourhood dynamics: New insights for neighbourhood effects research*. (pp. 161–182) Dordrecht: Springer.

Pettigrew, T. F. (1973). Attitudes on race and housing: A social psychological view. In A. H. Hawley & V. P. Rock (Eds.), *Segregation in residential areas* (pp. 21–84). Washington, DC: National Academy of Sciences.

Sampson, R. J. (2009). Disparity and diversity in the contemporary city: Social (dis)order revisited. *The British Journal of Sociology, 60*(1), 1–31.

Sampson, R. J., & Groves, W. B. (1989). Community structure and crime: Testing social-disorganization theory. *American Journal of Sociology, 94*(4), 774–802.

Sampson, R. J., McAdam, D., MacIndoe, H., & Weffer-Elizondo, S. (2005). Civil society reconsidered: The durable nature and community structure of collective civic action. *The American Journal of Sociology, 111*(3), 673–714.

Sidanius, J., & Pratto, F. (1999). *Social dominance: An intergroup theory of social hierarchy and oppression*. Cambridge: Cambridge University Press.

Snijders, T. A. B., & Bosker, R. J. (1999). *Multilevel analysis: An introduction to basic and advanced multilevel modeling*. London: Sage.

Statistics Netherlands. (2011). *Population figures*. Retrieved from online Statline database: http://statline.cbs.nl/StatWeb/publication/?DM=SLNL&PA=37325&D1=0&D2=a&D3=0&D4=0&D5=0,3,137,152,215,232&D6=l&HDR=G2,G3,G4,T&STB=G1,G5&VW=T

Tajfel, H. (1982). Social psychology of intergroup relations. *Annual Review of Psychology, 33*, 1–39.

Taub, R., Taylor, D., & Dunham, J. (1984). *Paths of neighborhood change: Race and crime in urban America*. Chicago: The University of Chicago Press.

van der Laan Bouma-Doff, W. (2007). Involuntary isolation: Ethnic preferences and residential segregation. *Journal of Urban Affairs, 29*(3), 289–309.

van Ham, M., & Manley, D. (2010). The effect of neighbourhood housing tenure mix on labour market outcomes: A longitudinal investigation of neighbourhood effects. *Journal of Economic Geography, 10*(2), 257–282.

van Kempen, R., & Bolt, G. (2009). Social cohesion, social mix, and urban policies in the Netherlands. *Journal of Housing and the Built Environment, 24*(4), 457–475.

VROM. (2000). *Mensen Wensen Wonen, Wonen in de 21e eeuw*. The Hague: Samenvatting Ministerie van VROM.

VROM. (2004). *Leefbaarheid Van Wijken* [Liveability of neighbourhoods]. The Hague: VROM.

VROM. (2007). *Actieplan Krachtwijken: Van Aandachtswijk naar Krachtwijk* [Action plan power neighbourhoods: From special needs neighbourhood towards power neighbourhood]. Den Haag: VROM.

VROM-raad. (2002). *Haasten en onthaasten in de stedelijke herstructurering, advies over de herstructurerig van stedelijke woonmilieus*. Den Haag: VROM-raad.

Williams, R., Nesiba, R., & McConnell, E. D. (2005). The changing face of inequality in home mortgage lending. *Social Problems, 52*(2), 181–208.

Wittebrood, K., Latten, J., & Nicolaas, H. (2005). Wonen, leefbaarheid en veiligheid in concentratiewijken. In K. Wittebrood, J. Latten, & H. Nicolaas (Eds.), *Jaarrapport integratie 2005* (pp. 132–147). Den Haag: SCP/WODC/CBS.

Woning Behoefte Onderzoek Nederland. (1998). *Data provided by the Centraal Bureau voor de Statistiek*. Data can be obtained from http://www.dans.knaw.nl/

Woon Onderzoek Nederland. (2009). *Data provided by the Centraal Bureau voor de Statistiek*. Data can be obtained from http://www.dans.knaw.nl/

www.rijksoverheid.nl. (2010). http://www.rijksoverheid.nl/nieuws/2010/04/16/minister-van-middelkoop-geeft-rotterdam-verlenging-rotterdamwet.html. Consulted 3 Aug 2011.

Zorlu, A., & Latten, J. (2009). Ethnic sorting in the Netherlands. *Urban Studies, 46*(9), 1899–1923.

Chapter 12
Community Choice in Large Cities: Selectivity and Ethnic Sorting Across Neighbourhoods

William A.V. Clark and Natasha Rivers

Introduction

A substantial literature has now documented the continuing separation of ethnic and racial groups and of separation more generally by socio-economic status within metropolitan areas. In particular, US, European and Canadian cities are still substantially segregated by race and income and this has generated a research agenda which attempts to understand how and why this separation occurs (Bayer et al. 2004; Clark 2007; Dawkins 2004; Fossett 2006; Iceland et al. 2002). That literature emphasizes one of three perspectives on why and how separation occurs within cities. One of the explanations focuses on resources and budget constraints. Although this explanation has been discounted by some sociologists, clearly resources matter and budget constraints and the cost of housing are factors basic to who can live in particular neighbourhoods. In this perspective higher housing costs and lower incomes are constraints on the ability of poorer households and minorities to enter affluent and often White neighbourhoods. A second perspective argues that much of the separation in the residential fabric is created by the expressed preferences and

W.A.V. Clark (✉)
Department of Geography, University of California,
1255 Bunche Hall, Los Angeles CA 90095-1524, USA
e-mail: wclark@geog.ucla.edu

N. Rivers
Centre for Studies in Demography and Ecology, University of Washington,
206 Raitt Hall, Box 353412, Seattle, WA 98195-3412, USA
e-mail: riversn@uw.edu

M. van Ham et al. (eds.), *Understanding Neighbourhood Dynamics: New Insights for Neighbourhood Effects Research*, DOI 10.1007/978-94-007-4854-5_12,

social networks of Whites and minorities. In particular it is the varying desires and willingness of households to live in neighbourhoods within the city where they are in the majority or at the very least a plurality that generates separation. The contrasting preferences lead to residential segregation as there are insufficient neighbourhoods to satisfy the varying preferences or both minority and White households. A third perspective emphasizes the continuing barriers to minority access to predominantly White neighbourhoods. This perspective emphasizes housing market discrimination and the role of real estate agents and lending institutions as gatekeepers in the residential mobility process. In this view it is structural forces which continue to reinforce the patterns of separation within the residential fabric.

All three perspectives have individually generated a substantial research literature and contributed to the debate about the relative effect of budget constraints, preferences and choice, and structural discrimination on the creation of the patterns of ethnic and socio economic sorting that characterizes modern metropolitan areas. Although there is a continuing debate about the relative role of the three mechanisms and considerable debate about the role of budget constraints in residential selection we are increasingly sure that a combination of budget constraints and preferences for particular ethnic and racial compositions are a central element of understanding why there is separation. That is not to argue that structural forces play no role but the research seems to suggest that those effects may be at the margin of creating the patterns we observe.

In part the explanation based on budgets and preferences reflects the operation of residential mobility in the city. There is substantial inertia in the structure of residential change – people move nearby often within the same neighbourhood and often within constraints formed by access to jobs, schools and other urban services. The distance decay curve for residential mobility and migration established that local moves predominate within the overall structure of relocation, and this in itself will necessitate that new choices are very likely to be like old locations. At the same time it is clear that some households move up and others move down in socio-economic status and some households move from areas of majority own race to more mixed areas. These changes eventually change the levels of separation and affect the "look of the residential fabric".

This chapter is about selection, about who chooses what kind of neighbourhood and the relationship of that choice to household characteristics. The research uses data from the panel study of income dynamics (PSID) and data from the decennial census of population and housing to examine the selectivity patterns of moving within metropolitan areas in the US. We first examine the patterns of selectivity in neighbourhood choices by neighbourhood racial and ethnic composition and then socio economic status, based on tract data. Second, we pose the question to what extent do the moves reinforce current ethnic and socio-economic distributions in neighbourhoods. Third, does the selection for majority-own race and majority White areas, and the selection across the socio-economic status scale differ on the dimensions of income, education, age, and by ethnicity?

Theoretical Background and Previous Research

Budget Constraints and Neighbourhood Choices

There has been a general tendency to argue that budget constraints cannot explain ethnic and racial separation. On the face of it, we would expect that income matters in residential selection as the hedonic housing models would suggest. However, with respect to racial and ethnic patterns there has been an argument, originally by Farley et al. (1978, 1994) but continued by Massey and Denton (1993) and Charles (2000), that largely dismisses the role of socio-economic status. The argument in brief, is that because there are neighbourhoods in suburban areas which are affordable for both Black and White households, but where there are few or no African Americans,[1] then the explanation must be discrimination. Fisher (2003) also provides a similar argument and concludes that income accounts for only about 25 % of the variance in residential choice. South and colleagues (2008) also suggest that economic status, and wealth in particular, is not a critical factor influencing choice. They use individual data to examine the mobility patterns of Black and White households and specifically include measures of household and parental wealth in their models. They conclude that racial differences in wealth appear incapable of explaining the disparate neighbourhood locations of African American and Anglo families. Putting aside the issue that we would not expect income or wealth alone to explain the patterns, as I have argued elsewhere (Clark 2007), they also conclude seemingly in contradiction to their argument, that greater household and parental wealth for African Americans is associated with migration into neighbourhoods that contain a relatively large percentage of Anglo residents. Albeit the effects may be small but it does appear that wealth and income do play a role. Perhaps it is a question of which of the perspectives we wish to privilege in our discussion of the explanations of selection.

Still, some data suggest more directly that there are differential choices by the available resources. Quillian (2002) and Pattillo-McCoy (2000) show that non-poor Blacks are more likely than poor Blacks to choose predominantly White residential neighbourhoods when they move. Blacks who move out of predominantly White tracts are significantly more likely to move to another predominantly White tract and make up a small percentage of all non-Whites in that particular tract. This mobility behaviour is consistent with mobility behaviour in general wherein minorities attempt to leave marginal lower class and lower middle class neighbourhoods for middle class neighbourhoods. This process means that single parent minority

[1] The nomenclature African Americans and Blacks are used interchangeably. Often in tables the term 'blacks' is used for space reasons.

households who tend to be poorer will end up in poorer neighbourhoods with lower probabilities of being able to leave those neighbourhoods. It is here that the intersection of changes in life circumstances and residential location can interact – thus unemployment and being unmarried can limit the accumulation of human capital and the income necessary for moving to and living in predominantly owner occupied housing.

Other research also suggests that the role of income is not insignificant. Clark and Blue (2004) showed that income does distinguish between levels of separation for Whites and Blacks: in the largest multi-ethnic metropolitan areas the levels of separation, measured by dissimilarity and exposure indices, decline with increases in income. Homeownership also plays an important role in increasing access to neighbourhoods which are predominantly White and increases the likelihood of staying in those neighbourhoods. As we know (from research on residential mobility) homeowners are less likely to move and therefore less likely than renters to leave a neighbourhood (Clark and Dieleman 1996; Quillian 1999, 2002). There is also research which shows that low income African American families are more likely to move back into predominantly Black neighbourhoods than high income African American families. This suggests that financial pressure intersects with homeownership as a factor in return migration. Further, examining the income and budget effects is one of the central questions in the neighbourhood mobility patterns.

Neighbourhood Preferences and Neighbourhood Choices

Clearly it is not only a budget constraint that influences selection. The substantial body of research on residential preferences shows that the differential willingness to live with combinations of other races and ethnicities is a powerful force in creating separation across neighbourhoods and communities. Theoretically the role of preferences was first outlined by Schelling (1971) who established that quite small differences in the desire to be with people of similar background could generate quite marked patterns of segregation. Empirically, a seminal empirical paper (Farley et al. 1978) established that, by and large, while African Americans preferred integrated neighbourhoods and specifically neighbourhoods which are close to equal combinations of Whites and African-Americans, Whites expressed preferences for largely majority White neighbourhoods. Further work showed that these preferences were translated into outcomes which emphasized separation (Clark 1991, 1992). Additional studies also documented the continuing separation of African Americans and White households although suggesting that there might be enough overlap in preferences to generate some level of integration (Farley et al. 1997).

There does not seem to be any question from a large number of empirical studies that African American households express a stronger desire to be in a mixed neighbourhood than do Whites. Indeed a study across several cities including analyses of all racial and ethnic groups revealed that very similar patterns of some level of inter-mixing are preferred (Clark 2002, 2007) It also seems to be true that in studies of other minorities that Hispanics and Asians express relatively strong own race preferences for neighbourhoods where they will be a majority. However, even if African American households slightly prefer more integrated neighbourhoods as we noted Schelling's theoretical contribution was to show that even relatively small differences in people's preference for neighbours like themselves can lead to quite significant levels of residential separation in the urban fabric. Showing how preferences can be translated into Schelling tolerance schedules was an important part of moving the study of preferences to a central role in the theory of residential separation (Clark 1991). Still, there are substantial differences in how these preferences are interpreted in their role in creating separation. Some see preferences as themselves generated form White hostility (Charles 2000; Farley et al. 1997) while others argue for a neutral interpretation of preferences as reflecting comfort and familiarity (Clark and Fossett 2008).

The Choice Context and Residential Mobility

Choices do not occur in a vacuum. The city is structured by race and by socioeconomic status. Choices are made within that context and this context does not provide a complete palette of choices. To begin, there are still few integrated neighbourhoods which can be used to make 50/50 residential choices. In fact there are very few truly 50/50 neighbourhoods but if we broaden the definition to include all neighbourhoods which are between 40 and 60 % White and 60 and 40 % minorities, less than a fifth of all tracts in US cities qualify as integrated tracts, or more specifically, tracts which would satisfy African American expressed preferences. This constraint will necessarily restrict the number of households who can choose such a neighbourhood. The choices of combinations of Hispanic and African American mixing enlarges the possibility of a mixed neighbourhood setting, but neither African Americans nor Hispanics express strong preferences for that mixing.

As we emphasized in the introductory remarks not only do we have a constrained context we know from the residential mobility literature that households move within familiar contexts within the city and often move a relatively short distance. We would expect, therefore, that many of the moves will be within areas that are similar both in origin and destination characteristics (Clark and Dieleman 1996). Research specifically on neighbourhood choice has shown the high probability that White households will choose and move to predominantly White areas but it also shows that Hispanic and African-American households tend to choose majority own race neighbourhoods even though they have expressed preferences for some form of integration (Clark 1992). The tendency of Black households to move to other Black neighbourhoods has been confirmed by South and Crowder (1998). In those studies it was quite clear that the predominant choices despite our evidence of 50/50 preferences was to choose own race residential selections. Of course all groups are influenced in their mobility behaviour by a variety of life cycle factors including age and children, homeownership and duration of residence (Clark and Dieleman 1996).

Much of the recent focus has been on whether or not Whites are avoiding neighbourhoods with substantial non-Anglo, especially Black, populations (South et al. 2008). Now whether Whites are avoiding racially mixed neighbourhoods because they do not want to live with non-Whites or whether this is a reaction to other factors that characterize the urban structure and may be associated with race (crime and housing values to note two important neighbourhood characteristics) is still debated (Emerson et al. 2001). While race is a factor in residential choices, Emerson, Yancy and Choi point out that about 25 % of Whites say they would buy a house when the racial composition was 15 % Black or less, about the national average if Blacks were distributed across neighbourhoods according to their percentage of the national population. Still, Whites were much less likely to choose such neighbourhoods than Hispanics.

There is survey evidence of growing tolerance and a greater willingness to live in moderately mixed neighbourhoods. The data show that Black college graduates (and by extension those with higher incomes) have considerably more exposure to Whites in their neighbourhoods than do Blacks with low levels of education (St John and Clymer 2000). Still, even this positive finding must be tempered by the evidence that many middle class Black households are choosing to live in majority Black middle class neighbourhoods especially when the numbers of middle class Black households is relatively large. Clearly, there are diverse outcomes in the changing intersection of race and class and it may be that the differences will exacerbate the differences between those in the minority communities who have more education and more income and those who are less able to move up the income ladder.

Previous work on preferences drew a distinction between a household's willingness to move into a neighbourhood and the likelihood of leaving a neighbourhood (Clark 2002). In general households had lower expressed likelihoods of leaving a neighbourhood than entering a neighbourhood. While White households expressed strong preferences for neighbourhoods which were more than 70% White, they were willing to stay in neighbourhoods that changed to become nearly 50/50 although with a majority of Whites. These findings from preference studies have been confirmed with simulations of the likelihood of moving and staying (Ellen 1997). In the simulation of the likelihoods of moving into or leaving a neighbourhood, the research suggests that while households who are resident within a neighbourhood are likely to have a good sense of the quality of the neighbourhood, its schools, crime rates and social context, it is more difficult for outsiders who may choose to use race as a signal of neighbourhood quality. In this conceptualization, a household's dislike of integration must exceed the costs of moving but for in-movers the preference for integration can be lower. The simulations show how much more important entry is over exit in creating racial change.

In the context of the way in which households make choices for varying combinations of ethnic compositions and socio economic status, this study examines the actual outcomes of residential change. What choices do households make and what are the links between their origins and destinations? The general hypotheses are (a) that moves are likely to be "on the diagonal", that is that moves will be within areas similar in ethnicity and status to those that are already occupied and (b) that resources and status play important roles in choosing off the diagonal either to more own race areas or to areas which are more or less advantaged in socio-economic status.

Data and Methods

To examine the evidence on choice and outcomes we use data from the Panel Study of Income Dynamics, (PSID) for the years 1999–2005 and construct matrices of choice by neighbourhood ethnicity and neighbourhood socio-economic status. During this period the PSID collected data every 2 years so we will use data from 1999, 2001, 2003 and 2005. As others have noted, the PSID is a rich source of data for examining neighbourhood mobility. Geo-coded files link the addresses of all respondents to their corresponding census tract which makes it possible to examine residential moves between tracts. Obviously tracts are not a perfect representation of neighbourhoods, but they are the closest available unit to represent the context within which mobility takes place. They are widely used in geographic and demographic research as a basis for residential studies of neighbourhood change and neighbourhood mobility. We use census data from the 2000 census for the 5-year period in which we examine mobility. We recognize that some tracts will have undergone ethnic change, and we may not estimate the racial and ethnic composition exactly. However, the amount of change in 5 years for most tracts will not be so great as to interrupt the broad outline of the findings. Moreover, because we are using fairly broad categories by race, ethnicity and socio economic status; the likelihood of tracts moving from one category to another is thereby limited. Finally, the 2000 data is the only tract data available for the analysis and the decision not to collect long form data[2] in the 2010 census will make these analyses more difficult in future analyses.

We select Black and non-Hispanic White, Asian and Hispanic heads of households during the period 1999–2005. Family members, who move with a head of household, are only counted as one move. The PSID data provides month and year of move and we are able to look back for the preceding year to see whether there was a move. We have data on the ethnicity/racial composition and socio-economic status of the respondent's census tract at each interview. Thus, we are able to create a matrix of all the moves between categories of racial and ethnic composition. We recognize that the 2-year interview interval could create additional moves, which are not part of our sample.[3] We also note that we have aggregated all tracts across metropolitan areas and a move could be between metropolitan areas.[4]

To explore selectivity the study uses two strategies. The first strategy focuses on race and ethnicity and constructs a set of racial and ethnic categories (30% White, 30–50% White, 50–70% White and over 70% White) to examine the changes in selectivity outcomes over the 6 year period of analysis. These categories effectively construct a continuum or more or less minority in combination with Whites.

---

[2] The "long form" collected data on a wide variety of socio economic variables for small geographic areas.

[3] From other research with the PSID we know that the number of moves by any one household in a 2-year period is relatively small (Clark and Withers 2007).

[4] A small number of moves are between metropolitan areas but we can still conceptualize these moves as between different kinds of neighborhoods. Later research will unpack the differences across choices within and between neighborhoods.

A second approach examines choices across socio-economic status. Four variables, tenure, value, percent in poverty and percent single parent families are used to construct a bi-polar index of neighbourhood status. Principal component analysis of all tracts (movers and non-movers) generated a factor score for each tract. The approach is similar to indices of neighbourhood deprivation where high levels of poverty, single parent households, largely rental stock and lower housing values create the least desirable neighbourhoods, and high values, high levels of ownership, low levels of poverty and few single parent households create the least deprived neighbourhoods. The scores on tracts are ordered in quintiles and moves between quintiles test the extent to which households make moves within, or up and down the SES hierarchy.

Findings: Racial and Ethnic Choices

The first set of findings focus on selectivity across neighbourhoods defined by race and ethnicity. The analysis reports (a) existing patterns of residence across the four categories of ethnicity and racial composition, (b) the distribution of destination choices, (c) matrices of mobility amongst the four categories of racial and ethnic composition and (d) patterns of own race choice for Whites, Blacks, Asians and Hispanics.

We report resident household locations across neighbourhoods defined by census tracts for White, Black, Asian, Hispanic and other race/ethnicity (Table 12.1). In 2001 the data confirm the tendency for Whites to live in all White neighbourhoods but the results are quite mixed across other racial and ethnic groups. Nearly half of all African-Americans live in tracts which are less than 30% White and the number is even higher for Hispanics (59.2%). Notable is the significant proportions of other races, Asians and African-Americans who live in tracts which are at least 50% White. These proportions vary from a high of nearly 60% for Asian ethnic groups to a low of just under 20 % for Hispanics. While Whites on the whole still live with Whites, there are significant numbers of Whites and other ethnic groups living in what we can define as mixed race neighbourhoods.

Table 12.1 Residence by neighbourhood type in 2001

	Percent distribution across neighbourhood type				
Neighbourhood percent white	White	Black	Asian	Hispanic	Other
0–30	2.5	49	18.7	59.2	22.8
30–50	3.8	17.2	19.6	18.3	12.1
50–70	10.0	17.3	21.4	9.9	18.1
70–100	81.8	15.3	38.4	9.9	42.3
No data	1.3	1.3	1.7	2.7	4.7
Total	4,422	2,253	112	333	149

Table 12.2 Residence by neighbourhood type in 2005

	Percent distribution across neighbourhood type				
Neighbourhood percent white	White	Black	Asian	Hispanic	Other
0–30	2.2	46.6	20.9	46.8	17.4
30–50	3.2	17.6	21.7	18.7	16.7
50–70	10.0	16.9	18.3	12.7	14.0
70–100	83.8	18.7	38.3	21.1	50.0
No data	0.9	0.2	0.9	0.7	0.0
Total	4,521	2,634	115	577	149

Table 12.3 Destination choices for all movers 1999–2005 by current neighbourhood type

	Percent distribution across neighbourhood type		
Neighbourhood percent white	White	Black	Hispanic
0–30	3.4	46.6	36.6
30–50	4.5	16.5	22.5
50–70	11.1	16.7	17.8
70–100	81	20.2	23
Total	2,020	1,285	191

The same data for 2005 reveals some important changes especially for the Hispanic population, but the changes for the African-American population are notable also (Table 12.2). African-Americans have increased their proportion in tracts which are more than 50% White (from 32.6 to 35.6) but the most dramatic change is for the Hispanic population whose proportion in 50% or more White tracts is over half by the middle of the decade. The "other" racial ethnic group has also increased their proportion in 50% or more White tracts. Clearly, there are significant changes occurring in the distribution of all racial and ethnic groups across neighbourhoods and these results confirm other data which has also documented these changes (Brookings 2010).

Mobility and Choices

The heart of the research in this chapter is about the selectivity process and the destination choices when households change residence and change locations (Table 12.3). As expected from other research, Whites by a very large proportion select mostly White neighbourhoods (over 80% move to 70% or more White tracts). The choices for other ethnic groups are much more diverse. While 51% of Asian households move to tracts which are 70% or more White, about a fifth (21%) of Black households, and 23% of Hispanic households make such moves. More importantly more than a third of Black households move to tracts which are 50% or more

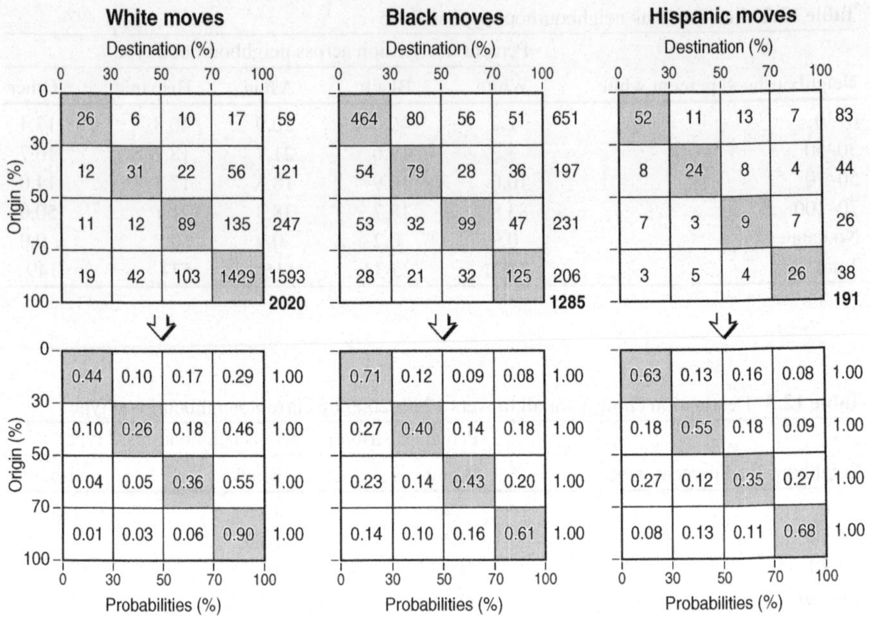

Fig. 12.1 Moves across neighbourhood codes by ethnic/racial characteristics

White and 66% of Asians do this, along with 40% of Hispanics. There is clearly a great deal of fluidity in the choice processes and outcomes in terms of racial and ethnic composition for these groups. Neighbourhoods are changing and becoming more racially mixed and selectivity is reflecting that change. Here we can point to the effect of overall demographic change creating the context for (and indeed being created by) further demographic changes. A very large part of this demographic change is the 15 million new immigrants that the US received in the last decade and a half. At the same time nearly half of African-Americans move to tracts which are largely minority (less than 30% White) and more than the third of Hispanics do this as well. This bifurcated pattern will be something that we will examine in more detail later in the research.

While the analysis of the marginals for destination choice reveal considerable detail about choice and selectivity, we can gain considerable additional understanding of the choice process by examining the matrix of moves between the varying compositions of race and ethnicity (defined as the various categories of White and other minorities). The analysis examines moves for Whites, Blacks and Hispanics (the numbers for Asians are not sufficiently large to carry out a tract to tract analysis). The analysis examines actual moves between the four categorizations of race and ethnicity (Fig. 12.1). As expected, Whites live in and move to neighbourhoods which are 70% or more White households. Most White households in majority White tracts do not move down to tracts which are less White. Only small numbers of Whites are in tracts which are 30 % or less White and about a third of them move up to majority White tracts. For Whites in the middle ranges, 30–70% White, about half move to majority White tracts when they move (Fig. 12.1). Seventy-eight percent of the White moves are on the diagonal – a finding which emphasizes the continuity in selection and choice and the tendency to re-assert the current patterns of White residence. About 12.2% of the moves are above the diagonal (more White) and 9.8% are below the diagonal.

The selections by Blacks and Hispanics reveal the potential for neighbourhood change. While in some ways the moves of Black households provide a mirror image to those of the White moves (about half of all Black households have origins in neighbourhoods which are 30 % or less White in composition), there is lower dominance on the diagonal. Nearly a quarter of all Black households are in neighbourhoods which are majority White (50 % or more White) and move within those neighbourhoods. Nearly 60 % of Black households move on the diagonal and slightly more move above the diagonal (23.2 %) than move below the diagonal. That is slightly more make upward moves in the sense of more mixing. In examining this matrix we can focus on either the glass half full or the glass half empty with respect to access to White (and presumably higher status SES neighbourhoods). In terms of the glass half full a large number of African-American households are in tracts which are majority White and a significant proportion of them are able to maintain those neighbourhood locations when they move. In contrast, a significant number of African-Americans are in neighbourhoods which are less than 50 % White and they do not move out of those neighbourhoods. It is these households that are either exercising a choice of more Black neighbours or they are locked into poor neighbourhoods with few opportunities for upward mobility.

The story of Hispanic choices is somewhere between those of the White and the African-American households who move. The data are sparse compared to the information available for the other two groups but they tell a story of significant proportions of Hispanics in, and moving to 70% or more White neighbourhoods and at the same time a significant proportion of Hispanics in, and moving within mostly minority neighbourhoods (Fig. 12.1). While there is again a strong diagonal preference (58.1% move on the diagonal) there is a distinctly higher likelihood of moving above the diagonal (26.2%) than below the diagonal (15.7%). Even though the numbers are small it resonates with census data which suggest strong changes in the distribution of Hispanic households (Brookings 2010; Iceland et al. 2002).

When we examine the diagonal probabilities, the extremes at either end of the diagonal have the highest values. Whites in highly White areas have very high probabilities of moving within those neighbourhoods. Similarly, though at somewhat lower probabilities African Americans and Hispanics also maintain their residence in these White and presumably higher status neighbourhoods. At the other extreme African American and Hispanic households in highly concentrated minority areas (non-White) are likely to stay in those areas. This is also somewhat true for White households but in their case there is a real probability that they will make the move to highly White majority areas, certainly at higher probabilities than for African Americans and Hispanics. These descriptive findings are the basis for models of mobility choices – how do we understand the role of income, education, family status and ownership in these choices.

Multinomial Models of the Choice of Race and Ethnicity

In the discussion of the varying perspectives on continuing separation in the residential fabric we emphasized the possibility of variations in resources as an important part of understanding choices by Black and White households. To test this proposition we conduct two modelling strategies, one which examines movements above and below the diagonal as against movement on the diagonal and a second modelling strategy, which looks at the choices of majority own race. We might think of the first strategy as a test of moving up (to a more White and probably up in the neighbourhood hierarchy), moving down or staying in the status quo and the second strategy as a test of self-selection. Each of these strategies however, is designed to evaluate the extent to which socioeconomic status is a force in g residential selections that we have examined descriptively to this point.

For Whites, movement above the diagonal is related significantly to education (Table 12.4a). Households with some college or college credentials are significantly more likely to move above the diagonal than below the diagonal. The measure on education is clearly the most important variable with the highest chi-square value. Education is related to income though certainly not in a linear fashion but it reflects resources and perhaps as importantly, status. White households are moving to less minority neighbourhoods in general. In addition, being a married family is marginally significant but interestingly has negative coefficients for both movements above and below the diagonal in contrast with moving on the diagonal itself. Without reading too much into this we might suggest that it hints at the inertia and stability that we discussed earlier in the conversations about choice and selection.

For Black households, resources are clearly important in movements within the matrix (Table 12.4b). Income is significant and significant for both movements above and below the diagonal and ownership is also marginally significant but negatively related to movements below the diagonal, which is consistent with the notion of resources as an important constraint on mobility behaviour. Households moving above the diagonal to less minority neighbourhoods not only have more income they are likely to be owners, while the coefficient for ownership for moves below the diagonal is negative. These findings are consistent with an explanation that greater resources enables choices other than in concentrated minority areas and opens up the possibility for moves to mixed residential areas, that is to areas that are less than 50 % minority.

The numbers for Hispanics are small, and so we must treat the results with some caution but we can suggest that the movement above the diagonal is related to education compared to movement on the diagonal and professional status is also related, marginally, to movement above the diagonal (Table 12.4a). These findings are consistent with the general arguments that we have been making. Resources and status are important variables in the decisions to choose particular combinations of neighbours. For Hispanics with small numbers the results can only be seen as indicative rather than definitive.

Table 12.4a Multinomial models for Selectivity within the mobility matrix (the diagonal is the reference category) variable coefficients

	White		Black		Hispanic	
Variable	Chi square	Pr > Chi square	Chi square	Pr > Chi square	Chi square	Pr > Chi square
Intercept	161.68	**<.0001**	30.38	**<.0001**	1.68	0.4317
Household income	0.13	0.9352	9.16	**0.0103**	0.56	0.7556
Some college/college	14.56	**0.0007**	0.52	0.7707	4.27	0.1182
Married family	4.53	0.1037	0.46	0.7693	0.94	0.6238
Professional/manager	2.32	0.3128	0.96	0.6186	3.43	0.1798
Owner	2.63	0.2684	6.73	**0.0346**	3.14	0.2081
Age	0.97	0.6164	3.26	0.1963	1.62	0.4458

Table 12.4b Maximum likelihood estimates for estimates above (1) and below (2) the diagonal (reference category)

		White		Black		Hispanic	
Variable		Estimate	Chi square	Estimate	Chi square	Estimate	Chi square
Intercept	1	−2.07	**93.07**[a]	−1.25	**25.41**[a]	−0.82	1.64
	2	−2.13	**88.89**[a]	−0.94	**11.52**[a]	−0.39	0.28
Household income	1	1.15E-07	0.03	6.82E-06	**7.47**[b]	−2.92E-06	0.28
	2	−3.13E-07	0.09	6.74E-06	**5.55**[c]	−4.81E-06	0.44
Some college/college	1	0.52	**13.55**[a]	0.1	0.44	0.76	2.97
	2	0.23	2.18	−0.02	0.01	0.88	2.83
Married family	1	−0.29	3.56	0.09	0.26	0.09	0.05
	2	−0.2	1.47	−0.06	0.08	−0.39	0.72
Professional/manage	1	0.26	2.29	−0.18	0.46	1.1	2.75
	2	0.08	0.15	0.14	0.25	1.21	2.29
Owner	1	−0.04	0.08	0.28	2.33	0.62	2.38
	2	−0.28	2.62	−0.38	2.61	−0.21	0.16
Age	1	0	0.12	0	0.04	−0.01	0.56
	2	0.01	0.92	−0.01	3.21	−0.02	1.37

Significance [a] ≥.001; [b] ≥.01; [c] =.05

Despite the general confirmation of the status variables, as explanations for overall movements within the matrix, more strongly for Whites and Blacks than Hispanics, the levels of fit for the models are modest. The gamma and Somers D values are also modest and the levels of concordance are not high which suggests that there is considerable complexity in the choice patterns across neighbourhoods. This of course is not unexpected as we have not factored preferences into the choice process for composition.

Logit Models of Own/Other Race Choice

The results from the multinomial models of status effects are confirmed with specific models of choices for majority neighbourhoods (White for White households and minority for Black and Hispanic households). For Whites, the logit model tests the choice of 70 plus percent White versus movement within less than 50 % White. For Blacks, the logit model is the choice of 70 % plus minority versus 50–100 % White and similarly for Hispanics, the choice is 70 % plus minority versus 50–100 % White.

Whites who moved within mostly White areas had strong and significant coefficients for married families. Neither income nor education were important explanations for movement and choice within the majority White areas (Table 12.5). Still, if we examine the incomes of those who move to or within own race areas, the incomes are 24 % higher than those who move to less than 50 % White areas. There are strong differences in education and ownership as well. The largest difference is for the married family variable – movement into less than a majority White area was on average about 20 % less likely for married households (Table 12.6).

It is Black households that exhibit the most significant pattern of resource effects. The income and married family coefficients are negative and significant – that is lower incomes and not married families are more likely to be moving within minority areas. The mean income for movement within majority minority areas for Black households is nearly 51 % less than for those households who move to areas which are more than 50 % White. Ownership and married households have the same differences (Table 12.6).

The Hispanic model is significant overall, but the individual variables do not distinguish between movements within largely minority and majority White areas. There are large differences in mean income for those households who move within minority areas and those who move to areas which have lower levels of minority composition. Education and ownership also reveal large differences. Still, the small number in the Hispanic sample makes it difficult to provide any sure conclusions from the variables.

The evidence from the logit and multinomial models on sorting and selection provide confirmation that resources do matter in the selections that occur, but the lack of stronger model fit emphasizes the overall complexity of sorting and selection by race and ethnicity. The implication is that hidden hand of preferences underlies much of the choice and selection that we see in the matrix. Clearly economics and

Table 12.5 Logit models of majority own-race selection versus 50 % other race/ethnicity:

White

Variable	Estimate	Chi-square	Pr>Chi square
Intercept	2.1	36.82	<.001
Household income	9.42E-08	0	0.9544
Some college/college	0.32	1.57	0.2109
Married family	0.79	8.27	**0.004**
Professional/manager	−0.05	0.03	0.8736
Owner	0.01	0	0.9853
Age	0.01	1.62	0.2037

Likelihood ration 15.15 Pr>Chi square **.019**; Somers D=0.26; Gamma=0.27

Black

Variable	Estimate	Chi-square	Pr>Chi square
Intercept	0.21	0.58	0.4454
Household income	−6.49E-06	4.74	**0.0295**
Some college/college	−0.04	0.06	0.8067
Married family	−0.88	18.65	**<.0001**
Professional/manager	−0.11	0.15	0.6975
Owner	−0.27	1.46	0.2277
Age	0.02	8.34	**0.0039**

Likelihood ratio 64.51 Pr>Chi square<**.001**; Somers D=0.31; Gamma=0.31

Hispanic

Variable	Estimate	Chi-square	Pr>Chi square
Intercept	−0.76	1.02	0.3131
Household income	−5.33E-06	0.7	0.4022
Some college/college	−0.91	2.17	0.1407
Married family	0.64	1.61	0.2046
Professional/manager	−1.29	1.15	0.2846
Owner	−0.81	2.26	0.1327
Age	0.03	3.52	**0.0607**

Likelihood ratio 16.97 Pr>Chi square **.009**; Somers D=0.43; Gamma=0.43

Table 12.6 Differences across variables by neighbourhood choice and race/ethnicity

Variable		White	[a]Black	[a]Hispanic
Income (mean $)	1	69,112	27,869	37,635
	0	55,700	42,068	56,239
College (%)	1	39.1	25.9	11.5
	0	30.7	30.4	28.2
Married/family (%)	1	50.7	15.3	61.5
	0	30.7	36.6	58.7
Professional/Manager (%)	1	19.7	6.2	1.9
	0	17.3	10.2	15.2
Owner (%)	1	47.1	13.6	23.1
	0	37.3	25.1	45.7

[a]Recall that Black and Hispanic logits use 1 for majority minority tract choices, as Whites have 1 for choices of majority White

status matter, and the fact that more than a third of all African-American households were able to move into or within majority White areas suggests that we treat with caution the notion that structural forces are limiting the opportunities for African American households. Almost certainly for some African American households discriminatory factors are still playing a role but to argue that money does not matter is not supported by this research.

Findings: Status Choices Across Neighbourhoods

Mobility and Socio Economic Sorting

As expected there are marked differences by race and ethnicity across the neighbourhoods by status (Tables 12.7 and 12.8). In 2001 more than half of White households are in the two top status neighbourhoods but only 12 % of African Americans. The reverse image, between the top and bottom status neighbourhoods, for Blacks and Whites is stark. Hispanic households have a similar pattern in 2001 but what is notable is the change by 2005 when Hispanics have an 11 % decrease in the lowest neighbourhood category in the 5 year period. Overall, a large number of Hispanic households moved "up" over this short time period. There was modest change in the Black distribution.

Again as expected status destination choices differ by race and ethnicity (Table 12.9). While nearly 50 % of Whites have a destination in the two highest socioeconomic status categories, African Americans with 14 % and Hispanics with 23 % have much lower proportions choosing and sorting into high status neighbourhoods. The real contrast is between the 49.3 % Whites who sort into the two highest status areas while nearly 73 % of African-Americans sort into the two lowest socioeconomic categories. It is this contrast in destination outcomes for White and African American households, that often generates the issue of equality of access. At first sight, this might suggest that there is little upward status movement for African Americans. However, a larger proportion of the selection in the lowest status neighbourhoods is the outcome of the one-third of all African Americans who are in the lowest category and stay within that when they move. A White household in the lowest SES category has about a 70 % chance of moving up and a Hispanic household has a 42 % chance, the same African American household has a 33 % chance of moving up in status. Still that a third of African American household and 40 % of Hispanics can make this change is again support for the argument that African Americans and Hispanics are making gains when they move.

There is more dispersion across the matrix of moves by the socio economic status of the neighbourhood than we observed across the racial and ethnic dimensions. Even so, there is still strong selection along the diagonal which confirms our arguments throughout the chapter that selection or sorting is very much an affirmation of choice within similar areas. Overall, if we include movement on the diagonal and in the

Table 12.7 Residence by socio economic status of the neighbourhood in 2001

	Percent distribution across neighbourhood type				
Neighbourhood SES status	White	Black	Asian	Hispanic	Other
1	26.1	3.7	44.5	5.6	10.6
2	28.1	8.4	15.5	10.2	20.4
3	25.5	15.9	10	17	23.9
4	15.2	30.2	19.1	23.5	23.2
5	5	41.8	10.9	43.8	20.8
Total	4,332	2,226	110	324	142

Table 12.8 Residence by socio economic status of the neighbourhood in 2005

	Percent distribution across neighbourhood type				
Neighbourhood SES status	White	Black	Asian	Hispanic	Other
1	27.1	5.4	43.9	9.8	22.1
2	28.4	9.1	7	13.4	19.5
3	25	16.6	19.3	19.7	23
4	13.7	26.7	19.3	26	17.7
5	5.4	42.2	10.5	31.1	17.7
Total	4,484	2,628	114	573	113

Table 12.9 Destination choices for movers 1999–2005 by current neighbourhood SES status

	Percent distribution across neighbourhood type		
Neighbourhood SES status	White	Black	Hispanic
1	23.1	4.8	8.9
2	26.2	9.3	14.1
3	25.7	13.2	23.6
4	17.2	27	27.7
5	7.8	45.7	25.7
Total	2,020	1,285	191

categories immediately adjacent to the diagonal there is substantial evidence which further emphasizes the tendency to reinforce current patterns in the residential mosaic. About 45% of Whites move on the diagonal while 50% of Hispanics and more than 50% of Blacks do so. All groups are likely to make gains in socioeconomic status with their moves. Nearly 31% all Whites and 30% of Hispanics made gains in status with moves during the period being studied. In contrast, 26% of African-Americans were able to make upward moves (Fig. 12.2).

To explore the variable associations with the choice and sorting that we observe in the matrix, we construct a series of multinomial logit models similar to those that we used for the analysis of racial and ethnic choices. Again, we examine moves above and below the diagonal with the diagonal as the reference category. In addition to examining the choices by Whites, African-Americans and Hispanics separately we also examine total moves and introduce race as an explanatory variable.

Transitions across Socio-economic Status

White

SES	1	2	3	4	5
1	233	93	52	46	7
2	93	219	84	51	31
3	63	115	258	73	28
4	61	79	88	147	35
5	26	23	38	31	56

SES	1	2	3	4	5
1	0.53	0.22	0.12	0.11	0.02
2	0.19	0.46	0.18	0.11	0.06
3	0.12	0.21	0.48	0.14	0.05
4	0.19	0.19	0.21	0.36	0.09
5	0.15	0.13	0.22	0.18	0.32

Probabilities

Black

SES	1	2	3	4	5
1	12	2	5	1	8
2	17	37	18	18	13
3	8	22	55	48	34
4	17	25	49	165	116
5	8	34	42	115	416

SES	1	2	3	4	5
1	0.43	0.07	0.18	0.04	0.29
2	0.17	0.36	0.18	0.17	0.13
3	0.05	0.13	0.33	0.29	0.20
4	0.05	0.07	0.13	0.44	0.31
5	0.01	0.06	0.07	0.19	0.68

Probabilities

Hispanic

SES	1	2	3	4	5
1	5	3	2	2	0
2	3	8	7	7	1
3	1	3	20	7	5
4	4	6	10	25	7
5	4	7	6	12	36

SES	1	2	3	4	5
1	0.42	0.25	0.17	0.17	0.00
2	0.12	0.31	0.27	0.27	0.04
3	0.03	0.08	0.56	0.19	0.14
4	0.08	0.12	0.19	0.48	0.13
5	0.06	0.11	0.09	0.18	0.55

Probabilities

Fig. 12.2 Moves across neighbourhoods coded by socio-economic status

Multinomial Models of Socio-economic Choice

The model of choices by all groups aggregated is significant (Table 12.10). Education professional occupations, ownership and being Black, are significant explanatory variables for choices above or below the diagonal. Recall that the choice below the diagonal in these matrices is a rise in socioeconomic status, while choosing above the diagonal is a step down in socioeconomic status. Education is important for choices, both above and below the diagonal; the coefficient is much stronger for choices which generate gains in socioeconomic status. Being an owner clearly brings about gains in socio economic status while the negative coefficient associated with choices for lower status areas suggests that it is renters who are moving down in status. The African-American coefficient is large and significant for movement down the socio-economic status hierarchy. That is, *controlling* for income, education, occupation, marital status and ownership there is still an effect of being African-American on the ability to exercise choices within the socioeconomic matrix. Thus, we cannot conclude that it is only resources which are associated with movement across neighbourhoods by status. It is here that we can invoke the role of preferences or structural factors in the choices by African Americans. That it may be structural or preferences in combination with income is emphasized by the lack of significance of being Hispanic in the choices across the matrix of neighbourhoods. Choices and selections by White households are significantly related to professional

Table 12.10 Maximum likelihood estimates for Multinomial variables (2-) loss in status) and below (1-) gain in status

		All movers		White		Black		Hispanic	
Variable		Estimate	Chi square	Estimate	Chi square	Estimate	Chi square	Estimate	Chi square
Intercept	1	–0.52	**14.53**[a]	–0.34	**4.48**[c]	–1.26	**25.74**[a]	0.15	0.06
	2	–0.62	**18.43**[a]	–0.56	**10.91**[a]	–1.13	**19.00**[a]	–0.76	1.26
Household income	1	1.09E-07	0.04	–3.97E-07	0.41	1.10E-04	**16.84**[a]	4.14E-06	0.66
	2	2.58E-07	0.17	1.74E-08	0	6.14E-06	**4.02**[c]	9.81E-08	0
Some college/college	1	0.25	**8.79**[b]	0.19	3.04	0.28	3.54	0.43	0.87
	2	0.18	**3.86**[c]	0.18	2.49	0.02	0.01	1.01	**4.48**[c]
Married family	1	–0.02	0.04	–0.23	**4.01**[c]	0.16	0.8	0.15	0.14
	2	0.02	0.06	–0.08	0.38	0.14	0.51	–0.07	0.03
Professional/manager	1	0.35	**8.69**[b]	0.34	**6.33**[c]	0.41	2.72	0.49	0.47
	2	0.39	**9.34**[b]	0.34	**5.50**[c]	0.4	2	1.32	3.18
Owner	1	0.33	**12.13**[a]	0.24	**3.93**[c]	0.37	**4.28**[c]	0.34	0.75
	2	–0.38	**12.11**[a]	–0.42	**10.37**[b]	–0.37	2.64	–0.41	0.72
Age	1	–0.01	2.71	–0.01	1.3	–0.01	0.13	–0.03	**4.43**[c]
	2	0	0	0	0.06	–7.70E-03	0.02	–0.01	0.22
Black	1	–0.17	3.39						
	2	–0.38	**15.34**[a]						
Hispanic	1	–0.01	0						
	2	–0.19	0.97						

The diagonal is the reference category
Significance [a] ≥.001; [b] ≥.01; [c] ≥05

status and ownership (Table 12.10). Again, the large negative coefficient for ownership emphasizes the choices by renters who are likely to be choosing lower status areas. It is the outcomes for African American households which are of particular interest with respect to the sorting process. Is it simply race or is there a significant socio-economic association with the selections by African American households. The argument for resources appears to be supported from the multinomial estimates (Table 12.10). The coefficients for income and ownership are large and significant. Additionally, they are much larger for moves which brought more gains in status than for moves to low status areas. The significant coefficient for gains is balanced by a negative coefficient, though not significant, for movement to lower status areas. The model for Hispanics, as in the case for choices by race and ethnicity is not significant (Table 12.10). Still, there are hints within the maximum likelihood estimates of the role of education in securing gains in status.

These results provide a certain level of confidence that resources matter in the sorting and destination choices that we observed across socioeconomic status. At the same time, the intersection of race and income appears to be determining at least some of the sorting for African American households. That Hispanic households do not have the same outcome suggests that race does play a role in the case of African-Americans. To examine this in greater detail, we turn to some specific movements across the socioeconomic matrix.

The Intersection of Mobility, Race and Neighbourhood Status

We can provide greater detail on the intersection of race and resources by examining the choices of households in the initial highest and lowest status socioeconomic areas and their choices of new locations. The analysis plots the income for White and Black households who move within the highest status areas and the moves of those who move within the lowest status area. We plot these outcomes for both Black and White households (Fig. 12.3).

Plainly income matters. Movements within the highest status areas, but either Black or White households have incomes in the 80,000–$100,000. In contrast movements within the lowest status areas have household incomes which range in the $35–$50,000 levels for White households and $25–$30,000 for Black households. Not only is income different across the categories of movement, ownership is also different. Ownership rates are in the 50 % and above range for movements in the highest status areas and in the 10–30 % for movements in the lower status areas. Owners prevail in high status areas and renters in lower status areas. Clearly income and ownership are related and they do define the most advantaged areas in the residential fabric.

These final results offer evidence of the important role of resources in residential choices. At the same time, it is fairly clear that this complex process involves more than simply income and the associated ability to buy into the homeowner market.

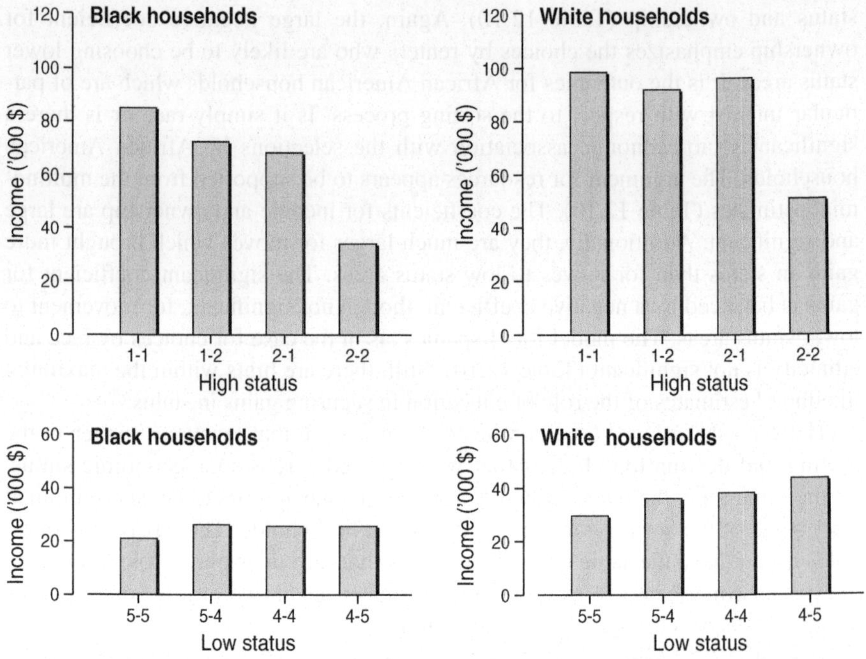

Fig. 12.3 Moves within the two highest and two lowest SES neighbourhoods by income. Note: 1–1 indicates a move within the highest SES category, 1–2 is a move one step down and so on

As the data on racial and ethnic preferences showed households are still choosing areas which have significant proportions of similar neighbours. The two processes in combination, choosing like neighbours and choosing within the constraint of economic resources, reminds us of the continuing power of both status and preference in creating the residential mosaic.

Summary Observations

The chapter began by posing three questions. What are the choices by Whites, African-Americans and Hispanic households within the residential structure? To what extent does the choice and sorting reinforce the current patterns of ethnic and racial separation and the separation by socioeconomic status? And, what is the association of income and status with the choices? The findings from this research on selectivity and sorting across neighbourhoods can be summarized simply. There are strong tendencies in choice and sorting which reinforce existing patterns of separation in the residential mosaic, strong ethno centric preferences by race and ethnicity means that racial separation is likely to remain an important dimension of the residential mosaic, and socio-economic status combines with racial combinations to exacerbate the levels of separation in the urban fabric.

The evidence for the tendency to reinforce patterns comes from the robust probabilities of selection on the diagonal across race and ethnicity and socio economic status. At the same time it is clear that substantial numbers of movers are able to increase both their socio economic status and in the case of Blacks and Hispanics their greater levels of integration – defined as living in White tracts. This occurs even when Whites on average are likely to choose more White tracts. The models which explain choices especially for African American households emphasize the importance of resources in the choices for "more White and less minority" areas.

Race and ethnic choices of neighbourhoods are similar to the origin neighbourhoods and range between 58 and 78% depending on whether it is White, Black or Hispanic moves. Overall, Blacks have a very high probability of originating in and remaining within the largest minority areas. Even though the sample is small the evidence from Hispanics is of considerable movement across the matrix of choices. It is Hispanics who choose the greatest variety of outcomes. Clearly the structure is not as constraining or Hispanics are willing to think outside their ethnic constraints or they can use their social networks more effectively to move to higher status neighbourhoods.

Socio economic choices are more diverse than those by race and ethnicity. Of course those choices are conditioned by the opportunities on offer in the urban structure. After all the urban structure provides a palette of choices and the moving household chooses, subject to their budget constraint a place in the hierarchy. As with much mobility and the choices that are made, their tendency is to outcomes on the diagonal or on the steps in close association with the diagonal. When we examine a model of all moves while income is a critical variable in the sorting outcomes, race plays a role for African Americans after controlling for income. We cannot say whether this is all a function of preferences or some combination of preferences and other structural factors.

In the context of understanding neighbourhoods this chapter argues that sorting within the existing fabric is the most powerful factor in understanding the process of neighbourhood formation and neighbourhood change. Neighbourhoods do change as we know from the shifts in the location of majority and minority populations. Those changes occur as households make selections based on race and socio economic status and they do not always choose the same neighbourhood type as their origin type. It is that change which in the end changes the distribution of population composition- across the urban fabric.

Acknowledgements We would like to thank Philip Morrison, Beate Volker and Maarten Van Ham for comments on drafts of this chapter, and Jeff Garfinkle for data analysis.

References

Bayer, P., McMillan, R., & Rueben, K. (2004). What drives racial segregation? New evidence using census micro data. *Journal of Urban Economics, 56*(3), 514–535.

Brookings. (2010). *Sate of metropolitan America: On the front lines of demographic transformation.* Washington, DC: Brookings Institution.

Charles, C. Z. (2000). Residential segregation in Los Angeles. In L. Bobo, M. Oliver, J. Johnson, & A. Valenzuela (Eds.), *Prismatic metropolis: Inequality in Los Angeles* (pp. 167–219). New York: Russell Sage.

Clark, W. A. V. (1991). Residential preferences and neighborhood racial segregation: A test of the Schelling segregation model. *Demography, 28*(1), 1–19.

Clark, W. A. V. (1992). Residential preferences and residential choices in a multi-ethnic context. *Demography, 30*(3), 451–466.

Clark, W. A. V. (2002). Ethnic preferences and ethnic perceptions in multi-ethnic settings. *Urban Geography, 23*(3), 237–256.

Clark, W. A. V. (2007). Race, class and place: Evaluating mobility outcomes for African Americans. *Urban Affairs Review, 42*(3), 295–314.

Clark, W. A. V., & Blue, S. (2004). Race, class and segregation patterns in U.S. immigrant gateway cities. *Urban Affairs Review, 39*(6), 667–688.

Clark, W. A. V., & Dieleman, F. M. (1996). *Households and housing: Choice and outcomes in the housing market.* New Brunswick: New Jersey Rutgers University, Center for Urban Policy Research.

Clark, W. A. V., & Withers, S. D. (2007). Family migration and mobility sequences in the United States: Spatial mobility in the context of the life course. *Demographic Research* (Max Planck Institute for Demographic Research) *17*(20), 591–622.

Clark, W. A. V., & Fossett, M. (2008). Understanding the social context of the Schelling segregation model. *Proceedings of the National Academy of Sciences, 105*(11), 4109–4114.

Dawkins, C. (2004). Recent evidence on the continuing causes of black-white residential segregation. *Journal of Urban Affairs, 26*(3), 379–400.

Ellen, I. G. (1997). *Race-based neighborhood projection: A proposed framework for understanding new data on racial integration.* New York: New York University, Wagner Graduate School of Public Service, Taub Urban Research Center.

Emerson, M., Yancey, G., & Chai, K. (2001). Does race matter in residential segregation? Exploring the preferences of white Americans. *American Sociological Review, 66*(6), 922–935.

Farley, R., Schuman, H., Bianchi, S., Colasanto, D., & Hatchett, S. (1978). Chocolate city, vanilla suburbs: Will the trend toward racially separate communities continue? *Social Science Research, 7*(4), 319–344.

Farley, R., Steech, C., Jackson, T., Krysan, M., & Reeves, K. (1994). The causes of continued racial residential segregation: Chocolate city, vanilla suburbs revisited. *Journal of Housing Research, 4*(1), 1–38.

Farley, R., Fielding, E., & Krysan, M. (1997). The residential preferences of black and whites: A four metropolis study. *Housing Policy Debate, 8*(4), 763–800.

Fischer, M. (2003). The relative importance of income and race in determining residential outcomes in U.S. urban areas, 1970–2000. *Urban Affairs Review, 38*, 669–696.

Fossett, M. (2006). Ethnic preferences, social distance dynamics, and residential segregation: Theoretical explorations using simulation analysis. *Journal of Mathematical Sociology, 30*(3–4), 185–274.

Iceland, J., Weinberg, D. H., & Steinmetz, E. (2002). *Racial and ethnic residential segregation in the US 1980-2000.* US Bureau of the Census, Special Reports, Series CENSR#3.

Massey, D., & Denton, N. (1993). *American apartheid: Segregation and the making of the underclass.* Cambridge: Cambridge Press.

Pattillo-McCoy, M. (2000). Negotiating adolescence in a black middle class neighborhood. In S. Danziger & A. Chih Lin (Eds.), *Ann arbor, coping with poverty: The social contexts of*

4 neighborhood, work, and family in the African-American community (pp. 77–101). Michigan: University of Michigan Press.
Quillian, L. (1999). Migration patterns and the growth of high-poverty neighborhoods, 1970-1990. *The American Journal of Sociology, 105*(1), 1–37.
Quillian, L. (2002). Why is Black White residential segregation so persistent: Evidence from three theories from migration data. *Social Science Research, 31*(1), 197–229.
Schelling, T. (1971). Dynamic models of segregation. *Journal of Mathematical Sociology, 1*(1), 143–186.
South, S., & Crowder, K. (1998). Housing discrimination and residential mobility: Impacts for blacks and whites. *Population Research and Policy Review, 17*(4), 369–387.
South, S. J., Kyle, C., & Jeremy, P. (2008). Inter-neighborhood migration and spatial assimilation in a multi-ethnic world: Comparing latinos, blacks, and Anglos. *Social Forces, 87*(1), 415–443.
St John, C., & Clymer, R. (2000). Racial residential segregation by level of socio economic status. *Social Science Quarterly, 81*(3), 701–707.

Index

M. van Ham et al. (eds.), *Understanding Neighbourhood Dynamics: New Insights for Neighbourhood Effects Research*, DOI 10.1007/978-94-007-4854-5,

The manufacturer's authorised representative in the EU is Springer
Nature Customer Service Centre GmbH, Europaplatz 3, 69115 Heidelberg,
Germany. If you have any concerns regarding our products, please
contact ProductSafety@springernature.com

Printed and bound by CPI Group (UK) Ltd, Croydon, CR0 4YY
30/09/2026
02225510-0009